J. B. WEST WAS THE MAN TO ⬚

ABOUT THE BE⬚⬚

To get new sla⬚ ⬚hen
the Trumans ⬚
To put in a k⬚ ⬚be
there to "reach ⬚⬚ ⬚is old bald
head."

ABOUT THE BOARD:

To see to the two kitchens the Roosevelts had:
one for him and one for her.
To scrounge up enough food for over a thousand
people when the Johnsons gave an impromptu
party.
To find cottage cheese for Mrs. Nixon—about the
only thing the White House kitchen didn't stock.

ABOUT THE BEAUTIFICATION:

To help Jacqueline Kennedy search the storerooms for antiques.
To help Mamie decorate for every holiday, Halloween to Christmas.

Now J. B. West "has applied his own magnifying
glass to the everyday detail of life at 1600 Pennsylvania Avenue (with) an astonishing memory for
detail," [1] "He is too discreet to tell Everything . . .
but he tells a lot more than we knew before." [2]
"The intimate family details he provides can help
all of us understand our First Families better." [3]

[1] *Time* Magazine   [2] Washington *Post*   [3] Cleveland *Press*

UPSTAIRS AT THE WHITE HOUSE

MY LIFE WITH THE FIRST LADIES

J.B. WEST
Chief Usher
of the White House
1941-1969
with Mary Lynn Kotz

WARNER
PAPERBACK
LIBRARY

A Warner Communications Company

For

KATHY *and* SALLY

WARNER PAPERBACK LIBRARY EDITION
First Printing: September, 1974
Second Printing: September, 1974

Library of Congress Catalog Card Number: 73-78738

A portion of this book appeared, in somewhat different form in
Ladies' Home Journal.

The photographs on pages 193-224 are from J. B. West's own collection. Where not otherwise noted, the photographers represented
are: Abbie Rowe of the National Park Service (Truman and Eisenhower periods), Robert L. Knudsen, White House photographer
(Eisenhower, Kennedy, Johnson and Nixon periods), and Captain
Cecil W. Stoughton, Signal Corps (Kennedy and Johnson periods).

This Warner Paperback Library Edition is published by arrangement with Coward, McCann & Geoghegan, Inc.

Cover art: Honi Werner

Front Cover photographs (left to right): 1. Bill Bridges; 2. Lisa
Larsen; 3. Carl Iwasaki; 4. Michael Renaro; 5. Don Uhrbrock;
6. D. Halstead

Back Cover photographs (top to bottom): 1. George Skadding;
2. Peter Stackpole; 3. Ed Clark; 4. Paul Schutzer; 5. John
Dominis; 6. John Olson

All cover photographs © Time Inc. All rights reserved.

Warner Paperback Library is a division of Warner Books, Inc.,
75 Rockefeller Plaza, New York, N.Y. 10019.

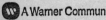 A Warner Communications Company

Printed in the United States of America

Contents

Foreword   7

The Roosevelts   11

The Trumans   52

The Eisenhowers   128

The Kennedys   190

The Johnsons   316

The Nixons   385

Bibliography   402

Index   409

White House plan follows

page 405

Foreword

On March 1, 1941, after my first day at work in the White House, I started to keep a diary. It was short-lived, however, because as the days became more frantic and filled with more responsibilities, and the working hours longer, I decided that I didn't want to "relive" each day.

And from that day until I retired on March 1, 1969, it was never my intention to write a book. Howell G. Crim, Chief Usher of the White House from 1933 to 1957 (when I was promoted to the position), had always said, when asked if he would write his memoirs, "I'm not the type to 'kiss and tell,'" although he was an avid reader of *42 Years in the White House* by Irwin H. ("Ike") Hoover, the first Chief Usher.

That book, covering the years from 1891 to 1933, has been cited as a mine of information by historians and authors. Since retirement, I have been encouraged by numerous people—including some First Ladies—to add my more recent recollections to bring the story up to date. That I have attempted to do. If this book is of some help to future historians, then my efforts will have accomplished my purpose.

I am most grateful to all those who gave me encouragement and assistance, most of whom are mentioned in the text.

I also wish to cite all of the dedicated, selfless people who staff the "President's House"—ushers, housekeepers, butlers, maids, chefs, cooks, doormen, housemen, florists, gardeners, electricians, plumbers, storekeepers, engineers —each one of whom has a passion for anonymity. And I apologize profusely to those few whose names I have had to use in telling a story.

Many times I was asked, "What does the Chief Usher do?" I usually replied, "I do what I'm told to do." Also I received many letters from students asking what educational background would be helpful for a job as Usher at the White House. I could only reply that experience on the job was the main requirement—since its duties are unique; no other government or civilian establishment offers a comparable position. And how to get this experience? To be at the right place at the right time, and have a lot of *luck*.

The title "Chief Usher" is a holdover from early times, when the principal duty was "ushering" expected visitors in to see the President and the First Lady. In recent years many have tried to change the title, but to date nobody has come up with an appropriate appelation.

To give you a better idea of what the job encompasses, I quote from the official U.S. Civil Service Commission Position Description form:

• Subject only to the general direction of the President of the United States, serves as "Chief Usher" of the White House. As such is the general manager of the Executive Mansion, and is delegated full responsibility for directing the administrative, fiscal, and personnel functions involved in the management and operation of the Executive Mansion and grounds, including construction, maintenance, and remodeling of the Executive Mansion.

• Is responsible for the preparation and justification of budget estimates covering administrative and operating expenses, and for the construction and maintenance projects of the Executive Mansion . . . , as well as for the allotment, control, and proper expenditure of funds appropriated for these purposes.

• Is responsible for the direction and supervision of the activities of approximately one hundred employees of the President's household including their selection, appointment, placement, promotion, separation, disciplinary

action, etc. In addition, exercises responsibility over the mechanical and maintenance forces in connection with the maintenance and repair of buildings and grounds.
• Serves as the receptionist at the White House, and as such is responsible for receiving and caring for all personal and official guests calling on the President or the First Lady. These guests include, among others, members of the Congress and their families, members of the Judicial Branch, governors, foreign dignitaries, and heads of state. Is responsible for arranging for accommodations for house guests, their comfort, their acquaintance with the customs of the household, etc. Is responsible and arranges for all personal and official entertainments, receptions, dinners, etc., in the Executive Mansion, which frequently include the heads of sovereign states, and several hundred persons. Is responsible for the procurement of all food consumed by the President's family and their guests. Makes personal appointments for the President and other members of his official family.
• Is responsible for answering a large volume of correspondence regarding the Executive Mansion, its history and furnishings, historical subjects, sightseeing, Congressional requests with regard to the Mansion and Grounds, State functions, etc.
• Is completely responsible for the efficient operation, cleanliness, and maintenance of the 132 rooms of the Executive Mansion containing 1,600,000 cubic feet; $2,000,000 of mechanical and air-conditioning equipment.

During all my years of managing the White House, I gave no interviews, sought no publicity. I felt articles about my activities would hamper my effectiveness. My loyalty was not to any one President, but rather, to the Presidency, and to the institution that is the White House. The Executive Mansion of the United States is more than a temporary home for the family who lives there for four or eight years. It is now a museum containing priceless works of art and furnishings, a national monument open to two million tourists a year, a guest hotel for entertaining visitors of state, and, in recent years, an impregnable fortress for protecting the life of the Commander-in-Chief.

In more than a quarter-century in the Usher's office just inside the front door, and in the private office of the Chief Usher upstairs at the White House, I came to know and admire Eleanor Roosevelt, Bess Truman, Mamie Eisenhower, Jacqueline Kennedy, Lady Bird Johnson, and, briefly, Pat Nixon. Each brought with her a different viewpoint, a different life style, and each, in her own way, using her own background and training, made a special imprint upon the President's House, and her own contribution to the heritage of the United States.

As First Ladies of the land, these women filled the most demanding volunteer job in America. They were not elected, they were legally responsible to no one except the man with whom they had exchanged marriage vows. They had no official title. First Lady was a term popularized by a newswoman many years ago, but it has remained the only designation given to the woman who is married to the man we call "Mr. President."

To me, each is indeed the First Lady, and will ever hold my greatest respect.

J. B. W.

The
Roosevelts

1

Contrary to published reports, Eleanor Roosevelt never walked anywhere. She ran.

She always raced down the halls of the White House from one appointment to another, skirts flapping around her legs. And then she would sail out the front door at full speed, jump into her waiting car, and call out to the driver: "Where am I going?"

Or she hurried down the driveway and out the front gates to the bus stop or, on a sunny day, marched resolutely a full ten blocks up Connecticut Avenue to her volunteer office on Dupont Circle—and on her way back, she gathered up people to bring home for lunch. There were no Secret Service men hovering around Eleanor Roosevelt.

I was introduced to this awesome study in human motion on my first day in the White House, March 1, 1941. I had just begun work as assistant to Chief Usher Howell G. Crim, a small, proper man in a black suit, and was sitting beside his desk near the front door. Suddenly, the First Lady of the Land appeared in the doorway of the Usher's office. I jumped to my feet.

"Mrs. Roosevelt, may I present J. B. West, my new assistant," announced Mr. Crim.

The tall, imposing woman smiled, showing more teeth than I'd ever seen, and extended a slim, graceful hand. It was surprisingly soft in my grasp.

"How do you do, Ma'am," I managed to say.

She was wearing a dark skirt and a white ruffled blouse, and wisps of gray were beginning to stray from her hair, which was loosely pulled back into a knot. When she spoke, her voice was high-pitched and shrill, and she talked so fast I had trouble understanding her.

Dismissing me with a pleasant nod, she turned to Mr. Crim, who handled all appointments in the mansion: "I'm having the Japanese Ambassador to tea," she said. "I'll see him in the Red Room, but please don't leave me in there too long with him—I don't know what to talk about!"

And she was off.

Mrs. Roosevelt well knew that American and Japanese leaders were engaged in a delicate verbal sparring match, while her husband sought to prepare the country for any eventuality, including war. And as a single male of twenty-nine, reading newspaper warnings of impending war, and reports about Japan's invasions, I, too, was concerned.

A few minutes after Mrs. Roosevelt hurried down the red-carpeted hallway, Secretary of War Stimson, Secretary of the Treasury Morgenthau, and Presidential Advisor Harry Hopkins entered the White House through the North Portico facing Pennsylvania Avenue. The liveried doorman brought the three gentlemen to the Usher's office, the first door to the right off the marble-floored main lobby.

Mr. Crim checked their names off the list of Presidential appointments and accompanied the three men upstairs to meet with Franklin Delano Roosevelt.

"That's the only ushering I do," the Chief Usher explained. "We always accompany guests to a formal appointment with the President and First Lady. We simply announce their names. The rest of the time, we run the place. I have a budget of $152,000 a year, a staff of 62, and a free hand to furnish and direct the mansion as I see fit." He added that he had working under him two ushers, Wilson Searles and Charles Claunch, on duty in shifts from the time the President awakened in the morning until his valet put him to bed at night.

And I, because I could type and take shorthand and, I was told, mind my own business, was sent over from my job in the Veterans Administration to be assistant to the Chief Usher.

"I'd like you to handle Mrs. Roosevelt's travel arrangements, the mail, and assist in the operation of the White House," Mr. Crim told me.

"The President's mail as well?" I asked, thinking I'd surely be snowed under.

"No, just the mail that comes to our office, concerning anything related to the mansion itself. The President's and Mrs. Roosevelt's mail is handled by their personal staffs."

That first day, I thought the Usher's office was a twelve-by-twelve-foot madhouse. People ran in and out of the room all day, the phone rang incessantly, and the buzzer buzzed.

Mr. Crim tried to explain the signal system, which registered on the electric callboard above his desk. Listed on the board were the names of every room in the house, the corridors, the elevator. When the buzzer sounded, an arrow popped up, indicating one of those locations.

"This is to alert everybody—police, secret service, doormen, ushers—when the President is on the move," he said. "Three buzzes are for the President, two buzzes mean the First Lady, and one is for a guest—and that includes the President's children."

One buzzer rang, the arrow pointed toward the word "elevator," and minutes later Mrs. John Roosevelt, the President's daughter-in-law, stopped in on her way to see her ailing husband at the Bethesda Naval Hospital. "I'll be bringing him back here this afternoon for a few days," the young woman said.

Mr. Crim made a note for the housekeeping staff to prepare a bedroom for John Roosevelt.

"Is he very ill?" I asked the Chief Usher.

13

"Indeed not," he said. "You sneeze around here and they call it pneumonia. This goldfish bowl is made out of magnifying glass."

Houseguests, including Alexander Woollcott—"The Man Who Came to Dinner," opera star Grace Castagnetta, Henrik Van Loon, wandered in and out trying to make themselves at home.

"We assign them to their rooms and hope they stay there," Mr. Crim explained. Then, in a whisper, he confided: "Mr. Woollcott is impossible. He was supposed to stay for two days and stayed two weeks. He rings for coffee at all hours of the night, and he invites guests right up to his room."

The short, balding Mr. Crim was easily horrified at anything he considered a breach of the highest standards in manners and morals. He was so correct, his eyebrows seemed perpetually raised. When his employers appeared, he almost bowed and clicked his heels.

"You 'Mr. President' the President," he instructed me, "and 'Ma'am' the First Lady."

My strongest impression that first day was of Eleanor Roosevelt, who kept popping in and out of the office, her gray hair more disheveled with every appearance. She thrust a new list of appointments at Mr. Crim and was off again. I could have sworn the wind whistled as she zipped into the office still another time.

"Frances Parkinson Keyes is coming for lunch," she announced and zipped out.

Mr. Crim pulled out a place card from his top desk drawer, carefully lettered the lady novelist's name, and took me down the hall where we made a right turn into the Private Dining Room. "Set up one more place for lunch," he ordered, introducing me to head butler Alonzo Fields.

The Private Dining Room, adjoining the larger State Dining Room, was set for sixteen. "It's hardly private," Mr. Crim said. "She has a luncheon here nearly every day."

During the noontime lull, while the luncheon guests chattered away, and between every visitor, Mr. Crim quietly instructed the staff—head butler and his men,

14

housekeeper Henrietta Nesbitt, doormen, gardeners, engineers, plumbers, carpenters, electricians, painters, drivers—in their duties for the day.

By afternoon, I had met most of the people who kept the President's House a going concern. And at four o'clock I watched Mr. Crim escort the Japanese Ambassador in to the Red Room, to have tea with Mrs. Roosevelt.

"She hasn't changed her dress or combed her hair," Mr. Crim reported when he returned to our office, only a few yards away. At the end of fifteen minutes, he looked at his watch, then, as Mrs. Roosevelt had instructed, marched into the Red Room to help her end the tense appointment.

When I got home, I wrote in my diary: "Spent the day wondering if I'll like the job. The first day wasn't too impressive, but I'll know more tomorrow."

On my second day in the White House, Charles Claunch, the usher on duty, took me on the elevator to the second floor. The door opened, and the Secret Service guard wheeled in the President of the United States. Startled, I looked down at him. It was only then that I realized that Franklin D. Roosevelt was really paralyzed. Immediately I understood why this fact had been kept so secret. Everybody knew that the President had been stricken with infantile paralysis, and his recovery was legend, but few people were aware how completely the disease had handicapped him.

I'd seen the President once before, three years earlier, when he brought his campaign train through Creston, Iowa.

"Why on earth do you want to see that man?" asked the owner of the store where I was bookkeeper. "I wouldn't step across the street to look at him!"

But after all, it was the first time a President of the United States had ever stopped in Creston, and I went to the train station to see him, even though he *was* a Democrat. (I spotted my boss in the crowd, too.)

We all knew he was supposed to be "crippled," that he walked with a limp or something, but then, standing with Mrs. Roosevelt on the back platform of the campaign

15

train, he looked strong, healthy, and powerful. He had a huge head, broad shoulders and a barrel chest, and he stood well over six feet tall. I don't remember a word of his speech, but there was something in his manner. He was truly dynamic, I thought.

Now, as I watched him in his wheelchair, the vitality was gone. His little black Scottie, Fala, ran into the elevator, the door closed, and Claunch introduced me to Mr. Roosevelt. It was a tight squeeze in the car, and I felt uncomfortable towering over the President of the United States. It was a long two minutes back down to the first floor. As he wheeled out, Mr. Roosevelt flashed that famous smile at me:

"You're going to have to go some to be able to type and take dictation as well as Claunch can," he said. Mr. Claunch beamed.

I soon learned that the White House staff took extraordinary precautions to conceal Mr. Roosevelt's inability to walk. Special ramps had been built all over the White House for the President's wheelchair. During State dinners, butlers seated the President first, then rolled the wheelchair out of sight. Only then were guests received in the dining room. For ceremonies in the East Room, the doormen would quietly close the double doors, which were covered with red velvet curtains, after all the guests had assembled. Mr. Roosevelt then rode to the doors in his wheelchair, someone lifted him from the chair, and we flung open the doors and curtains. The President, on the arm of an aide, swung his legs the two steps to the podium, on which he could lean while speaking. No photographs were permitted. His entrances were passed off as Presidential dramatics.

At formal receptions, the gardeners set up a wall of ferns at the south end of the Blue Room. A special seat, like a bicycle seat, was placed between the ferns. It protruded just enough for the President to sit on and still look as if he were standing. His legs, shrunken and useless, could not balance him. With his heavy, steel braces, he could only remain in an upright position with the assistance of someone or something.

My entire first week I spent observing the comings and

goings in the White House—Ambassadors, the Secretaries of War and Treasury, the omnipresent Mr. Hopkins. We were in the midst of growing international tension, first about the German armies which had swept through Europe and now threatened England, then also because of Japan's drive deeper into China. The President's visitors, I discovered, had to do with the Lend-Lease program of aid to the Allies, which he signed into law on March 11, and which was eventually to cost fifty billion dollars.

The mansion was always full of people. But sitting just inside the front door, I soon found that the White House had two kinds of visitors: there were the President's people, and then there were Mrs. Roosevelt's people.

2

For the Roosevelts, the White House was like a Grand Hotel. Eleanor Roosevelt's life was filled with visitors from early morning until late at night. Her house was full of guests, some of whom stayed for months, and some of whom she'd just picked up on the street. Sometimes she invited so many people, she forgot who they were.

Mrs. Roosevelt never took a meal alone, that I remember. Dressed in her wrapper, a flowing morning robe, she'd step out of her tiny, austere bedroom, to the chintzy, floral West Sitting Hall, where she presided over a table of assorted houseguests, business appointments, or just friends. The bacon and eggs, carried up two floors and served by two butlers, were usually quite cold by the time breakfast began.

She always had guests for lunch. Every day she was at the White House, the butlers served a formal seated luncheon for at least twelve, in the Private Dining Room on the first floor. She arranged the seating herself, stopping in at the Usher's office to pick up the place cards, sometimes scribbling the names herself, sometimes handing the cards to Mr. Crim to letter. There were always at least two more people to fit in at the last minute.

Her dinner guests, again in the Private Dining Room, wore black tie, although they were usually "working" guests, people involved in the projects in which she was interested—subsistence homestead, National Youth Administration, Work Corps for single women, WPA art, and anything else to do with public welfare or social justice. Unless the dinner were a State occasion, the President rarely appeared.

On Sunday nights, Mrs. Roosevelt's table was like a European salon. The President did attend, if he felt well, and listened to authors, artists, actresses, playwrights, sculptors, dancers, world travelers, old family friends—mixed in with Ambassadors, Supreme Court Justices, Cabinet officers, and Presidential Advisors.

Eleanor Roosevelt, using a large silver chafing dish she'd brought from Hyde Park, scrambled eggs at the table. But the main course was conversation.

We called the menu "scrambled eggs with *brains.*"

Mrs. Roosevelt often entertained her personal guests in her two-room suite on the second floor. Her sitting room, a drab parlor with sofa and desk, adjoined a small dressing room, where she slept in a narrow, single bed. As in her husband's suite, the walls were covered with framed photographs of official life. There were so many pictures that we had to draw a detailed plan of their arrangement each time we cleaned or painted the walls.

The Roosevelts were great collectors. President Roosevelt's books took every inch of space on the White House shelves, and they overflowed into stacks and stacks on the third floor. His intricate ship models and Naval mementoes were not appreciated by the staff, however. Each tiny sail and gangplank had to be carefully dusted, and he was in the room so much the servants hardly had time to finish their chores. His study was not air-conditioned, and in the summer, with the windows always open, his collections collected more dust.

Eleanor Roosevelt collected people. We could accommodate 21 overnight visitors at a time, but Mrs. Roosevelt often invited more. And it was always musical chairs with the guest rooms at the President's House. "We've got them hanging from the hooks," Mr. Crim told me one day as two new arrivals appeared, suitcases in hand, and we had to move one of the President's sons to his third bedroom of the week, to make room.

By 1941, the Roosevelt children, Anna, James, Franklin, Elliott, and John, were grown, with families of their own. When they visited the mansion, they were accorded no special privileges because they were Roosevelts. Mrs. Roosevelt saw them briefly by appointment or at breakfast, treating them just like any other houseguest.

Movie stars, political friends, just plain people she had met on her travels—Mrs. Roosevelt invited them all to spend the night at the White House. The First Lady was so busy with her own work, however, she sometimes didn't know who was sleeping down the hall. Once they came, she left the visitors to their own devices. They used the White House like a hotel, meandering in and out at will, sometimes stopping by the Usher's office for help in scheduling their day in Washington.

Some never went home. There were two "permanent guests" at the White House. One of them, Lorena Hickok, a former reporter who currently worked at the Democratic National Committee, lived in the little room on the northwest corner of the second floor, across the hall from Mrs. Roosevelt's bedroom. "Hick," as she was called, had become an intimate friend of Eleanor Roosevelt's while covering the first Presidential campaign, and moved into the White House after she left journalism to join the Roosevelt administration. A heavy-set, mannish woman, she kept to herself, never taking meals with the family or staff, never appearing at any social functions. Sometimes there were so many people in the house that Miss Hickok would have to relinquish her room to another guest and sleep on the couch in Mrs. Roosevelt's sitting room.

The other "staying guest" was Joseph Lash,* a young man in his early thirties, who when he was in Washington

* This same Joseph Lash, in the 1970's, published an intimate, two-volume, prize-winning biography of Eleanor Roosevelt.

slept in the small blue bedroom on the second floor, across from the President's study. Lash was executive secretary of the American Student Union. Because of her work with the American Youth Congress, Mrs. Roosevelt took a special interest in the young man.

Joe Lash occupied a unique position in Mrs. Roosevelt's life during my years in the Roosevelt White House. He was her closest confidante, her most personal friend. The two would sit in his room talking until late at night; she'd step across the hall to say good morning before her breakfast, and to say good night after everyone had gone to bed. They often walked together around the sixteen acres of White House lawn, or down Washington streets. When he was called to the Capitol to testify before a House Committee, Mrs. Roosevelt sat in the hearing-room audience like an anxious mother, her knitting needles clicking. Eleanor Roosevelt was closer to Joe Lash than she was to her own children, we thought. But then, her children didn't live in the White House.

Once, we almost caused an international incident because we moved Joe out of his room.

Mrs. Roosevelt had gone to New York. While the First Lady was out of town, Crown Princess Martha of Norway and her gentleman-in-waiting moved in for a personal visit with the President. We placed the Princess in the Queen's Room, at the east end of the floor, and her aide nearby in the small blue room, moving Joe Lash to a little room on the third floor.

But Mrs. Roosevelt came home during the night—actually it was early in the morning, she'd slept on the train—and nobody told her of the arrangements. Her first stop was the small blue room, Joe's room. As she usually did, she gave a little rap on the door and walked right in. And was greeted by a totally shocked—and totally undressed—gentleman-in-waiting for Princess Martha.

The First Lady was mortified.

At eight o'clock that morning, Mrs. Roosevelt phoned the Usher's office. In her iciest tones, she said, "Never, never move or change a guest from one room to another without first contacting me. The telephone operators can reach me wherever I might be."

In my early days in the White House, the President's closest confidante appeared to be his secretary. One morning shortly after I came to work there, I was alone in the Usher's office when the telephone rang.

"Is this the Usher?" a young woman's voice asked. "No . . ." I answered, and the lady hung up. Minutes later, the garage called. "Miss LeHand has ordered a car," the dispatcher reported. The garage, as well as the front door, was under Mr. Crim's supervision, and normally the Usher placed orders for all cars. When the Chief Usher returned, I mentioned the puzzling order.

"Who is Miss LeHand?" I asked.

Mr. Crim's eyebrows elevated. "She is the President's *personal* secretary, who lives in a two-room apartment on the third floor," he explained, noting her order in his "Garage" book. "In fact, she probably sees more of the President than Mrs. Roosevelt does. She acts as his hostess when Mrs. Roosevelt isn't here."

Thereafter, Miss LeHand ordered cars at will.

But in early June, Marguerite LeHand, acting as hostess at a small party in the Diplomatic Reception Room for the President's close personal staff, suffered a stroke, and after a stay in the hospital, went to Warm Springs to recover.* Her duties were taken over by her assistant, Grace Tully, who did not live in the mansion.

In contrast to Mrs. Roosevelt's close relationship with friends, and her husband's with his staff, we never saw Eleanor and Franklin Roosevelt in the same room alone together. They had the most separate relationship I have ever seen between man and wife. And the most equal.

When she met with him, it was usually in the evenings. She always brought him a sheaf of papers, a bundle of ideas. His secretary Grace Tully was usually there, or hers, Malvina Thompson. Mrs. Roosevelt reported to her husband not only to plead for her own projects and for liberal programs that she favored, but also to discuss other matters. The President had lots of people serving as his "eyes

---

* Miss LeHand was never able to return to her duties; she died in 1944, in Boston's Lahey Clinic.

and ears" around the country. But his wife was perhaps his most trusted observer.

Because of his infirmity, the President couldn't travel at the pace his wife did. He sent her out to assess the feelings of the people on just about everything, including his own policy statements. After eight years in office, he knew full well the awe that strikes most men when they walk into the President's office, that they are tempted to tell the Chief Executive only what he wants to hear. Because of that tendency to be less than frank, he felt he couldn't trust his regular channels to filter correct information to him.

Mrs. Roosevelt, therefore, performed a high-level intelligence operation for him. A skilled interviewer, she could easily instill confidence in anyone from an illiterate farm worker to a high government official, and draw out the person's true opinions or reactions. Her reports to the President were filled with facts and quite often went to the very heart of a subject.

The longer she lived in the White House, the more people found out about this "intelligence service," and an ever-increasing number tried to get to her, hoping she would filter their messages to Mr. Roosevelt. Which may have partially accounted for some of our overburdened guest lists.

The White House conferences between husband and wife did not occur all that often. The President spent far more time with his personal advisor Harry L. Hopkins. Mr. Hopkins had been one of the original Brain Trust; he was the first administrator of the National Relief Administration, then head of the Civil Works Administration and Works Progress Administration, and from 1938 until September, 1940, Secretary of Commerce. Now he was living in the White House, with his daughter, Diana. He walked up the hall from his bedroom to spend hours on end with the President. Mr. Hopkins, a widower, took the "Lincoln's office" guest room down the hall from the family quarters, and Diana lived on the third floor next to the sun porch.

A little girl of eight, Diana was the first child to live in the White House since "Sistie" and "Buzzie" Dall, Anna

Roosevelt Boettiger's two children, had lived there for a few years in the Thirties. But now the Roosevelt White House was not geared to life with children, and Diana was quite lonely. She had few visitors her own age, very few occasions to see the Roosevelts, and little time with her father. So the White House domestic staff "adopted" Diana.

Her father ate dinner with President Roosevelt, on trays in the President's private study, and worked with him there, often joined by Grace Tully, until late at night. The President also entertained his private visitors in that study. He was proud of his abilities as a bartender. A butler would place a tray of fixings atop the ornately carved desk, and, announcing that his specialty was a dry martini, Franklin Roosevelt mixed the drinks himself.

Two of the most important men in President Roosevelt's life, however, were his valets, Arthur Prettyman and George Fields. The two men worked a twenty-four-hour shift, taking turns sleeping on the third floor, so the President could call for assistance after retiring, for he could not get out of bed without their help. Every morning, the valet would call down to the kitchen to order Mr. Roosevelt's breakfast, and a White House butler soon brought up a tray.

The President's bedroom, on the south side of the second floor, was sparsely furnished, with a modified hospital bed—not much wider than a standard single bed. At about ten every morning, his aides, General Edwin "Pa" Watson and Press Secretary Steve Early, went up to his bedroom for their morning conference. The three would pore over the day's newspapers (except the Chicago *Tribune*, which was barred from the house), and the list of daily appointments.

Then Mr. Roosevelt's valet would dress the President and wheel him into his adjoining oval study. The room, painted a flat battleship gray, was like a naval museum. The study shelves were lined with hundreds of books, photographs, and a vast collection of ships' models. Mr. Roosevelt's massive oak desk, made from the timbers of HMS *Resolute*, was covered with personal mementoes. A cabinet radio, two breakfronts full of books, and a big green rug filled the room.

If the President was feeling well, he'd emerge from the second floor at about noon and his bodyguard or valet would wheel him to the elevator and down to his official office in the west wing. Mr. Roosevelt frequently suffered from sinus trouble, and he came down with a good case of flu every winter. When he did not feel well, he held all his appointments in that oval study upstairs.

Franklin Roosevelt loved to have a fire crackling in the marble fireplace of that room. But the valets were instructed to extinguish the fire if he were left in the room alone, even for a few minutes. He was afraid that the room might catch fire, and he knew that he could not get out by himself.

The valets, Mr. Hopkins, "Pa" Watson and Steve Early, Grace Tully—those were the Oval Room "regulars." The President shuffled other appointments in and out about every fifteen minutes, with an usher appearing at the door to announce the next guest. But there was one frequent visitor whom we never hurried.

Quite often, but only when Mrs. Roosevelt was out of town, the President invited his friend Mrs. Lucy Mercer Rutherfurd to the White House. An attractive, vivacious woman in her forties, she'd arrive at the front door, the north entrance. We'd watch her hurry up the steps, to be escorted by an usher to the second floor. The butler would serve tea, close the door, and leave the President and Mrs. Rutherfurd alone. After about an hour's time, the President rang for the doorman to escort her back to her car.

In good weather, the President enjoyed taking a drive in the Virginia countryside with his little dog, Fala, and the Secret Service guard. One day Mr. Roosevelt directed the driver to go along a certain wooded, dirt road. Suddenly, he ordered the driver to stop. "There seems to be a lady walking along the road. Let us ask her if she needs a ride," the President directed.

The fourth time this incident occurred, the Secret Service men following the President began to be aware that the same lady, on the same country road, always needed a ride. They'd take the long route to her destination, giving the President and his passenger a scenic spin in the big car. One of the agents mentioned those drives to the Usher's office, wondering if any of us might know the mysterious lady. So one day Wilson Searles talked the agent into letting him accompany them on an excursion. When he saw Searles in the Secret Service car, Mr. Roosevelt laughed.

"I see it's your turn to find out what's going on!" the President said. The lady was Mrs. Rutherfurd.

President Roosevelt's recreation—drives in the country, fishing from the yacht *Potomac*, weekends at Shangri-La —was limited by his desire for privacy and by the restrictions of his physical condition. At the White House, his sole form of exercise was swimming in the austere, fifty-foot pool under the west terrace. That swimming pool had been built for the President in 1933, from funds raised by a nationwide newspaper campaign. At first, Mr. Crim told me, Mr. Roosevelt had exercised there several times a day; now, at the age of fifty-nine, he seldom swam. He spent most of his time in his oval office in the west wing of the White House, or upstairs in his oval study.

If Franklin Roosevelt's days were spent more or less in confinement, Mrs. Roosevelt more than made up for it in activity.

After her "company" breakfasts in the West Hall upstairs, which all first families use as a sitting room, Mrs. Roosevelt joined her competent secretary, Malvina ("Tommy") Thompson, in the First Lady's tiny office by the elevator, overlooking the north lawn. There, she'd begin dictating her syndicated newspaper column, "My Day," which gave the country a running account of the Roosevelts' activities. She could never sit still for long, however, and she'd often jump up from her desk, "Tommy" at her elbow, and fly down the halls, dictating all the way. She'd even dictate—or write notes to herself—riding in limousines, on trains and planes.

Eleanor Roosevelt was very communicative. She wrote for magazines, talked over the radio, went on lecture tours, pouring out millions of words to the patient Miss Thompson. During the process, the two of them would cook up enough work to occupy the White House staff for the next 48 hours. It had to be done in eight, of course.

The President's wife delegated responsibility, requiring the same efficiency from her staff as she did of herself. Once she had given an order, she immediately forgot about it. There was no checking back with her for clarification. She didn't have time to give instructions twice.

She must have scribbled a million notes during her years in the White House—notes which had all the legibility of a doctor's prescription. One day Mr. Crim came down with two gold wristwatches. "Send the watches to the engraver," he told me. "Mrs. Roosevelt wants them to be sent out as gifts. Here are the inscriptions and the addresses." I tried all morning to read the instructions but couldn't make head or tail of them. Neither could Mr. Crim, which I suspect is why he turned them over to me.

Finally I went up and asked Mrs. Roosevelt's personal secretary. "Tommy" knew what to expect from her boss. "I'm not going to take those watches back to her," she said. "You'll have to do it yourself."

Embarrassed, I took the watches in to Mrs. Roosevelt's sitting room and found her at her desk, scribbling away. The First Lady looked up, then frowned. By that time she had quite forgotten which watch was for whom. She was not amused. "You are supposed to get things right the first time," she said.

One of the watches, it turned out, had been selected by Joe Lash as a gift to his future wife.

Although she dealt with thousands of details every day, Mrs. Roosevelt wanted trivial matters handled with dispatch. There were more important things on her mind.

She didn't have much time for housekeeping problems either, and the mansion suffered because of it. Even to me, an Iowa boy with little experience in such matters, it seemed dingy, almost seedy. She left things up to the housekeeper, Henrietta Nesbitt, who was more country gentlewoman than dirt chaser. Mrs. Roosevelt didn't pay much attention to White House food, either, but the President did. He couldn't stand it.

"I wish we could do something about Mrs. Nesbitt," he said to Mr. Crim, in mock surrender, "but Mrs. Roosevelt won't hear of it."

Henrietta Nesbitt prided herself on her friendship with the First Lady, and blithely instructed cook Elizabeth Moore to carry out her menus, no matter what the President requested.

"The food around here would do justice to the Automat," the President said.

On the third floor, they installed a diet kitchen, where meals for the President were prepared by his mother's old Hyde Park cook, Mary Campbell. As the years went by, the President ordered almost all his meals cooked there, separate from the White House kitchen.

Her feelings ruffled, Mrs. Nesbitt complained to Mr. Crim, "Mary Campbell's kitchen is so dirty, I'm concerned about the President's health." Mr. Crim, alarmed, reported the complaint to the President.

"You tell Mrs. Roosevelt I'll get rid of Mary Campbell when she gets rid of old lady Nesbitt!" the Chief Executive shot back.

And Mrs. Nesbitt stayed on. Once, during a White House luncheon where she was a guest, she looked up at a chandelier and remarked to the woman next to her, "My goodness, isn't that filthy?"

"As if she were a guest instead of the housekeeper," Mr. Crim sniffed.

Mrs. Roosevelt's personal maid, Mabel Webster, lived on the third floor and took care of the First Lady's clothing and personal laundry. Mabel had come down from Hyde Park with the Roosevelts, but was now on the government payroll. All the Roosevelts' servants were treated with great deference by the White House staff. They ate with the other domestics in the servants' dining room on the ground floor, which was decorated with paintings by WPA artists, but when Mabel Webster entered the dining room, the White House servants rose to attention, as if the First Lady herself had walked in.

The First Lady's table was more democratic. Neither the President nor Mrs. Roosevelt liked to sit at the head of the table, whether in the State Dining Room or in the

28

small Private Dining Room. Instead, they were seated across from each other, on either side of the table, where they'd have a chance to be near, and talk with, more of their guests. Mrs. Roosevelt also sat in the same central position at her luncheons, having worked out her seating arrangements on a chart in the Usher's office.

After the Private Dining Room had been cleared from Mrs. Roosevelt's luncheons, the First Lady herself went back upstairs with "Tommy" to her office for an hour or two, then came down again to greet official visitors.

When she received those appointments in the formal State rooms on the first floor, we had them lined up in every room. She might come down to meet someone in the Red Room, while others were waiting in the Blue Room, the Green Room, the East Room, and even in the Lobby. Each visitor garnered about fifteen or twenty minutes of her time. At the end of that time, one of us would go in and announce her next appointment, so that her present visitor would know it was time to leave.

When Mrs. Roosevelt served tea in the Red Room, pouring herself, she could see many people in a short period of time. Tea was an important ritual in her life. Eleanor Roosevelt, educated in England, was of an era, of a social class, where a young lady learned the niceties of serving tea at an early age, and expected to preside at a tea table as part of her daily life. She was also a strict teetotaler, the only one among my First Ladies, and tea was the one beverage she could offer graciously—and briefly.

For the huge teas, Edith Helm, her social secretary, sat at one end of the long table in the State Dining Room, Miss Thompson at the other, serving the hundreds of guests. On one occasion the efficient "Tommy" was presiding behind the silver urns at the south end of the table. Among the honored guests was the British Ambassador.

"Coffee, tea, or cocoa?" Tommy asked routinely.

"Madam, I was invited for *tea!*" the gentleman replied.

In the West Sitting Hall upstairs, Mrs. Roosevelt served tea every afternoon at five for family, personal friends, and houseguests. Eleanor Roosevelt had tea even on the rare occasions when she was alone, sitting at a table covered with a lace cloth, pouring from a silver teapot.

The First Lady served tea to the women attending her regular press conferences in the Monroe Room. Next door to the old Lincoln office, where Harry Hopkins slept, the Monroe Room was filled with reproductions of the original Monroe furniture—which President Monroe had taken with him. When Mrs. Roosevelt had parties for the entire Washington press corps, however, they served beer in the foyer and danced the Virginia reel in the East Room.

Mrs. Roosevelt held conferences in the East Room, too, meetings mainly concerned with public welfare projects. Seated in the front row, knitting away, she spoke out whenever an idea caught her imagination. During those conferences, she turned out more baby blankets than she had grandchildren, and began passing her handiwork along to her friends. Knitting, scribbling notes, marking a passage in a book, Mrs. Roosevelt had the busiest hands I ever saw.

She believed in physical exercise, and encouraged all her staff to square-dance or do calisthenics. Besides her walking, which was always *to* somewhere, she often rode horseback in Rock Creek Park, either alone or with her good friend Elinor Morgenthau, wife of the Secretary of the Treasury.

I'll never forget my first sight of Eleanor Roosevelt in her riding habit, jodhpurs, boots, striding into the Usher's office, calling for her horse. I would call the White House stable, at Fort Myer, Virginia, and they'd put the horse in a van and take him to Rock Creek Park. There Mrs. Roosevelt, who had arrived in a White House car, would mount, and trot around in the woods along the shallow creek. She refused to take a Secret Service man along when she rode—or when she walked or took the train. Despite the great passions she aroused pro and con, the agents bowed to her wishes and let her roam around by herself.

When she returned from her ride, tired, disheveled, and smelling of horse, Mr. Crim always turned up his nose a bit. I had the feeling that, despite his protestations of neutrality, he slightly disapproved of Mrs. Roosevelt's breezy informality. The Chief Usher, a stern and proper gentleman of the old school, was accustomed to the strict life of the Herbert Hoovers, who dined regally in formal attire in the State Dining Room even if they were alone. He never quite recovered from the shock of one of Eleanor Roosevelt's early-morning visits to the Usher's office.

"I was sitting in my office with the door open, and there she came padding down the back stairs—barefoot. She had on a yellow bathing suit! She came up to me with some letters and said she was on her way to swim, and wouldn't I please mail these—." Eight years later, Mr. Crim was still aghast.

Mr. Crim had an ally in Sara Delano Roosevelt, the President's mother. During her visits the staff snapped to attention, and the service was as formal as if a queen were being entertained—even though the atmosphere was somewhat tense. A formidable matriarch, the elder Mrs. Roosevelt didn't take to her daughter-in-law's collection of friends, and she let everyone know it. Sara Roosevelt enjoyed Mr. Crim's company, however, and she often stopped by to chat with him.

One morning during my early days, she was sitting in our office when Naval Officer Earl Miller walked through the hall. A frequent overnight visitor and great comrade of the First Lady, Miller's friendship with Mrs. Roosevelt dated from earlier years, when her husband served as governor of New York. At that time, he had been a private in the New York State Police. Then later he guarded the Roosevelt estate in Hyde Park. Now he was a lieutenant commander in the Navy.

Sara Delano Roosevelt recognized him.

"First it was Private Miller. Then it was *Sergeant* Miller. Then it was *Commander* Miller. Now it's *Earl, dear*," she sniped, imitating the First Lady's high-pitched voice.

"Mrs. Roosevelt, Senior," as the telephone operators called her, also let Mr. Crim know how she felt about Mrs. Roosevelt's determination to integrate the White House domestic staff. She disapproved.

Eleanor Roosevelt was deeply involved in fighting for human rights for Negro Americans, and though her efforts

31

seem, in today's world, naïve and even conservative, she shocked the New York socialites with whom she had grown up, and infuriated Washington, D. C., a very segregated town.

She begged, cajoled, pleaded with her husband to integrate the Armed Services, to propose sweeping civil rights legislation, and to integrate the defense industry. Perhaps his zeal was not so great as hers, perhaps he had other priorities before the Southerners in Congress, but she was continuously far ahead of Franklin D. Roosevelt on that subject.

She aroused the wrath of Washington, and of her mother-in-law, but raised the hopes of millions of Americans by inviting blacks to the White House. Most notable of these was her friend Mary McLeod Bethune, the distinguished Negro educator.

When Mrs. Bethune arrived, Mrs. Roosevelt always went running down the driveway to meet her, and they would walk arm in arm into the mansion. Few heads of State received such a welcome.

In those days, my job had very little to do with entertaining, however, so I glimpsed the famous visitors only as they went in and out of the White House. One day Mr. Crim caught me gazing out the window of our cubicle.

"See those people out there," he pointed to the crowd walking down Pennsylvania Avenue. "They'd give anything to be in here looking out."

Actually, I had little time to look out the window. Handling Mrs. Roosevelt's travel arrangements was a full-time job. Back and forth she crossed the country by train, bus, and car. Even though air travel was very limited in those days, she wanted to take commercial planes as often as possible to dispel the public's fear of flying.

She would go to the most remote places—to coal mining towns in West Virginia, to public works projects in Oregon or Arizona, to New York innumerable times. I had traveled only from Iowa to Washington, so I received quite a geography lesson as I pored over maps and train schedules. Many times, after I'd spent days arranging a complicated schedule, she would cancel her plans and go somewhere else.

Her close friend Elinor Morgenthau often accompanied her on those trips. One of my first jobs involved a complicated change of reservations for a West Virginia trip. Mrs. Roosevelt had gone on ahead, and Mrs. Morgenthau was to board the train at Union Station, planning to join the President's wife. It was after dark when I finally cleared the reservations, so I met Mrs. Morgenthau at Union Station and gave her corrected tickets for Mrs. Roosevelt. Even though the reservations were secure, I felt that people like to have correct tickets in hand before undertaking a journey. I didn't think anything about it, but Mrs. Roosevelt was quick to appreciate any small favor other people did for her. She thanked me profusely, and I guess it was then they decided that I could stay.

One night as I was working late over her schedules, she wandered into the office and said, "Poor Mr. West—I change my plans so many times. . . ."

Mrs. Roosevelt, like most in her social strata, believed in the "city in winter, the country in summer," and ordered her train tickets for the family's estate in Hyde Park, New York, accordingly.

Every summer she'd come by the Usher's office, and say to Mr. Crim, "I have the President's permission to send one car, one driver, and one maid to Hyde Park for the summer."

The car, filled with her suitcases and files, followed her to the estate, where the driver and the White House maid stayed with Mrs. Roosevelt in her cottage, "Val-Kill." (The President's mother lived in the "big house" at Hyde Park.) When the President joined her, he would travel on the special Presidential railroad car, which was equipped with a bedroom, dining room, and even its own galley.

Usually, the White House almost shut down in the summers, the heat was so intense. Even though the First Family fled to the Hudson River, we had to keep the place halfway decent for the few sightseers who straggled through. But in 1941 the President spent more time in Washington than on vacation, because of his concern over the buildup of the war in Europe. Since May of that year, the President had declared an unlimited national emergency, due to the German military successes in Europe, the Balkans, and Africa. Mrs. Roosevelt came back from Hyde Park on June 17, to welcome Crown Princess Juliana and Prince Bernhard of Holland, who had just escaped from their war-torn country, which Hitler had invaded. And in August she received the Duke of Kent.

The pattern of White House living was different in 1941 for personal reasons as well. On September 7, the President's mother died. Nineteen days later, Mrs. Roosevelt's brother, Hall, died in Walter Reed Hospital, and there was a quiet family funeral in the East Room.

With those two deaths, Mrs. Roosevelt, an orphan, had lost her closest relative, Hall, and her major nemesis and critic, her mother-in-law. An era had ended in her life, and because of the threat of war, a new one was beginning.

Mrs. Roosevelt threw herself into her new volunteer job that fall, in the Office of Civil Defense. Mayor Fiorello La Guardia of New York was the titular head of the organization, which had been established in May, for "civilian protection and volunteer protection and morale responsibilities."

The President's wife got into hot water with the Congress, however, for her idea of Civil Defense included nutrition, housing, medical care, education, and recreation for all Americans. She hoped to use the organization to launch programs fulfilling her special hopes for society. The incident that incensed Congress was her appointment of Mayris Chaney, a dancer who was a frequent White House visitor, as director of the physical fitness program. The Congress thought it was pure frivolity, and hounded Mrs. Roosevelt about her "fan dancer."

But the President's wife kept marching up Connecticut Avenue dressed in the blue-gray coverall she had designed for Civil Defense, saving White House gasoline and getting exercise besides. Although ominous headlines proclaimed that war was not far off, Mrs. Roosevelt still shunned Secret Service protection.

As a new employee, unfamiliar with workings at the top level in government, I had thought Mrs. Roosevelt's pace so frenetic, I wondered how she could possibly get anything done. But now, after months of observation, I realized that her life was filled with planned, purposeful activity, her motion directed toward specific goals. She was propelled by dedication.

Even though the Usher's office handled the President's appointments in the House and Mrs. Roosevelt's travel, our concern was not with politics or international affairs. We were often too busy to keep up with the world. Nevertheless, certain developments relating to the White House could not escape our attention.

3

On Friday, March 14, 1941, I wrote in my short-lived diary: "Saw Justice Frankfurter today, after his conference with the President. The President went to the office this morning but returned to meet the Japanese Ambassador at 4:30. Learned that the visit of the Japanese Ambassador was so secret that the Secret Service men made a list of everyone who saw him come in or leave—of course, that is a rather ticklish situation! It will be interesting to see future developments."

The future developments reached me on that Sunday nine months later, as I sat in my one-room apartment in the Pall Mall on Sixteenth Street. Sunday was a lazy day —I was usually so tired after my six-day (and sometimes six-night) work week at the White House, I didn't have much time to be lonely on my one day off.

On December 7, I woke up in the afternoon and turned on the radio. Every station was screaming about Pearl Harbor.

I called the office, first thing. "Do you need me?" I asked Mr. Claunch, who had drawn the Sunday duty.

"No, Mr. Crim is on his way," he replied. "They had the luncheon all right, but the President stayed upstairs the entire time. They've canceled everything else."

I spent the evening glued to the radio.

Reporting for work at six the next morning, I thought all the policemen in Washington had gathered on the White House grounds. As I walked up the front steps, soldiers were coming in from Fort Myer to guard the Executive Mansion. Then I remembered my first day at work, when Mrs. Roosevelt hadn't known what to say to the Japanese Ambassador. We all wondered if the White House would be bombed, too.

My first call was from Mrs. Roosevelt, asking me to arrange a trip to the West Coast. She soon left by plane, to help Mayor LaGuardia set up the Civil Defense organization in California.

Everyone was in and out of the mansion all day—the Cabinet, General Marshall, top military advisors, members of Congress. We watched as the President was lifted into his car to go to the Capitol for his declaration of war. We listened on the Usher's office radio, as he proclaimed the "date which will live in infamy—[when] the United States of America was suddenly and deliberately attacked by naval and air forces of the Empire of Japan."

Although the Roosevelts canceled the formal social season* for the duration, the wartime White House was by no means quiet for us. Presidential appointments in the mansion were still handled through our office. Quite often the Chief of Staff, Allied diplomats, and other officials would come for luncheon or dinner. And gold braid showed up at the Sunday night suppers.

Immediately after Pearl Harbor, Army engineers came in with plans to build a bomb shelter. To disguise this secret project, there was much to-do about the need for

---

* Traditionally, during the period from Thanksgiving to Lent, it consisted of ten large, official receptions and dinners held at the White House to honor members of the Diplomatic Corps, the Judiciary, Congress, the Cabinet, the Chief Justice, the Vice President, and the Speaker of the House.

extra Presidential office space, and the President requested a Congressional appropriation to build the east wing. Meanwhile, a tunnel was dug underneath East Executive Avenue to the Treasury Building, so that the President could go down beneath the North Portico and into a Treasury vault. This was set up as a temporary shelter until the permanent shelter beneath the new east wing was completed in September, 1942.

The White House police force, which had been increased, moved into the basement of the east wing, and military aides, Secret Service, and social offices occupied the two new floors above.

It is easy now to forget what life was like in the United States in the early days of World War II. There was genuine fear of military attack. The nation feeling threatened, precautionary measures were quickly organized everywhere. But the routine for the White House was especially stringent.

The military office ran practice drills for the staff. Every now and then, I'd be working at my desk, only to be blasted out of my seat by the urgent clanging of fire alarm bells. Our air-raid wardens, selected from among the staff, then took over. We grabbed our gas masks, and everybody who could squeeze in headed for the small, cramped room underneath the North Portico. There we stayed, breathing at one another, until the "all-clear."

The White House endured food rationing just as everyone else in America did. Henrietta Nesbitt faithfully trotted her stamp books down to the District of Columbia ration board every month, stood in line for her White House allotment, and planned her menus accordingly.

And with all the Roosevelts' stamp books, used to purchase the $3,000 worth of food each month for family, personal friends, and domestic staff, the White House kitchen was able to come up with adequate meals.

There were blackout curtains at the windows, and we went through all the blackout drills for Washington. But everybody from the President on down was adamantly opposed to the Army's scheme to cover the exterior of the White House with black paint. "It would be less of a

38

target for bombs," the engineers argued. That idea went back to the Army engineers' drawing board.

The President canceled all White House tours, stationed machine guns on the east and west terraces, and supplanted policemen with a twenty-four-hour military guard. Soldiers roamed outside the house and grounds. They lived in temporary barracks behind the battleship-gray State, War and Navy building next door. And I was officially inducted into the U. S. Navy, detailed to Headquarters, the Commander-in-Chief.

Although Mrs. Roosevelt stayed away from the secret Map Room, and rather archly prided herself on not being privy to any military secrets, the war entered her life in a very personal way.

James was on active duty in the Marine Corps; Elliott was in the Air Force; Franklin, Jr., and John were in the Navy; and son-in-law John Boettiger was also in the service, stationed in England.

And her great friend Joe Lash had been drafted. The First Lady tried unsuccessfully to get him an officer's commission. He was, however, stationed in the Air Corps at Bolling Field, near Washington, and retained his room at the White House. He commuted to his post in Mrs. Roosevelt's official limousine, complete with chauffeur and footman. When he was finally sent overseas, she managed to visit him at his base in the Pacific.

She was able to visit her sons, too, when she took wartime trips for the President. She traveled to England, visiting army camps and hospitals, to New Zealand and Australia, to Guadalcanal and other Pacific islands, to our bases in Latin America. Dressed in her Red Cross uniform, insisting on seeing "the boys" as well as the officers, she became a personal courier between individual servicemen and their families.

She brought messages to the President, as well. When the boys in England complained of cold feet, she petitioned President Roosevelt for wool socks. When the boys in Australia complained of discrimination, she begged that Negroes not be limited to menial jobs. Her motherly instincts poured out to the fighting men, and she spent long hours answering their letters, writing their families, channeling their petitions to proper government agencies.

When wounded servicemen began returning to Washington, Mrs. Roosevelt held afternoon teas for those who were able to travel to the White House. At her first servicemen's tea, for soldiers from Walter Reed Hospital, some of the men asked her for a souvenir. Thereupon the First Lady began handing out the silver teaspoons—engraved "President's House."

Mr. Crim was horrified. The Chief Usher is responsible, on personal bond, for every item in the White House, and he had visions of Congress, examining the austere wartime budget, and refusing to approve an appropriation to replace the silver teaspoons.

"Please, Mrs. Roosevelt, could you give them matches or something instead of passing out the silver?" he pleaded—and immediately ordered plain spoons with no markings of any kind.

The First Lady's assortment of visitors actually increased during the war. Several times, walking back from the Capitol, she'd run into a serviceman and invite him into the mansion for lunch. We'd have a time trying to spell the astonished soldier's name correctly on the place card.

The most colorful visitor ever to appear at the wartime White House was Winston Churchill. His living habits are still the subject of White House staff gossip, and every visitor who sleeps in the Queen's Room is compared to the crusty old Prime Minister.

He first arrived secretly, just before Christmas in 1941. When the Secret Service passed the word that from two until three o'clock in the afternoon of December 22 no one was to leave his office, no one was to enter the halls, we knew someone important was coming. We had been told to prepare for a VIP, but we didn't know who. It didn't take long for the cigar smoke to announce Mr. Churchill's presence.

Mrs. Roosevelt had arranged for him to stay in the Lincoln bedroom, then located off the West Hall, the favorite of most male guests. However, he didn't like the bed, so he tried out all the beds and finally selected the rose suite at the east end of the second floor.

The staff did have a little difficulty adjusting to Mr. Churchill's way of living. The first thing in the morning, he declined the customary orange juice and called for a drink of Scotch. His staff, a large entourage of aides and a valet, followed suit. The butlers wore a path in the carpet carrying trays laden with brandy to his suite.

We got used to his "jumpsuit," the extraordinary one-piece uniform he wore every day, but the servants never quite got over seeing him naked in his room when they'd go up to serve brandy. It was the jumpsuit or nothing. In his room, Mr. Churchill wore no clothes at all most of the time during the day.

One day the valet wheeled President Roosevelt up to the rose room, opened the door, and there stood his unclothed guest. The Prime Minister didn't mind, but the President did. He quickly backed out into the hall until Mr. Churchill could get something on.

One gloomy morning, little Diana Hopkins walked past the open door to the rose room, where Mr. Churchill was propped up in bed, this time in his undershirt, smoking one of his enormous cigars. The Prime Minister beckoned to the little girl. He mumbled something which she didn't understand, and she walked right up to his bed.

"Would you give us just a little kiss on the cheek?" he asked—and she complied, carefully avoiding the cigar clenched between his teeth.

There was little need for Mr. Churchill to go out; people came to the White House to see him. He and the President spent most of their time conferring in the makeshift Map Room, for which Mrs. Roosevelt had surrendered her press conference space in the Monroe Room, and which was off-limits to the White House staff. A special security officer guarded the room twenty-four hours a day.

At that meeting, the President and the Prime Minister began to plan the first steps on the long road back from defeat to victory. The United States would start reclaiming control of the Pacific in air-sea warfare in the Battles of Midway and Coral Sea. The two allies would start the counterattack in Europe with an invasion of North Africa.

Mr. Churchill was in and out of the White House

41

secretly several times during the war. Each time his departure was as sudden as his arrival. Many times the public had no idea he was in Washington.

After Prime Minister Churchill's twenty-four-day visit late in 1941, the Map Room was moved, under the greatest secrecy, from the Monroe Room down to the ground floor, adjoining the Diplomatic Reception Room. The room contained complete maps of the operations of the war all over the world, pointing out where the troops were, where the ships were, and where the next move was to be made. When the room was to be cleaned, the security guard covered the maps with cloth, standing duty while the cleaner mopped the floor.

The Signal Corps took up residence in the new bomb shelter, underneath the east wing. It was simply a forty-by-forty-foot-square concrete room, with walls seven feet thick, and ceilings of nine feet of steel-enforced concrete. It had two of everything—alternate heating and lighting systems, first-aid stations, and could hold about one hundred people. The President hated the room, and always tried to beg off during air raid drills.

The President himself enjoyed a great freedom of movement during the war years—freedom, that is, from public knowledge. For security reasons, the press agreed not to publish any of the President's travels—where he was or what he was doing. He often would go to Hyde Park for the weekend, to Shangri-La,* the secret Presidential retreat operated by the Navy in the Catoctin mountains of Maryland, or to confer with someone in the Atlantic or Pacific, and no one ever knew it. From the beginning of the war, the American flag, indicating that the Chief Executive is in residence, was flown from the White House every day whether or not the President was there, a practice which still continues. (Before the war, the flag was hoisted only when the President was in residence. When he went out the White House gate, it was lowered.)

Beginning in early 1942, we had a parade of royal refugees in and out of the White House. The Crown

* Now called Camp David.

Princess of Norway, who was living in Maryland, came in January; King George and Queen Frederika of Greece and King Peter of Yugoslavia, in June; Queen Wilhelmina of the Netherlands and her daughter, Princess Juliana, who lived in Canada, in August. Mrs. Roosevelt gave the Queens the rose suite, which Mr. Churchill had also claimed as his own, and from then on, the large bedchamber at the northeast end of the second floor, which also had been used by Elizabeth of Great Britain during a 1939 visit, was called the Queen's Room.

Except for small State dinners for the royal guests, there were no ceremonial functions attached to their visits. There was one small non-State ceremony in the White House in 1942, however. Harry Hopkins quietly married Mrs. Louise Macy in the President's oval study, with only a token glass of champagne to celebrate.

Though she was more often away from home than in residence, and had priorities other than running a household, Mrs. Roosevelt considered herself the only mistress of the White House. She was more than a little concerned about Mrs. Macy's moving in under her roof, as is evidenced by the letter she wrote shortly before the wedding:

THE WHITE HOUSE
Washington

Dear Mrs. Macy:

Since living as a guest in any house is always rather difficult, I think perhaps it will be easier for you if we have some things definitely understood.

I should like you to feel that the sitting room, known as the Monroe Room, next to the rooms which you and Harry will use, is yours at all times, except on the mornings when I have a press conference in that room, or when my children are in the house, because at such times they use that room to see their friends, just as I hope you will use it at all other times.

I hope you will feel entirely free to have anyone there for tea or cocktails at any time you wish to be alone.

I know that Diana would love to feel that she is at home with you and Harry next winter and can go to day

43

school instead of boarding school. She has her own room on the third floor, and I think if she is living in the house, it would be well for you to engage a maid whom you like and trust and who would look after both you and Diana, and perhaps take Diana to various things when you are not available.

I would, of course, hope that you three would have breakfast together in your own rooms, and whenever possible, that Diana would have her supper somewhere where you could be with her rather than upstairs alone.

Of course, I shall be delighted to have you ask any friends to lunch or dinner when the service capacity of the house is not already overtaxed. I hope that when I am in the White House you will always let me know whenever you want to ask anyone, and when I am away that you will let the usher know. I will be perfectly frank if, for any reason, it is not convenient and I will tell the usher to be equally frank.

It will probably often happen that the President will prefer to have Harry dine upstairs with him, even when I am there, and have other guests. In that case, of course, you will want to be with them. When I am away, the President usually has his meals upstairs and only those he wishes, like you and Harry, would be there. Of course, in this case, if you want to ask anyone else, you simply ask the President and then tell the usher how many there will be.

In the winter months, when I am of necessity away, there may be guests of mine to be looked after, and I usually ask Miss Thompson or Mrs. Helm, the social secretary, to act as hostess for me at tea or at any meals. If you wish to join them, you just tell the usher.

It will also be a help if you will remember to tell the usher in the morning whether you and Harry are going out for any meals during the day.

Mr. Crim will try to arrange to let you have a car whenever possible, but he has only two cars for the use of guests in the White House, and they cover any calls that may be made on them by my secretaries, as well as the meeting of trains and use by transient guests. If at any time, it is impossible to let you have a car, Mr. Crim will get you a taxi, unless of course, Harry has an additional car assigned to him. We will have to talk over what arrangements can be made for getting Diana back and forth from school if she is to go to day school.

I would suggest that you talk to Mrs. Nesbitt about some regular arrangements for your wash, so that you will know on what days it must be sent and when it will be returned to you, and what it costs. Mrs. Nesbitt makes all those arrangements.

If at any time you and Harry want people to stay in the White House, I hope you will let me know beforehand so that I can arrange with Mrs. Nesbitt about the rooms because I like, even when I am away, to know how they are being used. The White House telephone operators always know where I am.

Very sincerely yours,
Eleanor Roosevelt

If Mrs. Hopkins, with her maid and her little French poodle, ever upset Mrs. Roosevelt, nobody ever noticed it. The new bride moved into the old Lincoln office with Mr. Hopkins, and her comings and goings were quickly absorbed in the general White House traffic.

Taking a cue from the happily married Mr. Hopkins, I, too, brought a bride to Washington that year. Over the Thanksgiving holiday, I went to Baltimore to meet the train from Iowa, to wed the incomparable Zella. We moved into a cramped efficiency apartment across the street from the Russian Embassy, lucky to find it in crowded wartime.

In 1943, as the war raged on, the White House opened its doors to two most unusual official guests—Madame Chiang Kai-shek of China, and Soviet Foreign Minister Vyacheslav M. Molotov. The staff was nearly floored by each of them.

On her first day in the White House, President and Mrs. Roosevelt received Madame Chiang for formal tea in the West Sitting Hall. Knowing how the Chinese are about tea, Mrs. Roosevelt had secured some very special Chinese tea, supposed to be a hundred years old, for the occasion.

When the China doll, as Mr. Crim called her, sipped daintily without comment, Mrs. Roosevelt couldn't resist telling her about it.

"In my country, tea kept so long is used only for medicinal purposes," Madame Chiang replied sweetly.

Madame Chiang, who proved not to be so democratic as her publicity had us believe, traveled with an entourage of forty, many of whom were stashed away on the third floor, the others at the Chinese Embassy. With her on the second floor were her personal maid, and her closest aides, her niece and nephew, the Kungs. At first, we thought they both were nephews.

Miss Kung dressed like a man, and the White House valets, thinking she was *Mr.* Kung, went into her room to unpack her bags and help her undress. In a short time, they were in the Usher's office. "Your Mr. Kung is a *girl*," Caesar the valet told the horrified Mr. Crim, who immediately sent two maids up to attend to her needs.

But even the President was fooled, and called her "my boy" very expansively at dinner. ("I call *all* young people 'my boy,'" he tried to cover.)

Miss Kung proved to be quite a nuisance for the First Lady. Mrs. Roosevelt called down to the Usher's office, exasperated. "Mr. Crim, can you *please* explain to Miss Kung that she is to call *you* if she needs anything? She pops into my room a dozen times a day."

The tiny, delicate-looking Madame Chiang stayed at the White House nine days, and the White House maids were never so happy to see anybody leave. "Mrs. Generalissimo" brought her own silk sheets with her, which had to be laundered by hand every day, and stitched back inside the heavy quilted sleeping bag she had brought along from China.

Caesar, the same valet who unpacked Miss Kung, rushed into the Usher's office the day Mr. Molotov arrived. His hands were trembling.

"He's got a gun in his suitcase," the valet whispered excitedly. "What shall I do?"

Mr. Crim's eyes opened wide. That was a piece of hardware most unwelcome in the White House. But delicate international conferences were going on in the President's study. The Chief Usher called the Secret Service, explaining the situation, then hung up the phone. He turned to Caesar, who was still waiting.

"Just hope he doesn't use it on you!"

In 1943, Mrs. Roosevelt was always on the go. And the more train and airplane tickets I wrote for her, the more criticism she drew from Congress. If her critics bothered her, however, she never let on. It seemed to us that she merely ignored them. The main attacks came for the trips she took in military planes, trips to visit the servicemen abroad. Because many of Mrs. Roosevelt's trips now included visits to military installations, the Army took over planning that portion of her travel.

The President crossed the Atlantic to the Teheran Conference, visiting Algeria, Egypt, Tunisia, Malta, before he returned to the States aboard the U.S.S. *Iowa.*

When he returned on December 17, 1943, all kinds of doctors checked into the White House, and we knew the President was sick, though he kept his appointments. He was wheeled in and out of the Map Room, overseeing the war. At home, he juggled a railroad strike, finally seizing the railroads, placing them under military control. Though he still delivered his regular fireside chats from the Diplomatic Reception Room on the ground floor, he didn't go outside at all.

By January, 1944, the President had a raging case of influenza. He was not able to go to the Capitol to deliver his State of the Union speech. But by April, he was well enough to seek sunshine, and recuperated on Bernard Baruch's plantation in South Carolina.

He returned to the White House, much thinner, and we noticed that his hands trembled almost all the time. Later, in July, buoyed by the success of D-Day, the amphibious invasion of France on June 6, he announced that he would accept the Democratic nomination for an unprecedented fourth term.

We were all worried. It seemed that crews of doctors were being spirited in and out through the south entrance of the White House. The President quickly lost his Carolina tan and now looked gray as a ghost.

He took the train to California, arriving in San Diego

just long enough to accept his nomination, speaking from the back platform of the train, then went on a Pacific inspection trip to bases in Hawaii and Alaska.

When he returned to the White House from his month-long trip, his first visitor, on August 18, was Senator Harry Truman, the vice-presidential candidate he'd chosen to replace Henry Wallace of Iowa on the Democratic ticket.

We were curious about the newcomer from Missouri. "Wonder if he'll be coming around here any more than Wallace did," Claunch asked, as the two candidates, in their shirtsleeves, ate lunch beneath the Andrew Jackson magnolia. (Traditionally, Vice Presidents rarely were seen around the White House.)

"I doubt it," Mr. Crim replied. "You know the President!"

The strain of campaigning showed on the President's face when he returned from Hyde Park, victorious in the election. He'd campaigned in Philadelphia, Wilmington, Delaware, Camden, New Jersey, Chicago, Boston, Springfield, Bridgeport and Hartford, and took a final whistle-stop through his home state, New York. It was a lesser effort than in earlier days, but, to our thinking, a rather incredible feat for a man who, handicapped and tired, looked much older than his 63 years.

Mrs. Roosevelt went along on some of the trips, but we noticed that her various interests seemed to take precedence over the campaign. After the election, the President saw even less of Mrs. Roosevelt. Their daughter, Anna Boettiger, moved into the White House to take care of her father.

And it was Anna who got the new Vice President there to ride in the triumphal post-election parade down Pennsylvania Avenue. Mr. Truman, in Missouri at the time, tried to beg off because of a prior commitment to his old Army unit. "I wouldn't be able to get there and back in time," he said.

Anna fumed. "Hasn't the stupid so-and-so ever heard of a plane?" she said, and she arranged for a military plane to go to Missouri. Vice President Truman flew in for the parade.

The Hopkinses had rented a house in Georgetown, so

Anna and her six-year-old son Johnny moved into the old Lincoln office on the second floor of the White House. After quiet Diana, the antics of lively Johnny Boettiger kept the staff hopping.

It was Anna who dined with the President on trays in his study, Anna who now mixed his martinis and laughed at his jokes, Anna who listened to his speeches and threw him ideas.

But it was Mrs. Roosevelt who took charge of the fourth inauguration.

"Because of the President's health, we want to hold the inauguration here, rather than at the capitol. Can you manage it?"

The Chief Usher never says no to a First Lady's request, Mr. Crim had taught me. But he blanched at that question, knowing that we'd all be loaded down taking care of all the crowds.

"We shall certainly try, Ma'am."

When the joint congressional committee announced the White House ceremony, the statement cited the savings in inaugural expenditures, in view of war conditions, "which necessitate the abandonment of normal ceremonial activities, shortage of critical materials, the restriction of travel, shortage of hotel accommodations. . . ."

But we knew that if Franklin Delano Roosevelt had felt up to it, wild horses couldn't have kept him away from the Capitol. And the parade, which was canceled because of "wartime austerity," would have been used to incite patriotism.

The historic fourth inauguration of Franklin D. Roosevelt was by far the greatest assemblage of people ever to gather at the White House. By January 20, 1945, the staff, working with President Roosevelt's friend and military aide, General Edwin "Pa" Watson, had spent two double-duty months in preparation. The day began at ten in the morning with Episcopal services in the East Room, for two hundred seated guests.

At noon, the invited crowd, more than we'd expected, spilled over onto the South Portico, to watch Chief Justice Harlan F. Stone administer the oath of office to the President and to Vice President Truman, who was making his second visit to the mansion.

Colonel James Roosevelt, now a military aide to the President, physically supported his father to the platform. The President's speech was mercifully brief, and one of his most eloquent. Despite his doctor's instructions, however, Franklin Roosevelt wore no overcoat. It was a rainy, sleety, windy day, with snow on the ground. The throngs in the audience, standing beneath the South Portico in the raw weather, stamped their feet and rubbed their hands during the ceremony.

We'd spread out tarpaulins on the ground around the south entrance for top dignitaries to stand on. The rest, including many frozen Congressmen, had to stand behind a rope in the cold slush on the back lawn.

At 1:00, after the wives of the President and the Vice President greeted them in the lobby, we served lunch to 1,805 guests. It was a "plated" luncheon with covered dishes of food ready for the guests to pick up, served from long buffet tables in the East Room, the State Dining Room, and the ground floor corridor.

We'd barely cleared away after the first group when Mrs. Roosevelt began to hold her inevitable tea. At 4:00, the President and Vice President received two hundred Democratic members of the Electoral College in the State Dining Room; at five, Mrs. Roosevelt and Mrs. Truman greeted nearly seven hundred additional guests.

And there was more to come. That evening, as I changed from my formal morning clothes to evening dress, I felt that it was the most strenuous day I'd ever put in. Mr. Crim said as much, as did the doorman, John Mays, who'd been there since William Howard Taft's time.

The day came to an end after midnight, when the last of eighty close friends and political advisors left the White House. They had been guests of the Roosevelt family for a dinner in the State Dining Room.

Upstairs, the guest rooms, as usual, were packed.

"If we had one more person, we'd have to put him in the basket with Fala," Mays announced.

All thirteen of the Roosevelt grandchildren were spending the night, even though Mrs. Roosevelt had feared "an epidemic of chickenpox or something." All his sons, his daughter, his cousins Laura Delano and Margaret Suckley, made the solemn occasion a gala family gathering for the President.

But he went to bed early, exhausted.

Two days later, the President, taking Anna along to take care of him, left for Yalta and the fateful meeting with Josef Stalin and Winston Churchill, where the Allies reached controversial agreements on their various responsibilities and spheres of influence in the future world.

While he was gone, Mrs. Roosevelt carried on with all her usual activities. She entertained a Nigerian prince and a rabbi; held meetings with people involved in specifics of her various causes—civil rights, women's rights, labor. She was beginning her own next four years.

I was in awe of this remarkable woman. She was formal and distant with her staff, yet kind and warm to people everywhere. And she accomplished so much. None of us had a tenth of her energy.

It was after the President had returned from Yalta, tired beyond belief, and flown to Georgia to rest, that Mrs. Roosevelt held a luncheon for top women in government.

As I looked out the window over the north driveway, one of the guests, a short gray-haired woman, made her way up the steps. She looked vaguely familiar.

Mays, resplendent in his blue tailcoat and white stockings, grandly swept the lady in. I stepped out of the office, asking, "Ma'am, your name?"

"Mrs. Truman," she said.

Embarrassed, I led the wife of the Vice President of the United States into the Red Room.

The
Trumans

1

"I'm taking a long weekend," Mr. Crim said, as he worked his arms into the sleeves of his topcoat, "Why don't you go ahead and take the four days, too?"

I glanced at the Usher's log. Mrs. Roosevelt had absolutely nothing on the schedule Friday through Monday. With the President in Warm Springs, life was unusually slow at the mansion.

"Perhaps I can go on out to Iowa and bring back my family," I replied. Zella had waited until after the ordeal of the Inauguration to take our baby daughter to meet the relatives, but after so many weeks alone, I had come to dread weekends in the empty apartment.

"Very well, Mr. West," Mr. Crim nodded. "I'll see you Tuesday morning." Tipping his hat smartly, he marched out the door at the stroke of four. Mr. Crim is so formal he probably doffs his hat to his wife, I thought, arranging the desk for the night usher.

I walked from the White House to the barber shop on G Street, wishing I'd packed a suitcase so I could catch the 5:30 train to Chicago. Now, I'd have to wait until the next day.

It was chilly for April, and I remember thinking later, as the crowded bus jostled along 16th Street, how pleasant it might be to draw duty with the President in Georgia.

Mrs. Smaltz, the resident manager, was standing in front of the apartment house when I got home. "Isn't it just terrible!" she cried. "Isn't it awful!"

"Yes, it certainly is," I agreed, wondering what new turn the war had taken. I ran up the two flights of stairs and snapped on the radio as soon as I unlocked the apartment door. It was a few seconds after six, and every station was blaring out the news bulletin. For a moment I stood rooted to the rug, hat and raincoat still on, then I wheeled around toward the door.

Halfway down the hall, I remembered to call Mr. Crim. I knew he did not have a radio in his Virginia home. He answered the phone at the first ring.

"Have you heard?" I asked.

"No, what's happened?"

"The President died this afternoon. I just heard the news on the radio. It sounds like a stroke."

"I'll meet you in the office," he said.

I don't think there's a soul alive who was around on April 12, 1945, who doesn't remember where he was, how he heard the news, how he felt when Franklin D. Roosevelt died. There's something about the unexpected death of a President that we all take so personally that years afterward, when we talk about it, we always say, "I was in the kitchen when I heard the news"—or "I was walking down the street"—or "I was in a classroom." We seem to relate the experience to our own whereabouts. I can remember my surprise at finding a cab right around the corner in front of Walter Reed Hospital—sometimes it was just about impossible to find one during the war. I can remember the silent ride back to the White House, being grateful that the taxi had no commercial radio, because I didn't want to talk to the cab driver about it.

I remember thinking how frail the President had looked, how teams of doctors kept running in and out of the White House in the days after the Inauguration, how his daughter Anna had stayed on to take care of him, accompanying him to the Yalta Conference, and how he had no longer cared to disguise his paralyzed condition. He had even delivered his State of the Union message from his wheelchair, and, for the first time in his life, allowed public photographs and newsreels of that indispensable vehicle. He was too weak to pretend. There had even been talk that he wouldn't be able to make the trip to Warm Springs, where he found relaxation and therapy.

As the cab driver pulled up to the White House, I asked him to take me to a side entrance to avoid any press people who might be around. I noticed Anna Roosevelt Boettiger's car in the driveway. She'd been out at Bethesda Naval Hospital, where her son Johnny was recuperating from a stomach ailment. Once in the office, I checked the Usher's log—Secretary of State Stettinius, Anna, and her husband, John, were already upstairs.

Mr. Crim had arrived. "Mrs. Roosevelt is getting ready to go down for the body," he told me. "The swearing-in is going to be in the Cabinet Room."

It was all so sudden, I had completely forgotten about Mr. Truman. Stunned, I realized that I simply couldn't comprehend the Presidency as something separate from Roosevelt. The Presidency, the White House, the war, our lives—they were all Roosevelt.

But if Mr. Crim or any of the rest of the staff had any feelings about the President's death, they didn't show it. Every function, every movement, every reaction was business as usual. It could have been the day before. Have they no feelings, I wondered?

Steve Early, from the President's office, called. "Mrs. Roosevelt is preparing to leave by military plane. We'll have a meeting on the arrangements at eight o'clock, after the swearing-in ceremony."

Mr. Crim and I hurried down the ground floor corridor, through the glass doors to the Cabinet Room. Speaker Rayburn, Majority Leader McCormack, Minority Leader Joseph Martin, Admiral Leahy and General Fleming were already assembled.

Two Secret Service agents arrived from the east wing, bringing Mrs. Truman and her daughter, Margaret.

A gray-faced Mr. Truman, flanked by two agents and a tearful Secretary of State Stettinius, stepped out of the President's office to meet Chief Justice Stone. The two men shook hands, gripping each other's arms.

"Did you bring a Bible?" the Chief Justice asked Mr. Truman. "Oh, no—you see—I didn't know," the Vice President stammered.

Steve Early and Jonathan Daniels of the President's staff scrambled around the office, searching. There was an embarrassed silence. Mr. Crim snapped to the telephone and, in his best under-cover voice, called our office.

"Claunch," he said, "look in the bottom drawer of my desk for that Gideon Bible. Bring it over right away, and be sure to dust it off first."

Within seconds Claunch was over with one of the Bibles the Gideons had presented to Mrs. Roosevelt for the guest rooms.

The ceremony was brief. Chief Justice Stone raised the Bible, administered the oath, and the shaken, gray-haired man in the gray suit and bow tie, shorter than anyone else in the room, repeated:

"I, Harry S. Truman, do solemnly swear that I will faithfully execute the office of President of the United States, and will to the best of my ability, preserve, protect and defend the Constitution of the United States."

Mr. Crim and I melted into the background and disappeared back to the office, just in time to answer Mrs. Roosevelt's call.

"I will receive the Trumans in the Red Room," she said. I watched Mr. Crim straighten his back, walk back to the Cabinet Room, escort his charges to the Red Room and, in a ringing voice, announce:

"The President of the United States and Mrs. Truman!"

I couldn't help wondering how Mrs. Roosevelt felt at hearing those words, so formal, so matter-of-fact, so impersonal. For twelve years, Mr. Crim had announced, "The President of the United States and Mrs. *Roosevelt*" every time they entered the room. It was a custom as old as the White House, one we had inherited from the royalty our forefathers rebelled against.

But all I could think of was: "The King is dead. Long live the King!"

And at that moment I discovered the secret of White House existence—the secret that had kept everyone calm, performing smoothly, showing no reaction. It was a secret that sustained me through the years ahead, that kept me from developing emotional attachments, from becoming personally involved with any administration.

The secret was loyalty to the White House and to the Presidency, rather than to whoever happens to be occupying the office for four years, or eight. I discovered that there is a continuity to our government institutions and to the house where our Presidents live. I think it's a good thing that there are people who serve to maintain that continuity, and that all the Presidents have appreciated that. Of course, each has had his own ideas and has used them, but at the same time each has been very much interested in how things have been done in the past.

We had no time to mourn.

We stayed up all night. Mr. Crim and I met with the President's staff to plan the funeral. Because no one had yet replaced "Pa" Watson, Mr. Roosevelt's military aide who had died on the return trip from Yalta, a representative from the Military District of Washington read us the Army procedures for a State funeral. Then the State Department protocol officer read the official "List of Precedence" for diplomatic functions. The invitations had to be narrowed to a few because the East Room could hold only two hundred people. It was really no different from arranging any other appointment for Mrs. Roosevelt.

Our agenda set, we automatically ordered the housekeeper to ready the guest rooms and equip the kitchen—no extra work, because with Mrs. Roosevelt we'd learned *always* to be ready for guests.

But Robert Redmond, the head gardener, was not ready for the avalanche that fell on him. "What shall I do with all these flowers?" he asked in amazement. The wreaths had begun to arrive almost as soon as the announcement was heard.

"Arrange them in the East Room, around the walls," I said, setting up a flower brigade for Redmond and his eleven helpers.

At midnight, I looked out the window. There were throngs of people crowding the sidewalks, thousands massed in Lafayette Park across the street, all standing, crying, staring up at the darkened White House.

Tall and stately in black, Mrs. Roosevelt returned Saturday morning, entering the White House with the flag-draped casket, which had been drawn on a caisson from Union Station by six white horses. Her children, Anna and Elliott, walked behind her. In the car following them Mr. Roosevelt's cousin, Margaret Suckley, held Fala in her arms.

The undertaker placed the President's body on a catafalque in the East Room, where the honor guard was waiting.

Mrs. Roosevelt stopped at our office. "Can you dispense with the Honor Guard for a few moments," she asked, "and have the casket opened? I would like to have a few moments alone with my husband."

She waited in our office while we called the undertaker in to open the casket. When it was ready, she said to us, "Please don't let anybody come in." Mr. Crim asked the military honor guard to leave the room, and he stationed himself at one door, Claunch at another, and I stood guard inside the third door.

Mrs. Roosevelt stood at the casket, against the east wall, gazing down into her husband's face. Then she took a gold ring from her finger and tenderly placed it on the President's hand. She straightened, eyes dry, and she left the room. The coffin was never opened again.

We returned to the East Room for the funeral that afternoon. The air was heavy with the sweet odor of flowers that came by the thousands, from all over the world, to line the walls of the East Room, floor to ceiling. Just the wreaths. Mrs. Roosevelt told us to send fresh flowers in vases to the hospitals.

The chill of two days before had disappeared; the sun beat down on the White House roof, and the packed room was steaming. The service, fortunately, was short.

Ceremonies and officials then moved to Hyde Park for the burial. Mr. Crim, Claunch, and Searles all joined the family on the funeral train, leaving me in charge of the White House, with a twenty-four-hour respite before beginning the transfer from one family to another.

It took twenty big army trucks, jam-packed to the corners, to move the Roosevelts' monumental twelve-year collection of possessions out of the White House. We packed night and day, for one entire week. Every morning after breakfast, Mrs. Roosevelt took me through room after room, pointing out things that belonged to her—photographs by the hundreds, ships' models, books and books and books, tiny souvenirs from all over the world. But she saved the President's study for last. On the final day, when her last box was crammed into a truck, she called me in to the gray, oval room. The walls looked pockmarked without pictures.

But on the President's desk was the familiar clutter. Letter openers, bronze donkeys, a clock, some models of ships, a nautical ashtray. We had already received a note from Mrs. Roosevelt that the President had bequeathed $100 to each member of the staff in his will. Now, pointing out the desk, she said, "If you would like a remembrance, please take anything here."

I was young then, and had no idea I'd ever wind up with a collection of Presidential presents. Besides, the three Wests had already outgrown our small apartment. I knew what was needed.

"There's a playpen up on the third floor that some of your grandchildren used," I ventured, and she smiled. "Of course, Mr. West."

When she left that day, she shook hands with Mr. Crim, the ushers and me, at the front door. Then she hurried to her car, coat flapping, legs moving faster than they were designed to. Looking back only once, she drove away.

It took just one truck to move the Trumans from their three-bedroom apartment to the White House. All they brought was their clothes and Margaret's piano.

During the time it took to pack up Mrs. Roosevelt's

belongings, the three Trumans stayed at Blair House, the President's guest house across the street from the White House. The Secret Service insisted upon installing them in quarters where they'd be better protected, as crowds of news people and curious onlookers had begun to impede traffic at the Connecticut Avenue apartment house, where the Trumans had lived since a year after Mr. Truman's election to the Senate from Missouri in 1934.

We hadn't even had time to think what life with the Trumans might be like. From the swearing-in ceremony, we could see that they were quiet, modest people. They looked pitifully lost, surrounded by members of the impressive Roosevelt Cabinet. Perhaps the strangeness of their presence was increased because they had been around the White House so seldom.

During the week of packing for Mrs. Roosevelt, we asked for an appointment with Mrs. Truman. Notebook in hand, I reported to the new First Lady at Blair House. She was seated at a desk in the fourth-floor room she'd set up as her office. I was struck by the difference between her and Mrs. Roosevelt.

As I entered, she indicated a comfortable chair, and smiled. It was the smile of an equal, not of someone who considered herself of superior rank or status. When she spoke, I was aware from her words, from her tone of voice, that there was no distance of class or background between Bess Truman and myself. She seemed like an ordinary person, like someone from Creston, Iowa. Or Independence, Missouri. I felt at ease and I liked her immediately.

"I'm afraid I don't know much about the operation of the White House," she began. "You can appreciate how sudden this is for us."

"We're here to do everything in the world to help you," I answered. "I'll try my best to explain how the house operates and how the staff is set up. And then we'll be at your disposal to try to make it work to fit your family's needs."

Those first few days, we sat at Mrs. Truman's Blair House desk talking about how it would be to live in the White House. She was just feeling her way. From the beginning, I felt she'd be easy to work for—that there'd be no problem getting along with this very down-to-earth, personable lady. She was correct but not formal, hesitant but not indecisive. And she let us know how glad she was to find us there.

Our relationship—First Lady to administrative officer—was immediately different. The Trumans were new, and I had been at the White House four years. When I came to work for the Roosevelts, I had to fit into an established White House routine. Now, I had to help guide the Trumans into a new one.

She walked across the street to the White House the day after Mrs. Roosevelt's departure. It was like a ghost house. The walls of the second floor rooms were streaked with dust and faded around the outlines of all Mrs. Roosevelt's pictures. Much of the furniture was shabby, badly in need of an upholsterer. Draperies hung limply, many not blending with colors in the room. What little was left in the White House gave it the appearance of an abandoned hotel.

"How much redecorating can we do?" she asked.

"Actually, you'll be able to do quite a bit," I answered, "because Mrs. Roosevelt hadn't gotten around to doing it yet."

Then I explained that every four years, with each new (or reelected) administration, Congress allots $50,000 above our annual appropriation to paint the house white and refurbish the interior.

Mrs. Truman seemed immensely relieved. "We won't be bringing any furniture," she explained, "we'd planned to use what's already here." We walked through the guest rooms, borrowing a bed here, a table there, a mirror somewhere else, to set up the Trumans' private apartments.

During the next two weeks, she worked with me and with a Kansas City decorator, who brought paint samples, photographs, and fabric swatches, from which Mrs. Truman selected lavender and gray for her bedroom, raspberry pink for Margaret's bedroom, pastel green and blue for the President, and beige for the President's study. She did all the furniture arranging herself.

"I don't have nearly enough pictures to put on the

60

walls," she told us. The National Gallery of Art can lend paintings to the White House from their storage vaults, I explained. The three Trumans had one grand, art-filled evening when the National Gallery sent over painting after painting, from which they could select. They chose mostly landscapes.

For two more weeks our staff painted, hung draperies, cleaned, upholstered, and rearranged the White House for the Trumans.

During this time, Mrs. Truman was obviously concerned, as we all were, about what was going on in the world and in the President's office, as Foreign Ministers of Russia, China, France, and England trekked in and out of the west wing. But we were impressed by her calm, deliberate manner. One thing at a time, quietly, was her approach. Very different from Mrs. Roosevelt's juggling eighteen decisions at once, dictating while running down the halls. In the vernacular of today, the new First Lady kept her cool.

There was little glamour to Bess Truman. Like most Midwestern women I'd known, her values went deeper than cosmetics and color schemes. She was matronly and comfortable, often wearing gray to complement her soft gray hair. I don't think it ever occurred to her to tint her hair—it might end up purple, like that of so many of the berouged Washington ladies who came through our reception lines.

"She looks exactly as a woman her age should look," Harry Truman said proudly.

As a young girl, she had been considered a beauty; at sixty, she wore her age gracefully, and naturally. Her clothes were tailored—two-piece suits with hat and gloves for outside, simple dresses at home. In the evening, she wore long gowns cut with straight lines, usually with one strand of pearls. And I never saw her wrinkled or rumpled. She was always impeccably groomed.

Her eyes were her single most engaging feature. Her warm, expressive smile began with a twinkle there. But her eyes could freeze you with their steel-blue glint.

We saw very little of the President. He began early in the morning, walking across the street from Blair House to the President's oval office in the west wing, and every morning a huge crowd gathered on Pennsylvania Avenue to watch him make the trip and to walk back home for lunch. The traffic tie-ups were terrible.

He was too busy grappling with the huge burden of government that had so suddenly dropped in his lap to worry much about the White House. With the war still raging in Europe and in the Pacific, with the birth of the United Nations in San Francisco and the incredible secret of the atomic bomb, his days were filled with ambassadors, communications with Mr. Churchill, Stalin, General Eisenhower, General Marshall, Admiral King, and especially stormy sessions with Soviet Foreign Minister Molotov.

But on May 1, nineteen days after he took office, President Truman asked to be taken for a thorough tour of the White House. We had set up a table for his poker game on the third floor, and before the players arrived I took him upstairs. He was in a jaunty mood, perhaps because of the announcement of Hitler's death, and I was delighted to see the grim expression disappear from his face for a few moments as he expressed a lively interest in the history of the mansion.

"When you think of all the great men who've lived in this house, you can't help but feel a sense of awe," he said.

Up on the second floor, he wanted to see "where Mrs. Truman is going to put us all. . . ."

I explained that she'd decided to use Mrs. Roosevelt's living arrangements: She, too, would sleep on a little single bed in the First Lady's dressing room and use Mrs. Roosevelt's big room as her own sitting room. The President's bedroom was to be the same, with an antique four-poster from a guest room replacing Mr. Roosevelt's hospital bed.

The President decided to use Mr. Roosevelt's private oval study as his own. "It looks like I'm destined to work in oval rooms," he said. (On his first day in office, he had cleared the chaotic jumble off the desk in the President's oval office in the west wing. That desk was soon shipped to Hyde Park, and thereafter Mr. Truman worked behind Herbert Hoover's desk.)

Mrs. David W. Wallace, Mrs. Truman's aging mother,

would move into the guest room in front, over the north portico. Miss Reathel Odum, Mrs. Truman's secretary, could sleep across the hall and double as a companion to Mrs. Wallace. Mrs. Truman planned to use Mrs. Roosevelt's little office overlooking Pennsylvania Avenue, I explained.

We covered the second-floor territory at a brisk trot. The President walked as if he were marching, I observed.

As we talked, I was struck by the fact that President Truman evidently had very poor eyesight, even worse than mine. His glasses were so thick they magnified his eyes enormously, giving him a peering, owlish gaze. I had the feeling he was looking at me, all around me, straight through me.

The President moved quickly from room to room, murmuring approval at the progress, at his wife's choice of colors, at the furniture.

Then when we came to the Lincoln Room, one of the most historic rooms in the house, with its massive Victorian furniture and oversized bed, the President stopped, looked around, studying. And then the President said:

"Would we dare move Mr. Lincoln out of here? Would that be tampering with history too much?"

"Well, I'm sure Mr. Lincoln probably slept in every room in the house," I ventured.

"We'd like to put Margaret up in our end of the house," he continued, "and this suite seems the ideal spot, but the furniture isn't suitable for a young girl."

"The President may use the house any way he wishes," I assured him. "It's always been so. Actually, the room that Mrs. Truman has chosen for her sitting room was probably where Lincoln slept. The Coolidges kept the Lincoln furniture there, and President and Mrs. Coolidge slept in the room together. The Hoovers slept in the same room but they moved the Lincoln furniture across the hall to where it is now. You could just as easily move it down the hall over the East Room, because that was the Lincoln Cabinet Room, where he signed the Emancipation Proclamation."

"Now I know why they say Lincoln's ghost walks

around up here at night," President Truman chuckled. "He's just looking for his bed."

Much relieved at being able to "tamper" with history, Mr. Truman continued the tour, bringing up Jefferson, Madison, and Theodore Roosevelt, and how they had used the house.

President Truman was intrigued by the third-floor "diet kitchen," which had been installed for the convenience of President Roosevelt. "Well, well, look at this," Mr. Truman said. "Bess thought she was going to get out of cooking when she moved to the White House, but I've got news for her!"

On that exploratory walk around the White House together, I got some first impressions of the newest occupant, that would be reinforced in the years ahead. Harry Truman was his own man. There was no pomp or pretense about him, and he seemed to be at ease with every one of us. I had the impression that the new President knew who he was and was satisfied that his own personality would do just fine in the White House.

We were going to enjoy working for this family, I decided.

May 8, 1945, was a big day at the Executive Mansion of the United States. It was the President's sixty-first birthday. As if to celebrate, he made his first Cabinet shift (appointing Robert Hannegan of Missouri as Postmaster General), thus beginning the delicate process of turning the Roosevelt Administration into the Truman Administration. That day, also, was the Trumans' first full day in the White House. And most important from a standpoint in history, it was V-E Day. The war had ended in Europe!

As we brought Margaret's baby grand piano in the front door, crowds were gathering outside the fence. It brought to mind the thousands who had gathered three weeks before, a silent mournful crowd. But this was different. People were shouting, honking horns, celebrating long into the night. The President came out twice—raising his arms in victory, joining the crowds in their jubilation.

We discovered soon after they moved in that the Trumans had an extraordinarily close and stable family life, one that they had obviously enjoyed for a long time, and that gave strength to them all.

When Mr. Truman ascended to the Presidency, he and his wife had already settled into a simple pattern of living that reflected their small-town background, their age, and their economic status. Even in his three months as Vice President, Mr. Truman had been able to live quietly out of the spotlight, as he had when he was the U.S. Senator from Missouri. I think this was partly because Franklin Roosevelt was such an overpowering figure, partly because World War II, not personality, was the all-consuming public interest, but mostly because the Trumans preferred it that way.

The Trumans were the closest family who lived in the White House during the twenty-eight years I worked there. Some of the staff called them the "Three Musketeers," as they obviously enjoyed each other's company very much. They were essentially very private people who didn't show affection in public. But they did everything together—read, listened to the radio, played the piano, and mostly talked to each other. They had few private dinner parties; they ate informally together, in the third-floor solarium or, in good weather, on the South Portico. They lived as simply at 1600 Pennsylvania Avenue as they had at 4700 Connecticut Avenue or in Independence, Missouri.

The next four months held, in their capsule of time, the most tumultuous events within one short period of the twentieth century. The White House, with President Truman at the helm, remained at the center of those events. From May through September, the United Nations was born, the Potsdam Conference divided up Europe, the two atomic bombs were dropped on Japanese cities, Japan surrendered, and the war was over.

September 2 was V-J Day, the day when a battered Japan signed the unconditional surrender aboard the battleship *Missouri*. There has never, in my lifetime, been such jubilation in Washington. Thousands and thousands screamed and danced in the streets, in riotous celebration that the four-year holocaust had come to an end, that their boys were coming home. The President came out to speak to the crowds. But they became so raucous he feared they'd tear the fence down in their joy, so he spoke over a loudspeaker from the North Portico.

Four days later he introduced his bold, liberal domestic proposals to the Congress—a program so far-reaching, with its "economic bill of rights," to ensure all Americans a job at fair pay, decent housing, a good education, and increasing minimum wage and social security, and fair employment practices—that it brought the Republicans out of hibernation and began the vicious anti-Truman movement. On the other side, he was snubbed by the Roosevelt people, the men who had fashioned the country for the past thirteen years. The President of the United States was caught in a vise. At home, the Trumans tightened their belts and dug in for the duration. They didn't really emerge until spring.

Perhaps they were following a lifetime habit of private pleasures, perhaps they were limited in their activities by their personal finances, perhaps they felt bound by wartime austerity, or perhaps, as I said, they just preferred it that way. I rather think the President took very seriously the burden of office that had fallen on his shoulders, and, not being a young man, directed his private life first and foremost at the preservation of his health.

He was deeply aware of the role then being assumed by the United States in reshaping the world, and of his own predominant responsibility in these broadened international responsibilities. At home, the entire economy had to be restructured, as he had to formulate policies for converting from war to peace. He had no Vice President. He had to stay alive and keenly alert, if he were to cope with his job.

"A man in my position has a public duty to keep himself in good condition," he said. "You can't be mentally fit unless you're physically fit."

Our lives changed drastically to fit his Spartan regimen. He was up every morning at 5:30. I reported in at 6, and often met him heading for his brisk morning walk.

"It's the best part of the day," he told me often, as he took off, 120 paces a minute, marching his Secret Service agents around Washington for an hour, in heat, rain, or freezing cold. His walks were well publicized, but they were only the warmup of President Truman's daily physical fitness program. He went from his walk to the swimming pool, where he worked out with Master Sergeant Gaspar, the physical therapist.

From the pool—where he swam with his glasses on—to the rowing machines, to the exercise machines, and twenty-five sit-ups. Then to the sweat box, and back to the pool. Pretty soon he had certain overweight members of his staff going through the same routine.

Punctuality was the order for the Trumans. A hearty family breakfast was served at eight, and he expected Mrs. Truman and Margaret to be up and at the table with him. After breakfast, they all went to work.

I saw Mrs. Truman at nine every morning in her little office. She sat behind her desk, dressed for the day, decorous to a degree, often wearing a simply tailored housedress.

Mr. Crim had turned all the Truman family business over to me. "You're younger and sharper," he told me, "and since you're both from the Midwest, you seem to get along pretty well. I've got more than I can handle here in the office, what with the engineering, gardening, and all. And I've got to get ready for the Congress."

In October, I received my official discharge from the Navy, and entered "civilian" life at my same desk. So I went upstairs every morning, as Mrs. Truman's main contact with the operation of the White House. First I presented the day's schedule to her. Then the housekeeper presented the menu sheet. Sometimes the First Lady would scratch it up, sometimes not.

Mrs. Truman explained their diets at the beginning. There was to be no salt used, because she suffered from high blood pressure. We even had to remove the water-softening system from the cold-water plumbing, because it contained sodium.

The President was on a high-protein, low-calorie diet, and they shunned rich sauces and desserts. It was mostly plain, meat-and-vegetables, American food. ("I'm sorry to limit the kitchen so," she said at first, but she soon found that the kitchen was pretty limited anyway.)

After the menus, we got down to business, as Mrs. Truman was very conscious of economy in housekeeping. She kept her own books, went over the bills with a fine-tooth comb, and wrote every check herself.

It was during those morning sessions that I began to appreciate Mrs. Truman's humor. Her wit was dry, laconic, incisive and very funny. It's difficult to capture in words because it was so often silent.

She was at her funniest with a straight face, perfectly deadpan. If you weren't looking for one raised eyebrow, one downturned corner of her mouth, you might miss the joke entirely.

She undoubtedly performed her best material for the President and Margaret, who would howl with laughter at the dinner table while Mrs. Truman sat pokerfaced, enjoying her audience.

She made a big joke out of being grouchy in the morning. At eight, when she went upstairs to the solarium for breakfast, she might growl at her husband or Margaret and they'd tease her all through breakfast.

The butlers had a running wager on her mood for the day. "Is she wearing two guns this morning?" Fields would ask the butler who served breakfast.

"Just one today," he might answer, or if she had peppered her family with mock criticism—by mimicking their behavior of the night before, the butler's judgment would be: "Both guns smoking."

After our nine o'clock sessions, Mrs. Truman worked at her desk all morning, sometimes dictating to Reathel Odum, but most often handling her own correspondence, reading all her mail, writing her own letters in longhand.

She usually joined the President for lunch, or, if he had other plans, she ate lunch alone with her mother in Mrs. Wallace's room.

Mrs. Truman's mother, Margaret Gates Wallace, was as close to an aristocrat as the Midwest could produce, as formal a lady as ever lived in the White House. She called her son-in-law "Mr. Truman," even though he'd been in her family for twenty-six years by this time, and she delicately opposed a career for her granddaughter, Margaret. In the White House, where she lived for the rest of her life, she hardly ever left her room. Bess Truman visited her mother faithfully every day, and as Mrs. Wallace grew older, read the newspapers to her.

At two o'clock, after lunch, Mr. Truman went upstairs for a nap. He could go to sleep at the drop of a hat, and went to bed in the afternoon as if it were a long winter's night.

Mrs. Truman chose that hour to sit in her sitting room, reading. She liked to say that she didn't nap, but many times I went upstairs to see her about something or other and I'd find her sitting upright in her chair, sound asleep, her book open in her lap.

An hour later, the Trumans were off to their respective business. Mrs. Truman often received charity groups or servicemen in the afternoon, or appeared at charity functions such as a Salvation Army benefit, elsewhere in Washington.

At the end of the work day, the Trumans had cocktails in the West Hall, which is the family sitting room. One drink each, before dinner. But it took a while to learn their tastes. Shortly after they moved in, the First Lady rang for the butler. Fields came up, tray in hand.

"We'd like two old-fashioneds, please," she requested.

Fields, who often moonlighted at Washington's most elegant parties, prided himself on being an excellent bartender.

"Yes, Ma'am," he answered.

In no time flat, he was back with the order, in chilled glasses, with appetizing fruit slices and a dash of bitters. Mrs. Truman tasted the drink, thanked him, but made no other comment.

The next evening she rang for Fields. "Can you make the old-fashioneds a little drier?" she said. "We don't like them so sweet."

Fields tried a new recipe, and again she said nothing.

But the next morning she told me, "They make the worst old-fashioneds here I've ever tasted! They're like fruit punch."

The next evening, Fields, his pride hurt, dumped two big splashes of bourbon over the ice and served it to Mrs. Truman.

She tasted the drink. Then she beamed. "Now that's the way we like our old-fashioneds!"

They had dinner promptly at seven, usually in the third-floor solarium, after the first few days at the huge table in the high-ceilinged Private Dining Room. We had an electric "thermomator," which kept food warm in little ovens that the butlers, Fields or Charles, brought from the kitchen via the elevator and served elegantly, even though they were in the middle of a "game room." Although the Trumans sought informality, the traditions of waiting on Presidents are strong ones, so two butlers, dressed formally in black, served the three very informal Trumans.

In good weather, dinner was out on the South Portico, overlooking the Washington Monument, and again served formally, although the President fed the squirrels between courses.

After dinner, the Trumans watched movies, mainly because Margaret, a movie buff, often implored her parents to join her. Her mother spent more time with her in the theater than her father did, though I dare say neither of them sat through "The Scarlet Pimpernel" sixteen times, as Margaret did.

Mrs. Truman and her daughter played ping-pong in the third-floor hall; they played bridge on the second floor with some of Margaret's friends; they bowled in the new bowling alley.

But mainly, as a family, they talked to each other.

The second-floor scene was far different from the Roosevelt years: the sound of young college girls singing, playing the piano in Margaret's suite. The quiet voice of Mrs. Truman reading aloud to her mother, and the spunky retorts of the President's ninety-year-old mother, who arrived as the first weekend houseguest.

Like most mothers of Presidents I served, she had plenty of spirit. "When my mother arrives, she definitely will not sleep in the Lincoln bed," Mr. Truman told us. A Southerner to the core, she still fought the Civil War. "I'll sleep on the floor first," she said.

We then arranged for her to stay in the Queen's Room, but she'd have none of that either. "It's too fancy for me," she said, and slept next door in the small adjoining sitting room, offering the regal Queen's Room to her daughter, Mary.

We had taken President Roosevelt's wheelchair ramp out of the second floor and the President's mother tripped on the steps that weekend, injuring herself. She didn't tell anyone because she didn't want to be a bother.

That's the way the entire Truman family was. They didn't want to be a bother to anybody on the staff, they asked for very little. They treated the staff with respect—respect for us personally, and respect for the work that we did.

When a butler or doorman or usher would enter the room, the Trumans would introduce him to whoever happened to be sitting in the room, even if it were a King or a Prime Minister. They introduced all the staff to their visitors—something I'd never seen the Roosevelts do.

This personal touch revealed a great deal to me about the Trumans as people. They did not see the world as being composed of aristocratic leaders on the one hand and faceless servants on the other. They had a broad sense of humanity that bridged the divisions of job and status, which seem to wall us off from each other into so many compartments.

And Mrs. Truman always sent the maids home on Sunday afternoons. "I can turn down beds perfectly well by myself," she said when they protested that they'd be needed. For all these human courtesies, they received in return an extra amount of respect and admiration from all of us who worked there.

At nine o'clock, Mr. Truman picked up his briefcase, took Mrs. Truman by the arm, went into his study, and closed the door. They worked together until eleven o'clock almost every night, editing his speeches, discussing his policies, designing his politics.

In public, Mrs. Truman never said a word. She stayed as far in the background as Mrs. Roosevelt had projected her own personality into the foreground. Bess Truman guarded her privacy like a precious jewel. And in that privacy was hidden a great secret involving the role she played in public life. She probably had more influence on

71

political decisions than Mrs. Roosevelt had on social issues.

A keenly intelligent, well-educated, politically experienced person (she had worked in her husband's Senate office), Mrs. Truman knew her politics—and her husband respected her opinion. In that oval study every evening, she was more than a sounding-board, more than a "blue-penciler" for his speeches. Although it went unsuspected by nearly everybody in government, Bess Truman entered into nearly every decision the President made.

With the crisis of war ended, the new President found himself embattled on many fronts. In addition to the shellacking he was taking on domestic issues, he further infuriated Congress by insisting on civilian, not military control of atomic energy. He struggled to bring economic order in a country beset by strikes in the automobile, steel, oil, rubber, meat-packing, and lumber industries.

During those months of turmoil, as she had done almost every night since they moved in, Bess Truman applied her editor's touch to every statement, her analytical thinking to every action of the President's. Her mind was one of his greatest assets.

His staff always referred to Harry Truman as "The Boss." The President referred to his wife as "The Boss." Privately, she affected the role, and the President loved it.

"She's the only one who bawls me out and gets away with it," he bragged.

The President's salty language was a bone of contention. He was known to slip a "hell" or "damn" into his public utterances, causing quite a furor—unlike most Presidents who only cursed privately. Mrs. Truman was forever saying, "You shouldn't have said that!"

An apocryphal story that made the rounds had a famous woman Democrat rushing to the White House to plead with Mrs. Truman to have Harry clean up his language. It seemed that he'd called somebody's statements "a bunch of horse manure." Unruffled, Bess Truman is said to have smilingly replied:

"You don't know how many years it took to tone it down to that."

We often saw her look daggers at him if he got "out of line." But Mrs. Truman's rebukes were given because she

72

didn't want her husband to be hurt by an injudicious remark, not because she was prudish.

I often thought there was a twinkle in her eye, along with the daggers, for as her brother Fred told me, "Bess is not as shocked as they'd have you believe. She's heard cusswords all her life, and even knows how to use them. Why, she was the biggest tomboy in Independence."

Her tomboy years, when she pitched sandlot ball to her three brothers, were well behind her, however. She was circumspect in her conversation, ladylike in every way. No one entered her bedroom when she was inside. No one saw her in her dressing gown. All her conferences were at her desk. All her visitors were received in her sitting room. But she retained one childhood passion: She was wild about baseball. Mrs. Truman went to see every Washington Senators game that she could fit into her schedule, and she listened to the night games on the radio in her sitting room.

She kept up with her old friends, including the Senate wives, and she drove herself to her bridge club and to shops. Mrs. Truman was like Mrs. Roosevelt in her dislike of limousines. But where Mrs. Roosevelt walked or rode the bus, Mrs. Truman drove. I remember her first call.

"Please have my car brought up at two o'clock."

"Which car would you prefer," I asked, "the Cadillac or Packard?"

"My own car, the Chrysler," she replied.

"Would you like a driver?"

"Indeed not. I don't want to forget how to drive!"

And off she'd spin, sometimes alone, sometimes taking her mother for a drive. Sometimes she would tell us where she was going, sometimes she wouldn't. But the days when a First Lady could freely move around Washington were coming to an end.

Sadly, she stopped by the office one day and told us, "I'm going to have to give up driving. It just causes too much commotion. I can't stop at a traffic light without somebody running up. The Secret Service has laid down the law about my driving." Thereafter, Tom Hardy, Mr.

Truman's driver during his eighty-two days as Vice President, chauffered her around town.

Margaret, too, hated to use the limousines. "I'm so embarrassed to drive up to school in that big car," she told me. That big car was a Mercury.

Another time she called down to ask if I thought it would be all right to use a White House limousine to take her friends somewhere. "There are so many of us we can't fit into a regular sedan," she apologized.

"The White House cars are always at your disposal," I answered.

Margaret Truman was probably the most unspoiled of all the Presidents' children I have known. She was also the most over-protected.

At twenty-one, the President's college-senior daughter had her choice of escorts. She seldom went out on school nights that first year, but on the weekends her mother waited up for her when she was out on a date—even though two Secret Service agents had accompanied her every step of the way.

"I bet she gets it if she stays out past her curfew," Mr. Crim chuckled, when I told him of the First Lady's weekend vigils. Margaret herself despaired of any romance in the White House. "I ask you to consider the effect of saying good night to a boy at the door of the White House in a blaze of floodlights with a Secret Service man in attendance. There is not much you can do except shake hands, and that's no way to get engaged," she wrote.

Nevertheless, the bright, petite young woman appeared to enjoy her life in the White House.

Margaret's friends came often, and the second floor began to look like a college dormitory, with record players, bridge games, pincurls, corsages, and movies and slumber parties. The "formidable trio"—as the servants referred to Drucie Snyder, Jane Lingo, and Annette Wright—were almost part of the family.

Once, soon after the Trumans moved in, the girls decided to spend the night in Lincoln's bed—sleeping on the hard, lumpy, oversized mattress that every Presidential family just has to try out, for history's sake.

The President, much taken with the stories of Lincoln's

ghost, decided to give the girls a fright, and asked Mays, the lanky, dignified black doorman who also doubled as the President's barber, to dress up in stovepipe hat and lurk in the corner of the bedroom. But Mays called in sick on the day of the charade.

"I didn't feel right about impersonating Mr. Lincoln," Mays told me.

2

President Truman lived in the White House alone most of that first summer, except for his trip to Potsdam, but he rarely used the house to entertain his friends. During this period, he found that he had to surround himself with a new Cabinet, because the New Deal administrators all seemed to regard him as President by accident. One by one, he chose his own men to take their places. Mrs. Truman soon followed suit.

When Mrs. Truman and Margaret left for Mrs. Wallace's home in Independence, Missouri, at the beginning of June, the White House began to steam from the summer heat. The housekeeper, Mrs. Nesbitt, heaved a sigh of relief that her eagle-eyed boss was away.

From the beginning, Mrs. Truman had let it be known that she wanted the house kept clean!

"How does the housekeeping work?" was the first question she'd asked me.

"Well, technically the housekeeper works under the supervision of the Chief Usher—but actually, she works very closely with the First Lady. And that's the way it should be," I added.

"And how about the present housekeeper?"

I took a deep breath. Even Franklin Roosevelt hadn't been able to get rid of Henrietta Nesbitt.

"Usually, the First Family prefers to hire its own housekeeper," I said carefully. "Mrs. Nesbitt was brought in by the Roosevelts at the beginning—a country woman from Dutchess County. She will probably be all right with supervision."

Mrs. Truman nodded. "Does she give instructions to the maids, or do I?"

"Theoretically, she does. But as I mentioned, she'll need close supervision."

I passed the word along to Mrs. Nesbitt, who let it be known that she had been more concerned with the food end of the housekeeper's job, and that she was sure that the housekeeping staff was extremely efficient, because they had been there a long time.

However, Mrs. Truman soon found that the staff had fallen on easy ways, because housekeeping had been at the very bottom of the list of all Mrs. Roosevelt's varied interests. And since the housekeeper also was more interested in food than furniture, the cleaning staff went through the house with a "lick and a promise," as Mrs. Truman told me.

"They do a lot of turning down of beds at night, but I found cobwebs in the corners," she complained.

I passed the word along to Mrs. Nesbitt. "Mrs. Roosevelt never complained," she sniffed. "Anyway, they do like the food."

However, the White House kitchen was not exactly a gourmet's dream in those days, either, according to the Trumans. So when Margaret, her mother, and Mrs. Wallace, accompanied by Mrs. Wallace's long-time cook, Vietta Garr, escaped to Missouri for the summer, Mr. Crim and I had numerous conferences on how to handle the housekeeping. Then we called in Mrs. Nesbitt.

"We need some men upstairs to do that cleaning," Mrs. Nesbitt told us, "because the maids just do what they want, anyway, no matter what you tell them."

We explained that there was no budget for housemen upstairs—that our Congressional appropriation only allowed thirty positions, all of which were filled. And the maids would just have to do better.

"Well, I don't see how keeping house for three people should be more difficult than keeping house for the Roosevelts," said Mrs. Nesbitt.

When the confrontation finally came between the First Lady and the imperious housekeeper, it was over a stick of butter.

Mrs. Truman was off to a pot-luck luncheon with her bridge club. Her assignment was to bring a stick of butter, and she stopped by the White House kitchen to pick it up. Mrs. Nesbitt was there.

"Oh, no!" exclaimed the housekeeper to the First Lady. "We can't let any of our butter go out of the House. We've used up almost all of this month's ration stamps already."

That was the last straw. All the weeks of unwanted brussels sprouts at every meal, cobwebs, and general sluggishness from the staff came to a head in that one quarter pound of butter.

Mrs. Truman summoned Mr. Crim, as close to fuming as we ever heard her. "Our housekeeper tells me I can't take a stick of butter from the kitchen!"

"Why, of course you can," sputtered the horrified Mr. Crim. "She is entirely out of order!"

"Then I think it's time to find a new housekeeper," said Mrs. Truman.

And Mrs. Nesbitt, at the end of that summer, went the way of Secretaries Stettinius, Morgenthau, Stimson, Biddle, Wickard, and Wallace.

Mrs. Truman was no fussier than her predecessor, nor did she want to make life difficult for Mrs. Nesbitt. It was just that she had been brought up to be house-proud. But Mrs. Truman had never managed a large staff before. In their small apartment, she did all the cooking and Harry Truman wiped the dishes.

It frustrated her that people couldn't seem to keep the White House as clean as she had kept her own apartment, or as Vietta had kept her mother's house in Independence.

Actually, she had a point, because the White House is

not the most efficiently run establishment in the country, no matter how hard we tried. Some years were cleaner than others, because some housekeepers had a daily list of duties, and a daily check to see if they'd been carried out. But unless each task was followed through and inspected, more than likely the domestic staff slipped right back into the easy way out.

Individually, the domestic workers in the White House were some of the most loyal, conscientious employees any government could have. But as a work force, they were considerably less effective than their counterparts in any private house in America. What Mrs. Truman discovered was that their role was so ill-defined (their real role in the scheme of things, rather than their function as listed in the job description) and their hope for advancement so limited, that they had to establish their own code. This code was a subtle "we'll be here after you're gone" attitude that characterized the staff's relationship with every First Family. As eight-hour-a-day, time clock employees, the domestic staff were bureaucrats pretending to be old family retainers. And you simply can't be both at the same time.

Which is how Bess Truman ended up performing the duties of an assistant housekeeper at the White House. She'd stop a maid in the hall: "Could you take care of the fingerprints on the woodwork?"

The maid would stop dusting to wipe the doorsill—then, of course, it would be time to go home. The next day, Mrs. Truman found new fingerprints on the woodwork, and again she'd remind the maid to clean it.

Even after Mrs. Nesbitt left and things ran much more smoothly, the First Lady continued to "get in behind" the help until she wearied of the job.

Mary Sharpe, an assistant in the housekeeper's office, took over the job Mrs. Nesbitt left vacant, and spent much more time with Mrs. Truman herself. Her personality more nearly meshed with the First Lady's, and her wit soon reflected the Trumans. It first surfaced at Thanksgiving.

"We'd like to have Thanksgiving in the White House," Mrs. Truman told me. "A good traditional menu, but not too rich, just for the Truman and Wallace families from Missouri—very quiet and no publicity."

No sooner had Mrs. Truman said this than her politician husband had accepted as a gift a live turkey—from the newspaper carriers of Boston—and the presentation ceremony was carried out with great fanfare and picture-taking on the White House lawn.

As always happened, this kind of announcement brought a horde of questions to the publicity-shy Mrs. Truman. Each reporter, searching for an angle for the morning papers, thought up endless questions about the forthcoming dinner. The President's office referred all questions to Mrs. Sharpe.

Poor Mary was already overloaded trying to get the house in shape for the social season and to give it Mrs. Truman's concept of "a very thorough housecleaning."

But the phones kept ringing all day—reporters wanting to know the recipe for the stuffing, whether the President preferred light meat or dark, where the cranberries came from.

Finally, some newspaperman called and asked how she had killed the bird. Then, searching for detail, he went on, "In some South American countries they pour whiskey down the turkey's throat to make it tender."

"We pour whiskey down the guests' throats and they just *think* the turkey is tender!" Mary replied wearily.

Bess Truman, hearing Mrs. Sharpe's report of the conversation, roared with laughter.

The President of the United States gets to sleep in the White House free of charge, and the salaries of the servants are paid by the government, but he has to pay for his own meals and those of his guests. Before 1945, the President also fed the servants out of his own pocket, but when the Trumans came, we realized this system couldn't continue. Mr. Truman had no vast personal resources like the Roosevelts. So Mr. Crim's first order of business was to extract a little appropriation from an understanding Congress to feed the help. The Trumans had few guests and it didn't take much to feed them, but the First Lady investigated every item on the grocery list.

"How in the world could we have used so many dozens

of eggs?" she asked me. And I had to bring the house-keeper in to account for every item used.

The First Lady was every bit as scrupulous in accounting for White House expenditures as she was in her own set of books. She had no personal maid, and although Vietta Garr, the family cook from Independence, Missouri, had been placed on the White House payroll, Vietta's main duty was to care for Mrs. Truman's mother. Whenever the family went back to Missouri to visit, Vietta went with them.

Mrs. Truman, however, always insisted that Vietta be taken off the White House payroll during the time she was gone—something no other First Lady ever did, although all of them took White House servants along on weekends and summer vacations.

The Trumans also paid for refreshments they served on the Presidential yacht *Williamsburg*, which was operated by the U. S. Navy, and which they used often on weekends. Once, when Mrs. Truman was out of town, the President invited his pokergame companions to sail down the Potomac. He asked Mrs. Sharpe to send food from the White House kitchen.

The housekeeper looked in the refrigerator. There, melting (we had no freezer in those days), sat a large ice-cream cake that a friend had sent over as a gift for the President's birthday. It was made from the special, extra-rich ice cream formula used only for the White House.

Serving this will save money and please Mrs. Truman, Mary thought. As it was a warm day, she ordered dry ice to pack the cake for the trip to the *Williamsburg*, which was docked at the Washington Navy Yard.

Nothing escaped Bess Truman's eagle eye. When she was going over that month's bills, the First Lady called Mrs. Sharpe in.

"How did we happen to spend twenty-five cents for dry ice?" she asked. She was a very frugal lady.

There is absolutely no budget for official entertaining at the White House, nor has there ever been. The simple reason is that the word "entertaining" has always had a frivolous connotation with the Congress, from whose fists

81

we have to pry our annual appropriation. Entertaining is done, of course, but it is merely paid for from the President's travel budget (which was raised from the Roosevelts' $25,000 to $40,000 during the Trumans).

Beginning with Theodore Roosevelt, every President has been allotted this personal travel allowance, over and above his salary. However, beginning with the Trumans, the Presidents began traveling by plane, at the expense of the military, and we discovered that we could find a little money for entertaining in the travel fund.

The President's expense account, another $50,000 above his salary,* goes into his own pocket (nobody can spend it except on the President's authorization), and is taxed like regular income. This "expense account" was initiated because President Truman couldn't afford to live in the White House. He had no outside income when he suddenly succeeded President Roosevelt, and the law stated that a President's salary cannot be increased during his term of office. So, to get around the law, the Budget Bureau convinced Congress to add the $50 000 expense account for President Truman's living expenses in the White House—a bonus continued for future Presidents who were considerably more affluent than he. Harry Truman didn't spend much money in the White House, and I'd guess that he probably saved all the bonus, except for taxes.

The Trumans usually celebrated Thanksgiving in the White House, but they spent most Christmases in Independence, quietly, with their families. And every year they instructed the kitchen help to prepare two full Christmas meals to go to two needy families in the District of Columbia—and to tell nobody.

Especially at holiday time, when Margaret could put down her schoolbooks and invite her friends over for Christmas caroling, but actually all year around, music was a main ingredient in the Trumans' home life at the White House.

"Mr. West, do you think we could roll the little spinet

---

* As of 1969, the President's salary was $200,000 a year. In 1949 Mr. Truman's salary was raised from $75,000 to $100,000.

piano into my sitting room just for tonight?" Margaret asked me one morning. "Annette Wright is coming over to spend the night and we'd like to try a duet."

Her own piano, a baby grand, was a permanent and often-used fixture in Margaret's suite.

The spinet, purchased by Eleanor Roosevelt so there could be informal music in the State Dining Room to entertain the crowds of servicemen, was wheeled in and out of the Wedgwood-blue sitting room for Margaret and her friends as long as the Trumans were there.

President Truman sometimes played the piano there, sometimes played the baby grand piano in his own study, and even was known to use the concert grand Steinway in the East Room.

The piano people were overjoyed to find an *aficionado* at the White House. The Baldwin company had been rather miffed at the to-do when President Roosevelt helped design the elaborate, eagle-legged Steinway. Then, someone criticized the fact that the White House was displaying a German piano (even though it was actually an American-made Steinway). The Baldwin Company seized the opportunity and presented President Truman with a big, black "American" concert grand, which he promptly placed in the opposite end of the East Room, to the great displeasure of the Commission on Fine Arts.

But nobody played either piano, officially, that winter.

It's the custom, when the Supreme Court begins its session in the fall of each year, for the nine Justices to call upon the President at the White House, to announce that the Court is in session. It had always been a strictly formal afternoon occasion, with the Justices and the President dressed in formal day wear—striped trousers and club coats.

That first autumn, President Truman got all dressed up in his new outfit, having been schooled in the ceremony by Mr. Crim. But the Supreme Court, to everybody's surprise, appeared in regular business suits.

The jaunty Mr. Truman was not fazed in the least.

"I see I'm outvoted," he said, as the Justices left. "We'll just all dress in suits next year."

We soon discovered that Harry Truman, the former

83

haberdasher of Independence, enjoyed clothes. His suits were impeccable, always bandbox fresh and "matched-up," from his overcoat, hat, and gloves, down to his necktie and socks. In the White House, he never wore a sport shirt, nor even a sport jacket. Not once did we ever see him in his shirt sleeves, as we'd seen Mr. Roosevelt so often. In the most informal situations, or even at the end of the weariest day, Harry Truman wore a suit, white shirt, and necktie. Only on vacations, such as fishing at Key West, did he put on casual clothing and sport shirts.

But after the Supreme Court came to call, the President retired his club coat. Nor did he wear white tie and tails that first winter. There was too much war-devastation in the rest of the world to enter into a gala White House social season. More often than not, the State Rooms were dark night after night. Upstairs, behind the closed doors of the President's study, the sounds were not piano music, but papers rattling. At the same time that the President grappled with Congress and the new postwar economy, he was attempting to juggle Communist ambitions with allied national interests in Europe, while groping toward a new, definable American foreign policy.

One portion of that new foreign policy—a mutual defense treaty for the western hemisphere—was given a little boost by Mrs. Truman.

President Truman had come back from the Potsdam conference convinced that the Russians intended to take over the world. He decided that the beginning of any prudent policy was to do everything possible to keep the countries of this hemisphere together. He began a lot of out-and-out wooing of the Latin American countries, and so did Mrs. Truman, in her own way.

Beginning in October, 1945, her Spanish class met at the White House every Monday at 11:00 a.m. The enterprising instructor Ramon Ramos, with a spectacular flourish, managed to engage first the Green Room and then the library for his thirty-two-week course for struggling linguists. Among Mrs. Truman's classmates were the wives of the new secretaries of War and State, Mrs. Robert Patterson and Mrs. James F. Byrnes, along with Mrs. Leverett Saltonstall, wife of the Massachusetts senator, and Mrs. Dean Acheson, wife of the then Undersecretary of State.

During Pan-American week in the Spring, Señor Ramos and his students took over the White House kitchen.

Seven members of the White House class, including Mrs. Truman, cooked a complicated Spanish meal for the other sixty members of the class, who generally met elsewhere. Mrs. Dwight D. Eisenhower, dressed in a white apron, was among the waitresses who served the meal in the State Dining Room.

"You make a marvelous waitress," Mrs. Truman told her, and Mrs. Eisenhower laughed gaily.

That spring we had two quite different sets of guests to whom the Trumans extended their hospitality. The first was Winston Churchill, who, though no longer Prime Minister, stopped in Washington en route to Fulton, Missouri, to make his famous "Iron Curtain" speech.

The world had virtually set this great man aside, even as he won his place in the history books. He had been turned out of office; his step was slower, and the glint was no longer in his eye. As he walked slowly around the White House recalling his visits with Roosevelt, he shook his head and remarked sadly, "We got on well."

But he soon established rapport with the Trumans. Mrs. Roosevelt had coached President Truman on how to cater to the Prime Minister's various idiosyncrasies, to his interests in books. They most probably would have hit it off anyway, both because of their warm personalities and their mutual interest in preventing Soviet dominance of Europe.

Though it was not an official visit, Mrs. Truman entertained Mrs. Churchill and her daughter Sarah at luncheon.

The Trumans did not reserve fancy entertaining only for the great or near-great. They catered also to their old friends, who had never had an appointment with destiny. For example, the First Lady really put on the dog for her "bridge club" from Independence, Missouri, when they visited Washington. The eight ladies stayed at the White House for four days, chattering and clattering around in the guest rooms, running around Washington with the President's wife.

"It's not like the old days," Mr. Crim and I laughed together, recalling that Mrs. Roosevelt rarely paid any attention to her houseguests, and that it always fell to our lot to look after them.

But Mrs. Truman ran her own tour bureau. During the four days her friends stayed at the White House, she planned every moment of their time, took them sightseeing herself to the Capitol, the National Gallery, Mount Vernon, and even to the Shrine Circus, held a grand dinner in the State Dining Room, and generally rolled out the red carpet as if eight female heads of state were staying on the second floor.

The Trumans were being themselves. Their old friends were not forgotten or left behind. In fact, Mr. Truman had been sorely criticized for attending the funeral of his old benefactor Tom Pendergast, a Kansas City political boss of questionable repute. Loyalty to old friends and maintenance of friendships were very important to both Harry and Bess Truman.

Edith Helm, who served as Mrs. Roosevelt's social secretary and stayed on with Mrs. Truman, recalled that her entertaining of the enthusiastic Missouri women marked the return of social life to the White House after the war.

"I shall always think of the springtime visit of the Independence ladies as symbolizing that song this country so hopefully sang: 'When the lights go on again all over the world,'" Mrs. Helm stated.

Although the war was now over, the Trumans had followed the wartime pattern of very small-scale entertaining, and then only when there was some official reason, such as Churchill's visit, or the stag dinner President Truman held to honor the victorious General Eisenhower. Food was still rationed, and many young men were still overseas. The Trumans did not wish to appear frivolous.

For a short time, though, the social lights did go on again.

In the fall of 1946, Mrs. Helm and Miss Odum called a press conference to announce that the formal social season, Thanksgiving to Lent, would open again in Washington after five years of blackout. Dates for the various events were listed so that Washington hostesses could avoid conflicts with official White House functions.

We started where we had left off in 1941: Six official dinners for a hundred guests each, two honoring the Diplomatic Corps, and one each for the President's Cabinet, the Chief Justice and the Supreme Court, the President Pro Tempore of the Senate (since there was no Vice President), and the Speaker of the House—and five huge nine o'clock receptions, Military, Judiciary, Diplomatic, Congressional, and Departmental.

The Trumans threw themselves into the job of entertaining official Washington with such a flourish that, despite all the denying in the world (which he did), we could see that the President enjoyed it. He was an extrovert, a friendly man, and he liked company. On the other hand, Mrs. Truman did not, and was truly comfortable only with her family and close friends, but she dutifully performed the duties of hostess.

The press corps who covered the distaff side of the White House were pleased that there was going to be some social action. But they were very unhappy that Mrs. Truman herself never held any press conferences, in contrast to the loquacious Mrs. Roosevelt, who always was making news.

The contrast between the Trumans at home and their official social life was amazing. The Trumans followed to the minute the rules of White House entertaining—rules that hadn't been deviated from for half a century except for wartime. They brought back all the pageantry, all the formality, all the pomp that we had all but forgotten how to execute.

We had to work out the details, so that all the President and his wife had to do was to be in the right place at the right time. For a reception, they'd march down the stairs to the Blue Room and receive the guests, and then march back upstairs. But, behind the scenes, we spent weeks of preparation and scheduling for each detail of that "right place" and "right time."

In those days Mr. Crim and I worked out a list of

procedures and instructions for everybody involved. The Usher's Office was in charge of executing all arrangements for State entertaining. Our first was as follows:

Tuesday, December 10, 1946

FUNCTION:　　　　　Judiciary Reception followed by dance.

TOTAL INVITED:　　55 via Northwest entrance (Pennsylvania Avenue)
226 via Southwest entrance
1,052 via East entrance
1,333 Total

CHECKERS ORDERED (for coats): M. O. Carter

CAR PARKERS (door-openers):　　Harry Charnley

FIRE DEPARTMENT NOTIFIED:　Chief Murphy

NOTIFIED: 5 Doormen

DRESS:　　White Tie

AIDES:　　10 Army aides ordered through Lt. Commander William Rigdon (Mr. Truman's military aide)
10 Navy aides ordered through Lt. Commander Rigdon
(Aides have separate schedule in which they are assigned specific posts and specific guests.)

MUSIC:　Marine orchestra notified by Rigdon—22 members in lobby.
Marine orchestra notified for East Room—14 members

FOOD FOR ORCHESTRA ORDERED: Mary Sharpe

The Trumans didn't do any mingling afterwards. By the time they'd received more than a thousand people, they were ready to call it a night.

Cut and dried? Yes it was, and quite a bit of work for a Presidential handshake and maybe a few words, a glass of light punch and a couple of cookies. An aide would politely remove your cigarette, too, if you happened to violate the "No Smoking" rule. There were no objections from the Trumans, neither of whom smoked. The fire department frowned on that many people in the House anyway, and always stationed firemen around the House, to the dismay of the social secretary.

The best part of a reception was always the ten minutes before the guests arrived—all the butlers and doormen in place, lights dimmed, red-coated Marines sitting in the lobby. You could actually see the elegant arrangements of Mrs. Truman's favorite flowers, talisman roses, lighting up the State rooms.

And standing near the Grand Staircase, I always felt the magic of the House and the Presidency—listening to the drum tattoo "Ruffles and Flourishes," and the military march "Hail to the Chief" as the President and his party, preceded by the color guard bearing our country's flag and the President's banner, stepped smartly into the room.

The State dinners, elaborate, regal, almost cold in their formality, were welcome after all those dark wartime years. Always white tie, always at eight, they were always preceded by the same ceremony which began the receptions. The Trumans managed to execute them quite well.

Seated across from his wife at the head of the U-shaped banquet table, the gold White House tableware gleaming before him, President Truman presided over more social functions that season than during any other in his administration. There was only one near-mishap in that 1946–47 season. It involved the Diplomatic Dinner.

The diplomatic corps had grown so, since the Roosevelt days, that we simply couldn't feed them all at one sitting. With all the new nations that sprang forth after World War II, the number of ambassadors in the United States was now up to 62. There was no way that we could seat them, their wives, the Secretary of State and his wife, and the Trumans in the State Dining Room. Not one body more than 104 could squeeze in at the big horseshoe banquet table.

The Chief of Protocol, Mrs. Helm, Mr. Crim and I presented a plan to Mrs. Truman:

Protocol in Washington is governed by the length of

service of an ambassador, and diplomats were numbered in the State Department's blue book according to the time of their arrival in Washington.

According to our plan, the "even" numbers were invited to the first diplomatic dinner and the "odd" numbers to the second. The State Department took great pains to broadcast this system to all the ambassadors, lest someone feel slighted at broken protocol.

Someone did. In fact, one of the most touchy ambassadors canceled out at the very last minute, causing lots of embarrassment. Mrs. Truman was horrified and the President was incensed, not because he gave a hang about protocol but because Mrs. Truman was upset.

The next morning he called in Dean Acheson, the Undersecretary of State, and Stanley Woodward, Chief of Protocol. "I wish to have that ambassador recalled at once," he told Mr. Acheson firmly.

Mr. Acheson, one of the President's intimate friends, didn't hesitate to disagree with the President's impulsive request.

"No, I don't propose to overlook it," said the President. "That ambassador has been rude to Mrs. Truman. That is the end of that, and I don't want any more discussion."

Just then, the phone rang and it was Mrs. Truman.

The President was silent for a long time, then he handed Acheson the receiver.

"You must not let Harry do what he's going to do," Mrs. Truman told him.

So Mr. Acheson said, "Perhaps you could help me, Mrs. Truman," and, still holding the phone, began "repeating" to the President what Mrs. Truman was saying, although she, on the other end of the line, was saying nothing.

"She says the press will tear you up," Secretary Acheson said to Mr. Truman, ". . . that you're acting too big for your breeches . . . that you don't need that kind of criticism right now."

Finally, the President reached over and took the phone.

"Well," he said to his wife, "if you two gang up on me, I'm just lost."

Then the President picked up a little filigreed-gold

picture frame from his desk and took out a photograph of a young girl, dressed in 1917 style, with a note on the back to young Captain Truman.

And he told Mr. Acheson, "Any man who is rude to that girl is in trouble with me!" *

The late Congressman Adam Clayton Powell was in trouble with the President for just that reason. Although later history would prove that the young black Congressman had been a courageous pioneer for civil rights, as was President Truman, Mr. Powell was the one Washington official who was excluded from all the Trumans' guest lists. It happened because he criticized Bess Truman.

When the Daughters of the American Revolution, who own Constitution Hall, refused to allow black pianist Hazel Scott to play there, Powell, who was Miss Scott's husband, was rightfully incensed.

When Mrs. Truman later attended a D.A.R. function, Congressman Powell publicly called her "the Last Lady of the land."

President Truman was furious. He apparently felt that the insult to his wife was worse than the insult to Powell's wife and to American Negroes. And yet this same Harry Truman was an early champion of civil rights and the first President to integrate the armed forces. He was a complex man, but when it came to his family he was very single-minded. They came first.

State dinners, receptions, and smaller social events have been used successfully by a number of Presidents to win help from new Congressmen or to mend strained relations with old ones. Harry Truman needed all the help he could get, as he struggled with strikes, overly independent Cabinet officers, and a Congress that was ignoring his domestic programs. But the entertaining didn't seem to work too well for him in that respect.

The social season was curtailed in 1948, however, mainly because Bess Truman considered it in poor taste to put on sumptuous meals in the White House when the

---

* Told by former Secretary Acheson at ceremony unveiling portrait of Bess Truman, April 18, 1968. (Official White House transcript.)

President was publicly expressing his concern about hunger overseas, calling on this country's generosity to aid the war-ravaged nations.

It was a political matter, too. Knowing the whims and peculiarities of Congress, how could the State Department ask for billions in foreign aid for the Marshall Plan, while spending $3,000 to entertain each head of state who visited the White House? Our political leaders then were self-conscious about our growing wealth in a world that mostly lacked it.

President Truman himself went abroad—first on good-will visits to Mexico and Canada, then in September, 1947, to Brazil to sign the hemispheric mutual defense treaty, and in early 1948, to Puerto Rico, the Virgin Islands and Cuba. It was of paramount importance to him that anti-Communist bastions be established or maintained throughout the Americas.

And then, when he returned from all his travels he found his house was falling down.

3

By the beginning of 1948, his popularity had dropped to 32 per cent in the polls and the newspapers' favorite game was sniping at Harry Truman. If it disturbed him or daunted him, we never saw it.

Congress was in a rebellious mood. And as it looked for ways to put down this feisty, independent President, it found one in plans to expand the White House.

The Executive Mansion was plenty big as a home, but it had long since failed to meet the office-space needs of a President trying to direct a rapidly expanding federal government.

During his first year in office, the President had proposed expansion of the west wing Presidential offices. He wanted a $970,000 addition—to include a small auditorium for press conferences and motion pictures, a permanent stage, and a lunchroom for his office employees—mansion employees then ate in the servants' dining room, but high-ranking Presidential aides had nowhere to go.

In February, 1946, the Senate Appropriations Committee abruptly halted those plans. The reason given for rescinding the appropriation for the expansion was "to preserve the general architectural scheme."

"They've never done that to a President since I've been here," said an astounded Mr. Crim. "Heaven help us if they go so far as to cut back our budget" (then $171,940).

But Congress had not reckoned with Harry Truman, who may have been starting a counterattack when he called us to his study a few days later. It was late afternoon, after he'd come back from the office and he looked weary. But he was ready to do battle.

Beckoning us over to the window in the oval room overlooking the south lawn, he pointed over to the ellipse, to the Washington Monument.

"That's a magnificent sight, isn't it?"

"It certainly is," Mr. Crim nodded.

"I'd like to be able to take better advantage of that view," the President went on. "It would be far more correct, in an architectural sense, to have a balcony up here, on the second floor. And it would solve the awning problem downstairs."

Mr. Crim and I were pleased to think that the President was considering the awnings on the South Portico, which were always in need of cleaning and repair. Those awnings, under which the Trumans took almost every meal, were one of the biggest problems we had.

He showed us some drawings, with a balcony directly above the South Portico. We could see that it would serve as a roof for the porch.

"Is there any precedent for this?" he asked

Mr. Crim replied, hesitantly and a bit uncertainly, "Mr. Coolidge put on a new roof and a third floor, but they got a special congressional appropriation."

"Can we get this out of our own budget?" the President countered, in a determined voice.

"If it doesn't cost over $10,000 it can come out of what Congress left us for this year," Mr. Crim replied.

At which the President broke into a gleeful smile. "I'm going to preserve the general architectural scheme of the White House any damn way I want to!"

He first studied the original plans for the White House (with no balcony), and even all the other plans that had been submitted, including Thomas Jefferson's design for the Presidential Palace, which had won second prize in the original architectural contest. When Mr. Truman announced his balcony plan to the Fine Arts Commission (who advise and approve architectural plans for the nation's capital), however, the staid old committee went up in smoke. They started a hullabaloo through the entire country about that balcony and how it would destroy America's heritage. They called it "Truman's folly."

Mr. Crim chuckled at the furor.

"And all that because the President wants to eat supper on his back porch without traipsing through the Red Room," he said.

Mr. Truman called in an architect who swore that classic Georgian mansions had two balconies, the better to break up the line of the great columns. But Gilmore Clark, chairman of the commission, was not mollified.

"The President cannot make that change without the approval of the Fine Arts Commission," he thundered.

"The hell with them; I'm going to do it anyway," Mr. Truman told us. And he did. And Gilmore Clark was replaced, at the first opportunity, as chairman of the group.

That was the way Harry Truman was. He didn't have any fancy airs or pretensions, but he also wasn't cowed by experts, or people who had far more education than he did. He had the confidence to act on his own beliefs.

Ironically, after all the historical protests and Presidential determination, the balcony received very little use. Mrs. Truman would sit out there every now and then and watch a baseball game on the ellipse in front of the Washington Monument, and they sat on the balcony a few times at night. But they found it to be too public for comfort. Crowds would gather at the end of the south lawn and gape at them as they sat there. So after all that fuss, the Trumans went back to eating on the South Portico, off the first floor, underneath their controversial balcony.

But sparring about the balcony and added offices was nothing compared to what came next. The Trumans soon

95

noticed that the old mansion had begun to quiver and quake.

Actually, the telltale signs had been brought home to us earlier in the winter as Mrs. Truman held an afternoon reception for the D.A.R. The First Lady was receiving her guests in the large oval Blue Room.

Suddenly, she heard a strange tinkle of glass. Looking straight above her head, she saw the huge crystal chandelier swaying, clinking the hundreds of prisms back and forth.

Still smiling, still greeting the ladies, she motioned to an aide and sent for me. "Would you please find out what in the world is going on upstairs?" she asked urgently.

The Blue Room is directly below the President's oval study.

I hurried upstairs trying to imagine what kind of scuffle was going on that would rattle the White House. No earthquakes had ever occurred in Washington to my knowledge, and nobody had been given instructions to move around any heavy furniture that day.

Fields, the head butler, stepped out of Mr. Truman's bedroom.

"What's going on up here?" I asked.

Fields looked puzzled. "The boss is taking a bath," he said, "and he asked me to get him a book from the study."

Before the horror set in, I had to laugh.

"Fields, you need to go on a diet!"

He was the biggest man on the staff, six feet four and well over 200 pounds. He walked with a sturdy bounce, and when he stomped in and out of the pantry, dishes rattled. But we'd never known him or anyone else to make chandeliers tremble.

As he retraced his steps across the President's study, the floor creaked ominously beneath the thick carpet.

"This place has been squeaking like this for years," Fields said nonchalantly about the house, which was built in the 1790's.

By this time the reception was over and Mrs. Truman had joined us, with Mr. Crim in tow. Mr. Truman emerged from his bedroom and we all stomped across the floor, in an unscientific search to explain the shimmering chandelier.

"I was afraid the chandelier was going to come right down on top of all those people," Mrs. Truman said.

"And I would have come crashing through the ceiling in the bathtub, right in the laps of the D.A.R.," the President laughed. "That would have been something."

Later Mr. Truman told us, "You'd better get some engineers in here. They might have to shore up the floors."

Within a month, the Commissioner of Public Buildings, who had made a cursory structural survey, reported that we were indeed in trouble. He found that some of the timbers under the second floor had been notched out about five inches, causing the floor to incur many times its normal stress.

President Truman immediately formed an investigating committee, made up of the presidents of the American Society of Civil Engineers and the American Institute of Architects, the Commissioner of Public Buildings, and the Chief Usher.

The first thing the committee discovered was that the White House was a fire hazard.

It was a wonder that we hadn't burned to the ground—and there was ample precedent to give us warning. Fire was part of the building's history—the British burned it in 1814. A favorite story of that fire is how Dolly Madison ran bravely into a State parlor, cut the portrait of George Washington out of its frame and ran for her life, leaving her own precious things behind.

More recent and pertinent were the pictures of flames and smoke when the west wing caught fire on Christmas Eve, 1929, but I suppose we really didn't think through all the conditions that could lead to a holocaust.

We soon were forced to think about at least some of those multiple hazards. The wiring had been put in in 1891 and had been patched and added to ever since. And so we instituted a few emergency safety procedures.

Our first order was to cut down on the use of electricity on the second floor. When Mrs. Truman heard there would be even less vacuuming, she threw up her hands in mock defeat.

Our second order was that a really thorough study had to be made. One engineer told us that the whole building had to go.

"Before that happens," the President replied, "I'm going to have the most thorough study ever made of every nook and cranny, beam and pipe in this old house."

And the Congress, which had been simmering over the Truman balcony, suddenly got generous and provided $50,000 for such a study. Perhaps the Congress thought that the coming 1948 election would take care of its Truman problem and there would be a new man in the White House.

"This may be an inconvenience," I told the President. "They'll be drilling into the walls, tearing off plaster, and we'll have to put scaffolding in the East Room to hold up the ceilings."

"Don't worry about us," the President replied. "We're going to Missouri to gather up strength, and then, after the Democratic Convention, we just may be charging around all over the place."

The President had been planning ahead about a lot of things, including taking his family on the famous "Whistle-Stop" campaign of 1948, 21,928 miles on the Presidential railroad car, the "Ferdinand Magellan."

The whistle-stop tour, which became the vehicle the President used to turn around a nation, was appealing to Mr. Truman not only as a technique to reach people at the grassroots, but also because it was inexpensive.

The whistle-stop was an economy move that paid off. The private railroad car had been a gift (a $1 purchase actually) to President Roosevelt from the Association of American Railroads. The President took along a cook, a couple of waiters, his wife and daughter, and a seventeen-person campaign staff. The Trumans brought their own food, so all they had to pay for was the railroad tickets.

The rest of the seventeen cars were filled with newsmen whose newspapers paid for their tickets, and thus bore most of the cost of the train trip.

There also was a Signal Corps communications car. Whether the President travels by railroad, airplane, helicopter, limousine or mules, the Army Signal Corps always goes with him to keep in constant touch with the command post in the basement of the White House. The Secret Service preceded the train in two cars pulled by their own engine.

At each town, the President, Mrs. Truman and Margaret spoke to the crowds from the train's rear platform. Back in the White House, reading about their progress through the small towns and cities of America, I could imagine how people would come to hear him. In those days, anybody would go down to the station to see a President. I recalled how we'd turned out in Creston to see President Roosevelt—even the rock-ribbed Republicans among us.

I will always remember Harry Truman, standing out there on that platform and talking to people the way he talked to us in the White House—a plain man expressing his convictions in plain language. He wasn't concerned about his image or about developing a new one. He hadn't time to be. And besides there was no television set bouncing back his speeches to make him self-conscious. The audiences roared "Give 'em hell, Harry," and he did.

The entire campaign cost the Democrats only $1,368,-058, and gained Mr. Truman 24,179,345 votes, to the surprise and embarrassment of all the pundits and prognosticators—the New York *Times*, the Gallup Poll, and *Time* Magazine, which had referred to Republican candidate Thomas E. Dewey as "the next President."

The victorious Trumans rode their train into Washington November 5, and a huge crowd, estimated at 750,000, roared its greeting as he motored from Union Station to the White House.

The next morning when I appeared at Mrs. Truman's study, she was beaming. I'd never seen such a broad smile on her face. Before I could congratulate her, she leaned way back in her chair—unlike her usually erect posture—and waved over her head a copy of *Time* Magazine with Dewey's picture on the cover.

"Well, it looks like you're going to have to put up with us for another four years," she said.

It must have been a tremendous personal victory for the Trumans. They had come through together against

99

all the odds, and despite all the criticism. I guess there were a lot of people out there who liked Harry Truman's directness as much as I did.

But unfortunately, we had bad news for the victorious Trumans. "I'm afraid you're going to have to move out right away," I said. "The house is actually in very dangerous condition."

The President, who had joined us, was on his way to meet with Mr. Crim and the engineering committee. But he was still in an exhilarated mood.

"Doesn't that beat all!" he said. "Here we've worked ourselves to death trying to stay in this jailhouse and they kick us out anyway!" But after he met with the committee he grew much more sober about the prospect of getting out—quickly.

While the Trumans had been living in a railroad car, the President's bathtub had actually begun sinking into the Red Room ceiling. And one leg of Margaret's piano nearly went through the floor. In fact, the only safe place in the mansion was Mr. Truman's new balcony!

The White House, which had been under "improvement" with modern conveniences for almost 150 years, had chosen to collapse during the Truman administration.

The investigating committee found some really shocking engineering errors. In all the years Presidents had been living there, nobody had taken the trouble to review the entire structure.

There was no support for the interior walls, only soft clay footings. And on those walls hung a weight of 180,000 pounds. Any collapse of the interior walls would plunge everything into the basement. And it looked as if failure were imminent, because doors had been cut through the supporting walls.

The exterior, however, was in good shape. It had, after all, survived the British, and still sat firmly on a foundation of stones from Aquia Creek in Virginia.

In their haste to rebuild after the War of 1812, the young Americans just neglected to put strong footings under the interior walls. Nor did they plan for the technological revolution that would put wires and pipes of all varieties in those walls.

Inside those walls—certainly not planned for by the original architect James Hoban—we found heavy lead pipe that had been installed in 1840 for the first water system, gas pipes for lighting in 1848, pipes for the first hot-air heating system in 1872, and, of course, pipes for the current heating system supplied by the government's central heating plant in southwest Washington. The hundreds of yards of pipe from former systems increased the weight and undermined the building's stability.

Exploration of the walls turned up another fire hazard. Inside the walls were piles of woodshavings left by successive workmen during the various modernizations. A single spark could have lighted that tinder.

On top of those old walls, shoving the mansion down into Foggy Bottom, sat the third floor and the heavy slate roof.

As the engineers sifted through the place, they found a frightening split in a beam in the State Dining Room. In Margaret's sitting room, another beam was split badly, which may have occurred as long ago as the days Lincoln slept there. Many walls were cracked on the inside, and the floors sagged and sloped like a roller coaster.

Mr. Truman was understandably upset.

"My heart trembles when I think of the disasters we might have had," he said, "with 1,400 people downstairs at a reception, none of them knowing that tons and tons of ceiling might drop on their heads at any moment."

Our next problem was to find a place for the President of the United States to live. Mrs. Truman, at first, ruled out Blair House.

"We need to keep it as a guest house," she said. "We've already invited six foreign visitors."

And Mr. Truman spoke up.

"Wherever we go, it has to be a government house," he said. "It can't be somebody's private home. I've read about the criticism the Coolidges got when they moved into somebody's house on Dupont Circle." The President quickly let us know he didn't want to be beholden to any private individual for any favor as big as a place to live.

So we took Mrs. Truman around on a quick tour of "government" houses. First we went to the Peter Mansion, out in Bethesda, Maryland, on the grounds of the National Institutes of Health.

Mr. Crim and I thought it would do well except that it was located so far away from the oval office. "It's a very nice house," Mrs. Truman agreed. As we drove out the driveway, however, a dump truck let fly with a cloud of dust that almost blinded the driver.

"Is that an everyday occurrence?" Mrs. Truman asked, glancing at the big construction project going on next door. They were just beginning to build a huge office building and hospital for the N.I.H. The noise and dirt of construction would have been bothersome, if not unbearable. Besides, it would be a long commute from the office for an afternoon nap.

Then we looked at the Naval Commandant's house, on the grounds of the Naval Observatory on Massachusetts Avenue at the end of Embassy Row, which would have been much closer to the White House than the Peter Mansion. But the big frame house just wasn't set up to take care of all the entourage of the Presidency.

So then we looked at Blair House again—it had been our choice in the first place—and suggested to the Trumans that we connect it to Blair-Lee House, next door, on all the floors. Lee House was also owned by the government, and the two row houses together made one large residence. The Trumans finally agreed.

"We'll just have to put the President of Brazil and the other visitors someplace else," Mrs. Truman said.

Now confident that they'd have a roof over—and not on top of—their heads for the next four years, the Trumans packed up and went to Key West to recuperate from the campaign, while we set about making an alternate White House across the street.

Blair House, in my opinion, is one of the loveliest homes in Washington. Its scale, architecture, and its furnishings reflect the best of nineteenth-century American design, and like the White House, it, too, has figured in American history.

Built in 1824 by Dr. James Lovell, the first Surgeon General, the house was sold in 1836 to Francis Preston Blair, whose descendants held the home for a century. It was Blair's daughter, Elizabeth, who married a grandson of Richard Henry Lee, for whom Blair-Lee House next door was named.

The Blairs not only entertained the Presidents who lived across the street—Martin Van Buren, Andrew Jackson, Abraham Lincoln, William Howard Taft—but they also rented out the house to various Cabinet officers over the years. Henry Clay, John C. Calhoun, and Daniel Webster were frequent visitors. It was in Blair House that Robert E. Lee, a relative of the Lee side of the family, was asked—and refused—to command the Union Army.

The Blairs were concerned with keeping the house as a memorial to their family's place in history, and, in 1942, sold it to the State Department.

Blair House was exquisitely furnished, with genuine period pieces, unlike the hodgepodge in the White House, and Mrs. Truman remarked to me more than once how comfortable the house had been during the first two weeks of the Truman Presidency. "Everything except the plumbing," she added.

Making it comfortable as a permanent home was something else again. In the two weeks before Thanksgiving, we mustered all the White House carpenters, painters, electricians—and particularly plumbers—plus others from GSA. Every bathroom in the house was supplied with new fixtures. Doors were cut through on every floor, joining the houses together.

We didn't touch the furnishings in Blair House. But the adjoining annex, Blair-Lee House, was in pretty bad shape. It had been used mainly for overflow, to house a foreign visitor's retinue of servants, and had earlier been used for government offices.

After the painters had slapped on the last coat of paint, we moved the Green Room furniture into one room, the Red Room furniture into another, and the Private Dining Room furniture into the dining room.

We made a little study for the President right inside the front door at Lee House.

Our staff moved through the White House rooms with some trepidation, lifting furniture and paintings from beneath the big braces hastily installed to hold up the ceilings.

"I don't want the house to fall down on the President," said one of the movers as he hauled the heavy portraits of past Presidents down from the Green Room wall, "but I don't want it to fall down on me either."

We moved our staff and our equipment—china, silver, linen, curtains—across the street.

What was left—and that was most of the White House furnishings and chandeliers—was stored at the very obliging National Gallery of Art. What an inventory! What a job of cataloguing, cross-checking, packing and storing of all that furniture—that wasn't so great in the first place.

The President went to Congress. Five months later, in April, 1949, a law was passed establishing the high-level Commission on the Renovation of the White House—two senators, two representatives, and two Presidential appointees.* And they immediately set about to solve the problem of the collapsing mansion.

The Commission presented the President with three alternatives: (1) to demolish the building, preserving and storing the exterior stones for later replacement; and to rebuild the White House from the ground up; (2) to demolish the building and rebuild it entirely, in the same design but of new material; (3) to preserve in place the outer walls, to gut the interior completely, to add underpinning and strong foundations and basement, and rebuild from the inside.

President Truman strongly favored the third solution, as did all of us whose lives revolved around the old building. In my view, the first two plans were terrible. The White House would have lost its history and become just another brand-new office building.

I recalled the President's fascination with that history

* Senators Kenneth McKellar of Tennessee, Edward Martin of Pennsylvania; Representatives Louis C. Rabaut, Michigan, and Frank B. Keefe, Wisconsin; Presidential appointees Richard E. Dougherty and Douglas William Orr. The Commission hired a staff, headed by Maj. Gen. Glen E. Edgerton (Ret.), and three consulting engineering firms.

when I'd taken him on his first tour. He loved it even more now because he'd earned his right to live in it.

"There are so many memories here," he said, "so many events that shaped this country, and some that didn't. Why, I can almost believe in Lincoln's ghost myself. And I can almost smell the big hunk of cheese at Andy Jackson's inauguration. They say he sprawled around on the furniture with his boots on."

Mr. Truman pointed out the Commission's newest discovery, on the landing of the grand staircase.

"See?" The President pointed out some charred wooden beams uncovered behind the plaster and bricks. "That happened during the War of 1812 when the British set us on fire."

I wished that Mr. Churchill could have seen it. He would have enjoyed that visual reminder of Anglo-American history.

"I'll do anything in my power to keep them from tearing down the White House," the President told us. "If only we can get Congress to agree."

Congress, however, was giving serious consideration to a new White House. To gut the mansion and rebuild from the inside would be more difficult, more costly (the estimate was $5,412,000), and would take longer.

Rep. Clarence Cannon, a fellow Missourian, who was chairman of the House Appropriations Committee, thought it would be better to build a new, machine-cut marble Executive Mansion. Like most of President Truman's requests to Congress, this one was not going smoothly.

But finally the President got his way, thanks in a large measure to an uprising of popular support around the country. Americans, it turned out, were proud of this historic house and did not want to erase it.

The Congress authorized the $5.4 million in June, and the agreement to renovate the building was signed in August, 1949.

"It would have amounted to substantial desecration to have acted otherwise," commented the Renovation Commission.

B. Altman and Company of New York won the bid to

furnish the house. The general contractor was John McShain, Inc. When the work began, the builder put up a big sign on the north lawn: John McShain, Inc., Builders.

The President saw it as he walked across the street from Blair House.

"Take that thing down right now," he ordered Mr. Crim, and the sign disappeared immediately.

The scope of the reconstruction was immense. New footings had to be placed, and a new supporting structural-steel frame erected on those footings within the existing limestone walls.

First they built a high, protective fence around the job, partly to keep the curious workmen from peering in the windows at the President of the United States, as he worked in his west wing office.

Then, after they'd "underpinned" the outer walls, they had to tear down and remove the interior walls. Every door, every window, every length of woodwork, mantelpiece, piece of molding or wood paneling, was carefully removed, measured, and stored—because they had to be put back inside the house.

The inside work involved connecting the new steel frame inside the walls, building two new basements, and installing new, fireproof floors all over the house.

Next, they set about to replace the interior rooms and facilities in the ground floor, first floor, and second and third floors, restoring the architectural detail of the State floors.

Meanwhile other workers were digging vaults under the front lawn for the mechanical equipment for air conditioning and the extra power supply. Still others were installing modern plumbing, heating, electrical equipment, elevators, and central air conditioning, refurbishing the exterior, and replacing and landscaping the trampled-upon, dug-out grounds. It took fifty subcontractors and hundreds of workmen, all of whom got security clearance, to work on the White House.

Despite the inconvenience to the President, with all the dirt from the excavating, and noise from the machinery rattling the windows in his Cabinet Room, Mr. Truman took great pride in the rebuilding of his home and spent many hours as a sidewalk superintendent.

He was delighted with some of the discoveries—the decorative cornices of the Theodore Roosevelt renovation that later had been covered over with plaster, and underneath them the original 1792 decoration of architect James Hoban's cornices.

As workers gingerly threaded huge structural-steel beams in through the windows, excavation for the two additional underground floors brought forth more secrets. Among them was a well dug near the east wall, at the direction of Thomas Jefferson. In the foundation stones, they discovered numerous carved symbols of freemasonry, fishhooks, chevrons, and treelike sketches. Those early stonecutters would have been pleased to know that their signs would be cherished by a twentieth-century President, himself a Mason, and would be embedded decoratively in fireplace walls of his new broadcast room, which was the original kitchen.

Each swirl and fleurette of the ornamental plaster cornices, so elaborately molded, had to be carefully diagrammed, so that they could be copied in fresh plaster. But after this was done, they couldn't find a single craftsman in America who could replace the molding. Finally, the Commission imported skilled artisans from Italy, and the work went on as planned.

Mr. Crim was totally involved in the renovation of the White House, while I concentrated on life at Blair House.

By Inauguration Day, January 20, 1949, the Trumans were happily ensconced in their cozier quarters. We were delighted that the celebration itself would necessarily be less of a job for us than had the 1945 Inauguration.

Because the mansion was out of commission, the traditional after-the-parade reception was to be held at the National Gallery of Art. The White House staff was to serve and arrange flowers, but we had to purchase the tea-party sandwiches from caterers and food suppliers in town. Our only function at Blair House was a buffet luncheon following the swearing-in ceremony at the Capitol.

"Make it simple," Mrs. Truman told us, "but as nice

107

as any official luncheon. Guests will be strictly limited to members of our families.

"I'd rather be here with them than over at the Capitol," Mrs. Truman added, but she dutifully attended the luncheon at the Capitol, given for the President and the leaders of Congress by the Inaugural committee. The diplomatic corps attended another traditional post-Inauguration luncheon at the State Department.

All the dignitaries in Washington had some place to go, but Mrs. Truman, in a characteristic, gracious act, made sure that the Truman and Wallace clans also had a splendid luncheon. As we checked in the various Trumans and Wallaces from all over the country, however, a very familiar—but uninvited—guest arrived.

Perle Mesta, the Washington party-giver, stepped out of the back seat of her open car, gave the Blair House doorman a glittering smile and swept past the policeman as if she owned the place.

"What shall we do?" a policeman at the gate asked me. "She isn't on the list."

"Never mind," I answered. "She's a good friend of the Trumans."

"I'm sure she's had gate-crashers at her parties, but I wonder if this is the first time she's ever crashed one herself," Mr. Crim whispered.

Later, when we told Mrs. Truman, she just laughed. "That's all right," she said. "I'm sure she livened up the luncheon."

Shortly thereafter, the vivacious Mrs. Mesta was appointed Ambassador to Luxembourg, a role that later was fictionalized in the musical *Call Me Madam*. The "hostess with the mostest" entertained that day, flitting from table to table, seeing to Bess's brother, Fred, Harry's brother, Vivian, all the cousins and other relatives, as if they were her family visiting *her* home.

The Trumans and Vice President Alben Barkley rode back down Pennsylvania Avenue in open limousines to the reviewing stands in front of the White House. The sun beamed—such a contrast from that snowy, dreary wartime inaugural day in 1945, when there wasn't even a parade. And so did Mr. Truman, in his high silk hat and striped trousers. The old World War I artillery captain really loved a parade.

"When the band played 'I'm Just Wild About Harry,'" Margaret reported, "Dad did a little jig to the music."

It was a great day for the three Trumans, and the entire family never stopped smiling until Margaret and her friends came limping in at about 1:30 a.m., after being crushed in a crowd of 10,000 at the Inaugural Ball at the National Guard Armory.

Ever since Margaret had graduated from college, her second summer in the White House, she had been studying voice and trying to launch a career on her own. Now, her year of campaigning over, she was moving to New York to her own apartment and a serious singing career.

Her mother, protective as always, sent along a companion to chaperone the aspiring young singer. Mrs. Truman entrusted that job to Reathel Odum, her own personal secretary. Reathel's secretarial services had been greatly underutilized by the efficient Mrs. Truman, who almost always ended up writing her own correspondence.

"Now that we're going to be living a quiet life in Blair House, I can manage without her," Mrs. Truman told me.

The staff all missed Margaret and Reathel. It was strange at first, not to hear the young soprano vocalizing behind a closed door, hours and hours on end.

We had watched her grow up from a fresh-faced young college student to a sophisticated performer. And she'd remained amazingly unspoiled, despite all the attention.

Mrs. Truman insisted that her daughter learn the fine points of homemaking. I remember one morning, when the housekeeper and I went up for our meeting with the First Lady, we found Margaret sitting in her mother's office, stitching a long strip of lace onto the edge of a white slip. She had a thread about a yard long, all tangled, and Mrs. Truman was laughing uproariously at her efforts. "Have you ever seen such a seamstress?" the First Lady laughed.

"Why don't you have one of the maids do that?" Mrs. Sharpe asked.

"Indeed she won't," Mrs. Truman said. "She's going to learn to do this if it takes her all day!"

Even after four years as the President's daughter, Margaret did her own personal maid work, and washed her own hair, using the new vogue, a beer rinse.

Although none of us were music critics, we admired Margaret's determination and wished her well in her new career.

Her father, protective as always, kept an eye on her, concerned about her health in New York. He scribbled a note to me:

Memo to Mr. West
   Call Jills (No. 6020) and make an appointment for Mrs. Truman with Jean or Doris for any time Monday 8th.
   Tell Wilma to bring vitamin pills for Margaret to N.Y. They are wrapped in celaphane [sic] and probably are in Margie's cabinet.
   Tell Pennington to meet B&O National Limited at 7:30 a.m. Saturday at Union Station for baggage to go to N.Y.
                                                    H.S.T.

Without Margaret, without the official load of entertaining (State dinners were being held in the Carlton Hotel on 16th Street), Bess and Harry Truman got to spend a lot more time alone together. They'd sit out in the garden reading, having a light lunch, resting together. Very discreet, very private, they spent a lot of time behind closed doors in Blair House.

The butlers no longer bet on "Two-gun Bess" in the mornings. Nor did the maids joke about the Three Musketeers. Instead, it was "the lovebirds are upstairs."

When Mrs. Truman left to take her mother to Independence for the summer, the President was disconsolate. He'd pick at his food if he had to eat alone, and often, on the spur of the moment, he'd call over a crony for an evening's visit in the drawing room. Solitary thinking was not his favorite approach to solving problems. He liked a verbal sounding board. And he liked company.

The President had the poker game come to the White House only once, in his earliest days in office. We'd even bought a special poker table. However, he preferred to spend his evenings alone with his wife. But when Mrs. Truman was out of town, the President returned to the poker game.

When she returned that fall, the President was jubilant. He met her train at Union Station and they came back arm in arm.

"It's good to have the real boss back," he beamed at me. "But we'll have to mind our p's and q's around here from now on."

Mr. and Mrs. Truman were so obviously glad to see each other, butlers kept grinning as they went back and forth through the house.

After a light dinner in the President's library, they sent the maids downstairs.

The next morning, I was in Mrs. Truman's study at nine, as usual.

She scanned the day's menu, then, in a rather small, uncomfortable voice, she said:

"Mr. West, we have a little problem."

"Yes," I waited.

She cleared her throat, demurely.

"It's the President's bed. Do you think you can get it fixed today?"

"Why certainly," I said. "What's the matter?"

"Two of the slats broke down during the night."

"I'll see that it has all new slats put in," I said hurriedly. "It's an old antique bed anyway, and if he'd like a newer one. . . ."

"Oh, no," she said. "This one is just fine."

But the Trumans certainly aren't antiques, I thought to myself. The President's wife was blushing like a young bride.

In Blair House, we established a routine for the limited amount of entertaining, which seemed to work—at least for the staff.

We served formal dinners for semi-State guests for no more than twenty-two persons in the Blair-Lee dining room. The White House staff had simply moved across the street and taken over. Mrs. Victoria Geaney, who'd been housekeeper at Blair House, had become more hostess than housekeeper.

111

With the Usher's office in residence, and Bess Truman as the only hostess we needed, Mrs. Geaney's particular talents were going to waste. She was gently eased over as hostess at Prospect House in Georgetown, which the State Department took over as a temporary Presidential guest house.

The White House housekeeper, Mrs. Sharpe, had resigned, thinking she'd only be in Mrs. Geaney's way. So Mabel Walker, her young assistant whose principal job was keeping books, moved over to Blair House.

Miss Walker protested to me that she didn't know much about food—and after a month or two, Mrs. Truman agreed.

"I think she has a list of menus exactly two weeks long, and at the end of two weeks she just runs them through again," the First Lady chuckled. That gave me the idea for a long-overdue promotion.

I went to Mr. Crim. "How about dividing the duties?" I asked. "Miss Walker could run the housecleaning and books, and Fields could be in charge of food preparation and services."

As head butler, Alonzo Fields knew entertaining inside out.

Mr. Crim was dubious. He had never promoted from within the ranks. In the White House hierarchy, "servants" never became "executives." Assistants, like Miss Walker, were always hired to inherit managerial positions, if they worked out.

"Let's see what Mrs. Truman thinks," he said. As I already knew, Mrs. Truman admired Fields' abilities and she was genuinely fond of the huge, genial butler.

"I think that's an inspired idea," she replied—and even came up with the title for his new position: Maître d'hôtel.

It worked out well.

For State entertaining, we turned to the Carlton Hotel, which supplied a generally competent handling of our special needs, protocol, and very heavy guest lists.

The State Department quickly found out that it was a lot cheaper to entertain their foreign visitors at the White House than anywhere else in town. The food prepared in the Carlton was much more expensive than that which we purchased wholesale and cooked in White House kitchens. Also, all the culinary employees of the hotel had to be security-checked.

Mr. Redmond and his crew bought the flowers we used from local greenhouses, then arranged bouquets for the banquets in his quarters beneath the west terrace of the White House, which, like the social office, remained open during the renovation.

For every hotel dinner, we went into the vaults beneath the North Portico, packed up the china, crystal, and gold flatware and hauled it all down to the hotel.

We sent the White House butlers down to serve the President and his top-ranking guests. In fact, all the ushers, social aides, Marines, and others carried on as if it were a White House away from home. Fields worked out a tentative menu, Mrs. Truman approved it with the suggestion that room be left for the hotel chef's specialty, and I took the menu, with a suggested wine list, to work out the details with the hotel's maître d'.

But not even away from the staid traditions of the mansion did we ever serve cocktails before a State dinner. Mr. Crim was adamant about holding to that rule, as was the social secretary. The main reason, however, was not propriety, but protocol.

"They all march into the dinner according to order of precedence, and they are assigned specific dinner partners for the procession," Mr. Crim told the surprised hotel manager, who was not accustomed to "dry" banquets.

"If they drink too many cocktails, they'll forget where they are in the line of protocol and who they're supposed to be escorting!"

With the preparations for State entertaining taken from under their supervision, the Trumans were able to live in Blair House as they preferred to live—quietly. There were no sightseers trooping through, no elaborate functions. I think they rather appreciated the quiet time, too, because a new course of world events began to occupy the President's every waking moment. The Cold War, as it was now called, spread to new fronts.

Among the issues which Harry Truman struggled with and thought crucial to the survival of the Western world were the ill-fated attempt to support the Nationalist Government of China and the establishment of West Germany.

Mr. Truman was not making these decisions in a vacuum. At home, he had to cope with Senator Joe McCarthy's charges that the government was infiltrated with Communists. The Soviet Union had produced its own atomic bomb, creating a new balance of terror.

He countered the Russians' Berlin blockade with an air-lift; he made the tough decision to produce the hydrogen bomb.

And in July, 1950, North Korea invaded the Republic of South Korea. President Truman decided that the United States would fight. After receiving United Nations support, he named General Douglas MacArthur as his com-mander, and sent two divisions of American soldiers into Korea.

The seriousness of our new war brought a near mora-torium to the already limited entertaining in Blair House, except for one innovation by Mrs. Truman. She began afternoon parties for wounded soldiers, a hundred at a time, at Blair House. They were brought in from hospitals by the Red Cross to be entertained by the Marine band and young friends of Margaret's. Whenever she could interrupt her new concert career, Margaret came down from New York for the teas. And her father never failed to attend.

It was the day after one of those teas, November 1, 1950, that something occurred to change unalterably the life of Harry S. Truman and the lives of future Presidents of the United States.

4

————

At one in the afternoon, punctual to the second, President Truman walked into Blair House, nodding to Mr. Crim and me, as we sat in our little office just inside the front door.

The President went upstairs for a few moments, then came down to lunch with Mrs. Truman and Mrs. Wallace. Things were quiet, sleepy, back to normal after the previous day's entertainment.

I checked the Usher's log as Mr. Truman went back upstairs to take his nap. The President had one appointment for the afternoon, a ceremony at Arlington Cemetery.

"You can sleep until two thirty," I joked to Mr. Crim. "His car won't be here until then."

Mr. Crim laughed. "I'm afraid I might not wake up," he said.

I looked out the window—Blair House, like most period townhouses, is right on the street—at Officer Birdzell, dressed in his winter uniform, standing on the sidewalk.

"I bet he'd like to be in his shirtsleeves today," I said.

Mr. Crim and I were sitting in the office just inside the

front door with the window open, because it was so unseasonably warm outside. The house was so quiet, the day so close, it was a struggle to stay awake.

Suddenly a shattering noise brought us both to our feet.

"That's gunfire!" Mr. Crim exclaimed as we ran to the window.

I saw the White House policeman Davison and Secret Service agent Boring, their pistols drawn and shooting, running down the sidewalk from the police box, at the east end of the house. They were shooting at somebody near the front door of Blair House!

I ran out to the entrance hall and found the front door wide open.

Wade, the doorman, was just standing there, staring at a man in a dark striped suit, who was firing at the policemen.

"Close the door," I yelled and wheeled around to get at the open windows, when I saw Mrs. Truman coming down the stairs.

"What's happening?" she asked worriedly.

"There's a shooting outside," I said. "Somebody is shooting at the police."

Eyes wide, she turned quickly and walked back upstairs.

When I saw Officer Birdzell, who'd been standing out front only a few moments before, fall to the ground bleeding, I realized we were under attack. I had no idea how many gunmen there were or whether there'd be an invasion of Blair House. Then city police and Secret Service agents appeared in droves, and the shooting suddenly stopped.

The man in the striped suit lay on the bottom doorstep, another man was crumpled in a heap inside the hedge in front of Lee House. Office Coffelt was dead, and Officer Downs was seriously wounded.

"Get me a priest," Downs gasped, as they dragged him into Miss Walker's office at Lee House. I called St. Stephen's Church and asked a priest to meet him at Emergency Hospital. Fields and I stayed with the wounded, bleeding man until the ambulance arrived. There had

116

obviously been an attempt to kill the President. But who—and why?

One of the would-be assassins was killed. The other lived to explain that they were Puerto Rican nationalists, who had tried to kill the President because they hoped to set off a revolution in the United States so that their country could declare independence.

It was a frightening experience for all of us to see people murdered just a few feet away, as they tried to invade the residence to kill the President of the United States.

But we were astounded minutes later to see the President come downstairs and leave by the back alley door to make a speech, unveiling a statue of a British war hero, at Arlington Cemetery.

If the killers had arrived at 2:50, instead of 2:20, the President would have been walking out the front door of Blair House—a frighteningly easy target.

From that moment on, the Secret Service, the police, and the President were never allowed to forget the possibility of a madman's bullet. No longer could President Truman walk across the street to his office or take his constitutional. From then on, his car always picked him up at the back alley of Blair House, drove him around the back to the southwest gate of the White House to his west wing office. West Executive Avenue, between the White House and the old State-War-Navy Department building, was closed to traffic forever. Pedestrians no longer could stroll on the sidewalks in front of Blair House. We began to know the feeling of life behind a barricade, a feeling that never again left us.

Publicly Mr. Truman shrugged off the attack. "A President has to expect those things," he said, but he expressed great sorrow to the family of the dead policeman.

Mrs. Truman, however, was visibly upset for days. Her great concern was to keep the news from her mother, who was quite ill.

The confrontation with mortality must have had a deep effect on this President, who had so geared his personal regimen to staying alive. During the next month his responsibilities and burdens multiplied even more with what he termed "the worst situation we have had yet"—the invasion of Korea by 260,000 Chinese Communist troops. General MacArthur was pressing for retaliation, but the President felt that would draw the Russians into a Third World War.

On December 5, 1950, the President reacted to the great strain he was under, but in a very personal way that stirred limitless controversy.

It happened not long after a tense conference aboard the yacht *Williamsburg* with Prime Minister Clement Attlee of Great Britain, which was followed by the sudden death of Mr. Truman's close friend and press secretary Charlie Ross, who collapsed at his desk in the White House.

The President requested that nobody tell Margaret about her friend's death, because she was scheduled to sing at Constitution Hall that evening. She had been ill and he did not wish to upset her further.

The Trumans, with Attlee as guest, dressed for the concert, despite the grave international situation, despite Charlie Ross's death. If anything could lift the President's spirits, it was the sound of his daughter's voice.

But when the doorman took Mr. Truman his newspaper the next morning, the President exploded.

The reviewer panned Margaret's recital and the irate father scribbled a furious note to the critic.

I have just read your lousy review buried in the back pages. You sound like a frustrated man that never made a success, an eight-ulcer man on a four-ulcer job, and all four ulcers working.
I never met you, but if I do you'll need a new nose and plenty of beefsteak and perhaps a supporter below. Westbrook Pegler, a guttersnipe, is a gentleman compared to you. You can take that as more of an insult than a reflection on your ancestry.

The letter brought more unfavorable publicity to Mr. Truman than just about anything he ever wrote. But it was so in character. He could take anything himself, but just let somebody say a word aaginst his womenfolk: "There's just one thing I draw the line at," he said, "and that's any kind of attack on my family. Any man can make mistakes, even if he's trying with all his heart and mind to do the best thing for his country. But a man's family ought to be sacred. There was one columnist who wrote some lie about my family when I was in the Senate and instead of writing him a letter I called him on the phone and I said you so-and-so, if you say another word about my family, I'll come down to your office and shoot you."

The publicity didn't seem to hurt the budding singer's career, though, because Margaret was soon on magazine covers, television shows, all over the place.

The criticism of President Truman reached a crescendo on April 11, 1951, when he fired the insubordinate but popular General MacArthur. Congress was in the biggest uproar—there were even shouts to impeach the President.

It was on that same day, of all days, that Mr. Crim had to go before the House Appropriations Committee to ask for a $49,000 increase in our annual budget. It would take $315,600 to operate the renovated White House, he explained, and, as he feared, he received quite a grilling from Representative Albert Thomas of Texas.

All the new gadgets and space would have to be serviced, the electricity bill alone would be $25,000, with the new air conditioning, laundry, and two elevators. We also needed more staff to maintain the house and its physical plant. The interior was to be more than twice as big as it had been before.

The mood of Congress showed in the way Mr. Crim was treated. The Senate trimmed the figure to $300,000.

In addition, the Commission on Renovation had to go back in August, in the midst of the MacArthur hearings, to ask for a further $321,000 (above the $5,400,000 already voted) to complete the renovation of the mansion itself. The Korean War had driven prices up so that construction costs exceeded the estimates. And to further complicate the situation, a plasterers' strike stopped the entire construction for a while. Once again, a President had to assure Congress that the White House would not be a royal palace. The Senate chopped off $60,000 from *that* request, which had to be made up out of the budget for furnishings.

"I've been using a curry comb on the contractors to try to speed up reconstruction," Mr. Truman joked, but by the promised completion date of September 26, 1951, they were nowhere near finished.

The Trumans were more than a little set back by the delay.

Margaret, who had become a good-will ambassador for her father on an "enchanting" trip to Europe (which she'd financed entirely from her music earnings), had been entertained at Buckingham Palace. She returned the invitation to Princess Elizabeth, hoping that there'd be a sparkling new mansion to welcome her. When the Princess accepted with her husband, the Duke of Edinburgh, for November, we had to scurry around to entertain them at Blair House.

The Blair-Lee House bedrooms had been rather "hotel" in character, serving the official houseguests comfortably but with little charm. Margaret and her mother wanted to do something special for the future Queen of England.

"Let's put my bed in there," Mrs. Truman told me, "and make the room a little more attractive."

So we moved the four-poster canopy bed and curtains to match from Mrs. Truman's room into the guest bedroom. We brought in a small Oriental rug, with a table and a few books, to make it more cozy. But the Princess still had to use the concrete bathtub.

President Truman was quite carried away by his young guest, toasting her as a "fairy Princess" at a small formal dinner in the Blair-Lee House.

Another guest, General Eisenhower, drew no attention at all. He came into Blair House for an off-the-record afternoon appointment with the President in his study. The President had decided not to run for reelection, although he hadn't announced it yet, and both political parties were courting General Eisenhower as a candidate.

We felt sure that President Truman had called the General in to sell him on the Democratic party.

Later, after President Truman's State of the Union speech in January, when we again had Mr. Churchill in tow, Mr. Truman called Mr. Eisenhower a "grand man." But when it turned out that the General was a Republican, Mr. Truman said, "If Eisenhower wants to go out and have mud and eggs thrown at him, that's up to him." (As it turned out, both threw some mud, and General Eisenhower, a newcomer to the tough world of political rhetoric and attack, never forgave Mr. Truman for it.)

By now, the White House was almost ready for the Trumans. Mrs. Truman chose the colors and fabrics for her family's bedrooms—plum for herself, pink for Margaret and green for the President's oval study—but she left the decorating entirely up to the Commission on Renovation and to B. Altman Company.

"I'm only going to be around for a year," she said. "It would be unfair to the next First Lady to impose too many of my ideas upon the house."

As a result, the house had an impersonal, store-decorated look.

The original allotment of $208,000 for furnishings had been cut back to $150,000, not anywhere near enough to buy grand furnishings for sixty-six rooms. The State rooms were restored, as closely as possible, to their former grandeur. In the white-and-gold East Room, our equivalent of the Grand Ballroom, the heavy gold chandeliers that had dragged the ceiling down were reduced in size, outfitted with tiny "candle" bulbs and equipped with a dimming control. New draperies of lemon-gold silk hung at the seven windows.

In the adjoining Green Room, the green silk wall-covering was carefully rehung. A new rug, a copy of a green Aubusson with the Presidential seal, covered the floor. The Red Room wall had new silk damask, and the oval Blue Room, our formal reception room, had new, bright blue satin walls, with a gold design woven in. The dark oak paneling in the State Dining Room for the first time was painted a light green to complement a new dark-green marble fireplace.

President Truman's balcony remained, and he added one more final, personal touch to the house. He ordered that the Grand Staircase be relocated so that it swept up the center bay east of the Entrance Hall on the State floor.

Previously it opened on to the long corridor opposite the Green Room door. Now the State procession—(President, State visitor and color guard descending the staircase)—could be seen by the guests.

A few days before the Trumans finally moved back in on March 27, 1952, Mrs. Truman broke her own rule of silence to the press and took the women's press corps on a tour of the house, upstairs and down. Someone asked her if she'd like to spend four more years at the White House.

"That is a question to which you are not going to get a yes or no out of me," the taciturn First Lady replied.

"But could you stand it if you had to?"

"Well, I stood it for seven years," she replied.

Our first guest, also returning hospitality extended to Margaret in Europe, arrived five days later—Queen Juliana of Holland and her husband, Prince Bernhard. The Queen's Room was ready but the kitchen was not. Once again, we held a State dinner in the Carlton Hotel, the last time in the Truman administration we were to carry all our paraphernalia out of the White House for dinner.

But we unveiled the State Dining Room the next day (and used the new Truman Presidential china) with a smaller official luncheon for the Queen. Once again the President bowed to royalty and toasted the "fairy queen."

Mrs. Roosevelt was next. President Truman had appointed her to the United Nations as a representative on the Human Rights Commission. She visited the White House on April 10, to report on her trip to India and the Middle East.

President Truman proudly gave her a tour of her old home.

"I think it is lovely," she said. "The third floor is so much better arranged and nicer for guests!"

The third-floor solarium, where the Trumans spent so much time, was greatly improved. The Roosevelts' old porch was now almost a penthouse, with a blue-green window wall that afforded a spectacular view, yet was barely visible from the street. The most informal room in the House, it had tile flooring and was outfitted with rattan furniture.

As Mrs. Roosevelt walked through the bright new rooms, she made one more observation: "The closets are a great help!"

I recalled Mabel Webster's endless processions to the third floor to store Mrs. Roosevelt's dresses, because the old White House didn't have built-in closets.

We all agreed with Mrs. Roosevelt that closets would be a great help in the White House. So would the laundry room—we'd sent out the White House wash twice a week. So would the electric dishwashers—the butlers had washed millions of dishes by hand. So was the kitchen elevator— the butlers and maids had run up and down stairs for years. And so, above all, was the air conditioning!

As summer approached, we realized how miserable we had been all those years. The First Families always were able to escape for the entire summer, as did most of Washington. Before the war, the Congress, of course, disappeared from sweltering Washington. The diplomatic corps left, fancy shops closed down. Some government offices sent workers home in the afternoon. But we stayed on.

With air conditioning, Washington became a year-round city, the White House a year-round house.

Despite all the new conveniences, though, Mrs. Truman was worried about her pet concern—keeping the house clean.

She had opened the house to tours. Before the war, tourists could come through only by Congressional appointment. But the Trumans wanted the house open, accessible to the public. Thousands of people flocked through that first year of the "new" White House, leaving fingerprints on the woodwork, tracks on the floor.

"The Appropriations Committee would love it if we asked for more staff right now," she told Mr. Crim and me one afternoon. "Do you know of any way we can get some more in here?"

"Not unless it's through the military," I answered. "We have already had to go to G.S.A. for extra maintenance engineers, and to the Park Service to get some proper care for the lawns."

"It's sort of borrowing from Peter to pay Paul, isn't it?" Mrs. Truman said.

The next morning, as I met her for the daily schedule, she said, "Mr. West, I have an idea. We aren't planning to use the *Williamsburg* as much as we have been now that it's so pleasant up here. Could we bring some of the Filipino stewards in to be housemen and kitchen helpers? Do you think the Navy would approve?"

"I don't see why it couldn't be arranged," I replied, "if the Commander-in-Chief should request a transfer."

The Navy quietly acquiesced, assigning three seamen to the White House pantry and as housemen to help with heavy cleaning, vacuuming, waxing, washing walls upstairs.

Beginning with Mrs. Truman, they became a White House fixture. Some, after they retired from the Navy, stayed on as White House employees. Until that time, though, the Navy paid their salaries.

The Truman White House sported a new fleet of automobiles. Because General Motors executives contributed to Governor Dewey and Henry Ford supported the President, Mr. Truman got rid of the Cadillacs and ordered Ford products. Actually the cars were leased from the manufacturers for $500 a year, so a rapid turnover never surprised anyone.

Mr. Truman's new limousine was a specially built Lincoln Cosmopolitan, with gold-plated fittings in the rear compartment, special running boards for the Secret Service, a padded leather top, and at the President's own request, "sufficient head room for high silk hats." The garage also supplied the family with eleven other Lincolns, two Packards, two Mercuries, ten Fords, and three Ford trucks.

Mr. Truman did his best traveling in trains, however, and he took to the rails once again to go on the stump for Adlai Stevenson, the Democratic candidate opposing General Eisenhower, even though Stevenson chose not to run on the record of the Truman Administration.

None of us was surprised when the General won. After all, the World War II hero was so popular that both parties had wanted him.

Despite the Democratic defeat, President and Mrs. Truman hoped to enjoy their last two months in the White House. Right after the election, they began bringing in close friends to share their remaining days.

On December 4, we held a farewell dinner for the Truman Cabinet. Adlai Stevenson slept in the Lincoln bedroom, his only chance to spend the night in the White House.

The next day, at noon, Mrs. Truman stood in the Red Room receiving a group of ladies. As soon as they left, she hurried back upstairs. Her mother had suffered a mild stroke on December 1, and Mrs. Truman had scarcely left her bedside since.

At about 12:45, the President called me to his oval study. He and Mrs. Truman were seated side by side on the green damask couch.

"Mrs. Wallace has just passed away," he said.

Mrs. Truman was composed, sitting quietly beside the President while he talked.

"We'd like to make arrangements to go to Independence, but without any notice. Mrs. Truman would like it to be as private as possible. Would it be possible that we could travel in a regularly scheduled train, just go in a regular drawing room?"

"I'll see what I can do," I answered.

But the Secret Service would not allow it. The President of the United States cannot travel around like a private citizen, no matter how deeply he may wish it.

So they had to use the Presidential car, on the end of a regular train, to go to Independence for the funeral. The press, for once, respected Bess Truman's wish for privacy.

They came back to the White House for Christmas, for dinner with the family in the State Dining Room. But Mrs. Truman was sad, both at losing her mother and, I suspected, at leaving the White House.

We had three weeks to pack, but the Trumans left with little more than they'd brought with them. Margaret's piano went to Independence, her collection of Dresden china to her apartment in New York. The pink bedroom, with its antiqued ivory furniture, looked almost bare without her girl's clutter.

Mrs. Truman had one final request for me.

"Mr. West, Margaret would like to have her bedroom furniture from the White House, for sentimental reasons. Do you think we could replace it?"

"I don't see why not," I answered.

The three of us took the limousine to Mayers, the Washington furniture store, where we'd bought the pieces in the first place.

We selected an identical set on the spot, Mrs. Truman paid for it with a personal check, and exchanged it for Margaret's White House bedroom. No one was ever the wiser.

Mrs. Truman, by herself, gave Mrs. Eisenhower a tour of the White House on December 1, 1952. The two ladies, who shared the same Spanish teacher, had known each other for years and were much more cordial than their husbands.

It is a tradition that the President-elect ride up to the front door of the White House to greet the outgoing President, and then that they ride together to the Inauguration. In my thirteen years there, this was the first time I'd witnessed the ceremony, because there'd been no "outgoing" President since 1932. And I almost missed this one because the President-elect was so angry with the President he didn't want to go through with it. But he did, of course.

I watched the two grim-faced men step into the special, high-roofed limousine (General Eisenhower refused to wear a tall silk hat, for which the limousine was designed), and I was glad I wasn't in that car. But I had a strong feeling that Mrs. Truman should have been at her husband's side. She always had been, in every endeavor.

As Mr. Crim and I turned to go inside, hurrying to remove the big, black Steinway from the East Room before our new residents came back from the parade, I said to him:

"The White House didn't seem to change the Trumans too much."

"No," he replied. "I watched the Hoovers and the Roosevelts grow into something completely different from what they were when they moved in. They left as different

126

people. But the Trumans—Margaret grew up, that was all."

The Trumans had used the White House more or less as a temporary government residence. They didn't leave much of an imprint on the patterns and appearance of the mansion. Their strongest effect, I think, was on the lives of the help, who came to like and admire them as people. The times, rather, had imposed changes on White House life. More Secret Service, more police, less freedom of movement for the First Family, more people around to manage—we were becoming more of an institution than an official residence.

And yet, within this institution, Bess Truman had been successful in guarding the privacy she so dearly cherished. She simply set firm rules for her private life and never deviated from them.

The full impact of Bess Truman's contribution to the history of America, and, indeed, of the world, will probably never be measured. Only she can supply the details, and I'm sure that she won't. Her keen intelligence, calm reasoning, and unswerving devotion to her husband were rarely revealed to the public (perhaps they sensed it) because of her vision of her role as First Lady: To stand always in the background, showing herself only as a support for Harry Truman the man. Few people knew that she was his full partner, in every sense of the word.

There was a sign on President Truman's desk: "The Buck Stops Here." However, we knew the buck didn't stop there. He packed it in his briefcase every night, took it upstairs, and discussed it with "The Boss."

The
Eisenhowers

1

There'd be no separate bedrooms for the Eisenhowers. Mary Geneva Doud Eisenhwer made that perfectly clear her first morning in the White House, after she'd spent the night in Bess Truman's narrow, single bed in the little room known as the First Lady's dressing room.

That morning, January 21, 1953, she called for Mr. Crim and me.

We adjusted our neckties, picked up our notebooks, and hot-footed it upstairs for our first conference. As we stepped off the elevator, we looked down the hall to where Rose Woods, Mrs. Eisenhower's personal maid, stood beckoning to us from the First Lady's bedroom door.

Mr. Crim and I walked into the room and stopped in our tracks, both assuming our deadest deadpans to hide our surprise. For Mrs. Eisenhower was still in bed!

Standing awkwardly at the foot of the narrow bed, we managed to say "Good morning," as Mamie Eisenhower pushed away her breakfast tray. She was wearing a dainty, pink-ruffled bed-jacket and had a pink satin bow in her hair.

"I'd like to make some changes right away," she said, lighting a cigarette and surveying her new quarters.

"First of all, I'm not going to sleep in this little room. This is a dressing room, and I want it made into *my* dressing room. The big room"—she indicated with a sweep of her arm the mauve-and-gray chamber next door, where Mrs. Truman had sat listening to baseball games—"will be *our* bedroom!"

"Prior to the Roosevelts, it had been used that way," Mr. Crim ventured.

"Good!" Mrs. Eisenhower went on. "We need a 'king-sized' bed—with a mattress twice as wide as a single bed—and we'd like it as soon as possible, please." Taking a pencil from her bedside table, she quickly designed a double headboard for the bed, to be upholstered and tufted in the same pink fabric as the easy chair in Margaret Truman's sitting room, and a dust-ruffle to match.

The bed must have been an immediate success. The morning after it arrived in a White House truck from New York, Mr. Crim and I accompanied the butler bringing Mrs. Eisenhower's breakfast tray.

"Come in, come in," the First Lady sang out, as Rose Woods opened the door to the new bedroom.

She was nestled in the big bed, propped up against half a dozen pillows, deep in conversation on the white bedside telephone. Waving gaily at Mr. Crim and me to take a seat, she said, still talking to her friend, ". . . And I've just had the first good night's sleep I've had since we've been in the White House. Our new bed finally got here, and now I can reach over and pat Ike on his old bald head anytime I want to!"

That was Mamie Eisenhower. Gay, breezy, open—we all got to know her better than we did any other First Lady because she let us in on almost everything that went on in her life, and she took an interest in everything in ours.

She was feminine to the point of frivolity—for her, ruffles and flourishes were something to wear. She was affectionate and sentimental—nobody could celebrate a

129

birthday like Mamie Eisenhower. She adored the pomp and circumstance and grandeur that went along with the nation's top job, and she even embellished that, somewhat.

Yet underneath that buoyant spirit, there was a spine of steel, forged by years of military discipline. As the wife of a career army officer, she understood the hierarchy of a large establishment, the division of responsibilities, and how to direct a staff. She knew exactly what she wanted, every moment, and exactly how it should be done. And she could give orders, staccato crisp, detailed, and final, as if it were she who had been a five-star general. She established her White House command immediately.

President Eisenhower had scheduled a stag luncheon for business associates his second week in office. Alonzo Fields pulled out a menu from his "appropriate for stag" file, and we set about our usual preparations to serve fifty in the State Dining Room.

Two days before the luncheon, Ann Whitman, General Eisenhower's personal secretary, called the Usher's office. "The President wants to see the menu for the luncheon," she informed us. Fields sent it over immediately, and back it came by return messenger, "Approved DDE."

The morning of the luncheon, when I went upstairs for Mrs. Eisenhower's bedside conference, she looked over the day's menus.

"What's this?" she asked. "I didn't approve this menu!"

"The President did, two or three days ago," I quickly explained.

Mrs. Eisenhower frowned, shaking her head in annoyance.

"I run everything in my house," she said. "In the future all menus are to be approved by *me* and not by anybody else!"

Later that morning, she went down to inspect the table. It was set with the green-bordered Lenox china selected during the Truman renovation, and the "President's House" silver. We had brought up the new banquet chairs purchased by Mrs. Truman.

Mrs. Eisenhower was aghast at the size of the small bentwood chairs.

"Heavens! It looks like we're having a children's party in here!" she exclaimed.

The next day, she was ready for action. "We *must* do something about those little chairs," she said. "They won't do for men at all."

I explained that the twenty large, high-backed upholstered chairs in the State Dining Room were mainly for show.

"Have some more of the big ones made," she ordered, "enough to fit at the banquet table. We just won't invite any more people than we can seat."

The skilled craftsmen in the White House carpenter's shop set about copying the heavy, handsome, gold cut-velvet chairs, because it was soon obvious that President Eisenhower planned to use the State Dining Room often for men's business.

Whether for Presidential luncheons, stag dinners, or gala occasions of state, the new President's wife swiftly exercised her firm control as mistress of the Mansion. She needed no period of adjustment to learn White House routines, no slow introduction to her role as First Lady. The small, smiling lady in the curly bangs simply took over.

In Mamie Doud Eisenhower, the public saw a friendly, outgoing lady, rather like Mrs. Average America, the member of the garden club, the congenial suburban housewife. A closer look showed a vivacious, fun-loving grandmother, an uninhibited belle who adored her Ike.

Though many identified with her, she'd never, ever been a suburban housewife. From her earliest childhood, when maids and butlers waited on her in John Sheldon Doud's home in Denver, she'd been accustomed to large houses with servants in attendance. More recently, in a New York mansion, as wife of the president of Columbia University; in the spacious Quarters Number One in Fort Myer, Virginia, as wife of the U.S. Army Chief of Staff; and in an elegant estate at Marnes-La-Coquette outside Paris, as wife of the Supreme Commander, Headquarters of Allied Powers in Europe, she had managed large household staffs, entertaining with ease, surrounded by elegance. (A general has always at his disposal a trained corps of aides who are bound by military code to "pass muster" in operating his household.) For Mamie Eisenhower, the White House was a snap.

In Europe, the Eisenhowers had already been feted by royalty, and she seemed determined to bring to her Executive Mansion all the grandeur, all the autocracy of those palaces, as well as all the prestige, status, and deference she felt was due the First Lady of the land. Once behind the White House gates, though she appeared fragile and feminine, she ruled as if she were Queen.

She could be imperious.

"When I go out," she insisted, "I am to be escorted to the diplomatic entrance by an usher. And when I return, I am to be met at the door and escorted upstairs."

One day, dressed, hatted and gloved to go outside, she started to get on the elevator, and to her amazement it shot up to the third floor. So she sailed right up, curious to see who was using her elevator. It was George Thompson, a wizened little houseman.

"Never use my elevator again!" she admonished George, and she called Mr. Crim immediately to make an order that *none* of the household staff must ever use the "family" elevator.

The service elevator didn't open onto the second floor, however, so servants would have had to walk up and down stairs—or sneak into the family elevator. But fifteen minutes after she left the White House, George was riding on her elevator again. The servants had a long history of skirting around a First Lady's wishes.

Ever since the two "executive wings" were added to the White House, the west wing, installed by Theodore Roosevelt, had been used for the President's executive offices; the east wing, built by FDR, for the social office. And naturally there had always been traffic on the ground floor of the White House between the two wings. Mrs. Eisenhower stopped the traffic.

"You are *not* to use the mansion as a passageway," she informed both the President's staff and the social staff. "Please walk outside the House when going from one wing to another." And if she happened to run into anyone from east or west wings who didn't have specific business in the central mansion—whether he was a messenger or Sherman Adams, the President's top assistant—she'd chase him outside.

As the Executive Mansion command post, we'd always answered our telephone simply, "Usher's office." But one of the President's assistants complained that he never knew to whom he was speaking. So the next time the phone rang, I answered, "West speaking." Mrs. Eisenhower was on the other end of the line.

"*Never* call yourself 'West,' " she said. "You are *Mister* West, and you must insist that everyone refer to you in that way. You must establish your authority with everyone. You are not a servant."

The domestic staff were never addressed as "Mr." or "Mrs." Once one of the maids forgot, and referred to the maître d' as "Mr. Ficklin," and Mrs. Eisenhower reprimanded her. "You're to address him as Charles," said the First Lady.

2

It was important to Mamie Eisenhower to be set apart from the throngs. After she'd stood in her first receiving line at the White House, she asked for a platform "so everyone can see me."

Down in the carpenter's shop, we built a small platform, elevating her about a foot, so that the tiny First Lady could look her visitors in the eye as she shook hands. We covered the stand with an Oriental rug, and hauled it out for her second reception, for the D.A.R.

But it didn't work. "We almost lost me," she laughingly told me the next day. "They nearly jerked me off the platform."

So at the next reception, for the wives of conventioneering Shriners, she stood on the landing of the grand staircase, overlooking the Green Room, and waved to more than 2,000 ladies as they passed by. Except for a few hurt feelings from unshaken hands, this arrangement seemed to work all right. A few days later, receiving 1,500 Republican women, she stood on the bottom step facing the lobby, and four top Republican ladies stood on the second step, immediately behind her.

She rested for ten minutes after greeting each group of two hundred, while they were served tea. When she came back downstairs to meet the second group, she stopped by my office.

"Would you please have the social aides speak to the ladies standing behind me, and ask them to step back a couple of steps? They're so close nobody knows who is *me!*"

Mrs. Eisenhower loved the crowds of admirers who paid homage to the First Lady of the land. She also enjoyed riding in the back seat of the big White House limousine, waving to people on the street when they recognized her. In a parade, she usually rode in a car behind the President's car.

"Invariably somebody would yell 'Where's Mamie?' to the President up in the car ahead," her Secret Service agent told me, "and she'd roll down the window, poke her head out, and shout back, 'Here I am, here I am!'"

Even though she tired easily, she delighted in greeting the crowds who trooped through at White House receptions. We had thousands of political ladies, Girl Scouts, convention wives, Salvation Army volunteers, every possible group we could receive. To every lady who passed by the receiving line, she had something to say.

"I love your earrings"—or "What state are *you* from?"—"Oh, yes, I bought a beautiful shawl in Idaho. . . ." If there were a thousand people going through the line she'd have a thouand little items of small talk for them. In fact, she could charm the socks off anybody she met.

Mamie Eisenhower as a hostess was spectacular. In her diamonds and décolleté gowns, she fairly sparkled. She and the General applied more spit-and-polish, more pomp and circumstance, to their lavish, formal entertaining than any other President and First Lady in my White House existence.

She selected the flowers for every luncheon and dinner we had. She chose the linens for State dinners and place mats for luncheons, even the place cards and tiniest souvenirs. Rather than simply being in the right place at the right time, like the Trumans, she insisted on *our* being in the right place at the right time.

She disapproved of the U-shaped banquet arrangement in the State Dining Room, where previous Presidents had sat across the table from their wives. "I don't think the First Lady should have her back to so many of the guests," Mrs. Eisenhower said, and she devised a new seating plan for State dinners: The President and First Lady would sit side by side in the throne-like mahogany chairs, at the *head* of an E-shaped banquet table—just like royalty. The Eisenhowers were hosts to thirty-seven heads of state, in addition to the usual ten-event "social season." But it was the Annual Military Reception that General Eisenhower enjoyed most. Somehow his shoes had a touch more mirror-shine, his back was a little more erect when the thousands of top brass in Washington came by the White House to meet the Commander-in-Chief. It was as if he were on military review. "This is your reception, isn't it, Mr. President?" he was asked.

"You're darn right. This is the one I'm having fun at!" he replied. Mrs. Eisenhower, dressed in her flowery designer gowns, glowed with pride as she welcomed her old friends, the generals and admirals and their wives, to the gracious home of their commanding officer.

It wasn't just her position at the pinnacle or the elegance of her home that made Mamie Eisenhower enjoy living in the White House, however, for as she happily told me one morning, "I've got *my* man right here, where I want him!"

After all the years of separation during World War II and even the return to an official, though civilian, life at Columbia University, Mrs. Eisenhower was perfectly delighted that her husband's home and office were under one roof.

As a couple, the Eisenhowers were openly affectionate, unlike the more reserved, though devoted, Trumans, or the distant Roosevelts. He always knew the right sentimental touch, the proper number of carnations to send, the significance of the heart-shaped silver box to present her as one of his many gifts. It was perfectly natural for President Eisenhower to reach over and put his arm around "Mrs. Ike," as he called her. Having shared their home life with a staff for many of their married years, they didn't seem to mind if we observed them holding hands or exchanging a goodbye kiss. They simply ignored us.

Anyway, all of the mansion staff had years of training in pretending not to see or to hear the First Family, though it did seem to be a novelty to have a President and his wife sleeping together in the White House.

President Eisenhower awakened about six, dressed quickly with the assistance of Sergeant Moaney, took a few swings with his golf iron to limber up, ate breakfast in his own dressing room while reading the morning papers, or in the private dining room downstairs with visiting Congressmen, then, accompanied by Military Aide Robert Schulz, walked over to his west wing office.

The change in Presidential style from Mr. Truman to General Eisenhower was a marked one. President Eisenhower, with the ingrained habits of Army command, was much more formal in his official life than the plain-spoken Mr. Truman, who had grown up in the political world where give-and-take is a necessary part of the art of survival. And just as Mrs. Eisenhower quickly established the chain of command for her bailiwick in the White House, the new President established his own highly regimented command structure.

Unlike Mr. Truman, President Eisenhower confined his work to regular hours in his west wing office. It wasn't that he devoted less of himself to the job, though.

"I believe there is a point at which efficiency is best served," he told me. "After you spend a certain number of hours at work, you pass your peak of efficiency. I function best in my office when I relax in the evenings."

Painting was relaxation for President Eisenhower, as were golf, bridge, hunting, cooking and escape reading. And I learned early in the administration that he hated interruptions in his relaxation.

Late one afternoon, the White House switchboard announced an emergency call for the President, who couldn't be located. I knew where he usually was at that hour—standing at his easel in the little "painting room" overlooking Pennsylvania Avenue. There was a phone in there but he had it fixed so it didn't ring.

"Secretary of State Dulles is on the phone and says he *must* speak to the President," the operator told me.

I ran upstairs and knocked on the door to give the President the message. He was just painting a coat-sleeve on a portrait of golfer Bobby Jones.

"Damn!" he exploded, throwing his brush down on the little table where his paints were laid out. "I can't do anything around this place."

But he could—and he did.

President Eisenhower accomplished a great deal in his first six months of office. He quickly ended the wage-and-price controls imposed at the outset of the Korean War. He had come into office pledging to end the thirty-two-month-old war, and on July 27, 1953, the country breathed a sigh of relief as an armistice was signed at Panmunjom.

At sixty-two, Dwight David Eisenhower was tall and trim. He laughed easily, flashing the truly remarkable grin that was his trademark, throwing back his head in deep laughter of pure enjoyment. As quick to anger as he was to laughter, the President could turn the air blue when something displeased him. Accustomed to authority, his request was automatically a command and was delivered as such.

But around the house, he liked to be totally "at ease." He dressed casually in sports clothes—bright, open-collared shirts and slacks, and he often swung a golf club as he walked through the halls. Though he observed every formality of White House entertaining, he hated getting dressed up.

"I think white tie and tails makes for a very stiff evening," he complained to me.

At his Inaugural the new President had insisted upon the less formal day dress of striped trousers, shorter club coat rather than cutaway, dark overcoat and dark Homburg hat. When the Congress complained that he was breaking tradition, he retorted: "If we were going back to tradition we would wear tri-cornered hats and knee britches."

The changing flavor of the government from President

138

Truman to President Eisenhower could be found also in the Cabinet room and at the game table. Whereas Mr. Truman played poker, mostly with old political cronies, General Eisenhower's game was bridge, and his playing partners generally were corporation executives such as W. Alton Jones, board chairman of Cities Service, New York investment banker Clifford Roberts, public relations counsel Bill Robinson and publisher "Jock" Whitney. Around the President's bridge table in the Monroe Room, the bidding was as spirited and the competition as serious as a day on the Stock Exchange.

Also reflecting American business and finance were members of his new Cabinet: Wall Street lawyer John Foster Dulles, the architect of the Cold War strategy against Communism; Midwest industrialist George Humphrey; and General Motors President Charles E. Wilson, who angered Congress at first by refusing to sell his GM stock. Another important appointment was California Governor Earl Warren, named Chief Justice of the Supreme Court in 1953, and who, less than a year later, led the court to its historic decision outlawing segregation in the public schools.

Those were the faces we saw most often at the Eisenhower White House. Except for official or ceremonial occasions, the new Vice President, former California Senator Richard M. Nixon, rarely came over.

3

Mrs. Eisenhower was not an early riser.

She called for me anytime from 8:30 until 10:00. Carrying my note pad and pencil, I appeared with the butler who served her breakfast in bed. She'd already been up to put on her makeup, and to tie the pink ribbon in her neatly curled hair. And every morning, she asked for fresh flowers for her bedroom—two brandy-snifters full of pink rosebuds and a tall vase of pink carnations, her favorites.

Three days a week, masseuse Helen Smith came into her bedroom in the early morning.

"I've just had a six-mile walk," Mrs. Eisenhower laughed, after her massage. "This is the only exercise I need!"

It was soon evident that Mrs. Eisenhower wanted to be "in the pink" at all times. Taking her color cue from the giant, custom-made pink headboard and dust-ruffle we had outfitted for her bed, she brought over Margaret Truman's floral sitting-room curtains, which had some pink in them, and we had a fitted king-size bedspread made to match the curtains. Also from Margaret's room, the President's wife moved in a couple of upholstered chairs in the same pink-and-green floral print, as well as the solid-color pink waffle-weave chairs that matched the new headboard and dust-ruffle.

At first, she was terribly disappointed that she couldn't transform the entire mansion. But since the house had been so recently—and entirely—refurbished, Congress deleted the $50,000 usually granted each new administration to paint and decorate. Looking around at the bland department-store reproductions, she asked brightly, "Can't we bring out the real antiques?" When I answered that we had none stashed away anywhere, she was crestfallen. "But isn't there any way we can *get* historic furniture for this house?"

"Donations only," I answered, pointing out the few genuine pieces.*

"Well, I guess I'll just have to make do!" she said, marching resolutely off. But Mrs. Eisenhower had a long history of moving into an official house and making it hers. Instead of redecorating, she improvised.

For her bedroom she switched carpets with Margaret's sitting room, taking the green in exchange for the mauve-and-gray. From the West Sitting Hall, Mrs. Eisenhower borrowed the kidney-shaped kneehole desk Mrs. Roosevelt had used, to store all her checks and stationery. Then the President's wife decorated her dressing room and bathroom entirely in pink, too, except for the green rugs.

She had brought her own bedside tables and cigarette tables (the rest of the Eisenhower furniture went into storage), a large collection of oil paintings, mostly landscapes by her husband; a trophy case containing all of the General's military decorations, medals, and jeweled swords; and racks and racks of dresses.

Never, before or since, has a First Lady had quite so

* Even the President tried to help. He met me in the hall one day, and explained that he had a "little money" left over from his office appropriation. "Couldn't we use it to do some of the things Mrs. Eisenhower wants to do in the White House?" I had to explain that it would be fiscally impossible and illegal to transfer funds from the President's office to the President's house. Ours is a separate appropriation.

many clothes! We found that the new closets in the White House were nowhere near sufficient for the vast Eisenhower wardrobe. At first she was disturbed that there wasn't enough room for them in her dressing room. "I want my clothes with me," she said. Soon the third-floor storage rooms were overflowing with dresses, in addition to those in the dressing room. "I've never been able to throw anything away," she laughed, and to prove her point, she showed me her wedding dress, neatly encased in plastic as if it might be used tomorrow. Mamie Eisenhower liked to wear full-skirted Mollie Parnis dresses, imaginative little Sally Victor hats, and strapless evening gowns. (She was also fond of colorful costume jewelry, although the safe in her bedroom contained quite an inventory of expensive jewels.) To take care of all those dresses and of her, she installed Rose Woods in Vietta Garr's room on the third floor and into her slot on the White House payroll. Rose rinsed out the First Lady's stockings in the bathroom lavatory every night, and dressed her mistress in the late mornings.

Mr. Eisenhower's valet, the same Sergeant Moaney who'd laid out his clothes throughout Europe and at Columbia University, also joined the staff. George Thompson, who filled in for the valet on Moaney's day off, was astounded at his duties. "I even had to hold his undershorts for him to step into," he told us.

Mrs. Eisenhower brought her mother, too, settling Mrs. Doud across the hall from her own bedroom, in what had been Margaret Truman's little bedroom.

Gay, sprightly, with a personality much like her daughter's, Mrs. John S. Doud had been widowed in 1951. Although she retained her home in Denver, she actually lived with the Eisenhowers in the White House. But as far as we were concerned, she kept her own counsel most of the time, staying quietly in her room, as had Mrs. Truman's mother.

Like her daughter, Mrs. Doud stayed in bed until noon. And every morning, they chatted across the hall by telephone, each sitting up in her own bed, resting against dozens of pillows. "This is a long-distance call from Mother," Mrs. Eisenhower joked one morning, waving her ever-present cigarette in the direction of Mrs. Doud's room.

Because the First Lady used her bed as her office—she had a little standup bed tray where she signed letters, paid bills, wrote notes to herself—she didn't need the small room where Mrs. Truman and Mrs. Roosevelt had worked. Directly above the Usher's office overlooking the north lawn, Pennsylvania Avenue, and Lafayette Park, that little office was now the President's painting room. In the late afternoon or on weekends, Mr. Eisenhower stood by the hour at the tall easel, painting landscapes from memory or portraits from photographs.

With the limited amount of rearranging finished—Roosevelt's and Truman's official portraits were removed from the front hall, replaced by Washington and Lincoln —Mrs. Eisenhower gave up on finding antiques and concentrated on running the 132-room establishment.

"I have but one career, and its name is Ike," Mrs. Eisenhower once announced. But as far as we were concerned, she made a career of the President's house.

On the wall opposite the elevator, she nailed a little plaque, "Bless This House." It had hung in twenty-eight previous homes, from a one-room apartment to a French mansion, and now in the B. Altman White House.

She never treated the mansion as government property, it was *hers.* And she took such fastidious care of it that we almost believed it was hers. She became truly alarmed if things went wrong.

One such problem rated a 7:00 a.m. phone call to the housekeeper.

"Come up to my bedroom as soon as the President goes to his office!" Mrs. Eisenhower ordered. Miss Walker, alarmed, stopped by my office first. "Perhaps you'd better come up with me," she said. "It sounds like disaster."

It was the earliest we'd ever seen Mrs. Eisenhower. And she wasn't in bed.

But the bed was a mess. All over the sheets, covers, pink dust-ruffle, headboard, everything, were big black spots—or, to be exact, dabs and blotches and swipes of indigo.

"What on earth can we do?" the First Lady wailed.

143

Miss Walker began jerking the sheets off the bed herself. "I'll take these down to the laundry room to soak, and one of the maids will bring up some spot-remover for the rest," she said.

Once the housekeeper had disappeared with the soiled linens, Mrs. Eisenhower began to explain.

"You see, my nose was all stopped up," she began, "and I had a jar of Vicks on my bedside table. So during the night when I woke up, I reached over to put some in my nostrils. Well, it seemed to just get drier, instead of moister," she went on, "so I kept applying more and more. I didn't want to wake up Ike, so I didn't turn on the light. Then this morning, I discovered that I was using *ink* to cure my cold."

She had begun the conversation very earnestly, but now, knowing that it could all be set right, she began to smile.

"But you should have seen me," she laughed. "Black and blue all over—and the President, too."

I held down the chuckle that rose up in my throat. The President and the First Lady, in all their dignity, *covered* in ink.

"I don't think anything is permanently damaged," I assured her. "I'm sure it will all come out in the wash."

"Now don't you tell a soul," she admonished, still laughing.

"Certainly not," I promised, and beat a hasty retreat. Not since Harry Truman's four-poster broke down had I heard such a good bedtime story.

If Bess Truman had an eagle-eye for the housekeeping, then Mamie Eisenhower had a built-in microscope. But where Mrs. Truman's main concern was the woodwork, Mrs. Eisenhower focused her attention on the rugs.

Perhaps being closer to the ground than most people (at slightly under five feet four, Mrs. Eisenhower gave the impression of being much tinier), she got a closer look at the floors.

Footprints, especially, bothered her. The carpets, all new and thickly piled, did show shoemarks when people walked on them. Before every party, with the housekeeper in tow, she made a thorough inspection of the State floors.

"Have this rug vacuumed one more time," she'd point out, until finally, she hit upon the idea of brushes. "The last thing to be done, before the guests arrive, will be to brush the rugs," she directed. "Not one footprint must be showing when they walk into this room!"

She even ordered a separate brush for each color of rug. And at the last minute, as the butlers dimmed the lights for the evening, the Filipino housemen scurried around behind them, brushing away their footprints.

The biggest carpet culprit, however, was Heidi, the irrepressible Weimeraner somebody had presented to the President.

Heidi lived in a little doghouse outside the President's oval office, and gave Mr. Eisenhower a great deal of pleasure, bounding over the south lawn to retrieve a stick, or toy, or golf ball. But Heidi was not always well behaved.

One Sunday I was relaxing at home when Mrs. Eisenhower called me, in great distress:

"Mr. West, can you come down right away? We have a terrible problem in the Diplomatic Reception Room."

It took about twenty minutes before Brooks, my indispensable driver, pulled up to the White House. Mrs. Eisenhower was waiting in her entrance off the south grounds, the only one she ever used, where her friends came in. It was called the Diplomatic Reception Room because earlier Presidents stood there to receive credentials from foreign ambassadors. During the Truman renovation, the room had been outfitted with a brand-new, pale green oval rug.

Now, two of the housemen were down on their knees, scrubbing at a big yellow spot near the door.

"Heidi!" Mrs. Eisenhower wrung her hands in agitation. "I'm just sick about it."

"Let me see if I can rouse any cleaning experts," I offered, and I finally found a dry cleaner at home. He was pessimistic. "No solution known to man will completely remove that stain."

We summoned all the male strength in the house—butlers, doormen, housemen, engineers, to move out the furniture, pick up the rug, turn it completely around to

145

try to hide the spot. But there was nowhere that it wasn't highly visible. The next day, we sent the rug out to be dyed. The spot came back only slightly diminished in hue.

Shortly thereafter, Heidi went to live on the Eisenhower farm at Gettysburg, Pennsylvania, banished forever from the White House for her felony.

Later, when the National Society of Interior Designers presented to the White House a refurbished Diplomatic Reception Room, Mrs. Eisenhower was delighted with the new rug, specially woven with the seals of the 50 states in its border. At the ceremony where she graciously accepted the gift, she shot me a knowing glance. "You and I know how much we appreciate this," she whispered.

4

She was every bit as frugal as Bess Truman. Mamie Eisenhower could think up infinite ways to cut corners, in handling her own budget and making suggestions for ours. And the lengths to which she went soon became the talk of the Washington business community.

Every morning, she perused the newspapers, looking for bargains in foods and household items. Shopping by telephone from those newspapers, she always called the head of the department store, who must certainly have been startled to take an order from the First Lady of the land. "When you go into a store, go straight to the top," she advised all of us. "Don't fool around with some clerk."

Time after time, she'd notice some "special" in a chain-store ad, and dispatch the storekeeper's truck to the local grocery, where a Secret Service man would hop out and purchase the desired item.

Although the White House traditionally did its grocery shopping wholesale, sending an unmarked truck with a daily list to the old market area of Washington, where the security guard and a security-cleared employee of the establishment picked the food off the shelves, Mrs. Eisenhower was horrified at the cost.

The wholesalers provide us with the finest quality of meats and vegetables, we explained, and therefore their prices are apt to be higher than the weekly "loss leaders" at the chain stores. So the thrifty Mrs. Eisenhower still insisted on shopping for bargains, for the White House as well as for her own personal use. The truck sped all over Washington, from the supermarket to military commissaries, to seek savings.

Charles Ficklin, who'd taken over as maître d' when Alonzo Fields retired, always joined us at Mrs. Eisenhower's morning bedside sessions. Not only did the First Lady scrutinize every item on his menu list, she questioned the source of supply, freshness of the lettuce, compatibility of the combinations. She practically squeezed the tomatoes by remote control.

And she kept careful track of the leftovers. "I don't want one morsel wasted around here," she told Charles. Every morning she asked for a list of food that hadn't been eaten the previous day. "Three people turned down second servings of Cornish hen last night," she'd remind Charles. "Please use it in chicken salad today." The cooks learned to turn out lots of casseroles and ground-meat dishes. And fortunately the Eisenhowers were fond of hash.

Although she had never learned to cook herself, she was an avid reader of advertising and wanted the cooks to try out everything new on the market.

"Have you tried the new cake mixes?" she asked Charles. "They're infinitely more economical than doing it the old way," and promptly stocked her private pantry, as well as the official kitchen, with cake mixes.

Taking advantage of the new "walk-in" freezers in the renovated White House kitchen, she set up vegetable gardens at the Gettysburg farm. Soon fresh corn, beans, spinach, squash came to us in truckloads each summer, to be frozen and served on the Eisenhowers' wintertime trays or at their private dinner parties. It had been many a year since a President grew his own food, but this economical family managed to cut corners in every possible way.

Although the Eisenhowers were comfortably well-to-do when they came to the White House, they did not have a limitless outside income. Mrs. Eisenhower soon realized that White House living could quickly eat into their resources, and she tailored her budget accordingly.

Their food bills were never over $100 a month, and this was mainly for staples. The meat they used came from a friend in Kansas City, the vegetables from their farm, and wild game for the President's stag luncheons from his hunting trips.

Mrs. Eisenhower always scheduled luncheons and dinners so they wouldn't interfere with anything else. And she insisted that the kitchen and pantry not be overworked—she wouldn't let them have a dinner one day and a luncheon the next day.

"The staff needs a breathing space between functions," she said. More than just consideration for the staff, however, this was to ensure good performance. "If you constantly operate on a large scale, you're not putting out top-quality anything," she told me one morning, smoothing the sheets that covered her nightgown.

The housekeeper, Mabel Walker, began to attend our bedside staff meetings, because Mrs. Eisenhower didn't give orders to the maids; she knew that people, like soldiers, respond more readily to their next-in-command. She knew perfectly well what a domestic staff was supposed to do, and she held Miss Walker accountable if it wasn't done.

At the White House, the beds are fully changed, with clean, fresh sheets, every time they've been occupied—if only for a cat-nap.

During the Roosevelt and Truman years, the sheets sometimes found their way to the sewing-room, for a little careful mending here and there. But not for Mrs. Eisenhower.

"Please see that the best bed-linens are used at all times," she'd say to Miss Walker. "I don't want to see mended linens again!"

149

The White House was easier to operate during Mrs. Eisenhower's regime. She knew her own mind, and we appreciated it.

Furthermore, despite all her demands, all her commands, Mamie Eisenhower was personally a most thoughtful First Lady.

When a State dinner had gone especially well, she was lavish with compliments. And although she squeezed pennies in her household, she was more than generous to her employees. There was a personal touch to her kindness; it was not done by rote or in a perfunctory manner. She came to know a great deal about us all, and her knowing revealed her interest in those who served her, as human beings with lives outside the White House.

The personal lives of her domestic employees seemed to intrigue Mamie Eisenhower. Drawing them into lengthy discussions about their activities, their families, their homes, their state of health, she seemed, for a First Lady, to bestow an unusual amount of concern. When anybody got sick, she always sent flowers from the bouquet room; even if she heard that one of our relatives was ill, she sent flowers, too.

"She wants to be everybody's godmother," said Mr. Crim.

I've never seen anybody so happy as Mamie Eisenhower spending her first Christmas at the White House. She had selected something for everybody in the House—for all the domestic staff as well as the carpenters, plumbers, and electricians.

"Well, I've finally done it," she said, when the gaily wrapped boxes were at last all piled under the tree in the West Hall. "It's been my desire, all of my life, to be able to give a Christmas gift to *everybody* who works for me!" On Christmas Eve, she invited all the employees up to the second floor, in small groups, to present us our gifts.

She had even bought presents for my wife and my daughters.

One morning, she opened a small white box on her bedside table.

"Isn't this pretty?" she said, showing me a pearl-and-rhinestone necklace, bracelet, and earrings set. "I want to give this to your wife for Christmas."

"That's very thoughtful of you," I began. But she hardly heard me. "Now, you should go out and buy her a ring to match."

"I will," I nodded.

"Bring it back and show it to me!"

Realizing that I was in a bind, I hurried to a store on Connecticut Avenue and selected a gold ring with a cultured pearl for Zella. When I brought the ring back for her inspection, Mrs. Eisenhower said, jangling her own bracelet with its "Ike" charms—helmet, tank, five stars, map of Africa—"That's perfect. I couldn't do better if I had shopped for it myself."

But on one occasion Mrs. Eisenhower's ideas about gifts contrasted rather sharply with my family's income and needs. She had ordered a mink stole for inspection, then decided it wasn't right for her. "Why don't you buy it instead and give it to your wife?" she suggested. I replied that my next gift would have to be a new washing machine. Mrs. Eisenhower made a wry face. "Ike had better not give *me* any household appliance for a gift!" she said.

Over the years, she was extremely generous to me. One year she gave me a battery radio, another year a Polaroid camera. Then a set of trays, a silver salad bowl, a silver silent butler, a set of eight silver julep cups (two each for four years), and a brass tray table, and finally had the President present me with an original oil painting signed "D.E."—all gifts that I could use, and which I still treasure.

Every Christmas she sent each of my little girls a U.S. Savings Bond. Kathy, born during the Roosevelts, and Sally, who arrived during the Trumans, thought Mrs. Eisenhower was their best friend.

One afternoon I came home to a wonderful fragrant kitchen. "Daddy," Sally yelled happily, "we're making some cookies for Mrs. Eisenhower."

The next day I told the First Lady about her gift, which I'd forgotten to bring. She immediately wrote the girls a little thank you note, telling them how much she looked forward to tasting their cookies.

But when I proudly brought the note home, the girls shrieked in horror.

"We ate them all up!" wailed Kathy.

But they cooked up another batch, which Mrs. Eisenhower shared with us at the next morning's conference.

The First Lady insisted that the housekeeper keep a "birthday calendar" along with the household records. Every time a member of the household staff celebrated a birthday, Mrs. Eisenhower ordered a cake baked in the White House kitchen. She personally selected a birthday card to accompany it.

All our children were treated to presents from the "toy room," a great storage closet on the ground floor filled with gifts provided by toy manufacturer Louis Marx. And at Christmastime, when Mrs. Eisenhower was overwhelmed by thousands of letters from poor families throughout the country, she directed Miss Walker and me to dip into the toy room to supply as many requests as we could fill.

For the maids, butlers, housemen, everyone with whom she was in daily contact, she sent Christmas and birthday gifts as well, which she chose from her bulging "gift closet" on the third floor, stocked from calls to department stores, from gifts she'd received herself, or from one of her out-of-town shopping expeditions.

On those excursions to stores (she especially loved the five-and-dime), she was always accompanied by her Secret Service agents. "I've never seen anything to beat it," agent Stewart Stout told me. "She always insisted that I buy my wife a present. Every single time we stopped at a store."

I soon discovered that the new vogue for television dictated certain aspects of life in the Eisenhower White House.

Although two television sets had been installed during the renovation, one in the West Sitting Hall and one in the President's study, the Trumans hadn't cared much for the electronic novelty. Now, however, the medium had begun to come of age, and it fascinated the Eisenhowers.

In the evenings, President and Mrs. Eisenhower, with Mrs. Doud, took dinner on their tray-tables in the West Hall, while watching the television news. Along with the rest of the country, they were that caught up in the new TV mania.

For the first time, this major revolution in American communications had begun to influence national politics, as well as the life style of the First Family. The first two Eisenhower years in office were also years of dominance for Senator Joseph McCarthy and for the phenomenon that became known as McCarthyism. Without question, television fueled the controversy of McCarthy's Communist "witch hunt," making internal security in government a political issue with which President Eisenhower had to deal constantly.

Television also provided an effective medium for President Eisenhower. His wide smile, his proud, erect posture, his direct manner were magically carried to homes around the country by the TV cameras. With much ado, he made the first telecast from the White House ground floor broadcast room in May, 1953. (Thereafter, actor Robert Montgomery came in to advise him on his performances.) Then Mr. Eisenhower became the first President to hold televised press conferences, giving the public its first opportunity to watch how a chief executive handles himself under pressure of questioning. His critics came away pleased that President Eisenhower indeed appeared to be fallible. They saw his flashes of anger and his occasional twisted syntax. But for most Americans, these qualities only showed that the popular Ike was also human.

Even more than the press conferences or the TV dinners, "As the World Turns" initiated the Television Era in the White House. Watching the daytime serial was a daily ritual for Mrs. Eisenhower, as I found out early in the administration.

I'd been out to lunch, and when I returned there was a note to "see MDE upstairs." But when I knocked on her bedroom door, the First Lady pointed me toward the pink overstuffed chair, never taking her eyes off the television set.

"Let's just wait till this is over," she said. And I watched

153

while one tragic dialogue after another unfolded on the twelve-inch screen. Not even during the commercials could I find out what she wanted from me.

Every afternoon, while the President napped in his dressing room, Mrs. Eisenhower avidly followed the adventures and perils of her soap-opera heroines. She wouldn't miss a program for anything! I learned to avoid the second floor at that time if I possibly could, for if I went up there I'd be trapped with "As the World Turns." You just can't say, "I'm sorry, I have more important things to do," to a First Lady—especially to Mrs. Eisenhower.

When they moved from the official, ceremonial world of the Presidency to the private world of their families and close friends, the pomp and circumstance which the Eisenhowers seemed to enjoy and accept as a highly important part of their official roles gave way to a very easygoing, informal style of living. They were just being Mamie and Ike at home.

The Eisenhowers were great weekenders in the White House. In the mornings, President Eisenhower was up early to tee off. Wearing a jaunty golf cap, he'd hit a drive from the garden just outside his office to the south grounds, where the faithful Sergeant Moaney retrieved the golf balls. We always had to turn off the fountains during those practice sessions.

In good weather, it was golf for the President at Burning Tree Country Club, where he often took his young grandson, David, and several old friends to make a foursome. Then back to the White House for cards.

Their weekend guests were old friends, not official friends, and card-playing was the Eisenhowers' main form of private entertaining. The lively games went on all afternoon, at two tables—one in the Monroe Room for the President and his bridge group, the other in the solarium for their wives, who played Bolivia, a form of Canasta.

After the game, President Eisenhower, dressed in an open-collared sport shirt, treated his guests to a cook-out on the White House roof, flipping hamburgers and Kansas City steaks on the charcoal broiler. In the wintertime, he boiled up a pot of stew in the third-floor diet kitchen.

"Ike's stew," a recipe passed reverently around official

154

Washington, was known unofficially at the White House as "Moaney's stew." The good-natured sergeant chopped up the meat and onions in the diet kitchen on the third floor, assembled all the ingredients, and stood patiently beside the pot like a surgical nurse, handing the President parsley, paprika, garlic, as Mr. Eisenhower asked for each.

At first, the Eisenhowers spent almost all their weekends at home.

To Mamie Eisenhower's way of thinking, the decor at Shangri-La, the Presidential retreat in Maryland's Catoctin Mountains, left a great deal to be desired. Because the Trumans rarely went to the mountains, preferring the yacht *Williamsburg** to the lodge, the latter still looked as it had when President Roosevelt escaped there on weekends, only shabbier. It was rustic, paneled in rough wood and furnished with big, heavy pieces.

"It would be nice if we only had the money to redecorate it," Mrs. Eisenhower said wistfully to Mr. Crim.

"The Navy still operates the lodge," he explained, "and I don't see why they couldn't pay to have it redecorated."

Mrs. Eisenhower's eyes sparkled at the idea. "I think I'll just pass a hint along to the Commander-in-Chief," she said.

Soon came the order for the Navy to redecorate Shangri-La, with Mrs. Eisenhower as consultant, and the rustic lodge soon took on a "1950's modern" look, in greens, yellows, and beiges.

When it was finished, the President renamed the retreat "Camp David," in honor of his little grandson, and there the Eisenhowers spent many weekends, held some Cabinet meetings, and entertained foreign visitors until their Gettysburg remodeling project was finished.

Whether at Camp David or at the White House, Mamie Eisenhower kept to one steadfast rule when entertaining her friends: No liquor was to be served before 6:00 p.m. And she always insisted that dinner be served promptly at 7:00.

* President Eisenhower retired the yacht soon after taking office.

"Don't give them time to have more than one drink," she instructed Charles, thinking not only of her guests' sobriety but also of a frugal liquor cabinet. A persistent, vicious rumor to the contrary, Mrs. Eisenhower was a very moderate social drinker. Occasionally President and Mrs. Eisenhower would take one scotch and soda (his) and one bourbon old-fashioned (hers) in the evening, before their dinner trays were set up. Before State dinners, cocktails were never served in the Eisenhower White House. The butlers poured only American wines at the table, with dinner. Neither were drinks offered at the large receptions. Mrs. Eisenhower followed the White House tradition of serving a "spiked" punch at one end of the State Dining Room table, a nonalcoholic fruit punch at the other end.

Even when her closest friends came to play cards in the afternoon, Mamie Eisenhower served only coffee, colas, and mixed nuts.

Those afternoon card games with "the girls" gave Mrs. Eisenhower considerable pleasure during her White House reign. In the 1950's, Mamie Doud Eisenhower had a passion for Bolivia. Practically every day, after the big public receptions at noon, after her private time watching television, a group of her old friends appeared at "her" Diplomatic entrance. Sometimes, dressed in her customary hat and gloves, she'd take the limousine to their homes. But more often, they'd come to the White House, playing cards and chatting merrily in the Monroe Room or the solarium.

The same group had been playing together for years, the game having been their main diversion while their husbands were overseas.* At the White House, the Bolivia players usually took a break for tea at 5:00 p.m., and sometimes they'd stay for dinner. Afterwards, a frequent treat for the friends was a movie in the ground-floor theater—

* Many were the wives or widows of military officers, like Mrs. Everett Hughes, Mrs. Walton Walker, and Mrs. Ruth Butcher; others were Mrs. Pell Miller, Mrs. James C. Black, Mrs. George E. Allen, Mrs. Howard Snyder, and Mrs. Eisenhower's sister, Frances "Mike" Moore.

usually a light, romantic comedy. Mrs. Eisenhower confessed to enjoying sentimental love stories as well.

The President's taste in movies, however, was more restricted. Providing Mr. Eisenhower with enough Westerns became a major task for the Usher's office—because he'd seen them all, perhaps three or four times. Every night the projectionist prepared a list of the films available from the motion-picture distributors for White House screening.

"Can't you find a new Western?" President Eisenhower kept asking. And we hunted through the amusement ads in the newspapers, the Library of Congress film collection, or approached the producers themselves.

Colonel Schulz, the military aide, had the same assignment to search for reading matter. Mr. Eisenhower escaped into Western novels, whodunits, and cookbooks. Every four years, the American Booksellers' Association sent several hundred new books for the White House library. But when it was reported that the President's favorites fell into the Western category, we were flooded with paperbacks of all sorts, guns blazing on the covers, most of which the President read after dinner, while Mrs. Eisenhower concentrated on popular magazines and romantic novels.

The President's pride and joy was his putting green, a gift from the American Public Golf Association, installed on the south lawn just outside his office window. He liked to stop by on the way home from the office to practice his shots.

Keeping that green in perfect condition became an obsession with Dwight Eisenhower. He ordered the gardeners to flick the dew off the green with fishing poles every morning. The squirrels, which Mr. Truman had almost tamed by feeding them scraps under the table, infuriated Mr. Eisenhower because they buried acorns and walnuts in the putting green.

"The next time you see one of those squirrels go near my putting green, take a gun and shoot it!" he thundered to the faithful Sergeant Moaney.

But the quick-thinking Secret Service talked him out of that order. "If there's shooting out here, we'd have to first inform the police," they explained, "and it's not exactly as if the squirrels were facing a firing squad and we could schedule it in advance, so there'd be bound to be some fuss made, the press would get hold of it, and the humane societies would never let you forget it. Couldn't some traps be set instead?"

Somehow the gardeners caught most of the offending animals in nets. They were evicted by White House van to Rock Creek Park.

The ubiquitous squirrels found a friend in the President's little grandson, David Eisenhower, and a foe in David's terrier, Skunky. Skunky chased the squirrels around the south lawn on weekends and holidays, when the children came to visit, and David chased Skunky.

Mrs. Eisenhower took great delight in her four grandchildren—David, Barbara Anne, Susan, and Mary Jean—the children of their only son, John, and his wife, Barbara. (John's older brother, Dwight Doud, had died of scarlet fever at the age of three, a great tragedy in the Eisenhowers' life.)

"Every moment I spend with my grandchildren is the best moment in my life," Mrs. Eisenhower once said.

When the Eisenhowers had moved in, John, then a major in the Army, was stationed in Korea, and his young family lived in Highland Falls, New York. We first met the younger Eisenhowers in 1953, when President Truman ordered John flown back to Washington for his father's Inauguration, and John and Barbara slept in the Queen's Room.

David was only five then, Barbara Anne three, and Susan one. Wide-eyed on his first visit, little David asked his grandmother, "Mimi, why do you live in such a big house?"

Thereafter, Barbara and the children came down frequently on weekends until 1955, when her husband was assigned to nearby Fort Belvoir, Virginia, and then to the White House as an aide. The youngsters came much more often to visit "Mimi," as they called their grandmother. The children always stayed in the third-floor bedrooms. But Mrs. Eisenhower decided, after the first Inauguration, that only a Queen should sleep in the Queen's Room on the second floor, so John and Barbara had to sleep elsewhere in the house.

The "White House baby," born in 1955, was Mary Jean. Barbara Eisenhower's doctors recommended that the birth take place in a hospital rather than in a bedroom upstairs in the White House, but Mary Jean managed to be christened in the Blue Room.

Those Eisenhower children were exceptionally well behaved—their grandmother insisted upon good manners. Although they had no nurses or nannies to look after them, they caused no trouble for anybody. They swam in the big Roosevelt swimming pool, practically the only time it had customers during the Eisenhower years, rode their tricycles up and down the ground-floor corridor and their little battery-operated cars outside on the circular south driveway. Mrs. Eisenhower kept a good supply of their dolls, electric trains, and toys stashed away in a room on the third floor.

The children were a special joy also for their great-grandmother, Mrs. Doud, who joined in all the family gatherings. President Eisenhower appeared to be especially fond of his wife's mother. Teasing her unmercifully, he always called her "Min," after a character in the old Andy Gump comic strip. Mrs. Doud played the harmonica in her room and sometimes accompanied her Mamie, who played, by ear, a small electric organ in the West Hall.

Mrs. Doud was a permanent resident in the White House, although another daughter, Frances, Mrs. George Gordon Moore, whom everyone called "Mike," also lived in Washington. Mrs. Moore and her daughters, Mamie and Ellen, frequently dropped in on their famous relatives.

Although her mother, sister, son, daughter-in-law, and grandchildren were often around the house, Mrs. Eisenhower took great precautions that none of them would appear to be taking advantage of her position. The First Lady stressed that if any White House services were needed by her family, she'd be the one to request them.

One morning, as I was in conference with the First Lady, Mrs. Doud came into the bedroom and mentioned that she had a dentist's appointment at 11:30 and would like a car, if possible. "Certainly," Mrs. Eisenhower said.

When I went downstairs, I ordered a car to be there for the First Lady's mother. About thirty minutes later, Mrs. Eisenhower called me.

"Who ordered the car for Mother?"

"You did," I answered.

"Why, I just called the garage and they said it had *already* been ordered," she said.

I explained that I called her order into the garage after I'd heard it mentioned in her room. "Oh, good," she said, "just so the order came from me!"

She rode in a Chrysler limousine, which was replaced by a new model every year. Those White House cars always came under the special scrutiny of Mamie Doud Eisenhower. Every time the manufacturer sent down a new model for our approval, she'd try it out first. "The seat is too high" or "The seat is too low," she'd report, among other assessments, after a spin around the block. And back to the factory went the new limousine.

"She's the best critic we've ever had," the Chrysler representative told me one day, waiting for her to return from a test-run.

5

More than any other task I performed for the Eisenhowers,
I liked working at Gettysburg. It was a change of pace
from the White House routine, the 160-mile ride back and
forth through the Pennsylvania countryside was scenic,
and the creative process involved in building or rebuilding
had always excited me.

The huge farm, near their friend George Allen's farm,
became the only permanent home the Eisenhowers had
ever known. Although they'd purchased it in 1950, when
they came back from Europe, they began to remodel the
farmhouse after they moved into the White House. Since
1954, I had been commuting back and forth from the
Usher's office to Gettysburg.

The farmhouse was small, more than 200 years old, and
in pretty bad shape. Over a period of three years, the
Eisenhowers had it expanded and remodeled into a large,
attractive, rambling two-story white brick and natural
stone home with seven bedrooms, and plenty of space for
the guards and Secret Service in the barn.

"You're my general supervisor at Gettysburg," Mrs.

Eisenhower laughingly told me, but added firmly, "I don't want anybody working up there—decorators, carpenters, anybody—unless either you or I are there."

My job at the farmhouse was to make certain that the contractor followed Mrs. Eisenhower's wishes—covering over a window here, cutting through a door there, enclosing the porch with sliding glass panels so the President could have a light-filled painting corner.

The Eisenhowers paid for every piece of material used in connection with the Gettysburg house and kept careful records of their expenditures. For every house gift they received, they made a public ceremony or statement of acceptance. However, some of the work—kitchen cabinets, bookshelves, and other fine woodwork—was done in the White House carpenter's shop, as was our own house gift, two large glass-enclosed "Louis XV" curio cabinets.

Sometimes, during the three-year project, White House carpenters and electricians accompanied me to Gettysburg, Mrs. Eisenhower scrupulously paying all their expenses—though not their salaries for the time they put in. A White House car always was at our disposal, and occasionally I had a chance to ride along with Sergeant Dry, the Army driver assigned to the First Lady.

As the house neared completion, I spent even more time at Gettysburg, because Mrs. Eisenhower wanted to be sure, with last-minute changes such as new wallpaper on the stairway, that workmen didn't traipse over the rugs or tear the draperies.

Because the trip took about an hour and a half each way, I often stayed from Monday until Friday. Mrs. Eisenhower urged me to stay in the house, but I preferred a motel in town. Even though I knew that the First Lady regarded me as a friend and confidant, I still felt it more proper that I separate myself from the personal lives of any Presidential family.

One evening, after a long day at the farmhouse, I said goodnight to Mrs. Eisenhower, and put on my overcoat.

"I want you to call your wife and thank her for lending you to me," Mrs. Eisenhower called down from upstairs.

"I will," I answered, laughing.

"No, you call her right now, where I can hear you,"

she insisted. So I picked up the living room phone, placed the call to Virginia, and relayed her message to Zella. ("That's all right," Zella replied. "Tell her she can lend me Ike for a day or two.") Only then could I head for my motel.

Sergeant Dry, however, always stayed in a room on the third floor at Gettysburg, when the Eisenhowers were in residence. He served as the operating engineer, caring for the air conditioning, furnace, and mechanical equipment.

After early 1955, when the house was comfortable enough for occupancy, the Eisenhowers spent almost every weekend there, as well as most summer vacations. In addition to Sergeant Dry, they brought along Sergeant Moaney, whose wife, Delores, became the cook at Gettysburg, and Rose Woods, all of whom had rooms at the main house; two Filipino housemen, Enrique and Lem, who stayed in Navy barracks at Camp David and commuted to the Gettysburg farm; the President's doctor, General Snyder; several Secret Service men; and, of course, the Signal Corps, who stayed in motels in Gettysburg.

For the first time since I'd been working for the White House, getting away had become quite a cumbersome proposition for the President. Having to take that number of staff around, seeing to their food and housing was an operation in logistics—far different from the days when Eleanor Roosevelt needed a single train ticket.

We had to pack White House linens for each trip, ship them back by truck daily for laundering, take food from each of the mansion's refrigerators for the help and the Eisenhowers, and, if there was official business, from the White House storerooms. When the Eisenhowers came home, everything was packed up and brought back again.

When Mrs. Eisenhower went up to the farm alone, she took along Dr. Walter Tkach, General Snyder's assistant. The young Air Force physician was quite a violinist, and during the quiet afternoons he played the fiddle in his second-floor bedroom.

It was not music to Mrs. Eisenhower's ears, however. "Please tell him if he has to play, please go to the barn," she laughingly told Delores in exasperation.

When the Gettysburg house was finally finished, the

163

Eisenhowers held a celebration in July, 1955, combining a housewarming with their wedding anniversary—an all-day picnic catered by the Navy from Camp David. The Gettysburg kitchen wasn't big enough to handle all that crowd.

All the White House was invited—carpenters, painters, plumbers, everybody, and their spouses. It was the first time a President had ever entertained like that for all of us. After everybody had trekked through the house, we ate fried chicken on the back lawn, then presented the Eisenhowers with a surprise anniversary gift—two folding tray tables like the ones we'd used at the White House, and a silver serving tray, which we'd all chipped in to purchase. Thus, Gettysburg was "launched."

Whether at Gettysburg, Camp David, or at home in the White House, it always seemed to us that President Eisenhower had everything under tight control, and that Mrs. Eisenhower's "taut ship" approach to directing activities in the Executive Mansion only reflected the way the General ran the Presidency. It was as if a military command post had been set up in the west wing, with the Executive branch operating under a staff system. Under the next-in-command Sherman Adams, the staff worked from early morning until late at night preparing information for the President's decision. Everything and everybody who received consideration from the President went through Governor Adams first, although the President's closest working alliance was with his Secretary of State, the stern John Foster Dulles.

During those first three years of his Presidency, General Eisenhower relied to a considerable extent on Mr. Dulles' ideas about foreign policy in waging attacks in psychological warfare against the Soviet Union and China, and in building a massive nuclear force.

He said that he would do his utmost to prevent the admission of Red China to the United Nations; that the United States would employ "massive retaliation" with nuclear power (later modified to mean small nuclear weapons) in case our allies were attacked by Communists.

The President, under attack from Senator Joe McCarthy, felt that his own hard line against Communism was plenty sufficient. (During 1953–1954, 8,000 cases of security risks were identified, out of tens of thousands of records examined.) However much he deplored McCarthy's methods, which whipped the nation into a mood of anti-Communist hysteria and fear, he refused to dignify the attacks by answering them. But the President was especially distressed over the Wisconsin Senator's attacks on the President's "own," the U.S. Army, in 1954. General Eisenhower's sense of rank and military honor was deeply offended when the issue boiled down to the Senator's grilling the Secretary of the Army over the matter of a mere private. During these hearings, the President spoke out pointedly about "demagogues thirsty for political power," and was privately relieved when McCarthy was finally condemned by the Senate in December, 1954.

In 1955, at sixty-four, Dwight Eisenhower still looked physically fit, tall and lean. But the strain of the Army-McCarthy hearings, in addition to the other burdens of his office, were beginning to tell on the President.

In July, just after their anniversary celebration at Gettysburg, he and Mrs. Eisenhower, who, he said, "had never completely convinced herself that an airplane flies," took off for Geneva for a five-day summit meeting with European leaders*—a meeting that had been two years in preparation.

When they returned, both the President and Mrs. Eisenhower looked exhausted. As soon as the Congress adjourned in August, they left for Mrs. Doud's home in Denver. The President had set up a Summer White House office nearby, and spent his vacation time hunting in the woods and fishing in the Colorado streams.

Mr. Crim had taken a vacation, too, and as things were quiet on Pennsylvania Avenue, the White House staff was going through a general "September slowdown." Nevertheless, Mrs. Eisenhower telephoned from Denver every day, checking on the staff, on details at Gettysburg, on the coming social season.

On Friday, September 23, 1955, when she called, she

---

* Prime Minister Anthony Eden of Great Britain, and Premiers Edgar Fauré of France and Nikolai Bulganin of the U.S.S.R.

mentioned that the President had been out to Byers Peak Ranch in the Rockies. "You should have heard what he cooked himself for breakfast," she laughed.

The next afternoon, I smiled when I read the little item in the evening paper about President Eisenhower's "digestive upset." But the headlines on Sunday's paper were far more serious. The "digestive upset" was now being described as a "moderate coronary thrombosis." The President had been taken to Fitzsimons General Hospital in Denver with a heart attack.

6

I arrived in the office within minutes, newspaper still in hand. At 10:00 a.m. the Usher's office telephone rang. I was startled to hear Mrs. Eisenhower's voice on the line.

"I wanted to be sure you knew about the President," she told me. "I wanted to tell you myself."

Almost speechless, I tried to convey my wishes for his recovery.

"He is resting comfortably now," she said. "In fact, I'm right here with him to keep him quiet. I've moved into the hospital," she added, cheerfully.

I was amazed at her even thinking to call us.

Almost every day during the next seven weeks, Mrs. Eisenhower phoned from the hospital, giving reports on the President's health—"He's painting a fine Colorado landscape today"—or "He's out in his wheelchair this morning"—and giving detailed instructions for finishing touches on their Gettysburg home.

"I want to be sure it's all done by the time we get back," she told me, "so there are no workmen around."

I practically moved up to Gettysburg, to supervise the additional work.

On November 11, the President and Mrs. Eisenhower returned from Denver, taking the big, closed limousine from the airport to the White House. (The President had ordered an open car, because he wanted to be able to wave to the crowds, but his doctor, General Howard Snyder, prevailed.) All the staff lined up outside the south entrance to greet him. As he stepped out of the car, he waved to everybody, breaking into a huge grin.

I stood just inside the Diplomatic Room door, waiting to accompany the Eisenhowers upstairs. The President looked healthier, more suntanned and trimmer than I'd ever seen him.

"Welcome home," I said, and we shook hands.

"Mrs. Eisenhower tells me you've been looking after Gettysburg for us," he said, as we walked toward the elevator.

"I think everything is in pretty good shape for your stay up there," I replied.

"Some time while I'm there I'd like you to come up, because I'd like to add some bookshelves in my den."

"Certainly," I replied, stepping back for the Eisenhowers to enter the elevator. But the President stopped short.

"No," he said firmly. "General Snyder tells me I should use the stairs," and to the back stairs he went, slowly but determinedly walking up the white marble steps.

On November 14, Mrs. Eisenhower's birthday, they moved to the Gettysburg farm to complete the President's period of recovery.

When they returned to Washington in January, Mrs. Eisenhower immediately canceled the social season and set about to enforce the President's afternoon naptime, his recreation and relaxation, taking care of him almost like a trained nurse. They didn't go to Denver again.

The President's doctors advised him to spend more time painting, playing golf—relaxing. As in every other era, when a Presidential pastime was well publicized, the country followed suit. Men who'd never touched a paintbrush were suddenly advised to paint for relaxation.

President Eisenhower gave paint-by-the-numbers sets to all of his staff, and people all over the country turned out landscapes and portraits by the millions. There was also a definite sales boom in golf clubs.

The President and Mrs. Eisenhower spent rest-and-recuperation time in Georgia, in the two-story "Mamie's Cabin," a white-columned plantation house, decorated in pink, on the grounds of the Augusta National Golf Course, where he exercised by playing twice daily. He also enjoyed birdhunting nearby at Treasury Secretary George Humphrey's Thomasville plantation.

At the White House, the stag dinners for business and political leaders continued—with the addition of quail, pheasant, and other wild game bagged by Mr. Eisenhower and his hunting party. And at every table setting, we placed a souvenir color photograph of the bird to be consumed.

Although the White House entertaining had been curtailed to lessen strain on the President, Mrs. Eisenhower found an outlet for her talents as a hostess by dressing up the mansion as if it were a giant shopwindow.

On Halloween she held a luncheon for wives of Presidential staff members. The ladies were amazed to find witches and black cats flying around the State Dining Room, and skeletons hanging from the ceiling. In the dignified foyer of the State floor, shocks of corn circled the stately columns, jack-o'-lanterns marched down the halls. Mrs. Eisenhower had stationed ghosts and goblins, owls and witches all over the tables, which were decorated with Indian corn, nuts, gourds, dried leaves, and chrysanthemums.

The White House never celebrated the change of seasons so heartily as it did under Mrs. Eisenhower. For St. Patrick's Day, she twined the columns with green ribbons and top hats, with shamrocks hanging from the chandeliers, leprechauns in the State Dining Room and green carnations and bells-of-Ireland in the flower bowls. At Eastertime there were butterflies hanging from the chandeliers, artificial birds singing with tape-recorded voices ("Would you please shut off the birds?" Mrs. Eisenhower said to the butler), Easter bunnies hatching from pale

169

blue shells on the mantel, ropes of cherry blossoms climbing the marble columns, and masses of fresh spring flowers throughout the White House.

But at Christmastime, she outdid herself.

Unlike most of the previous First Families, who went "home," the Eisenhowers spent nearly every Christmas in the White House with their grandchildren, opening presents on Christmas morning underneath the family Christmas tree in the West Sitting Hall.

Heretofore, Christmas decorating had been the province of the White House gardeners and electricians. At about the same time that the President turned on the lights at the giant outdoor Christmas tree on the ellipse every year, they brought in a fresh green tree to the East Room, dressing it with the lights and icicles stored in the electrician's shop. Another box held the Christmas balls and ornaments for the second-floor family tree that every White House family also requested. In past years, a few fresh wreaths at the windows, holly in the vases—and that was all.

Mrs. Eisenhower, however, spread Christmas throughout the entire White House. Together with her social secretary, Mary Jane McCaffree, the First Lady scoured all of Washington's department stores for ideas and baubles. In the State Dining Room, they put wreaths on all the candelabra, little Christmas trees on each side of the mantel, hung red ribbons and holly from the chandeliers. Hundreds of poinsettias decorated with white-sprayed branches lined the halls; green roping and big red bows adorned the white columns; giant dressed-up spruces stood in the East Room, the Blue Room, and even outside on the North Portico.

One year she placed a large nativity scene, with piped-in Christmas carols, beneath the East Room tree. Another year a tall Santa Claus stood there. Mamie Eisenhower decked the halls with more than holly.

7

Throughout the country in 1956, the main concern among Republicans was whether the President would be able to run for office again. While he recuperated at Gettysburg, and during the weeks after his return to the White House, speculation was building up all over Washington.

Then Ann Whitman called to order a top-secret dinner for "eight of the President's friends" Tuesday, January 10, and Mrs. Eisenhower duly approved the menu. But somehow word got out, and the President personally called to postpone the dinner.

"Make it for Friday the thirteenth. It's to be an absolutely confidential gathering," he insisted.

The dinner was so confidential that the President laid out the place cards himself, after his advisors arrived. After dinner in the family dining room, they went upstairs to the oval study, now the President's trophy room, which had been freshly painted white. There, after everyone*

---

* Herbert Brownell, Leonard Hall, John Foster Dulles, Henry Cabot Lodge, Sherman Adams, General Wilton Persons, George Humphrey, Arthur Summerfield, James Hagerty, Howard Pyle, Thomas Stephens, and the President's brother, Milton Eisenhower.

was polled by the President, he later recounted, he decided to run for reelection.

On February 29, the President announced the decision for which a concerned nation had been waiting.

Explaining that "I may possibly be a greater risk than the normal person of my age," he went on to describe how well he felt, and that he had not the slightest doubt that he could now perform as well as ever all the important duties of the Presidency. Throughout the spring, he held conferences with political leaders, went out campaigning, and, we thought, never looked better.

We were more than a little stunned on June 9, when an ambulance pulled quietly up to the south entrance of the mansion. Two uniformed medical corpsmen rushed in with a stretcher.

The President's heart attack was so fresh in our minds that we assumed he'd had another. Silently, we waited for the news from upstairs. The entire house was quiet that late afternoon, until my buzzer rang urgently. It was General Howard Snyder, the President's physician.

"Please send someone to help," he said. "The stretcher is too big to go on the elevator."

I immediately sent Ray Hare, one of the ushers. Moments later, a strange procession came down the Grand Staircase: Hare, Dr. Tkach, and the two Army medical corpsmen, bearing the stricken President on a hospital stretcher, followed by Mrs. Eisenhower. They maneuvered carefully down the marble stairs to the ground floor and out the Diplomatic room door, so that press people in the west wing wouldn't be able to see.

The President's illness was announced just after he checked in to Walter Reed Army Hospital. It was an attack of ileitis, an inflammation of the small intestine, requiring immediate surgery.

Once again, Mrs. Eisenhower moved into a hospital with her husband—into the special Presidential suite at Walter Reed, where there's a big living room, a dining room, a separate kitchen, two bedrooms, and two baths. The Secret Service set up shop across the hall.

During the weeks she stayed in the hospital, Mrs. Eisenhower called every day to give us reports on the President's health, and to check, as usual, on the operation of her house.

Despite two serious illnesses within a year, the President bounced back, and on July 1, reconfirmed his decision to run for reelection. After easily winning the Republican nomination, he and Mrs. Eisenhower opened the campaign on September 12 with a picnic at Gettysburg for 500 campaign workers.

I had nothing to do with the picnic, since it was political.

I did, however, get to take a free ride on a campaign trip.

A few days after the picnic, I noticed on the President's schedule a trip to Iowa, to the national plowing contest near Mrs. Eisenhower's birthplace at Boone.

"I wish I could go along, to see my father," I remarked to Mr. Crim, never imagining there'd be a chance to do so. But Mr. Crim evidently went right to Mrs. Eisenhower, because the phone was ringing within minutes.

"The President and I would like for you and Mrs. West to accompany us on our trip to Des Moines," the First Lady said. And I accepted immediately. "We leave at two this afternoon," she finished.

"Pack a bag and get a sitter," I telephoned my surprised wife. "We're spending the night in Iowa!"

"But my hair . . ." Zella protested.

Somehow she got herself together in the four hours we had left, and we drove to Andrews Air Force Base, for our first ride in a Presidential plane. The *Columbine,* which Mrs. Eisenhower had named for the Colorado state flower, was a four-engine Super-Constellation, piloted by Colonel William Draper, the President's Air Force aide. It was like a flying apartment.

Somewhere over Indiana, Mrs. Eisenhower called for Zella to join her in her private cabin. All the way to Des Moines, the two women in my life discussed children, hair-dos, and Iowa.

"She asked a hundred questions about all of our family," Zella reported. "Is she that interested in everybody?"

She was.

The Eisenhowers spent the night with Mrs. Eisenhower's uncle, Joel Carlson, in Boone; Zella and I stayed in Des Moines with our relatives. I daresay the Republicans could justify our tagging along. I'm sure there were now a few even more definite votes in Iowa—the West family's.

It was a mark of President Eisenhower's immense popularity with the American people that, despite two major illnesses, he won the November election by 27,000,000 votes. He was also helped, the polls later showed, by two sudden developments in international affairs in October and early November, which caused the public to fear a change. The invasion of Egypt by England, France and Israel, and the Hungarian Revolution occurred almost simultaneously, and each could have drawn this country into war. We managed to stay aloof from the Mideast crisis, and sheltered thousands of Hungarian refugees without getting into the fight, and the voters expressed confidence in the President once again.

And the very next day after the election, Mr. Crim had some news that would affect my life.

"I have told President and Mrs. Eisenhower that I am in poor health and cannot carry on the job of Chief Usher any longer," he said. "I told them I'm scheduled to retire next year anyway, and they said all my work should be turned over to you. And when I do retire, you should take over the job." Practically speaking, I had been in charge of household details since the Truman Administration, while Mr. Crim had concentrated on fiscal affairs of the White House. But, I thought, things really wouldn't be that different if I accepted the full work load without the title.

I explained my position to Mr. Crim: "The arrangement you've outlined will not relieve you of any responsibility. As long as you have the title of Chief Usher, people will insist on going to you, first. I cannot accept under those circumstances." I felt sorry to say this, because I knew how much he wanted to retire. His health had been failing for months.

The very formal, very correct Chief Usher went back

to Mrs. Eisenhower with my answer. Mr. Crim was made a special assistant to the President, until his retirement in eleven months, and I was promoted to Chief Usher immediately.

Mrs. Eisenhower had only one reservation about the arrangement.

"What about Gettysburg?" she asked me.

"Don't worry, I'll take care of Gettysburg first," I assured her.

In January, President Eisenhower was inaugurated twice. Because Inauguration Day, January 20, fell on a Sunday, a small, private ceremony was held at the White House, with only the Eisenhowers, their relatives, Vice President Nixon and his family. Only forty-eight people gathered in the East Room of the White House to witness Chief Justice Earl Warren administer the solemn oath of office. The ceremony was repeated the next day at the Capitol, followed by the traditional luncheon, the parade, and two gala Inaugural balls. The Eisenhowers entered his second term glowing.

Their energy for entertaining was limited, though. The President was concerned about Mrs. Eisenhower's health, as well as his own. At 60, she began her husband's second term with her usual flourish, but he soon stopped her practice of shaking hands with the thousands of reception visitors. "She insists on talking to everyone," he complained. "It's a strain on her."

But Mrs. Eisenhower learned how to conserve her strength well. Although she had been quite ill with rheumatic fever as a child, and had contracted a heart murmur as a result, she had learned to discipline her time and energy so that, after a strenuous day as a hostess or traveling, she always collected adequate rest for herself.

"I believe that every woman over fifty should stay in bed until noon," she said, quite seriously.

Rejuvenation—at Elizabeth Arden's Main Chance farm in Arizona—was among her projects. She spurned physical exercise, hated to go outdoors. "I'm not an outdoor girl," she laughed. Instead, she depended on the masseuse who came to the White House three mornings a week to give her a good workout. Taking such good care of herself paid off. She didn't have one wrinkle in her face. Most of our women visitors commented on Mamie Eisenhower's smooth, unlined complexion.

8

It seemed that we'd saved all the entertaining for Queen Elizabeth.

Our most glittering—and strenuous—occasion of 1957 came in October, when the Queen of England and Prince Philip came with a party of fifteen for a State visit.

It was the first visit to the White House for the young Queen. It was as Princess Elizabeth that she had stayed at Blair House during her last visit, when she had presented President Truman with a gift from her father, an antique floral over-mantel with mirror, now in the State Dining Room. This time she slept in the Queen's Room, Prince Philip in the Lincoln Room, and their various ladies- and men-in-waiting in the second-floor and third-floor guest rooms. The highlight of their visit was a State dinner, for which we'd brought out all our formal regalia.

Strictest protocol was to be followed, White House elegance to be unsurpassed. This was very important to Mrs. Eisenhower, who had been entertained by the Queen's parents in Europe, and wished to return the honor in the grandest manner.

Timing was of the utmost concern. To us the logistics of clearing the State Dining Room after dinner became a major matter, for which we held many a strategy session.

There was to be a concert in the East Room after dinner, to which two hundred additional guests had been invited. As soon as the President and Mrs. Eisenhower led their hundred dinner guests out of the State Dining Room, we were to close the doors, remove the elaborate place settings, flowers, linens, and banquet chairs, dismantle the big banquet table, and take everything, piece by piece, out onto the terrace.

Then, while the audience sat enthralled by the strains of Fred Waring's orchestra and chorus at the other end of the House, we'd set up the dining room with a small table for a champagne reception after the musicale.

It was quite an operation, one that required swift, delicate, and silent movement. We'd labored over it for days, rehearsing carpenters, butlers, and housemen for their part in the transformation. The carpenters, normally unaccustomed to State dinners, were to wait outside on the terrace, then enter the room through the terrace doors to dismantle the banquet table.

"Wait until *everybody* leaves the room and we've closed the doors to the main hall," I instructed them. "Be ready to *move*, and move fast as soon as the room gets quiet—I'll signal you, but remember, the main thing is to move fast!"

Up to a point the dinner went beautifully. Through all the courses, the butlers performed smoothly, Mrs. Eisenhower smiling her approval. After dessert, the President rose and proposed a warm, lengthy toast to the Queen, and the guests applauded.

Queen Elizabeth has a very soft voice, and when she spoke, returning President Eisenhower's toast, the room became breathlessly silent. I was standing discreetly in the corridor, looking in, when I heard the terrace door begin to rattle. My heart sank, as I realized the carpenters had taken the silence to be their cue. They were trying to get into the room! Then, just before I had a heart attack myself, I remembered that I'd locked the door from the inside.

178

Now, if they don't decide to break the door down, we'll be safe, I thought, holding my breath.

When the toasts were finally over, and the guests had all filed out to the Red and Green Rooms for coffee and liqueurs, I ran to unlock the door.

"We thought you weren't coming!" exclaimed "Tojo" Benton. "We thought we'd have to bust in."

When I told him how perfect his timing nearly was, his face turned as white as his carpenter's overalls.

"You mean I nearly broke in on the Queen of England!" he said. "God save her!"

The next morning, when I went up to see Mrs. Eisenhower, she was propped up in her king-sized bed, radiant.

"Everything was just perfect last night," she said. "I don't think we've ever performed more smoothly."

I threw all my papers down on the floor and sat down, shaking my head.

"What's the matter?" Mrs. Eisenhower said.

"If you didn't see the things that went wrong—or that almost went wrong—I'm not going to tell you," I said. And I didn't.

We found out later that morning that *our* First Lady sometimes required more in the way of service than did the Queen of England.

It had been, after all, a very late evening. But as usual, Rose Woods stayed up until her mistress retired, undressing the First Lady, taking her diamonds and carefully locking them in the bedroom safe, then rinsing out the little items of personal laundry.

As I left the jubilant First Lady's conference, pleased that she'd been so delighted with the State dinner, I ran into the White House maid who'd been assigned to straighten the Queen's Room. Wide-eyed, she told me, "Queen Elizabeth sent *her* personal maids to bed early last night—she told them not to wait up for her because she'd be so late!" Then, in utter astonishment, she described the morning scene in the Queen's Room: The fabulous diamond tiara, the heavy diamond necklace, the beribboned medals—all the precious jewels Elizabeth II had worn the night before—tossed casually on a dresser.

Her gown and underthings were folded neatly on a chair. The Queen of England had undressed herself.

The President thoroughly enjoyed the visit of the young monarch and her husband, even though their rigorous four-day schedule left everyone else huffing and puffing.

After the couple said their last goodbye at the door of the White House, before moving on to New York and a United Nations visit, the Eisenhowers waved to them until the limousine disappeared out of sight.

Still flashing his big grin, the President turned to me.

"If they'd stayed a day or two longer we'd soon be calling them Liz and Phil!"

Despite President Eisenhower's geniality with his royal guests, however, the burden of government had begun to fall heavily on his shoulders. The apparent lull that had quieted the nation after the cessation of hostilities in Korea seemed to be over.

The fall of 1957 brought with it a deluge of national and international problems to confront the President of the United States. The American economy floundered in the midst of a recession which left millions unemployed. The school integration issue reached its most serious crisis as Governor Orval Faubus defied a federal court order and the President dispatched federal troops to Little Rock, Arkansas to assure peace at Central High School. Constant crises brought the threat of renewed war in the Middle East. And the Soviet Union severely shook U.S. self-confidence by launching Sputniks I and II, the first man-made satellites to orbit the earth.

Nevertheless, by November, the President appeared to have weathered the strain. The afternoon of November 25 was dreary, not our favorite weather for a party, because Mrs. Eisenhower worried so about the rugs.

"Be sure that the rubber mats are out along the North Portico and outside the Diplomatic Reception Room," she called down to caution me, although the long, black runners were already in place.

Extra door-openers, with umbrellas, were detailed to the south entrance, extra coat-checkers and racks were installed, to take care of dripping raincoats. All our stormy-weather plans rolled into action before the State dinner.

At 3:15, I checked the State Dining Room, where the butlers were putting on finishing touches. The E-shaped table was set with the Truman china and vermeil flatware. Huge tureens of wine-red carnations, arranged according to Mrs. Eisenhower's own color scheme for the evening, were waiting in the bouquet room refrigerator, to be centered on the tables just before eight o'clock. The First Lady had spent her usual long time preparing for the dinner, which was to honor the King of Morocco.

Less than an hour later, we began to sense that something had gone wrong.

There's always a swift undertone of communication among the staff when there is trouble in the White House. Perhaps it is our years of intuition, second-guessing the comings and goings of the First Family, that prompts our coded signals to one another. The first indication that things might be amiss that afternoon came from our buzzer, touched off with three rings by a policeman when the President enters the mansion, to alert the ushers and doormen all over the house.

This buzzer rang at 4:00, when the President, accompanied by his military aide, returned from his office. That was slightly unusual in itself, because President Eisenhower was a man of habit, and walking slowly back to the White House in the middle of the afternoon was not part of his daily ritual.

Our second signal was General Snyder, President Eisenhower's physician, flying down the ground-floor corridor from his office to the elevator, heading for the second floor.

Moments later, Mrs. Eisenhower called me, her voice trembling.

"Can you come up right away?" she asked.

It was serious, I knew immediately, because John Eisenhower, who now served as his father's aide, was at his mother's side in the west sitting hall. The President's dressing-room door stood ajar, and I could see the President, in pajamas and a robe, seated on the edge of his bed, talking with his doctor.

"The President has taken sick," Mrs. Eisenhower explained gravely. "We must be prepared to cancel the dinner this evening."

181

"I'm sorry to hear it," I murmured. "I'll wait for your instructions." By now, we had only a few hours before the guests were to arrive. I began mentally disassembling all of our arrangements; first, call the social office; second, call the maître d'; third, call. . . .

The President, obviously in an argument with General Snyder, came to the door.

"The dinner will not be. . . ." He couldn't seem to finish his sentence.

". . . canceled?" Mrs. Eisenhower asked.

The President nodded vigorously.

"Sir, you *will* not be able to attend," General Snyder told his old friend.

President Eisenhower looked straight down at his wife, and with great difficulty—his tongue seemed to be thick—said, "The only way I won't is if Mrs. Eisenhower attends." Turning, he went back to his bed.

The First Lady looked at me, raising her hands in defeat.

"Continue as planned," she said. "I'll call Vice President Nixon to act as host."

Walking with me the few yards to the stairway, she said rather formally, as if organizing herself, as if I had not been witness to the previous scene. "The President has had a slight stroke, but he insists on going ahead with the dinner, so I will just act as hostess."

At 6:20 the President's press secretary, James Hagerty, gave a terse announcement: President Eisenhower is suffering from a chill, and will not be able to attend the dinner tonight.

It was a ghostly-white Mamie Eisenhower who descended the elevator with Vice President and Mrs. Nixon that night. She sat in her throne-like chair at the head of the E-shaped banquet table, visibly nervous, obviously wishing to be at her husband's bedside.

She went upstairs immediately after dinner, pausing to file an unusual complaint with me.

"The State Dining Room looked so dull, tonight. Those red carnations were much too dark," indicating the flowers she'd chosen for the banquet table. It seemed to me that the room may have seemed dull because the light of her life lay ill upstairs.

She stayed with the President until midnight, and her son sat watch in his bedroom, all night.

It was not until the next day that Press Secretary James Hagerty made the announcement about the President's cerebral hemorrhage. The stock market dropped $4,000,-000 in twenty minutes. But it quickly recovered, and so did the President.

After three days he was well enough to attend Thanksgiving services at the National Presbyterian Church, determinedly carrying on his duties thereafter—even flying to Paris to participate in a NATO heads-of-government meeting.

During the next three years, his physical stamina and mental skills were put to more severe tasks than he had faced before, as he set out, by plane and by diplomacy, on a search for peace in the world. At the same time, he was meeting threats from the Soviets with a firm show of American military strength. And that fall, he hosted what had to be one of the strangest State dinners I ever witnessed.

Nikita Khrushchev and his wife, daughter and son-in-law arrived in Washington on September 15. For weeks, Mrs. Eisenhower had worked on the menu for that evening's State dinner, which turned out to be a "typically American" offering of curry soup, roast turkey with cranberry sauce, sweet potatoes and tossed green salad.

Out on the south lawn that afternoon, the President was preparing to take his visitor for a sightseeing tour of Washington by helicopter. Mr. Eisenhower had judged the machines safe enough for Presidential use during a civil defense drill in 1957; since then, the fascinating whirlibirds had practically become a fixture, hovering over the south lawn to carry the President back and forth to Andrews Air Force Base, to the Gettysburg farm and now, with Chairman Khrushchev, on a tour of the nation's Capitol.

I stood in the door with Mrs. Eisenhower, watching the helicopter take off.

"They've refused to dress for dinner," Mrs. Eisenhower

said. "Did you know that? They're going to wear business suits and street dresses to a formal State dinner."

Then, with a little laugh, she said, "My husband would just as soon dress that way, too—if I'd let him."

But for the Khrushchevs, the President was decked out in white tie—we certainly wouldn't bow to the Russians' wishes—and Mrs. Eisenhower wore a long, sweeping gold brocade gown with diamond earrings and a diamond-and-pearl necklace.

The atmosphere at the State dinner was edgy. Mr. Khrushchev's after-dinner statement was part toast, part boast. And after President Eisenhower treated his guests to a performance by his favorite musicians, Fred Waring and the Pennsylvanians, everybody let out a general sigh of relief as the Eisenhowers escorted the uneasy Russians to the front door.

To the disappointment of the diplomatic community and most of the women's press corps, the Eisenhowers canceled that winter's formal social season. As the Trumans had done in 1948, the Eisenhowers placed other matters before official hospitality. The steel industry was entangled in a crippling strike, the economy slowly climbing out of the deep recession. The President had lost two trusted friends from his official family in 1958: Secretary of State Dulles had died, and Assistant to the President Sherman Adams had resigned under fire. Facing a hostile, Democratic-controlled Congress for the fifth year since the 1954 Congressional elections, Mr. Eisenhower was struggling to push through his domestic programs. Although his health was his own concern as well as the country's, the President decided that his first priority was attending to business, his second priority was taking care of himself.

On December 3, the President with his son, John, and his daughter-in-law, Barbara (Mrs. Eisenhower, terrified of flying in the new jet planes, chose to stay at home), took off on a "peace and goodwill" tour which took them nineteen days and 22,000 miles into eleven countries.

When the party returned, Mrs. Eisenhower, with the Nixons, drove out to the airport to greet them. The White House glowed with all her Christmas decorations, but a bigger glow came from Lafayette Park, across Pennsylvania Avenue, where a midnight crowd had gathered to greet the President with thousands of sparklers.

Inside, another welcome was staged on the second floor, in the West Hall, where General Gruenther, George Allen, Bill Robinson, and Ellis Slater sat around their usual bridge table.

President Eisenhower reported: "As we came in, Al Gruenther turned around slightly and said 'Hi,' turned back to his bridge hand and said, 'I double.'"

It was a warm homecoming.

In February, the President announced his intention to visit Russia in the summer, after an important Paris Summit Conference—a trip that was stopped by the downing of a U.S. reconnaissance plane over Soviet territory.

The U-2 plane incident, and the consequences of it, came as an enormous blow to everything Ike had worked for for two years. All those worldwide trips, cementing old alliances, and developing international understanding, were a prelude to reaching better relations with the Soviet Union.

Instead, a summit meeting was shattered and Dwight Eisenhower left office with the Cold War almost as frigid as before.

Mrs. Eisenhower clung more closely to her quieter pattern of living, spending more time with her grandchildren, playing cards with her close friends, entertaining only for State visitors. She turned the East Room over to John and Barbara for a spring dinner-dance for their friends—the only time the young couple had ever used the mansion to entertain. In October, Mrs. Eisenhower celebrated her husband's seventieth birthday with a lively party in the State Dining Room.

As the 1960 Presidential campaign got underway, Mr. Eisenhower at first hesitated to become involved. Then, in the fall, he did go out campaigning for Vice President Nixon, against his doctor's advice. But the election was won by the Vice President's opponent.

Mrs. Eisenhower had planned a gala victory celebration for the Nixons. Instead, her considerable talents as a hostess were extended to her own family—a grand debut for her two nieces in the East Room of the White House on November 25.

"I want it to be like the debuts I remember, with old friends and their daughters," the First Lady said proudly as she and her sister "Mike" introduced Ellen Doud Moore, 19, and Mamie Eisenhower Moore, 18, to Washington society. And it *was* like a page from the past.

Bouquets sent by friends and guests for the afternoon tea began arriving at the White House days before the debut. "Keep them fresh, in the refrigerators, then bank them along the East Room wall," directed Mrs. Eisenhower. (And when we did, florist Robert Redmond whispered, "It looks like the Roosevelt funeral in there.")

Dressed in a blue, sequined afternoon gown, Mrs. Eisenhower stood with her sister and the two girls in the Green Room, greeting the 500 guests. There were two tea tables, in the State Dining Room and the Blue Room, for Mrs. Eisenhower's last big occasion in the White House.

"Wasn't it a wonderful thing for Aunt Mamie to do?" said Mamie Moore, as she watched her aunt spread her own particular charm throughout the crowd.

After the debut, Mrs. Eisenhower moved into Christmas. . . .

"I want it to be the most beautiful Christmas ever," she told me. "It's our last one in this wonderful house."

Her sentiment about the mansion she had ruled so majestically over the previous eight years was echoed in her choice of music for her farewell dinner for the President's Cabinet, staff and close personal friends. As the Army chorus sang "Auld Lang Syne" and "Bless This House," the First Lady's eyes glistened with tears.

More than any of the others, Mamie Eisenhower hated to leave.

Shortly before Inauguration Day, we were at Gettysburg, arranging for the Eisenhowers' last move. There were still changes she wanted made, but now it was almost too late.

"I'd like to have had these stairs widened," she said, indicating the narrow steep stairs leading from the kitchen to the upstairs bedrooms, "So the servants could carry the big tray you gave us more easily, but I guess we won't bother, now."

Then, with a sad little smile, she shrugged. "Oh, well, instead of having my trays carried upstairs, I'll probably be downstairs with a dustrag in my hand."

Later that afternoon, she went on a shopping trek to Gettysburg. "Stop here," she said to Sergeant Dry, pointing to a bakery. "I want to get a cake for the help's dessert tonight."

Thoughtful of every detail as always, Mrs. Eisenhower carried the little bakery cake into the kitchen of her Gettysburg home. But there she found Delores Moaney merrily whipping up her own cake batter, using fresh eggs, butter and milk.

The First Lady quietly set her little present down on the counter and walked through the swinging doors into the dining room, where I stood checking a list of items to go in the big, new storehouse behind the barn.

"They might as well live high on the hog while they can," she said drily, "because they won't be able to live like that after we move back, when they're living off me."

Moving out has been a sad occasion for all the First Ladies. Even Mrs. Truman, who had expressed such relief at getting back to Independence, missed the hustle-and-bustle, the instant service, all the little pleasantries of White House life. It was even harder for Mamie Eisenhower, who had so thoroughly established herself as "Lady of the House."

When she first came there, she'd been disappointed at the furnishings. Now, on leaving, she thought they were grand.

During the Eisenhowers, there had been more drastic changes in White House life than in any previous administration, but the changes came gradually and the Eisenhowers adjusted easily. Television, for one thing, had become a permanent part of the Presidency, as well as an entertainment medium for the First Family; air conditioning made it possible for the family to use the mansion all summer long; jet planes carried them all over the world and back within days, and brought friends and supporters in from all over the country for an evening, revolutionizing

White House guest lists; the office of the Presidency had grown so that it filled the west wing, halls and basement, and the old State-War-Navy Building next door.

Our White House had grown, too, in this postwar era, and not just because of the increased size of the renovated mansion. Now, we had a staff of seventy-two, ten more than when I began during the Roosevelts. But this work force was nowhere near sufficient to take care of the enlarged patterns of White House living. Rather than ask Congress to increase our appropriation (all Presidents are reluctant to ask for a household raise from Congress), we found it necessary to draw upon resources and manpower from other government agencies to run the place. And those agencies, ever delighted to get a foot in the White House door, were only too happy to lend assistance.

The Navy, which came in through the ground floor during the Trumans, operated a little "staff mess" underneath the President's offices in the west wing. Cooks and waiters were primarily Filipino servicemen from the same Navy personnel force that had staffed Presidential yachts since the Spanish-American War. This little dining room was operated like an exclusive private club, with Presidential assistants during the Eisenhower and succeeding administrations vying for the status of membership there. When the renovated mansion needed extra help, Mrs. Truman requested additional Navy stewards to work as pantry-helpers; Mrs. Eisenhower added two more Navy Filipinos to help with heavy cleaning upstairs. And so nobody ever had to ask Congress for salaries for more servants.

During the evolution of the White House, the military moved in in other ways, too. The Air Force now provided all the President's transportation—three planes, helicopters, and personnel to fly, navigate, maintain and serve on them.* Gone were the days of the Presidential railroad

* The Air Force estimated that the Presidential plane, the *Columbine III*, which cost $3 million, cost $711 per hour to run. And although the yacht *Williamsburg* had been put in mothballs in 1953, the Navy still spent about $60,000 a year to maintain the smaller craft, the 92-foot *Barbara Anne*, and the 60-foot *Suzie E.*

car, "Ferdinand Magellan," and the President paying for his own train ticket—although Mrs. Eisenhower still used the trains and paid her own way. For years the Army had supplied drivers and gasoline for the fleet of twenty White House limousines and utility trucks. Then, of course, there was the Signal Corps, who handled all the electronic communications and photographic equipment, with at least a fifty-man contingent in the White House. And the Marine Orchestra, a twenty-two-man unit at the President's disposal. And General Snyder and Col. Tkach, the physicians. If the military didn't run the White House, they still staffed a great deal of it.

From the Treasury Department, the President's protective force had been increased to at least twice the personnel and equipment of Roosevelt days. (This peacetime President was barraged with more threats, his house surrounded by more pickets than had ever occurred during the "hot" wars.) From the Park Service came workmen to care for the sixteen acres of White House grounds. And from General Services, engineers, plumbers, builders, to assist the regular maintenance staff.

The complexities of the modern Presidency thrust upon General Eisenhower and his wife a different style of living from past Presidents. But it was a style that they easily adjusted to, and even designed, themselves, because of their experience with the attendant personal power of a high military command. They enlarged the scope of the White House, taking, for the first time, personnel and equipment out of the mansion itself to Gettysburg, a non-government weekend and summer retreat. The White House was now beginning to be looked upon as anywhere the President happened to be, rather than just the eighteenth-century mansion at 1600 Pennsylvania Avenue.

It was a complex world in which we found ourselves in January, 1961, as we packed up paintings, trophies, and gowns for the Eisenhowers. Regal, sentimental Mamie Eisenhower was the last First Lady born in the nineteenth century. She was the first to leave the White House in the Space Age.

The
Kennedys

1

Jacqueline Kennedy whispered. Or so I thought, at first. Actually, she spoke so softly that one was forced to listen intently, forced to focus on her face and respond to her direct, compelling eyes. There was wonder in those eyes, determination, humor, and—sometimes—vulnerability.

When she looked around a crowded room as if searching for the nearest exit, people assumed that she was shy, uncertain. I don't think she was ever shy. It was merely her method of studying the situation: memorizing the room, or assessing the people in it. She spoke no small talk —no "I'm so very glad to meet you and what does your husband do?" She limited her conversation merely to what, in her opinion, mattered.

Her interests were wide, however, as was her knowledge, and she had a subtle, ingenious way of getting things accomplished.

I soon learned that Mrs. Kennedy's wish, murmured with a "Do you think . . ." or "Could you please . . ." was as much a command as Mrs. Eisenhower's "I want this done immediately."

Mrs. Eisenhower had called me to her bedroom one morning several weeks after the 1960 election.

"I've invited Mrs. Kennedy for a tour of the house at noon on December 9," she said. "Please have the rooms in order, but no servants on the upstairs floors. And I plan to leave at one thirty, so have my car ready."

"Mrs. Kennedy's Secret Service agent phoned from the hospital this morning," I told the outgoing First Lady. "She asked that we have a wheelchair for her when she arrives."

At that moment, Mrs. Kennedy was still at Georgetown Hospital, recovering from her Caesarian surgery of November 25, when John F. Kennedy, Jr., was born.

"Oh, dear," Mrs. Eisenhower frowned. "I wanted to take her around alone."

The thought of Mamie Eisenhower, the grandest of the First Ladies, pushing a wheelchair through the corridors of the White House—especially when the passenger had been a political enemy—was too much for me.

"I'll tell you what . . ." her carefully manicured fingernails drummed the night table. "We'll get a wheelchair, but put it behind a door somewhere, out of sight. It will be available *if she asks for it*," she said.

On the morning of December 9, the house was spruced up in its Christmas best, the wheelchair hidden in a closet beside the elevator, and I was waiting at the south entrance to meet the future First Lady.

Just before noon, the Secret Service agent who had been assigned to Mrs. Kennedy drove a dark blue station wagon into the circular driveway. She was sitting in the front seat, next to him.

Harriston, the silent, genial doorman, opened the door for her.

"Thank you," she smiled at him, and stepped out.

I was struck by how young she appeared. Dressed in a dark coat, wearing hat and gloves, she could have been a young Congressman's wife paying an obligatory call. She was taller than I had realized, as tall as I, even in her low heels. Very thin, it seemed to me, and quite pale.

"I'm Mr. West, the Chief Usher," I introduced myself.

"I'm Jacqueline Kennedy," she whispered. As if I didn't know.

She stepped, a bit hesitantly I thought, into the Diplomatic Reception Room, looked around at the walls, sofas, and rug, and, without saying another word, walked with me through the green-carpeted hallway toward the elevator. Her wide, uncertain eyes took in everything around her, and I could tell she was somewhat ill-at-ease.

"Mrs. Eisenhower is waiting upstairs," I explained, as we entered the elevator.

She did not reply.

I thought suddenly of my daughter Kathy, who is always shy at first, and reveals nothing of herself until she is perfectly sure of her surroundings. Once sure, however, she takes over completely. Every time.

As the elevator door opened to the second floor, Jacqueline Kennedy took a deep, audible breath.

Mrs. Eisenhower stood in the center hall, a tiny figure under the high ceilings, surrounded by the beige expanse of hall. And very much in command.

"Mrs. Kennedy," I announced. Mrs. Eisenhower did not come forward.

As I escorted the young woman across the room to meet her formidable hostess, I was very much aware that neither lady had looked forward to this meeting.

"Hello, Mrs. Kennedy," Mrs. Eisenhower gave a nod and extended her hand in her most gracious meet-the-visitor pose. "I do hope you are feeling much better now. And how is the baby?"

I turned and left them, and waited in my office for a call for the wheelchair, a call that never came. At 1:30 on the dot, the two buzzers rang, indicating First Lady descending, and I dashed to the elevator.

The two women walked out the south entrance, where their cars were waiting. After the goodbyes and thankyous, Mrs. Eisenhower stepped regally into the back seat of her Chrysler limousine and disappeared, off to her card game. Mrs. Kennedy walked slowly over to her three-year-old station wagon. As I caught up with her, to give her blueprints and photographs of the rooms, I saw pain darken her face.

192

TOP: A favorite picture of President and Mrs. Franklin D. Roosevelt, photographed the summer before Pearl Harbor, which they sent to friends at Christmas, 1941. Mrs. Roosevelt's hands were always busy. If she weren't writing, she would be knitting, as in this picture. BOTTOM: President Roosevelt never let his simple wooden wheelchair show in his public appearances until the last year of his life. Here, in his bedroom, it sits in a corner next to the window. In addition to ship prints and photographs of family triumphs, Mr. Roosevelt collected small donkey statues —the symbol of the Democratic Party.

TOP LEFT: Mrs. Roosevelt's sitting room was "papered" with photographs of the Roosevelt family and friends, including her uncle, Theodore Roosevelt. Here she entertained family and personal visitors and listened to the radio (corner, on chest). Mrs. Roosevelt herself slept in a single bed in the smaller room attached. BOTTOM LEFT: President Roosevelt's oval study on the second floor of the White House. His desk, a gift to the United States from Queen Victoria, was used in this room by President Truman prior to 1948. President Kennedy had it in his office in the west wing. ABOVE: President Roosevelt's bedroom, adjoining his oval study on the second floor, contained a modified hospital bed and a heavy wardrobe. Interspersed with the President's naval prints are early scenes of the White House and photographs of the President's family, including (left) a large photograph of Eleanor Roosevelt.

TOP LEFT: President Truman's bedroom, with the antique four-poster later used by Presidents Kennedy and Johnson as well. In corner beside bed is a replica of the Presidential seal, on top of radio. Andrew Jackson, one of Mr. Truman's favorite Presidents, looks out from the wall. MIDDLE LEFT: President Truman's study, early 1948 (prior to the renovation of the White House). On the desk are photographs of his daughter, Margaret, and a young Bess Truman. On the wall to the left of the fireplace is a portrait of Mr. Truman's mother. To the right of the fireplace is the White House piano placed in the room by Mr. Truman. BOTTOM LEFT: Mrs. Truman's bedroom, formerly Mrs. Roosevelt's bedroom. As in her sitting room, the colors were lavender and gray, and she had her wardrobe doors covered to match the curtains. At left is a corner of the narrow single bed in which she slept, as did Mrs. Roosevelt before her. Beside the fireplace, the utilitarian hair dryer. ABOVE: Mrs. Truman's sitting room, prior to the renovation. Mrs. Truman selected the colors, lavender, gray, and mauve, and the flowered chintz curtains during her husband's first two weeks as President. The furniture, all White House property, had been used elsewhere in the White House under the Roosevelts.

TOP LEFT: Inside the White House—upstairs, downstairs, and no stairs—during the renovation of the White House. In this photograph, made June 6, 1950, steel braces support the outside walls while excavation begins for a new basement. At left is the north wall, which faces Pennsylvania Avenue. BOTTOM LEFT: President and Mrs. Truman move back into the White House after 1948–52 renovation, March 27, 1952. To welcome the Trumans, left, behind the President, Usher Charles Claunch; behind Mrs. Truman, Chief Usher Howell G. Crim; at door, right, Alonzo Fields, maître d', whose sturdy steps caused the chandeliers to tremble; and the author, J. B. West, then assistant to the Chief Usher. ABOVE: Heavy Victorian mirrors such as this were prominent in all the family rooms and guest rooms in the prerestoration White House. (This room, across the hall from the President's study, overlooking the North Portico, was used by Joseph Lash under the Roosevelts; then by Reathel Odum, Mrs. Truman's secretary.)

LEFT: Chief Usher J. B. West stands to the right of Mary Jane Mc-Caffree, social secretary to Mrs. Eisenhower, and Major Armand C. Elzey, senior social aide, in the Diplomatic Reception Room, ground floor of the White House. The portrait above the mantel, one of the finest in the White House collection, is of Angelica Singleton Van Buren, daughter-in-law of and White House hostess to President Martin Van Buren (painted in 1842 by Henry Inman). TOP ABOVE: The Center Hall, second floor of the White House, prior to the renovation. Mr. Truman's official portrait by Greta Kempton is on left (north wall). William M. Chase portrait of President James Buchanan on right (south wall). Doorway, center right wall, leads to the President's Study; arched doorway, center of photograph, leads to East Sitting Hall. President Truman's portrait was later (January, 1953) placed on the state floor. BOTTOM ABOVE: West Sitting Hall, under the Trumans. Greta Kempton's portrait of Margaret Truman is on the north wall. This White House furniture, all reproductions, was retired to the warehouse during the 1961–63 restoration.

TOP LEFT: The President's bedroom, used by Mr. Eisenhower as a dressing room and for naps, was decorated during the 1948-52 renovation. Above the bed is a Colorado landscape painted by Mr. Eisenhower. Painting at left is of the President's grandchildren, David and Barbara Anne Eisenhower. MIDDLE LEFT: The Eisenhower's king-sized bed, with the pink-tufted headboard designed by Mrs. Eisenhower, was covered with a bedspread in the same pink-and-green fabric as the curtains, which the First Lady had brought across the hall from Margaret Truman's sitting room. The walls and carpet were Williamsburg green, the bench, chair at left, and dust ruffle in the same pink as the headboard. The painting above the bed is a landscape by Mr. Eisenhower. BOTTOM LEFT: The Trophy Room, also used by President Eisenhower as a study. The room, on the second floor, is oval, as is the President's official office in the west wing. Mr. Eisenhower's desk was a gift to the White House during the 1948-52 renovation. The portrait on the wall is of President Eisenhower's father, David Jacob Eisenhower. ABOVE: President Eisenhower's study was known as the Trophy Room because it contained a large case displaying all of his medals, military decorations, and citations from foreign governments. On the round table is the Order of the Elephant, presented to General Eisenhower by the government of India.

TOP LEFT: The West Sitting Hall, under the Eisenhowers in the same red "George Washington" toile fabric of the Trumans' renovation. Here, the President and Mrs. Eisenhower, with Mrs. Doud, Mrs. Eisenhower's mother, had dinner on tray tables, nearly every night, while watching the news on the new television set (built into the north wall, at right). Portrait on south wall (left) is of the Eisenhowers' son, John, while a cadet at West Point. MIDDLE LEFT: President and Mrs. Eisenhower celebrating their wedding anniversary at Gettysburg, Pennsylvania, July 1, 1955. The party for White House staff was also the occasion of a housewarming at the newly renovated farmhouse. Here J. B. West presents President and Mrs. Eisenhower with a gift from the White House staff—an engraved silver tray and table. BOTTOM LEFT: "I want to make this the most beautiful Christmas ever," said Mrs. Eisenhower of her last Christmas in the White House, 1960. As in past years, she decorated the front lobby with ropes of holly, Christmas-tree balls, wreaths, big red bows, lights, red poinsettias with white-sprayed branches. ABOVE: The Grand Staircase, seen from the main entrance hall of the White House, early in the Eisenhower administration. Portrait of President Franklin D. Roosevelt, by Frank O. Salisbury, faces the lobby; on the staircase wall are earlier Presidents, from the collection of official White House portraits.

LEFT: The Center Hall on the second floor, after the Kennedy restoration, was filled with antique furniture and objets d'art. In the right corner, beside the door, is the black baby grand piano that had been in President Truman's study. Chinese lacquer screens, a gift to the White House, add interest to the doorway. On the north wall, right, are paintings of American Indians by George Catlin that Mrs. Kennedy borrowed from the Smithsonian. TOP ABOVE: The Center Hall, as used by the Eisenhowers, was decorated in beige during the renovation, with accents of red in the sofa and chairs. The crystal chandeliers were acquired during the renovation. Portrait of George Washington is at left. BOTTOM ABOVE: In the Inaugural Parade reviewing stand in front of the White House, January 20, 1961. In the front row, left to right, Ambassador Joseph P. Kennedy, Mrs. John F. Kennedy, the newly inaugurated President, Vice President Lyndon B. Johnson, Mrs. Johnson, and the Kennedys' friend William Walton. Second row, behind President Kennedy, is Mr. West, greeting former President and Mrs. Harry S. Truman. Seated beside the Trumans is Speaker of the House Sam Rayburn.

TOP LEFT: The rose, white, and blue Monroe Room, where President Eisenhower played bridge, was changed to the Treaty Room during the Kennedy restoration. Here, as it was under the Eisenhowers, portraits of President and Mrs. James Monroe hang over the mantel. The fireplaces were never used by the Eisenhowers; Mrs. Eisenhower placed gold paper fans in each. MIDDLE LEFT: President Kennedy's bedroom, with the antique four-poster that Truman had used. To ease his painful back Mr. Kennedy used the heating pad, on night table shelf, and the rocking chair. The President's bedroom was off-white, with blue and white fabric for the canopy and bedspread. Painting on the wall is "Flag Day," by Childe Hassam in 1917, a gift to the White House in 1963. This bedroom remained unchanged during the Johnson administration. BOTTOM LEFT: Mrs. Kennedy's bedroom was white, with accents of light blue in the silk curtains, bedspread, chair covering, and mats on the pictures. Above the chest, left of fireplace, is a pastel drawing of Caroline. On the floor, behind the silk-covered round table, is Caroline's gingerbread house. ABOVE: The Treaty Room was the one room Mrs. Kennedy conceded to Victorian decor. The carpets and walls are dark green; draperies and wall pattern, dark red. Used as the Cabinet Room during the administration of Andrew Johnson, it contains copies of treaties signed in this room. On the wall to the right of the mirror is a portrait of President Andrew Johnson. The table, swivel chair, and clock were originally used in this room; the chairs at the table were used in the family dining room. The large crystal chandelier originally hung in the East Room.

same color as panel for screen – SA
went left central – Or you could keep the
ballns desk by that window flush with wall
+ pull it out at right angles to wall when
setting is going on – If a just the same –
You + Bill beside which looks best –

Another idea for table – One panel at
the screen rectangle – not with carved leg –
want bass stills – just laid across 2 columns
painted black – at the right height – simple
as carpenter shop could make –

This may be a nuisance
not + in or in furniture
+ costs etc – but let us
start at once with any table available – at just
the right one – (the old possible but that size in 2nd
the hall under banisters to stick with – got have in there
I day had with ink) as everything is soaked – But
a Kansas from us so that this has only we got it here

Bill – give to Mr West.

THE WHITE HOUSE
WASHINGTON

Mr West –

The President tells me that J.K. McNally
(always against selling quakes in beginning) and
says he'd move would be sold one way out – but
finally says this is your province + doesn't have
opinion it – which is rather sweet of him

I agree + we can use the B. Hall
you have a table set up at Entrance Hall 9-12
during public tours – where guards sit –
I suggest 3 bridge or washed tables (like I have
by bar bookcase in West Hall) in a row – or – a
trestle table – long plank of wood on 2 supports
that could be easily stacked away when not in use
It could be covered with a piece of red felt

TOP LEFT: Mrs. Kennedy's dressing room, adjoining her bedroom via the mirrored door (right corner), was decorated in light-blue silk taffeta, with white rug and woodwork. On the table and right corner wall are family photographs. A trompe d'oeil painting decorates the closet doors. BOTTOM LEFT: Mrs. Kennedy's memo to Mr. West for selling the White House guidebook. TOP ABOVE: The West Sitting Hall, during the Kennedy administration, was transformed with antiques. At left, on the south wall, is a French Empire desk that belonged to Mrs. Kennedy's father, John Vernou Bouvier. In the center of the hall is an antique mahogany and satinwood octagonal desk, a gift to the White House from New York entrepreneur Jules Stein. On the north wall, right, is an antique marble-top French commode, a gift to Mrs. Kennedy from President Charles de Gaulle of France. BOTTOM ABOVE: The yellow oval room on the second floor, formerly a study for Presidents Roosevelt, Truman, and Eisenhower (Trophy Room), opens onto the Truman balcony. It became a Louis XVI drawing room during the Kennedy restoration and was the favorite room of Mrs. Kennedy, Mrs. Johnson, and Mrs. Nixon. Above the mantel is Rembrandt Peale's portrait of George Washington. At the doorway leading to the President's bedroom stand the colors—the United States flag and the President's flag.

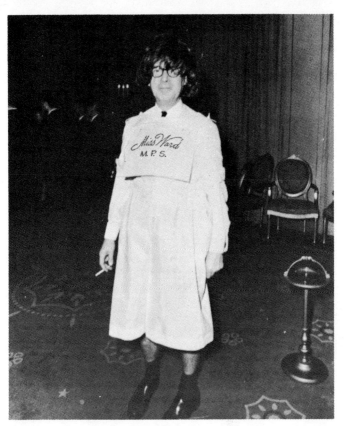

TOP LEFT: Former President Harry S. Truman plays Paderewski's Minuet in G on the Baldwin concert grand piano which was given to the White House during the Truman administration. The 1961 program in the East Room featured pianist Eugene List (standing behind Mr. Truman), who, as a soldier, had entertained the participants at the Potsdam Conference. President Kennedy, standing, is on his way to his front-row-center chair. Seated, left to right, former Secretary of the Treasury John Snyder, Mrs. Kennedy, Mrs. Johnson, and Mrs. Tom Clark, wife of the former Supreme Court Justice. Standing in the East Room doorway is J. B. West, Chief Usher of the White House. BOTTOM LEFT: Chief Usher J. B. West, with Mrs. Kennedy's two social secretaries, Nancy Tuckerman (left, white dress) and Tish Baldrige (center, back to camera), at a farewell party for Tish in the China Room, on the ground floor of the White House. At right is Marine combo, who sang "Arrivederci Tish," written by Mrs. Kennedy. ABOVE: "Miss Ward," Jacqueline Bouvier's housemother at Miss Porter's School (M.P.S.), as portrayed at the First Lady's suggestion by J. B. West at a birthday party for Nancy Tuckerman, Mrs. Kennedy's social secretary and former roommate at Miss Porter's.

THE WHITE HOUSE
WASHINGTON

In this room lived John Fitzgerald Kennedy with his wife Jacqueline — during the two years ten months and 2 days he was president of the United States January 20 1961 - November 22 1963

LEFT: The first snowfall of 1962 brought Mrs. Kennedy and the children to the south lawn, for a ride in an old-fashioned "one-horse open sleigh," complete with sleigh bells. When the snow began to fall, Mrs. Kennedy sent for Caroline's pony, Macaroni, and the sleigh, both of which were at Glen Ora, the Virginia country place the Kennedys had rented. TOP ABOVE: Prayer card selected by Mrs. Kennedy and presented at the door of St. Matthew's Cathedral to all attending the President's funeral, November 25, 1963. BOTTOM ABOVE: Mrs. Kennedy's note, of December 2, 1963, with the inscription she wished to leave in the White House, to be placed on the mantel in her bedroom. The mantel already had one plaque, stating that Abraham Lincoln had slept in the room.

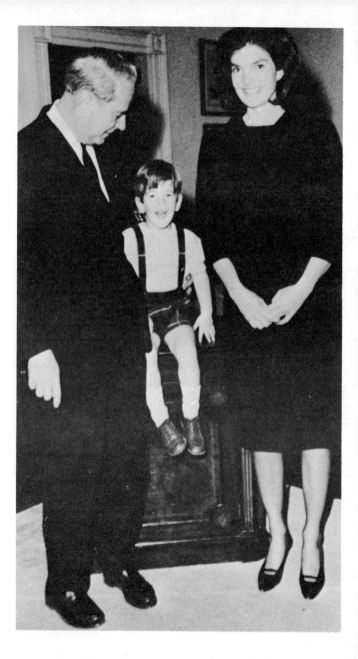

LEFT: On her last day in the White House, December 6, 1963, Mrs. Kennedy pauses in the West Hall upstairs (second floor—known as the Family Sitting Room) to say good-bye to Mr. West. John F. Kennedy, Jr. is seated on an antique octagonal desk presented to the White House during the Kennedy restoration. TOP ABOVE: The Johnsons move into the White House, December 7, 1963. Chief Usher J. B. West was at the Diplomatic (South) Entrance to greet Mrs. Johnson (carrying a photograph of the late Sam Rayburn, Speaker of the House of Representatives) and sixteen-year-old Luci Baines, who arrived in the convertible at right with Him and Her (foreground). BOTTOM ABOVE: Mrs. Johnson's bedroom, with the white walls and carpet that Mrs. Kennedy used, was decorated in green velvet, yellow silk, and rose-and-green curtains and bedspread. Over the fireplace is a French Impressionist landscape owned by Mrs. Johnson; to the left is a portrait of President Johnson.

TOP LEFT: The West Sitting Hall, redecorated by Mrs. Johnson, was rarely used by the First Lady because there were too many doors. Doors at right, on north wall, opened onto the second-floor kitchen; those at left, to Mr. Johnson's dressing room and bedroom. Above the commode on which Mrs. Johnson displayed photographs of Caroline Kennedy with her pony, Tex, is a French Impressionist painting on loan to the White House. BOTTOM LEFT: State dinner in the Rose Garden, honoring Dr. Ludwig Erhard, Chancellor of West Germany, was an innovation under the Johnsons, on June 12, 1964. President and Mrs. Johnson received the guests in the East Room before dinner was served on the round tables just outside the President's office window. During dinner, the red-uniformed Marine orchestra played (center). After dinner, the National Symphony Orchestra played from the band shell on the south lawn, and dancers Maria Tallchief and Jacques D'Amboise presented a ballet program. Afterward champagne was served from tents. ABOVE: J. B. West, Chief Usher of the White House, and Mrs. Johnson's social secretary, Bess Abell, planning final details for a State dinner in the Rose Garden, June 12, 1964.

LEFT: Mrs. Johnson appeared on the grand staircase early on the morning of her daughter Luci's wedding, August 6, 1966, to survey the masses of pink-and-white flowers decorating the state floor of the White House. Luci was married to Patrick Nugent at the Shrine of the Immaculate Conception, and their huge wedding reception was held at the White House. TOP ABOVE: The Catlin Indians, in the Center Hall, were much admired by Mrs. Johnson, but were sent back to the Smithsonian early in the Nixon administration. (At right is a Copley portrait, then on loan to the White House.) BOTTOM ABOVE: For the reception following Lynda Bird Johnson's wedding to Marine Captain Charles Robb, December 9, 1967, guests overflowed from the State Dining Room into a heated pink tent covering the West Terrace (over the swimming pool). Seated inside the tent are Chief Usher J. B. West, (right) White House Curator James Ketchum, and their wives.

LEFT: J. B. West, Chief Usher of the White House, confers with Head Butler John Ficklin, before a dinner in the State Dining Room, during the Johnson administration. On the round table, set for ten, is the Lincoln china, the Monroe vermeil flatware, and the West Virginia "President's House" crystal. The multicolored flower arrangement is typical of those used during the Kennedy and Johnson administrations. *Photo by James P. Blair, National Geographic.* ABOVE: On November 11, 1968, Mrs. Lyndon B. Johnson invited Mrs. Richard M. Nixon to the White House to discuss the day-to-day operation of the President's home. In the West Sitting Hall Chief Usher J. B. West shows the two First Ladies blueprints of the mansion.

TOP: Chief Usher J. B. West, at his headquarters just inside the front door of the White House. BOTTOM: His last day in the White House, March 1, 1969, Chief Usher J. B. West passed up the traditional farewell party for luncheon in the kitchen. Chef Henry Haller (center) and pastry chef Heinz Bender (right) served Mr. West and his wife, Zella, a four-course gourmet luncheon.

"Could you please send them to Palm Beach for me?" she asked. "We're going there to rest until Inauguration Day."

Two months later, as we were tromping around the third floor, Mrs. Kennedy suddenly turned to me.

"Mr. West, did you know that my doctor ordered a wheelchair the day I first went around the White House?" she asked.

"Yes, I did," I answered.

She looked bewildered.

"Then why didn't you have it for me? I was so exhausted after marching around this house for two hours that I had to go back to bed for two whole weeks!"

She stared into my eyes, searching for an explanation.

"Well," I answered carefully, "it was certainly there, waiting for you. Right behind the closet door next to the elevator. We were waiting for you to request it."

To my surprise, she giggled. "I was too scared of Mrs. Eisenhower to ask," she whispered. From that moment, I never saw Jacqueline Kennedy uncertain again.

Mrs. Eisenhower's feelings about the young Mrs. Kennedy were never spoken, only intimated.

The morning after Mrs. Kennedy's arduous tour, Charles Ficklin, Mabel Walker, and I went up to the Eisenhowers' bedroom for our daily conference. As usual, the First Lady sat propped up against her pink headboard, with a bow in her hair, picking at the breakfast on her tray.

". . . See that the maids begin packing all my summer clothes first," she finished instructing the housekeeper, then dismissed her.

"Change the lamb stew to beef, and leave out the potatoes," she approved Charles' menu, dismissing him, too.

The President's wife took a bite of grapefruit, then looked at me.

"Well . . . ?" she asked, one eyebrow raised quizzically.

"The moving vans are scheduled to arrive on January 2 to take the first load to Gettysburg," I answered innocently.

"She's planning to redo every room in this house," Mrs. Eisenhower said. "You've got *quite* a project ahead of you." Then, in the voice she reserved for disapproval:

225

"There certainly are going to be some changes made around here!"

Little did I realize how prophetic Mrs. Eisenhower's statement was. Throughout the next thirty-four months, not only would I become involved in coordinating the transformation of the mansion—from historic house to national monument—but also, I would have to adjust White House management from a regimented, stylized order-of-business to that of running an impromptu, informal household.

I would find myself dealing with Empire tables and rabbit cages; housing Maharajahs and ponies; steaming down the Potomac and wearing disguises; and thoroughly enjoying the most creative and challenging work to which the Chief Usher had ever been put.

The new First Lady turned the White House inside out, and she imprinted her own rarefied life style upon the mansion. But the greatest change in the White House was brought about by the presence of Jacqueline Bouvier Kennedy herself. She was thirty years younger than any of the First Ladies I had served, and, I was to discover, had the most complex personality of them all. In public, she was elegant, aloof, dignified, and regal. In private, she was casual, impish, and irreverent. She had a will of iron, with more determination than anyone I have ever met. Yet she was so soft-spoken, so deft and subtle, that she could impose that will upon people without their ever knowing it.

Her wit—teasing, exaggerating, poking fun at everything, including herself—was a surprise and a daily delight. She was imaginative, inventive, intelligent—and sometimes silly. Yet there were subjects that did not amuse her one bit.

Relaxed and uninhibited, she was always popping up anywhere, wearing slacks, sitting on the floor, kicking off her shoes, her hair flying in every direction. We all had fun along with her. Yet she also drew a line against familiarity which could not be crossed.

It was only with the cameras grinding or guests coming in the front door that the seriousness, the poise, the coolness that were also part of her, began to appear.

She had a total mastery of detail—endless, endless detail —and she was highly organized, yet rarely held herself to a schedule. For others, she insisted upon order; for herself, she preferred spontaneity. She took advice readily, but only when she asked for it, and she strongly resisted being pushed.

The trick was to read her correctly, to accomplish everything she wanted, and not to oppose her in anything. And it *was* a trick, because sometimes she was so subtle she needed a translator.

I saw her move swiftly into three different roles: wife and mother to her young children; commander-in-chief of the White House restoration; and chatelaine of the Great Hall.

The changes in the White House began on Inauguration Day, 1961.

"Please put me in the Queen's Room," Jacqueline Kennedy had told me the week before, "and my husband will stay in the Lincoln bedroom. We'll move into the family quarters as soon as they're done over. But I do wish there were some way we could get the decorating finished before the Inauguration!"

The morning of January 20, Mrs. Eisenhower read in the newspaper that Jacqueline Kennedy would sleep in the Queen's Room.

At our breakfast meeting, she confronted me:

"Who suggested that sleeping arrangement? . . . *You*, I suppose!"

Mrs. Eisenhower kept the Queen's Room as a special guest room, and you had to *be* a Queen to sleep there. She didn't think Mrs. Kennedy fit that requirement.

Inauguration Day is easily the busiest day of the year for the entire Executive Mansion staff. While the changing-of-the-guard takes place officially a mile away at the Capitol steps, it happens physically at the White House. Not only do we gear up for receiving important visitors from all over the country, sometimes with a formal reception after the Inaugural Parade, but we also must move the outgoing President's belongings out, and the incoming President's belongings in during the two hours of Inaugural activities at the Capitol. Every carpenter, plumber, electrician, engineer, doorman, butler is put to work.

The rule, of course, is that one Head of State occupies the mansion until his successor takes the oath of office. But White House tradition also has it that not one box, not one dressing table, not one book of the new President's must enter the mansion until he is duly sworn in. And we make it a point of pride to do all the moving, unpacking, hanging-up and putting-away, installing the new President in his home within those two hours of his Inaugural ceremony.

So, at noon on January 20, 1961, while President John F. Kennedy stood in front of the Capitol steps urging his fellow Americans to ". . . ask what you can do for your country . . . ," we were *doing*. Two sets of vans rolled down to the tradesman's entrance underneath the North Portico: One to carry what was left of the Eisenhowers' furniture to their Gettysburg farm; the other to bring in the Kennedy's clothing and personal effects.

Actually, very quietly and at the request of Mrs. Kennedy's social secretary, I had been receiving numerous boxes of toys and children's furniture from the Kennedys' Georgetown home during the two weeks prior to Inauguration. Lest anyone accuse me of breaking tradition, I stored them in the Usher's dressing room until noon, Inauguration Day, when a helicopter spirited away the last of Mamie Eisenhower's treasures, the portrait of her mother and a small electric organ.

When Mrs. Kennedy returned, exhausted, from the Inaugural Parade, I accompanied her up the stairs. Her tired eyes twinkled conspiratorially.

"I understand you and Tish [Baldrige] have been sneaking things into the White House under cover of night."

I laughed. "All those things now have been put in storage rooms on the third floor."

"Good. We'll bring them out as soon as the children's rooms are ready." She smiled as she stepped into the Queen's Room. "We've got a lot of work ahead, Mr. West. I want to make this into a grand house!"

To begin that work, Mrs. Henry Parish II, known to all as "Sister," arrived the very next day, with swatches of material, paint chips, closet designs. During the previous month, the New York interior designer and the new President's wife had pored over the color photographs I had sent via Secret Service to Palm Beach.

Mrs. Kennedy had done her homework well. By the time she moved in, she knew every inch of room space, every piece of furniture she would bring with her, every detail of where her family would live in the White House, and every penny of money in the federal budget to take care of the transformation.

Beginning on January 22, crews of White House painters, carpenters, plumbers, and electricians worked simultaneously in the seven family rooms on the second floor of the White House. As the paint in each room dried, the same workmen hung pictures and rolled down rugs, unloaded furniture and arranged it according to the decorator's instructions.

The household staff stood awed by all the changes.

"I can't believe what they're doing," housekeeper Mabel Walker told me.

At every step, Mrs. Kennedy roamed the mansion, discovering "treasures" and removing "horrors." ("If there's anything I can't stand, it's Victorian mirrors—they're hideous. Off to the dungeons with them," she declared, laughing.)

Within the next two weeks, while the President and his wife reigned from the Queen's Room and the Lincoln suite, the "Mamie pink" of upstairs disappeared, the Grand Rapids furniture and heavy Victorian mirrors were packed away in storage. The carpenters and painters changed the dark walls to soft white, a background for the paintings, drawings, and prints from the Kennedys' private collection, and a new sophisticated blue dominated the President's living quarters.

The hotel-suite decor of Truman-renovation guest rooms made way for Caroline Kennedy's pink rosebuds, white-canopied bed and rockinghorses. A wine-floral guest room became John-John's blue-and-white nursery, with white crib and playpen, and stuffed animals.

Between their bedrooms, we changed a dressing-room closet into a room for the nurse, Maude Shaw. ("She won't need much," Mrs. Kennedy whispered merrily. "Just find a wicker wastebacket for her banana peels and a little table for her false teeth at night.")

After a disastrous first-night dinner in the White House, when the Kennedys learned that the State Floor, even with its Family Dining Room, could not lend itself to the intimacy of their private entertaining, Mrs. Kennedy determined to install a dining room on the second floor.

"I want my children to be brought up in more personal surroundings, not in the State rooms," she told me. "That 'Family' Dining Room is just too cavernous." (Previous First Families had thought so, too, I told her.) Because of the location of the servants' elevator, I advised her to place the dining room across the hall from her bedroom, where she had originally wanted the nursery. In this arrangement, the children were down the hall, giving the President and his wife more privacy.

"We'll need a kitchen up here," she mused. "Do you think that could possibly be done?"

"Certainly," I said, looking at our shrinking budget. "Would you like to see some kitchen designers?"

"Heavens no," she laughed. "I couldn't care less about the kitchen! Just make it white and ask René what he wants in there."

René Verdon, the new French chef, Mrs. Parish and I designed a stainless-steel-and-white kitchen, with commercial-size ovens and refrigerators, which I ordered from a local wholesaler. Within two days it replaced the dusty-rose bedroom where President Eisenhower's mother-in-law had slept.

Hallmark of the new upstairs was Art: Gallery walls, filled with paintings and watercolors, original art in every corner: in the President's bedroom, in Mrs. Kennedy's bedroom, in the children's rooms, and in the halls.

From the Smithsonian, she "borrowed" twenty portraits of proud American Indians, painted by George Catlin. She selected the frames herself and displayed the paintings prominently on the walls of the wide center hall upstairs. And she set about to retrieve some magnificent Cézanne landscapes originally bequeathed to the White House, which President Truman had placed in the National Gallery of Art.

One morning during those first whirlwind days of re-decorating, Mrs. Kennedy poked her head in my office. "Guess what?" she announced. "Mrs. Vincent Astor is presenting us with some fantastic wallpaper for the President's Dining Room, and. . . ." She stopped in midsentence.

"Oh, Mr. West, you have a Grandma Moses!" she exclaimed, indicating the Fourth of July scene by the famous American painter, presented to the Trumans. President Eisenhower disliked the primitive oil painting so much that he banished it from sight, and it hung exiled on my wall.

"No, Mrs. Kennedy, *you* have a Grandma Moses," I replied. "It belongs to the White House."

"What a marvelous discovery—how I'd love it for Caroline's room," she said. "Would you mind terribly, Mr. West?"

We hung the colorful painting on Caroline's wall, across from another American primitive and a French Impressionist landscape.

The President's bedroom lost the murky green of the Eisenhower years, and acquired the canopied four-poster from the wine-floral guest room. For the old bed, Mrs. Kennedy ordered a special, extra-firm mattress to ease the President's back. She also ordered an identical, horse-hair mattress for the President to take on trips, and another for one side of the queen-sized bed in her own bedroom.

In a note to me, she vetoed the first design for the First Lady's bedroom, the big room the Eisenhowers had shared. Although she realized the decorator was thinking of a room "severe enough for a man to share," she explained, "it is mainly my room and I do not want it *too* severe."

Her room was French in style, decorated in light blue chintz, accented with leopard-skin throws and good pictures—a boudoir fit to entertain a President. It was soft, relaxed, and elegant.

By the end of two weeks, we had used our entire $50,000 appropriation just to redecorate the family living quarters. Because the exterior of the mansion had been dressed in its four-year coat of white paint the previous summer, there was absolutely no money left to put grandeur into the State rooms.

"I know we're out of money, Mr. West," she said wistfully, "but never mind! We're going to find some way to get real antiques into this house."

During those first weeks, I had discovered two things about Mrs. John Fitzgerald Kennedy: her innate sense of organization and planning, and her irrepressible humor. Every day, she said something that was just plain funny.

Comic metaphors cropped up in all her notes to me, amusing me no end. She thought the bedroom curtains were "seasick green," their fringe like a "tired Christmas tree." The ground-floor hall was a "dentist's office bomb shelter," the East Room floor a "roller skating rink." Guests had to use "Pullman car ashtray stands," but the lobby, finally, was "just like De Gaulle's." When she despaired of *ever* being able to adjust the thermostats, she thought surely "the greatest brains of army engineering can figure out how to have this heated like a normal rattletrap house!"

For their first State function, a diplomatic reception on the afternoon of February 9, Mrs. Kennedy made three requests to liven up the State Rooms: no receiving lines, more "natural" flower arrangements, and fires in all the fireplaces.

For two days, black smoke poured from the chimneys as we checked out one fireplace after another, to test their first actual use in eight years. (Mrs. Eisenhower had installed gold-paper fans as fireplace screens, and never had fires lit in any of the rooms.) It took two days to get them all working properly. Or so we thought.

Meanwhile, Mrs. Parish and I prowled the State rooms, switching lamps, placing ashtrays, looking for likely flower bowls.

"She wants to put pictures of the children and pets

around on the tables here to make it cozy," said Mrs. Parish, and laughed, as we went through the dull, imposing Green Room. We went searching—even to the National Botanical Gardens—for flowers that were not too "stilted."

Finally, the florist set out vases of tulips and wildflowers, the engineers lit the fires, and the diplomatic guests assembled in the Blue Room for cocktails and conversation.

All the ushers were dressed in formal day wear: club coat, striped trousers, gray cravats. I was determined to be excused from sight, because I had dislocated my shoulder sledding with my daughters. Just in case, though, I dressed in my "formals," and tied a black silk Navy regulation scarf around my neck for a sling. I was manning the Usher's office when a frantic call came from Bruce, a doorman on the first floor.

"Mr. West, come quick—the East Room. . . ."

I sailed down the hall to find the four East Room fireplaces belching smoke.

"Close all the doors to the room!" I ordered the doormen. "Open the windows, and bring up two big fans from the electrician's shop. Bruce, get a bucket and shovel to carry out the logs."

I stood at the fireplace, arm in black sling, directing the frantic traffic, and praying that the President and his guests would stay in the Blue Room and not call the fire department, when the door opened. Mrs. Kennedy and General Clifton, the President's military aide, stepped into the East Room. I braced myself as they walked over to the fireplace.

"Oh, Mr. West," Jacqueline Kennedy purred, "you look so glamorous—just like Zachary Taylor!" and making no mention of the commotion or smoke, she went back to her reception.

The next day I made a special trip into the Red Room to take a close look at the stern, military portrait of the twelfth President. I wondered how many fires he had put out. (Actually, I rather hoped Mrs. Kennedy meant John Tyler, the tenth President, who had posed for his portrait wearing a black scarf around his neck, and was, it seemed to me, a good bit better-looking than Zachary Taylor.)

Instead of having a regular 9:00 a.m. staff conference at her bedside, as Mamie Eisenhower did, Mrs. Kennedy might pop up anytime with a new plan for a room arrangement, a surprise dinner, a request for a stage or a stepstool. Our daily conferences took place in my office, in a storeroom, on the back stairs, on the south lawn, in a boat. She and I sat on the floor with drawings spread out all around us, we sprawled on the marble stairs to discuss the ceilings above, or we poked around in a dusty warehouse for some lost White House possession.

She learned quickly to put everything in writing, and kept on her desk a yellow legal-size pad with my name on it. Any time of day or night, when she thought of something to tell me, she'd jot it down. Anything that happened to pop into her mind, from picture frames for Caroline's drawings or sleeping arrangements for Kings and Queens, would find its way to me, on her notepad. Her incredible attention to detail, in every subject she put her mind to, made the difference for me in managing an institution (for by now, the White House had indeed become so) without the morning staff meetings to which I had been so accustomed.

For Mrs. Kennedy herself never kept regular hours. Despite the discipline that imposed order on everything around her, she usually did what she pleased, whenever she wanted to. The only truly inviolate time of her day was the children's hour, in the evening, when she read to or played with John and Caroline.

She had breakfast served on a tray, in bed, whenever she woke up. Sometimes at 8:00, sometimes, after a long evening of partying, at noon.

The President was usually up at 8:00, however, and Miss Shaw brought the children in to visit with him while he ate breakfast.

Caroline walked him over to his west wing office every morning, then walked back to the kitchen, where she picked up her little brown-paper-bag lunch, and headed for the play school that Mrs. Kennedy had designed and installed in the third-floor solarium.

After greeting her children, Mrs. Kennedy dressed in pants and a sweater or shirt (I can't remember her ever wearing a dress in the White House unless she had company) and took a brisk hour's walk, alone around the sixteen acres of White House grounds.

Before she developed her system of memos, she'd stop by my office on her way out, to discuss her plans for the day. After the memos started appearing, our meetings, though unscheduled, were actually more frequent. I learned to carry *my* yellow legal pad (with her name on it) around under my arm whenever I left my office. No telling where I might run into her, for a full-scale executive conference.

Following her walk, she'd return to the West Hall, where she worked at her desk. That ornate French Empire desk with big brass appointments was her most prized possession. She worried more about scratches-in-transit, or its improper care, than about any other piece of furniture or art in the White House or in her own house. The desk had belonged to her late father, stockbroker John Vernou Bouvier, whom she had adored and of whom she spoke quite frequently.

If she had no appointments or visitors, she joined the children in the "high-chair room," where they had lunch, then she ordered a grilled cheese sandwich, served to her in bed, before her nap.

2

After lunch, the Kennedy children were bedded down, the maids and houseman scuttled away, and silence reigned upstairs at the White House. For the President of the United States, after a dip in the pool, came home from the office.

Just after they first moved in, Mrs. Kennedy had walked with me down the ground-floor corridor, out of the west door, and along the colonnade by the Rose Garden, to the President's oval office in the west wing. A brisk January breeze whipped at us as we opened the door to Franklin D. Roosevelt's heated swimming pool.

"Do you think we could have this colonnade enclosed in glass, like the east entrance is, so that the President can get back from the swimming pool without walking in the cold air?" she asked. "He doesn't like to dress after a swim."

Without even glancing at the budget, I knew we couldn't stand that kind of expenditure, nor could I see changing the stately colonnade for one President's pleasure.

Instead, we cut a door through the flower shop, another through the exercise room, and when President Kennedy left the office at 1:30 every afternoon, he stopped by the pool, shed his clothes, swam nude for half an hour, wrapped himself in a towelrobe, and padded through the exercise room, through the banks of flowers, through the ground-floor corridor, to an elevator which took him upstairs, where he shed his robe, climbed into bed, and ate lunch (usually a hamburger or a glass of Metrecal) from a tray. He closed the door, firmly.

Mrs. Kennedy dropped everything, no matter how important, to join her husband. If she had visitors in tow, they would be left for me to entertain.

During those hours, the Kennedy doors were closed. No telephone calls were allowed, no folders sent up, no interruptions from the staff. Nobody went upstairs, for any reason.

At about three, the President, showered and dressed, walked back to his west wing office. Mrs. Kennedy went outside on the south lawn with her children, and then back inside to resume her business with redecorating, or to have her hair done. Usually at 5:30 she came upstairs to read, paint, or relax, and at 6:30 she would spend an hour with John and Caroline in their bedrooms or the West Hall.

The President, on his way back from the office, stopped at the swimming pool, and went through the same ritual again—swimming nude, walking over in his bathrobe, then changing clothes for dinner. George Thomas, his valet, had been over to retrieve his morning suit and deposit another bathrobe. (Some of the servants had bets on what the President would do if George forgot to take over the bathrobe: Would he dress, again, in the clothes he took off, or would he stride through the flower room and up the elevator, stark naked?) John F. Kennedy wore three separate suits of clothes every day of his White House life.

While he swam, Mrs. Kennedy dressed for dinner, then joined her husband for cocktails upstairs.

Rather than the White House tradition of dinner on-the-dot at 7:30, the Kennedys' dinner hour was different

237

from day to day. The butlers might serve two or twenty, the menu might feature grilled cheese sandwiches, or pheasant-under-glass.

Jacqueline Kennedy accomplished an astounding amount of work during her husband's short administration. And she drew amazing work out of the White House staff and her personal staff.

When she came to the White House on Inauguration Day, Mrs. Kennedy brought the statuesque Letitia Baldrige, who was to change the job of social secretary into a Position; petite Pam Turnure ("What in the world do I want a press secretary for?" Mrs. Kennedy asked me); good-natured Providencia (Provy) Parades, her personal maid; George Thomas, who as the President's valet learned to delegate authority and shoeshining to the upstairs housemen, ("George opens the door for the butler to bring in the breakfast tray," President Kennedy joked); Pearl Nelson, their oversized cook; and Mary Gallagher, who took dictation and helped with the Kennedys' personal bills. They were all put on the government payroll, which posed a few problems for me.

The Chief Usher is personnel officer for the mansion, which makes life simpler for the President, but probably makes it rather frustrating for people who work for the President. For they no longer work for the family, they work for the White House. As manager of the household staff, I was responsible for hiring—and firing. And through the years, I found that the First Families' personal servants took more delicate handling than those on the regular White House staff. Provy and George, for example, both had families, and they did not "live in" at the White House. Yet, as family servants, they often worked longer hours, staying to dress the President and Mrs. Kennedy, for example, than those on the regular eight-hour White House shifts. We could not pay them less than the minimum wage, neither could we afford to pay them hourly overtime, for they'd soon be making more than the White House staff, who had achieved government seniority. The solution was to "give" them servants' rooms on the third floor of the White House.

"Why am I paid less than the butlers [who made $4,000 a year]?" George demanded to know one day.

"Because the President's personal servants are allotted a room in the White House," I explained, "and the regular staff do not have that allocation."

"But I don't *live* in my room," he argued.

"Yes, but the room is there, and it is assigned to you ...," I explained.

George would take care of the President's clothes, but the housemen would do the cleaning; Provy would take care of Mrs. Kennedy's personal effects and dresses, but the upstairs maids were to attend to the linens and rooms. And other matters, they soon found out.

That first evening, after dressing for the Inaugural Ball, Mrs. Kennedy sent Provy home. I asked Wilma Holness, the trusted second-floor maid, to spend the night, in case the First Lady should need her.

"I'm sure glad I was here last night," Wilma told me the next morning. "She couldn't have gotten out of that ballgown by herself if her life depended on it. There were so many buttons on that thing and hooks and all —why, I'm sure she'd have had to sleep in it."

From then on, Provy stayed late whenever there was an Occasion.

Mrs. Kennedy was thoroughly prepared for one aspect of White House life—running a large mansion. Jacqueline Bouvier Kennedy had grown up in a privileged, sophisticated environment, had the advantages of a superior education, both in this country and in France, and the experience of eight years of marriage to a very wealthy man. All her life, she had been surrounded by servants. She knew what to expect from them, how to evaluate them, and how to get a polished performance from them.

The morning after Inauguration, Mrs. Kennedy was up bright and early.

"I'd like to meet all the staff today," she phoned me from the Queen's Room. "Could you please take me around the White House to meet them at their work?"

I thought fast. In the first place, I didn't *want* her going all over the house. There are many areas in which our work goes smoothly without the First Lady's knowledge. Or intervention. No President's wife had ever looked into the electricians' shop, for example. Or the staff lunch room, where servants eat. I knew there would be enough to do in the weeks ahead without Mrs. Kennedy's taking note of conditions in the linen closets or the butler's pantry.

"Mrs. Kennedy, I've already arranged for the employees—those with whom you will be working most closely—to come up to the second floor to meet *you*," I answered. "I realized that you still might not be strong enough to make a strenuous tour of the entire house, so they are waiting to come to you. There'll be plenty of time later on for you to meet the maintenance staff—carpenters and so forth—since you won't have much communication with them anyway. I can bring them up two or three at a time to meet you, if that is all right. . . ."

"What about the florist?" she asked. "Flowers are going to be very important to me. I couldn't *stand* the arrangements around here!"

"Shall we set up an appointment to meet the garden staff separately?" I countered. "That way, you can discuss your plans in detail."

"Fine, Mr. West," she acceded. "I'm going out for a walk around the south driveway. You can bring them up at eleven."

Our staff had never before been subjected to such formal review by a First Lady, and they were a bit apprehensive. With the first group of three, I rode the elevator to the second floor. There, perched on a corner of the large octagonal desk, was the new President's wife. She was wearing jodhpurs, a shirt, and low brown boots, and her hair, so carefully coiffed the night before, was tousled.

"Mrs. Kennedy, these are the ushers," I introduced them, "Ray Hare, Tom Carter, and Rex Scouten." Smiling, the First Lady repeated their names. Mabel Walker, who had been waiting on the elevator, walked over. "Miss Walker supervises the maids and housemen, the linen room, and household bookkeeping," I explained. Next, I brought up the maître d', Charles Ficklin, who supervised food preparation and service. "Charles." Mrs. Kennedy nodded, brushing back her unruly hair.

Charles was followed by the four butlers, his brother John, Eugene Allen, Fate Suber, and John Johnson. Next were the kitchen staff—three cooks and their helpers, who plainly were startled by the sight of a First Lady in pants. The second- and third-floor maids, five of them, then came forward. "Wilma, Lucinda, Julia, Viola, Clara . . . ." she repeated their names, slowly. Mrs. Kennedy was not taking notes, nor was there a secretary present. I wondered whether she could remember any of them. (She did, I soon discovered.) Following the maids were the two upstairs housemen, the Filipino Navy stewards.

"Is there enough work for everybody?" Mrs. Kennedy asked, as the parade ended.

"Plenty!" I assured her.

(Yet I remembered Margaret Truman's comment when I took her around the renovated third floor in 1951. "What are those two bedrooms?" Miss Truman asked. "Those are for visiting servants," I said, meaning the servants brought by such house guests as the Queen of England.

"*Visiting* servants? That's an appropriate name because that's what they do around here all day long. Visit and visit and visit!" said Margaret Truman.)

By the time all the employees had trooped in and out, Mrs. Kennedy's eyes were glazed.

"Is that all?" she asked.

"Well, there are three men in the flower shop, two women in the laundry, five downstairs housemen and three plumbers, three painters, two in the storeroom, twelve engineers, seven carpenters, and eight gardeners."

"You're right, I will see them another day," she laughed. Then she asked, "How much, again, is our total operating budget, Mr. West?"

"$500,000 a year," I replied. "But that does *not* include your personal expenditures."

"Well, just remember this. I want you to run this place just like you'd run it for the *chinchiest* President who ever got elected!" she stated.

Then her voice dropped to its near-whisper.

"We don't have nearly as much money as you read in the papers!"

There was a buzz as the servants went back downstairs. Mabel Walker, the housekeeper during the entire Eisenhower Administration, commented:

"How could she tell what she was looking at, with all that hair falling in her face?"

And Mabel Walker was the first to go.

The cardinal rule in the White House every change of administration is Adjust. (There are always dozens of others waiting in the wings for the honor of working in the President's house.) Strangely enough, if you are wise enough to last long enough to make the adjustment, it soon turns out that "they"—the First Family—are the ones to adjust. And life resumes the old tried-and-true ways. There never can be any personal loyalties to any President or his family. So the normal, workaday gripes and snipes at the boss have to be suppressed. At the White House, the walls have ears. Literally.

For those reasons, the servants never hinted to me what they thought of Mrs. Kennedy. But Mrs. Kennedy told me, often, what she thought of *them!*

The President's wife began scribbling notes to me, concerning ashtrays, empty cigarette boxes on the third floor, current magazines for the guest rooms. More than once, she wrote, "Could someone please rev up Miss Walker?"

I was surprised to find that at first the White House staff never quite came up to Mrs. Kennedy's standards. Bess Truman inspected for cobwebs and dust; Mamie Eisenhower erased footprints; Jacqueline Kennedy judged servants on performance and style. Her first assessment of the upstairs maids (written in her breezy, mock-autocratic fashion), arrived shortly after she did.

Mr. West

I just saw a new maid named Gloria—Apparently she has been here 6 months & isnt allowed to come to 2nd floor (she didnt tell me that—dont blame her) She seems bright & willing. My suggestion is this—In fact tell Miss Walker I want it done—let her come to 2nd floor—she can help Provy & Cordenia—they are the only ones who

242

would be nice to her—if she follows Provy around 2 days a wk—she will be trained lady's maid in no time.

But our maid situation is this:

Wilma—excellent—but getting on

You will be lost when she goes—like Julia

Lucinda—very good—good maid for guests

Cordenia is shaping up beautifully—I know I am monopolizing her for the children

But she has learned so much & is bright & a wonderful person

Gloria looks same—nice bright type as Cordenia—but big problem with W.H. maids is they are so terrified of being in W.H.—of First Family, etc, that they are rigid with fear & get panicky—even Lucinda who knows me well still apologizes 10 minutes if she drops a pin.

I can't teach them anything—nor have time—when they are that scared—as they are too panicky to remember—The only way they will get to be good maids—like Wilma—easy is to be around the family & house enough so some terror leaves them.

So Gloria should come off 3rd floor & be told to follow Provy 2 days a wk (She can do my room & bath—Provy will tell her how—while Provy does my clothes) She can learn how to lay out clothes etc etc etc

Provy is the only good maid who will be nice to her— Wilma is too grand! And Provy can train a ladies maid— she is tops—about 90 times faster than Miss Walker can.

JBK

As she assessed the abilities of the staff, Mrs. Kennedy quickly learned to utilize their particular talents. Lucinda Morman, she discovered, was an excellent seamstress. Before long, that maid who was "good for guests" spent most of her time making alterations on the First Lady's Oleg Cassini originals—many of which were designed from Jacqueline Kennedy's own preliminary sketches.

Later, when she had established a smoothly running household, she came to appreciate each of the maids for their own individual contributions to the White House and to her family. She was quick to show gratitude, as well as concern about their getting adequate days off and raises in salary. And, I observed, she held them very high in her affection.

And finally the President's wife decided to bring fellow Vassarite Anne Lincoln over from the social office to take over as housekeeper. ("She knows how I want cigarette boxes placed, and everything else about the kind of house this should be," Mrs. Kennedy told me. "Couldn't Miss Walker be curator of the warehouse or something?") Mabel Walker, who was nearing retirement age, was put to work on an inventory of White House furnishings, in an office out in our new warehouse. Janet Bowen, who had begun as Miss Walker's assistant during the Eisenhowers and always declined promotion to the taxing job of housekeeper, remained as assistant housekeeper to provide the necessary continuity from one administration to another.

Unfortunately, Tish Baldrige was not with me to hear Mrs. Kennedy request a tight—or "chinchy"—budget. Instead, the new social secretary breezily told the maître d', "Just serve them champagne and caviar every day, and they'll be happy!"

The maître d' did, but they were not.

In fact, both President and Mrs. Kennedy almost went through the ceiling when they saw the first month's bills. Entertaining in February, 1961, had been lavish, but strictly private—which meant that it came out of the President's own pocket.

"We've got to cut down drastically, Mr. West," Mrs. Kennedy complained. "Do you think we could buy our food where the White House buys its food?"

And so we arranged for the Kennedy grocery account to be transferred from the expensive French Market in Georgetown, to the same wholesalers who had supplied the Executive Mansion for years.

One of Mrs. Kennedy's most important early White House staff decisions was to hire the French chef René Verdon.

The President, nervous about the country's reaction to his importing "foreigners" for the White House kitchens, ordered the Secret Service to speed up citizenship papers for René and his assistant, Julius Spessot.

"It can be stated," reported the press office to the President, "that one is French and the other Italian by birth, but that they are in the process of becoming United States citizens."

But the President's father, Ambassador Kennedy, had a better suggestion: "Tell them that the President feels there are so many Irishmen in the White House, the French and Italians ought to be given a chance, too!"

When he arrived, René and his assistant, Julius Spessot, prattled away in the kitchen in French, much to the annoyance of the three demoted cooks. Also demoted was Charles Ficklin, the maître d'. From now on, René made out the daily menus, René ordered the groceries, René took over.

As soon as the second-floor kitchen was completed, Pearl, the Kennedy's Georgetown cook, was assigned to prepare the family meals. Mrs. Kennedy, however, soon realized that too many cooks just might spoil the *pot au feu*. And René and Pearl weren't communicating very well.

One morning, as we were shifting ashtrays in the Green Room for the hundredth time, Mrs. Kennedy said to me, "I'm going to have to fire Pearl, because we just don't need her with René here. Wish me luck."

Several days later, the President's wife knocked on my office door.

"Help," she whispered, dropping into a chair. Fixing her huge brown eyes on my face, she said, "Mr. West, would you please fire Pearl for me? I've tried to do it three or four times, but she just talks me down."

"Yes, Ma'am," I said. "I'll speak to her."

In the White House, you have to "release" people very smoothly, or else they can cause a big row. I called Pearl up to my second-floor private office, which overlooks the North Portico of the White House. She dropped her ample frame comfortably into the same chair Mrs. Kennedy had just vacated.

"You know, Pearl, with the new French chef here, your talents are just going to waste," I began. "You really should be working somewhere where your services could be appreciated more."

She shifted in the leather armchair, ready to do battle.

"But the President *likes* my cooking!" she argued indignantly.

I looked out the window. Spring was here, warming Pennsylvania Avenue for the tourists. No matter what the problems are, nobody ever wants to leave the White House.

"Let's work it this way, Pearl," I told her gently. "I'm going to turn all the cooking over to René—for the family as well as for the guests. But you will *live* here, as a guest of the White House, for two weeks. All of your meals will be served you, and you will have every privilege of the House while you look for another job. . . ."

Pearl, our guest, was on top of the world for two weeks. The maids made her bed. The chef prepared her meals, which were served by the butlers. She rode around in White House cars.

Mrs. Kennedy ran into me in the center hall during Pearl's first week in residence.

"I just saw Pearl!" she exclaimed, eyes wide. "Did you give up, too?"

"Not at all," I said, and explained my delicate maneuver.* Mrs. Kennedy was delighted.

"That's splendid," she said. "Just splendid!" She grinned impishly. "Now can you ease out Julius, too? What we really need is a pastry chef, rather than an assistant for René."

Julius had become known as the "platter prettier-upper," and his specialty was ice sculpture, which was Mrs. Kennedy's least favorite form of table decoration.

So I eased Julius out, then hired Ferdinand Louvat, the pastry chef.

I discovered the sensitivity of President Kennedy's political antennae as I carried out "the West plan" to relieve Julius of his job. The morning I assigned Julius to his guest room on the third floor, I met the President at the elevator, and walked with him to his west wing office.

* With Pearl's special references, she was employed in Georgetown within days after she left the White House.

"Mr. President, I have released Julius Spessot from the kitchen today, because Mrs. Kennedy would like to have a pastry chef," I informed him. "Could you give him an autographed picture?"

"Sure, I'd be glad to," the President answered. Then he frowned. "But aren't you afraid he might want to write something?"

"No, he doesn't know enough to write," I replied.

Several days later, Mrs. Kennedy called me to the second floor. "Mr. West, I've had some statements drawn up by my attorney. Do you think it's all right for the employees to sign a pledge that they won't write anything about their experiences in the White House?"

I was taken aback a bit. "I'll certainly check on it," I said and I telephoned her attorney, James McInerney, to check out the legal implications. In effect, the pledge was purely psychological, he explained. "Legally, it really has no force of effect."

The attorney had drawn up the statement "to conform to Mrs. Kennedy's requirements and those of the Presidential Office," and he had also written Mrs. Kennedy a warning that "if publicly disclosed, the agreement may be falsely construed as a further advance in the area of executive privilege (of non-disclosures), which had come under attack by the Congressional Freedom of Information Committees."

So, under the instruction of Mrs. Kennedy, I had the household employees sign the pledge. I assume the President, himself, asked his own staff.

As the lawyer warned, the pledge did come under attack. Pierre Salinger, the President's press secretary, let it slip out at a press conference, and newspapers across the country went up in smoke about the White House muzzling its employees. Pierre, who protested lamely that "we just felt that it is a step to ensure that the President's wife will have privacy," was besieged by newsmen.

And the President, who had just squeaked by in the election, was in a tight spot. He called me from the west wing.

"Mr. West, may I come to see you in your office?"

"Certainly, Mr. President," I answered, startled.

President Kennedy strode in, looking so official I all but saluted.

"I want you to help me, Mr. West," he began. "This 'pledge' business is causing a lot of trouble. Would you take the blame for it?"

"I did ask the staff to sign it, Mr. President," I answered.

"Good. We'll put out a statement saying it was your idea, and you initiated it. It will look more official, and less of a personal thing coming from you."

President Kennedy, perhaps because of his constant exposure during the television age, was more interested than any of the other Presidents in every nuance of what the press and the public would think about him and his family in the White House.

He fretted about the color of the walls, the height of the fences, any departure from tradition. Unfortunately, we were never treated to samples of his famous humor. He was always entirely serious about the White House. At the same time, he also had an interest in having the house reflect the issues and people who concerned him. His wife, who set the pace, made the choices, chose the style of living for the Kennedys in the Executive Mansion, was closely attuned to that interest.

For example, Mrs. Kennedy's purchase for the President's House of crystal from Morgantown, West Virginia, was a direct outgrowth of what the President had learned about that state and its problems when he campaigned for the Presidency there in 1960. John F. Kennedy had prevailed in that West Virginia primary, proving his popularity there, but he also was exposed to and struck by the pervasive poverty of the Appalachian region. He was determined to shape government programs to eliminate that misery.

It was Mrs. Kennedy's idea to buy the West Virginia glassware, which we filled with fine French wines. She wanted not only to bring to the White House an authentic piece of traditional American craftsmanship, but also to symbolize the President's interest in the economic problems and potential of Appalachia.

3

Jacqueline Kennedy devoted considerable time, energy, and concentrated attention to her children, yet you could hardly call her the typical American mother. Even when she pleaded for a "simple, unspoiled, normal life" for the children, it would mean the simple, normal life of a very wealthy family.

She did want to shield Caroline and John from public curiosity, from the pomp and pomposity of White House life. And yet there were always nannies and nurses, chauffeurs and clowns, and a butler who served hamburgers on a silver tray.

It was evident that Mrs. Kennedy intended to keep their lives separate from the White House operation. Caroline and John, in fact, never were a problem for the staff, as nurses were in attendance at all times. They never ran up and down the State halls by themselves, never slid down the banisters or romped in the East Room, as Teddy Roosevelt's boisterous youngsters are said to have done.

Instead, Caroline and John played in their rooms—or in the third-floor solarium. When they did appear, the staff was delighted, for they were well-behaved if exuberant youngsters, and totally charming.

"I don't want them to think they are 'official' children," she told me. "When I go out with them or when they go out with their nurses, please ask the doorman not to hover around to open the doors for them."

At first, with three-year-old Caroline at her heels, the President's wife pushed her baby son's carriage around the circular driveway, under the trees, and back again. When little John learned to walk, they took the same route, Caroline skipping merrily ahead and Mrs. Kennedy slowing her pace to match the toddler's.

She designed a play-yard, hidden underneath the trees near the President's west wing office. I directed the carpenters to follow Mrs. Kennedy's sketches, and we soon had a treehouse, rabbit hutch, a barrel tunnel, a leather swing, and a slide. As the "family" grew, we added a snow-fence pen for the lambs, a stable for the ponies, Macaroni and Tex, guinea-pig pens, and doghouses for Pushinka, a gift from Nikita Khrushchev, and Charlie.

The President could look out on the play-yard from his office, and he often stepped out to shrieks, hugs, quacks, barks, cackles, bleats, and all sorts of commotion. He seemed to delight in the mad scene.

"Do you think you could manage a big hole in the ground on the south lawn?" Mrs. Kennedy asked me, looking down from the Truman balcony.

"I'm certain we could . . . ," I agreed, my curiosity piqued. Swimming pool? Wading pool? Pirates' cave? I wondered what was next.

"Good! Let's put in a trampoline right there." She pointed to a spot alongside the tennis court. "They're too little for a high one, so could you place it at ground level so we won't have to climb up to jump. And hide it somehow, *please*."

Out came the gardeners with shovels, and out came the Park Service with holly trees, because Mrs. Kennedy wanted a natural "screen" around the trampoline. The First Lady, in slacks and sandals as usual, came out to supervise planting of the seven-foot holly trees.

"Oh, this will be perfect!" she whispered, as the trees

went into the ground. "Now, when I jump on the trampoline, all they'll be able to see is my head, sailing up above the tree tops!"

Actually, I believe that Jacqueline Kennedy enjoyed playing as much as the children did. Many times, when I watched her play with them, exactly as a child plays, I felt, strangely, that *this* was the real Jacqueline Kennedy. She was so happy, so abandoned, so like a little girl who had never grown up. Many times, when she was performing with such grace and authority the role of First Lady, I felt she was just pretending. She really longs for a child's world, I thought, where she can run and jump and hide and ride horses. I thought of her as an actress—constantly playing a role.

Caroline, Mrs. Kennedy and little John all loved animals and birds. But enough was enough!

The ducks had to go back to Rock Creek Park, even though at first they had seemed a wonderful idea. With great glee, Mrs. Kennedy had me install a pen for the fluffy baby ducklings. Then, as they grew, we acclimated them to the majestic fountain on the deep south lawn. But the ducks ate the tulips. And Charlie, the terrier, ate some of the ducks. And Caroline kept falling into the fountain, accompanied by great whoops from the tourists lined up at the fence.

Mrs. Kennedy ordered a showing of *Bambi* for Caroline and her friends in the ground-floor movie theater. Afterwards, she sent me a note:

"Mr. West—will you see about getting some deer for the south grounds?"

But before I could go on a deer-hunt, we learned that we'd be receiving a pair of Irish deer, a gift from the President of Ireland. I called the National Zoo, to inquire about the care and feeding of the animals, but was discouraged by the zoo-keeper.

"The zoo says deer are dangerous and unpredictable," I advised Mrs. Kennedy.

"Oh dear," she said. "Then I guess we don't want any after all." And the Irish deer took up residence at the zoo.

Several weeks later, Mrs. Kennedy sent another note:

251

"Mr. West—will you see about getting a pair of peacocks."

This time I didn't bother to check with the zoo.

"The zoo says peacocks are dangerous and unpredictable," I lied. Enough, as I said, was enough.

Mrs. Kennedy designed the play-schoolroom for Caroline in the third-floor solarium, and we built it, complete with sandbox, rabbit cages, guinea pigs, goldfish and plants. We ordered sand from National Parks, and put up low bookshelves, for which Mrs. Kennedy selected hundreds of schoolbooks from the list the teacher had prepared. It soon became a full-fledged nursery school—a co-op with ten pupils, whose parents shared the teacher's salary with the Kennedy's.

"Somebody's been up here making the biggest mess!" the teacher, Alice Grimes, complained one morning. "And it's not the first time, either. Something is going on in this nursery school at night!"

Determined to get to the bottom of the mystery, I summoned Wilma, the maid.

"It's just Mrs. Kennedy and Caroline," she reassured me. "They come up here at night and play in the sand."

Despite its after-hours use, the school followed the strictest regulations for educational institutions in the District of Columbia. As she was filling in Caroline's required medical form, Mrs. Kennedy sent me a note:

"As the White House school comes under your administration, it would give me a great sense of security if you would fill out the enclosed physical examination form and return it to Miss Grimes."

But the President's wife had already filled in some of the blanks on "my" medical form. On the question of "heart diseases," she wrote "almost too old but heart still palpitates at times." Recommendation of oculist? "Not to look at any more portraits of First Ladies." Does he have a midday rest? "Sneaks one in occasionally when lady boss has one." And finally, to the question as to whether the school child tires easily, she replied for me, "Yes, after tramping around house with decorators."

One morning, as we were roaming around the ground floor, Mrs. Kennedy said, "Mr. West, will you take me to the bomb shelter?"

252

I was a bit startled, hoping there wasn't a disaster brewing.

"Why, certainly," I said, and walked toward the elevator.

The ground floor of the White House, accessible to the south, west and east entrances, is underneath the State floor. Below that, a Truman renovation addition, are two basements, which are used for storage, for laundry rooms, and for servants' dining rooms and locker rooms. All the way through the basement lower level, and to the compartment beneath the east wing, is a protected corridor leading to the bomb shelter, built during World War II. Underneath that is the new bomb shelter, set up for use by the President anytime.

So I took Mrs. Kennedy down to the bowels of the White House, and we opened the door to the bomb shelter. She gasped, as an army of Signal Corps men sprang to their feet. The bomb shelter doubles as a command post for the Signal Corps, with their fantastic communications control rooms laid out underneath the east wing.

We looked around, then left.

Once outside, Mrs. Kennedy began to laugh.

"How amazing!" she said. "I didn't expect to find so much *humanity!* I thought it would be a great big room that we could use as an indoor recreation room for the children, I even had plans for a basketball court in there!"

Mrs. Kennedy sent a note to me: "Mr. West, please do not send my folders up for me to look at after 11 a.m. I want to keep my afternoons for the children as much as possible."

She read to her children for an hour every evening before dinner, and even though she and her husband usually did not dine with them, she sat in while they were eating.

When she went on a trip, Mrs. Kennedy always wrote and pre-addressed postcards for John and Caroline, one for every day she would be gone. "Please mail them for me, Mr. West," she asked. "One every day. I don't trust anybody but you to do this, and I don't trust the mails from overseas." I found canceled foreign stamps in the mailroom, and glued them onto her postcards.

When the First Lady was away from the mansion, she communicated to me via the Secret Service. Wherever she was, her agents were, and their walkie-talkies or car radios were always in touch with "home base," one floor below my office.

One dreary Monday in 1961, I was sitting in my office, poring over the latest estimate for fabric for the Red Room walls. A steady spring rain washed the boxwoods on the north lawn, outside my window. I looked out at the umbrellas on Pennsylvania Avenue, glad to be inside. Suddenly a call came from the Secret Service.

"Mrs. Kennedy is on her way back from the country," the agent reported. "She wants you to meet her at the south entrance. And she says to wear a raincoat."

Armed with my old trenchcoat, I dutifully waited just outside the diplomatic reception room door, until Sergeant Lee drove the Mercury station wagon up in front. Her Secret Service agent sat in the front seat and Mrs. Kennedy hopped out of the back. She was wearing Pucci pants, and her beat-up old trenchcoat matched mine. She greeted me with a big smile.

"Mr. West, will you take a little walk with me in the rain?" she asked sweetly, and took my arm.

The south lawn looked especially dead in the drizzle, and I wondered if the President, whose pet peeve was the condition of the White House lawns, had more complaints against our sixteen-acre headache. Mrs. Kennedy and I walked along the circular driveway, toward the children's play-yard, looking out over the wide expanse of wet grass. We walked past Andrew Jackson's magnolias, past Franklin Roosevelt's lindens, underneath dripping oak branches, finally coming to the carefully hidden spot between the Jefferson mound and the pin oaks President Eisenhower had planted. The treehouse and slide were mounted in Herbert Hoover's white oak tree.

"Please thank the carpenters for doing such a great job," Mrs. Kennedy murmured. "The slide comes down from the tree just exactly right. In fact, Caroline wants to push her baby brother down, carriage and all."

We walked until we approached the southwest gate. Then she stopped suddenly and pointed to the iron-grill gates.

"We've screened off the playground on the south by the mound and by the trees," she said. "But if you stand right here, you can get a good view of the children playing. Do you think you could plant rhododendrons or something along this fence so that everybody can't stare in?"

As we headed back, full circle, around the tennis courts, under Grover Cleveland's maples, she kept talking about her desire for privacy. How she didn't want her children to become "spoiled." How she had a fear of exposing her children to the unknown public.

"Oh, well," she sighed. "I guess you can't block off any more than that. They're entitled to *some* view of the White House. . . . But I'm sick and tired of starring in everybody's home movies!"

If Mrs. Kennedy had her way, I thought, the White House would be surrounded by high brick walls and a moat with crocodiles.

Thoroughly drenched, I phoned the National Park Service right away: "Mrs. Kennedy would like rhododendrons around the southwest gate."

The next day, three trucks, with six Park Service gardeners, arrived with thirty large rhododendrons.

"What's that army doing out there?" the President asked.

"Shielding your children," I answered. He shook his head.

"I hope it doesn't obstruct the tourists' view of the house," he said, seriously.

The first flak came from the Washington newspapers. And the second barrage came from the White House police.

"What in the world are you doing out by the southwest gate?" Major Stover demanded to know.

I explained the First Lady's wishes.

"What? How the hell do you expect us to guard this place if we can't see who's climbing over the fence?" he sputtered.

"I guess you'll just have to find a way," I answered evenly. "It's Mrs. Kennedy's request, not mine."

With much grumbling, the police put another man on post at the gate. Then they electrified the fence. But that didn't work because the alarm went off every time a bird flew over. Finally we were able to install ground lights among the bushes, and the police, at last, quit complaining about the rhododendrons.

Mrs. Kennedy, though, never was satisfied that Caroline and John were sufficiently screened from the public scrutiny. Yet those two were the most photographed American children since Shirley Temple. Every magazine, every newspaper, every television news show carried pictures of Caroline and John. What the public didn't realize was that Mrs. Kennedy carefully planned and directed all the publicity that the children received.

This apparent contradiction was puzzling, but I do believe that she was sincere about abhorring publicity. When she married John F. Kennedy, she married into a family that actively courted publicity, whose political success depended upon becoming known. President Kennedy was acutely conscious of the news media. His best friends were reporters, and he held sixteen stag luncheons for newspaper publishers from every state of the Union.

So Mrs. Kennedy had to fight a constant battle between her own desire for privacy and her husband's continuous campaign. And she also learned to exercise control over her children's exposure to the news media in a very subtle way. As a former journalist herself, she knew that she had to give the press something on her children, or else they would hound her to pieces or write articles that she didn't want. And so she would think up little stories, or agree to certain photographs, and filter them to the press via Pam Turnure. As long as she was the director, it was all right.

She guarded her own social life in the White House as jealously as she guarded that of her children, and invited "working" press only to those elaborate private parties—such as the one for forty-nine Nobel Prize winners or for André Malraux, France's Minister of Culture—which she deemed to be in the "national interest." The others—the dinner dances until dawn or the intimate little parties on the second floor—were strictly off the record.

The Kennedys entertained often, and rather lavishly, at their private dinner-dances—certainly more lavishly than any of their predecessors. They simply had more money of their own to spend. We set up a bar between the Red Room and the Blue Room, served cocktails and hors d'oeuvres in the Red and Green Rooms, where the President and his wife wandered around as host and hostess.

Lester Lanin and about twelve members of his orchestra played sprightly, nonstop music in the Blue Room, from eight o'clock cocktail hour to the last gasp before dawn. ("Tell them I don't want any 'breaks,'" Mrs. Kennedy said. "They can figure out how to do it without breaking their union rules.") After dinner, the guests had coffee and liqueurs in the Red and Green Rooms, and danced on the gleaming oak floors of the candle-lit Blue Room.

I noticed that Vice President and Mrs. Johnson were often on the guest list for those private parties, which was unusual only in that my Presidents rarely included their Vice Presidents in their private lives. Mr. Truman's Vice President Barkley, I believe, came closest to being a personal friend. I had the feeling that the Vice Presidents all were chosen to balance the ticket and not the White House social life.

The order of the Kennedys' big, private evenings in the State Dining Room, the decor, and the menu followed the plan for black-tie State entertaining, because Mrs. Kennedy couldn't abide "theme" parties.

Though those swinging private dinner-dances were the talk of Washington, the most envied White House invitations were those hidden from the public entirely, the intimate little black-tie dinners with Mrs. Kennedy as hostess, upstairs in the new President's Dining Room.

She used candlelight, antique china, and had René prepare his gourmet specialties. And even when only two people were dining, the chef scrupulously followed his State dinner pattern of four courses: fish, entrée, salad, dessert. Tish prepared place cards, and seated all dinners and luncheons—even for only a few people.

257

For their intimate upstairs dinners—for four to twenty—the guests were rarely politicians, not even members of the Cabinet (with the exception of the President's brother, the Attorney General, and his wife), nor were they members of his family. Their most frequent visitors were newspaper people: old Georgetown friends Benjamin Bradlee, then of *Newsweek*, and his wife, Toni; Charles Bartlett of the Chattanooga *Times* and his wife Martha; artist-author William Walton.

Mrs. Kennedy purposely selected visitors from the arts and from the entertainment world, rather than politicians or statesmen—with the exception of their long-time British friend Ambassador David Ormsby-Gore (Lord Harlech).

"I want my husband to be able to leave the office, even for a few hours," she told me. "I want to surround him with bright people who can hold his interest, and divert his mind from what's going on over there!"

These dinners set a trend in town, and Washington all but abandoned its huge, crushing cocktail parties in an attempt to follow the Kennedy style—black-tie meals for twelve, with after-dinner dancing in the living room, hostess gowns, French cooking. Lobbyists and labor leaders, merchants and secretaries began copying the sophisticated mode of entertaining favored by Mrs. Kennedy and her Georgetown friends. Social life sparkled.

But Mrs. Kennedy didn't entertain her own friends in the White House. She put them to work.

The women who worked for Mrs. Kennedy—either in the White House or on the Committee for Fine Arts—were women who had grown up in the same social milieu, who reflected her tastes, and who knew how to achieve the particular life style to which the President's wife had always been accustomed. Her two social secretaries, Tish Baldridge and Nancy Tuckerman, and Caroline's nursery-school teacher, Betsy Boyd, all were graduates of Miss Porter's School in Farmington, Connecticut—as was Mrs. Kennedy. Tish, Betsy, and housekeeper Anne Lincoln were graduates of Vassar College, as was Mrs. Kennedy. And another schoolmate, Janet Felton, who'd attended grades one through six at Miss Chapin's school with Jacqueline Bouvier, was in line for a White House job.

"I certainly could use her to work with the Fine Arts Committee," Mrs. Kennedy said. "Actually, Janet would be great, because she'll know instantly whether I'd agree, and you won't have to bother me as much. . . ."

The salary for a secretary was only $6,300 per year.

"Do you think she will be able to accept?" I asked delicately. (One of her other friends couldn't afford to move to Washington.)

"Oh, it won't matter, she has a private income," Mrs. Kennedy answered.

So Janet Felton came down for her official interview at a time when Mrs. Kennedy was entertaining Henry Francis du Pont, chairman of the Fine Arts Committee.

"May we invite Miss Felton?" I suggested. "It will be a good time for her to meet Mr. du Pont."

"Oh, she already knows him," Mrs. Kennedy replied. "They're old family friends."

Mrs. Kennedy didn't seek out the companionship of other women. She had no clique who came by for canasta or Spanish lessons, no confidantes in the outside world, except perhaps her sister, Lee Radziwill, with whom she spoke frequently over transatlantic telephone.

Her sisters-in-law, the Kennedy "clan," never stopped by for lunch, nor did the women who came with their husbands to the private evenings-with-friends. She seemed to enjoy being in the company of men far more than she enjoyed women, and often invited men, usually older men who were involved in the arts, to tea in the mansion. When she was hostess at large functions, private as well as official, she held long, animated conversations with male guests, and had few words for their wives.

Nancy Tuckerman, her second social secretary, I believe, came closest to being a confidante. Yet I always felt that Mrs. Kennedy let nobody come really close to her, despite all her jocular ways, despite the easy informality with which she greeted, teased, and talked with her friends.

When she entertained her sister, who lived in London, it was always a production, as if entertaining a visiting dignitary. Princess Radziwill slept in the Queen's Room, her husband in the Lincoln bedroom. The Radziwill chil-

259

dren stayed in the White House only once; during other visits, they stayed at Merrywood and in Georgetown with Mrs. Kennedy's mother, Mrs. Hugh D. Auchincloss.

Mrs. Auchincloss came to the White House for special occasions. She was always available to help her daughter, standing in for her at functions when the First Lady couldn't attend, or taking the children for a weekend. Nevertheless, Mrs. Kennedy seemed to me to be rather formal with her mother.

The First Lady's relationship with Mrs. Joseph Kennedy was not particularly close, either. The President's mother, a very religious woman, was always sending prayers, rosary beads, and religious artifacts to her son and his family. And Rose Kennedy came to the White House more often when her daughter-in-law was away, than when she was in residence. The Ambassador's wife acted as hostess for her son at official functions during those times, and she was definitely in charge when her son visited *her*.

As she wrote to the White House:

When the President used the house in Palm Beach late last spring, after we had gone, a lot of dirty dishes, pots and pans, and linens were left strewn around the kitchen. I should appreciate it if you would tell the staff to leave everything clean in the future, as we have had trouble with rodents.

Please use your own judgment when you speak with them, because I do not want them to think that our help are complaining. Thank you.

Sincerely
/s/ Rose Kennedy
Mrs. Joseph P. Kennedy

One exception to the arms-length distance between Jacqueline Kennedy and her family was her feeling for the "Ambassador," Joseph P. Kennedy. When the President's father came to visit, she fairly danced down the halls, arm-in-arm with him, laughing uproariously at his teasing. Her face was animated and happy, as it was when she was playing with her children.

When the Ambassador suffered loss of speech and

partial paralysis, Mrs. Kennedy was more distressed than I had ever seen her; when he came for a visit to the White House several months later, she took pains to provide for his every comfort, sending me a seven-page memo with detailed instructions for his accommodations and those of his nurse. While the stricken Ambassador was staying at the White House, Mrs. Kennedy spent every possible moment with him, though he could not communicate.

The Kennedys' most frequent guest was Lemoyne Billings, the President's old roommate at Choate school. Lem, a bachelor, was always at the White House. A close friend and outside the government, he appeared to provide comic relief. Along with the Boston-Irish politician Dave Powers, Lem Billings was court jester at the Great Hall.

When the Kennedys first moved into the White House, Lem came down every weekend, and just moved into his room without anybody ever knowing he was coming. (Maybe the President knew it, but nothing was ever said about it.)

One Friday, as Mrs. Kennedy was preparing to send Caroline's pony, Macaroni, down to Virginia for the weekend, I mentioned to her that Lem Billings had arrived. (He was one of the few people who joined the Kennedys on their weekends in the country.)

"Oh, Mr. West," she whispered in mock despair. "He's been a house guest of mine every weekend since I've been married."

4

The President and his wife were gone from the White House every weekend, with the exception of national emergencies, from Friday night until Monday morning. They were accustomed to many homes. They had their own house in Hyannis, and visited frequently with President Kennedy's father in Palm Beach. We found, however, that the Ambassador's home wasn't big enough to accommodate all the entourage and accoutrements of the Presidency: Secret Service, electronics equipment, staff and friends, and the Kennedys had to rent another Palm Beach house.

When President Kennedy was a Massachusetts Senator, he went to Hyannis every weekend, or in the winter to Palm Beach, which gave him a reputation as a "four-day Senator."

Knowing that becoming a "four-day President" wouldn't go over too well with his slim majority, they selected a retreat closer to Washington. The President acceded to his wife's interest in riding and rented Glen Ora, Mrs. Raymond Tartiere's French villa in the wealthy Virginia fox-hunting country.

The Eisenhowers had used Camp David, the Presidential retreat in the Cactoctin Mountains of Maryland, so frequently that the Kennedys, without even a look at the place, knew *they* wouldn't enjoy it. Mrs. Kennedy selected Glen Ora even before the Inauguration, and she had "Sister" Parish redecorate the country home at the same time she was planning the second floor of the White House.

After storing Mrs. Tartiere's furnishings in the White House warehouse, she swept through the rented villa to the tune of $10,000, including wallpaper, paint, rugs, curtains, and furniture. When she was finished, the President raised hell.

Mrs. Parish came to me with the bill.

"Mrs. Kennedy wants to know if there's any way the government can pay for this," she said.

"Absolutely not," I declared, thinking of Camp David and the enormous cost of running a perfectly good Presidential retreat. "It has to be a personal expense. The government can't pay a penny of it."

Mrs. Kennedy loved Glen Ora. She could ride horseback through the rolling Virginia pastures—the one place she could go without the Secret Service at her side. (They were probably hiding in the bushes, though. The government *did* pay for surveillance equipment, White House police posts and rest quarters and Secret Service stations to surround Glen Ora.) There could be no more casual riding through Rock Creek Park, as Eleanor Roosevelt had done. But Jacqueline Kennedy did get to ride at Glen Ora every weekend. The children played happily there, President Kennedy swam in the Olympic-sized pool, with its elegant French poolhouse, and they enjoyed a little of the privacy Mrs. Kennedy had been seeking.

Then the President and Mrs. Tartiere had a falling-out and the Kennedys had to leave Glen Ora and spend another sum to decorate it exactly as it had been before. And Mrs. Kennedy, Secret Service in tow, began looking for other houses in Virginia, but she found none that she really wanted. So she decided to build one.

While Wexford (the new house on Rattlesnake Mountain named for President Kennedy's ancestral county in Ireland) was under construction, the Kennedys weekended at Camp David. And, to their surprise, they liked the government's Presidential retreat. The young President's wife found that she could have her horses brought in vans, and the riding was as fine as it was in Virginia.

"If only I'd realized how nice Camp David really is, I'd never have rented Glen Ora, or built Wexford," she wistfully told me.

Built as President Roosevelt's Shangri-La, the secret mountaintop retreat, surrounded by forest, is miles from civilization. Yet it is like a little resort—with swimming pool, bowling alleys, movie theater, cabins for guests and police, and breathtaking views. When the Eisenhowers redecorated it from the rustic mountain lodge President Roosevelt enjoyed, they made it super-secure.

Glen Ora had only a makeshift bomb shelter, and Wexford's, while it met the grudging approval of the Secret Service, was hardly better than one of those hastily dug by thousands of American homeowners during the Cuban missile crisis. This lack of total security may also have been one of the reasons President Kennedy didn't like Wexford.

But I honestly don't know why he didn't care for his new country home. Nor could I understand why he didn't speak his mind about it until after the expensive country estate was finished.

I was puzzled that the man who fretted over every little detail of White House decorating—the size of rugs, the color of walls, what the public might think—would not take the time to approve his own home, to go over details and make sure the place was to his liking. I only know that he spent only two or three weekends at Wexford, and kept going back to Camp David even after his new home was finished.

Mrs. Kennedy and I were in the back seat of the White House station wagon, on our way to the Virginia warehouse to find some of her stored furniture for Wexford.

"Mr. West, has a President ever sold a house while he was in office?" she whispered.

"Not that I remember," I said.

"Well, do you have any idea what the repercussions would be if we were to sell Wexford?"

"You'd probably get twice what you paid for it," I said, and she laughed. But I could tell that the wheels were turning.

Because Jacqueline Kennedy did want to please her husband.

In public, and even in front of the staff, John F. Kennedy and his wife were rather formal and correct with each other, as if the marriage were another of their press agent's concoctions. Yet the discreet White House staff, which always must know when to stay away from the second floor, was attuned to the intimacy that actually existed between the young couple. The Kennedys' early afternoons, while the children were napping, were spent in absolute privacy. Quite often, music was heard floating out into the hall, from the stereo that Mrs. Kennedy had installed in the passageway between her bedroom and her husband's. And many a morning, when George Thomas, whose job it was to wake Mr. Kennedy, would find him absent from his bedroom, the valet would tiptoe into the room next door, and gently shake the President—so as not to awaken the President's wife.

Many of us noted how cool and aloof Mrs. Kennedy appeared in public. Yet we also knew that she tried very hard to please the President, to amuse him, to bring him into her world of the arts, and at the same time to step gingerly around the edges of his world of politics, which she never really enjoyed.

After their triumphant trips abroad, I think President Kennedy realized what a political asset his publicity-shy wife actually could be. And I felt that she was slowly beginning to enjoy the adulation. After all, when the crowds all over the world cried "Jack-ie, Jack-ie, Jack-ie," she realized that the applause was indeed for herself and not simply for the political stereotype of the devoted woman behind the great man.

Jacqueline Kennedy and her husband of nearly ten years had not yet become as truly close as they might

265

have been, but I think they were getting there. They were not knit-from-the-same-cloth and mirror-close like the Trumans; they were not openly sweethearts, like the Eisenhowers; but neither was their relationship formalized and "official," like the Roosevelts'.

I think Mrs. Kennedy was trying to grope through the maze of differences between them—differences in interests, background, and personality.

5

_____

"I want to make this a grand house," Mrs. Kennedy had told me at the beginning, and she started then to make it so.

A few days later the familiar two buzzes sounded on my telephone.

"Mr. West, could you come up here a moment?" Mrs. Kennedy called.

Notebook in hand, I was at her bedside in a moment's time; she was in the pink-canopied Queen's bed, propped up for all the world like Mamie Eisenhower. She held out an old, battered copy of a magazine on antiques, which featured a photograph by Hans Huth, depicting a pier table which had been used by President Monroe in the White House.

"Do you know anything about this table?" she asked.

"I'm sure I can find it," I answered, for the White House keeps an annual inventory of all its possessions, both those in the mansion and those in the warehouse. Sure enough, in the Fort Washington warehouse, we found the Monroe pier table, dusty and rickety, with the gilt peeling off. I sent a White House truck to bring it to the mansion, and stored it in the carpenter's shop until Mrs. Kennedy got a chance to see it.

When she did, she was delighted. "We must have it restored," she exclaimed. Then "May I go with you to the warehouse?"

I was startled—not being accustomed to First Ladies stumbling about in our warehouse. Neither Mrs. Roosevelt, Mrs. Eisenhower, nor Mrs. Truman had ever ventured there.

"You can see a list of everything in this inventory," I countered, handing her the huge bound book.

"Oh, Mr. West, please let me see your warehouse," she begged. Laughing, I agreed, and off we went to search for treasures.

The Fort Washington warehouse, located on the Maryland side of the Potomac, had been filling up with furniture since the Roosevelt administration. We scrupulously followed the law, which stated that anything donated to the White House immediately became government property, and could not be returned or resold. The same law ordered an annual inventory of all White House property, to be kept by the National Park Service. Prior to this 1929 Act of Congress, the Presidents could either give away their White House gifts, take them home with them, or sell them at public auction. (Presidents James Buchanan and Chester A. Arthur had staged notorious public auctions of White House furnishings, and many of James Monroe's French acquisitions disappeared during those sales.)

When I first took Mrs. Kennedy to the warehouse, she found it filled with broken-down, no-longer-usable furniture. There were few discoveries like the Monroe pier table.

What she did find was china—and she was delighted. Following the 1929 law, every broken piece of china or silver had been stored in a special cupboard in the White House butler's pantry until inventory time at the end of the year. When they were duly recorded as broken, we ceremoniously carted them off to the carpenter's room, where we smashed the broken or chipped pieces with a sledgehammer. We then sent a butler to toss the pieces off Hains Point, into the Potomac River.

Only after enough plates were broken and dumped in the river were we able to order new Presidential china. We couldn't replace the broken pieces, because the manufacturer always destroyed the mold. So when the White House no longer had enough dishes to make a complete "set" for the State Dining Room, we retired the remaining pieces to the Fort Washington warehouse.

As the Kennedys had no State china of their own choice, Mrs. Kennedy was happy to discover some remaining pieces of the Polk service, the Harrison service, and even some Lincoln pieces, during her warehouse tour.

"Oh, Mr. West, we can use these in our upstairs dining room," she whispered excitedly, wiping the dust off the Lincoln plates with her hand.

Our lack of success in finding historic furnishings in the warehouse, however, only made Mrs. Kennedy determined to bring in outside help to carry out the project. From the very beginning, she assembled advisors, named a Fine Arts Committee,* and appointed as its chairman the distinguished American furnishings authority, Henry Francis du Pont. The Committee's purpose was to locate authentic furnishings reflecting the history of the Presidency of the United States, furnishings that were both historically accurate and of museum quality. Though the fourteen members of the Committee didn't have regular meetings, or decide as a group what should or shouldn't be accepted, each person was simply expected to go around the country, search out antiques, and persuade people to donate them to the White House.

By the time Mrs. Kennedy announced to her Fine Arts Committee's first formal meeting that, "My main project here will be to make this a truly historic house," she knew that our budget would barely cover the cost of

* Members of the Fine Arts Committee: Mrs. C. Douglas Dillon, Mrs. Charles Englehard, Mrs. Henry Ford II, Mrs. Albert Lasker, Mrs. Henry Parish II, Mrs. George Henry Warren, Mrs. Paul Mellon, Mrs. Charles Wrightsman, Charles Francis Adams, Leroy Davis, David Finley, John L. Loeb, Gerald Shea and John Walker.

paint and window shades, that there was no appropriation or hope of an appropriation for the kind of a grand-scale restoration ("Not redecoration!") Mrs. Kennedy had in mind. She knew her only hope of achieving it was from private sources.

Originally Mrs. Kennedy hoped to find furniture that had actually been used in the White House or by the Presidents at some time or other. Members of the Committee soon learned, however that either such furnishings didn't exist or were jealously guarded by museums. Moreover, they found that what was in private collections cost plenty, especially if the White House was known to be interested.

The Fine Arts Committee brought in the money and the antiques, and she quickly named two experts to head actual restoration projects. Mr. du Pont was to be the one authority on historic furnishings. M. Stephane Boudin, of the Jansen decorating firm in Paris, was to be the decorator. He was selected because Mrs. Kennedy wanted the restored White House to recall the time of President Monroe, when it was finished in the then fashionable French style. Du Pont and Boudin, both in their sixties, brought strong opinions to the project. Each naturally thought his was to be the final word.

From the first day the two men met, it was apparent they'd never see eye to eye on anything. Mr. du Pont, a dignified Eastern millionaire, was interested only in authenticity, and didn't care about arrangement or proportion or compatibility. M. Boudin, a bubbly, dramatic little Frenchman, cared only about pleasing the eye.

Mrs. Kennedy and I gave them a tour of the White House early in 1961.

Mr. du Pont, who was slightly deaf, spoke rapidly, walked slowly, and mumbled. M. Boudin was also hard of hearing, spoke halting English, and bounced energetically around the room. They tried desperately to be polite to each other. There were so many "beg pardons" and "so sorrys" and "I'm afraid I don'ts" and "but don't you means . . . ," Mrs. Kennedy and I both had to interpret. We wove in and out of the State rooms, dumbfounded by their total lack of communication.

"This is *not* going to work!" Mrs. Kennedy whispered to me.

"We'll just have to see to it that they aren't here at the same time again," I ventured. She broke into laughter.

"Absolutely!" she said, still convulsed. "Must keep them apart!"

Mrs. Kennedy was in command at every step of the restoration, entering every decision, judging like a Solomon every conflict between Boudin and du Pont. In the Green Room, for example, du Pont submitted his choice of green for the walls, and Boudin submitted *his* choice of green.

Mrs. Kennedy sent me a memo:

Mr. West,
  Could you send Mr. du Pont Boudin's 3 samples for green room 1) big ocean on green design 2) smaller green-on-green piece 3) tiny bit of moiré. Also return his own darker green stripe material, on white board. Please enclose this humble letter soliciting his approval. If we don't get it he will have the shock of me doing it anyway!

Mrs. Kennedy selected design 3, the moiré, for the Green Room walls. Despite the selection of his favorite green silk for the walls, however, Boudin was never happy with the Green Room. "It is full of legs!" he shrieked, indicating du Pont's choice of delicate chairs and tables in the American Federal style of the late eighteenth century.

Mr. du Pont, on the other hand, was never satisfied with the Blue Room, with its white walls by Boudin and the traditional blue only in accent.

"It's too *French*," he mumbled.

President Kennedy, also, was unhappy with the Blue Room. He was not at all sure that the change to white walls would meet with the approval of the American people.

"He's scared to make the change," Mrs. Kennedy whispered. "Let's cross our fingers!"

But she assured the President that the white walls were more historically accurate, and he allowed the change. Before it was opened to the public, however, President Kennedy went through the Blue Room on his own. I waited outside the door.

When he came out, he had no compliments for the room.

"Before you open it up, have the floors darkened and get a great big blue rug on the floor," the President ordered.

I sent Mrs. Kennedy a note with her husband's instructions.

"Fine—Darken floors," she scribbled back. "I'll talk to Pres. about rug."

In the end, she talked him into keeping the present rug, a valuable antique Savonnerie donated by Mrs. Albert Lasker, which had a gold-and-pink scalloped design on a light blue field.

Just before we opened the Blue Room to the press, Mrs. Kennedy stopped by the Usher's office, Caroline swinging on her hand.

"Mr. West, could you please get Mr. du Pont and David Finley (Chairman of the Commission of Fine Arts) up here and brief them enthusiastically on the Blue Room—and have them here when it's opened to the public? I want to be sure they praise it for the press."

They both agreed to come early on the day of the unveiling.

When they arrived, I took them on a preview tour, explaining in detail each of the changes, pointing out what great pains were taken to avoid a "clash" between the Red Room and Green Room, by using a soft white rather than a bold blue.

At the end of fifteen minutes, Mrs. Kennedy stepped in, on cue.

"How do you like it?" she asked, smiling expectantly.

"It's great—a great improvement!" Mr. du Pont beamed.

Mrs. Kennedy winked at me. The master would perform well for the press.

As each room took shape, the President's wife maintained a very delicate sense of timing, knowing that it would not be politely or aesthetically proper to make over the White House overnight—even when we had found the money to do more. Just after we completed the Blue Room, she wrote a note asking me to warn Mr. du Pont "not to say anything about plans for the Gold and China Rooms—as I feel we have done enough this year."

All during the restoration, when decorators, committee members, or anyone else was there, Mrs. Kennedy insisted that I accompany her at all times, as mine was the responsibility for executing (and budgeting) all changes.

The tours with Boudin were always a show: Mrs. Kennedy and the irrepressible Frenchman chattering away in French, I following along with a notebook for her occasional translations; Boudin standing on tiptoe to indicate the height a picture should hang, then trying the picture first on one wall, then another, then in another room, then in another, until the perfect spot was found. Two carpenters stood by on these expeditions, to hang pictures and move furniture. Then Mrs. Kennedy would be apt to call the next day, and ask if it could please be moved back to the first location.

Round and round the rooms we went, trying art in every possible combination. With the acquisitions from a Special Committee for White House paintings,* we soon had 150 historic paintings to hang, including five life portraits of early Presidents. And she was finally able to persuade the National Gallery of Art to return to the White House two Cézanne landscapes—her favorite paintings in the house.

Boudin and Mrs. Kennedy preferred to hang pictures in multiple groupings on each wall, rather than the one-picture-to-a-wall style of recent years. When General Eisenhower came back to the Kennedy White House for luncheon with the Prime Minister of Japan, he noted the picture arrangement with great delight.

---

* Its Chairman, James Fosburgh, did the collecting and he assigned ten art connoisseurs throughout the country to be his scouts. Members of the Special Paintings Committee: Mrs. Joseph Alsop, Mrs. J. Cheever Cowdin, Mr. Lawrence Fleischman, Mrs. Walter Halle, Mr. Stanley Marcus, Mrs. William S. Paley, Mr. Joseph Pulitzer, Mr. Vincent Price, Mr. Nathaniel Saltonstall, Mr. Whitney Warren and Mrs. Susette Morton Zurcher.

"*I* wanted to do that here," he told me, "but the Commission of Fine Arts wouldn't let me."

Mrs. Kennedy and Boudin conferred on every detail in the house, from the wardrobe doors in her boudoir (they cost $800 and were painted with realistic trompe l'oeil representations of great moments in her life: the cover of her husband's prizewinning book *Profiles in Courage,* a photo of Caroline, a model of a yacht), to the chandeliers in the East Room, to the ashtrays in the upstairs halls. The Frenchman missed nothing. "The tablecloth on the round table in the Blue Room must go," he ordered, indicating the gold fringed cloth selected by Sister Parish. "It looks like a fat Spanish dancer."

"I've learned more about architecture from Boudin than from all the books I could ever read," Mrs. Kennedy told me. "He has a superb sense of perspective."

And Boudin wrote me hundreds of letters discussing all those little details—letters in French all signed, "Croyez, cher Monsieur West, à l'assurance de mes sentiments bien dévoués," or even more affectionate terms.

"You are carrying on one of the great French correspondences of the century, Mr. West!" Mrs. Kennedy wrote, after translating one of his letters. "Do you sign your letters to Boudin, 'please believe dear sir in the assurances of my most respectful sentiments'?" As his letters grew more flowery, Mrs. Kennedy was even more amused. "I think you two are having a great affair!" she teased.

Every lampshade, every vase, every andiron came under her scrutiny and that of Boudin. Even the chandeliers moved from room to room in their march toward perfection. And the contributions poured in.

Nobody had expected the donations to come in such quantity. The White House was barraged with everybody's old quilts, spittoons, and paintings. Some were unthinkable, some were real prizes. Most of the acquisitions were authentic pieces from the period of a particular Presidency, or from a President's private home. Mrs. Kennedy was overjoyed to recover from generous donors the few pieces that actually had been used in the mansion, such as President Monroe's Bellangé chairs. Some treasures were too rare. The antique rugs, for example, did not hold up under the heavy traffic. We had to order exact copies rewoven, and what was left of the originals was banished to the warehouse, to be brought back for smaller parties.

When the "accepted" antiques moved, one by one, out of the Map Room to their place upstairs in the White House, the "rejected" reproductions they replaced started piling up next door in the spacious ground-floor room which had first been the kitchen, then the broadcast room.

I had to call in the Park Service.

"We need another warehouse badly," I said, "This stuff is all White House furniture for storage, and we've run out of space."

"Too bad we can't sell it," came the reply. "We might be able to finance your whole project that way."

But they quickly found space, in a government warehouse near National Airport, for the department-store furniture chosen by a committee and disliked by three First Ladies. In a matter of months, both warehouses bulged at the seams with the massive Victorian mirrors and heavy Grand Rapids copies used during Roosevelt, Truman and Eisenhower years.

Jacqueline Kennedy seemed to possess endless ingenuity when it came to persuading various persons and groups to make particular contributions that she wanted for the restoration. When the Colonial Dames wished to make a gift, the President's wife confided to me that a "marvelous idea" would be for them to donate the chandeliers and lanterns, for which we had already paid $5,000 and installed in the ground floor, "saving our precious money to pay for all the little things—chintz, lampshades, carpets, etc., that we will never find donors for."

She took the restoration upstairs as well, to every room in the White House. But she never forgot her need to make every dollar count. When she began to decorate the north guest room so that it would reflect the elegance of the rest of the house, she wrote me:

275

Could you let me know how much chintz (50 inches wide) we would need for the double north guest room for curtains, bedspreads, and maybe a couple of chairs? The price is $13.50 a yard, hand-blocked in England. Maybe you know some charming way of wooing the wholesale dealer so we can get it with a decorator's discount—so, you can figure out how much it might cost—and then, I will tell you where it (the money) comes from etc.

On another occasion, we were trying to negotiate purchase of an Oriental rug for the President's Private Dining Room on the second floor. I advised Mrs. Kennedy that I could scrape up the money—more than $10,000—but that I thought "Rug dealers and antique dealers are all alike—no good." She replied in a memo: "I so like the rug, but we are short of dollars and I am ENRAGED at everyone trying to gyp the White House. Tell him if he gives it (to the White House) he can get a tax donation and photo in our book—if not—goodbye!"

As the restoration progressed, Mrs. Kennedy noticed more lampshades to replace, more footstools to cover, and again realized that the problem of money would not be solved entirely by gifts.

One day, while having lunch with John Walker, director of the National Gallery of Art, she hit upon an idea.

"They don't even have a brochure for all the tourists who go through here," she reported back to me. "But if we could *sell* one, we could finance the restoration!"

There was no precedent, except at the National Gallery of Art. President Kennedy, at first, was opposed to the idea. It seemed to him like profiteering, and he was touchy on any subject that might cause unfavorable publicity. Yet, eventually, he was won over by John Walker's assurance that all the books and reproductions of paintings sold by the National Gallery had only enhanced the Gallery's reputation as a great museum—and by Jacqueline Kennedy's saying plaintively: "I want to make the experience truly memorable for everyone who comes here. I want to make a truly impressive guide book."

So Jacqueline Bouvier Kennedy, collector of antiques

and art and restorer of White House rooms, became an editor.

She set up the White House Historical Association[*] as a nonprofit organization to research and publish the guidebook. The Association contracted with the National Geographic Society for its design.

She knew exactly what kind of book she wanted—educational rather than political, and of a high print quality. The editor of the *National Geographic,* after much time and effort, showed her some sample color photographs of White House rooms, livened by people.

"I want photographs of rooms and articles, not people," Mrs. Kennedy replied. "This should be a guidebook which can last from administration to administration with a minimum of change." Back to the drawing board went the layouts—as did every word of the copy she did not approve. She was the editor in every sense of the word. And a shrewd businesswoman, it turned out. The book entirely financed the restoration.

With priceless art and antiques filling the State rooms and living quarters, the White House was fast becoming a full-fledged museum.

In the early spring of 1961 Mrs. Kennedy took her children to the Kennedy summer home in Hyannisport for the week. Before she left we took a walk through the rose garden. The sun beamed on rows of tulips, not roses. Our greenhouse genius managed to produce and transplant blossoming flowers of every season for the White House garden.

"Please see if you can't do something about the grass," she murmured. "The President is after me again."

"We're going to have an opening in the Usher's office this summer," I reminded her. "Have you anybody in mind?"

She brightened.

[*] Board of Directors were: David E. Finley, chairman, John Walker, treasurer, Clark M. Clifford, Melville Bill Grosvenor, Leonard Carmichael, Conrad Wirth, and T. Sutton Jett, executive secretary.

"Oh, Mr. West, do you think you could get me a little curator, instead?"

"We'll look into it," I promised. I knew that the inventory of furniture was becoming too much for me to handle, and that, as a result of the restoration, both the social office and my office had to refer a great amount of mail to Mr. du Pont at Winterthur, his museum of American furnishings in Delaware, causing great delays for the sender. So I called the director of the Smithsonian, to ask for recommendations.

And, with a great deal of fanfare, we selected Lorraine Pearce, who'd trained at Winterthur, as the first curator of the White House. Perhaps there was too much fanfare.

Mrs. Pearce immediately won popularity on the Washington lecture circuit, and became the primary news source for stories on the restoration. At first, Mrs. Kennedy was highly pleased with her new curator—and insisted that Mrs. Pearce write the text to the White House guidebook, even though the prestigious John Walker himself had offered to do so.

"It needs to be written by a trained curator," Mrs. Kennedy scrawled on one of her innumerable memos to me. "Lorraine can do it."

The "little curator," however, wasn't about to be content sitting in a cubbyhole, cataloguing the White House furnishings. From the beginning, Lorraine was determined to build a position out of her job.

"I must have a secretary," she demanded, "and an assistant."

I explained to her that the government would not allow us to create satellite positions around her job because, technically, she was on loan from the Smithsonian.

"But, Mr. West," she argued. "Surely you can see the necessity of a permanent curator's office, if the White House is to be preserved properly." I had to agree, knowing that otherwise the responsibility for keeping records on those priceless antiques would be mine.

Inevitably, Mrs. Pearce became the one casualty, besides the Truman furniture, of the restoration—for breaking the unspoken White House rule: One does not provoke the First Lady.

First, Lorraine acted rather grandly toward Mrs. Kennedy's social staff in the east wing, expecting them to do the secretarial work she needed. Second, she felt free to talk to the press without consulting the press office, and twice made public statements on behalf of the First Lady that contradicted Mrs. Kennedy's personal feelings. Third, her interpretation of "what Mrs. Kennedy *really* wants" was at odds with Tish Baldrige's interpretation of what Mrs. Kennedy really wanted.

As the donations of antiques and paintings increased, so did pressure on Lorraine, and so did the tempers of the ladies in the east wing. One day Mrs. Kennedy stopped me as I walked past the bolts of cerise silk piled on the floor in the Red Room. "What is going on with Lorraine, Mr. West?" she murmured. "I'm getting notes about her from Pam, Janet, Tish, and everybody. I do like her work, though. Do you think you can solve this?"

"Perhaps you could ask Lorraine for a memo outlining her thoughts about the curator's job," I answered, since I had been receiving many such a memo from the new curator.

So the memo was requested, written, and received. Twelve pages long, the letter poured out all the frustrations of its writer, and ambitions for the office of curator.[*]

Mrs. Kennedy called me up to the second floor to show me the letter. She was seated in the West Hall at her father's desk.

When I finished reading it, she said, "Well, this settles it. She's come down with White House-itis. [White House-itis was our private term for the disease that swept through the mansion periodically, claiming a few victims among the employees. Its symptoms were enlargement of the cranium and a sudden desire for assistants.] But she must finish the guidebook."

That afternoon, I called Mrs. Pearce to my office.

"Since your principal job is writing the text for the guidebook right now," I said, "Mrs. Kennedy suggests that

---

[*] Ironically, the office of Curator eventually surpassed Mrs. Pearce's ambitions. In 1964, an Executive Order of the President established a permanent office of Curator and the Committee for the Preservation of the White House.

it might be best for you to isolate yourself, and write full time. . . ."

"Oh, I certainly agree," she broke in. "It's so hard to get anything done here, with all this furniture coming in, that has to be looked at, and—"

"So we're setting up an office for you in the Department of Interior," I continued, "where you'll be much better able to write."

By the time she finished the copy for the guidebook, Lorraine realized that her duties as curator had been taken over by Bill Elder, who soon was replaced by James Ketchum, a personable young man whose interest lay in American history. The entire broadcast room, across from the Diplomatic reception room, became his curator's office. Soon he had both an assistant and a secretary and, ironically, the "little curator" job began to carry all the weight and responsibility that Mrs. Pearce had hoped for.

But even in easing Mrs. Pearce out, the First Lady wanted to appear kind, as well as politically tactful. After reading my proposed letter telling the curator of her reassignment, Mrs. Kennedy noted to me: "This is a little strong . . . put in a couple softening sentences regretting to see her go, or something. . . . Announce her departure in terms most flattering to her. It has all gone so well. We don't want the last letter to make it bitter."

In a letter to John Walker, she wrote, "They should have sent Mr. West to Geneva with Gromyko."

And Mrs. Kennedy, along with everybody else, was delighted with the guidebook.

At the end of a year, the transformation of the house was well on its way. One January afternoon, in 1962, Mrs. Kennedy, Boudin, the carpenters and I were in the Green Room with a "new" painting, J. F. Kensett's "Niagara Falls."

Boudin suddenly sank onto Daniel Webster's own New England sofa, newly upholstered in creamy silk.

"The Benjamin Franklin—he must be alone," the tired little decorator insisted.

The carpenters duly took the fine old portrait from above the Cézanne landscapes, and placed it above the mantel.

"Madame, the proportion is all wrong," he said for the hundredth time. "These should not be so—dainty!" He indicated Mr. du Pont's white Federal sofas, Martha Washington's armchair and looking glass.

"But the wall covering *is* lovely," Mrs. Kennedy said gently. The green watered-silk had been Boudin's choice. "Now let's go into the room you like," she smiled, "for I have something to tell both of you."

It was nearly 5:30 when we walked into the newly finished Red Room.

"That's all for today," she told our patient picture-hanging carpenters, "and please send a butler in here."

She ordered Daiquiris for herself and for Boudin and me.

"Happy anniversary," she said. "We've been at this for one year."

"May it go on forever," said Boudin, raising his glass.

We sipped our drinks in our favorite of the downstairs rooms, the cerise-and-gold nineteenth-century parlor. President Kennedy had been nervous about changing the color from the traditional fire-engine red, but Mrs. Kennedy and Boudin won, as usual.

Presidents Jefferson, Truman, F. Roosevelt, T. Roosevelt, and Hoover, along with Alexander Hamilton, looked down from the rosy walls.

"I'm going to be a television star," Mrs. Kennedy announced. "What do you think?"

Boudin and I both drank to that.

On February 14, the publicity-shy First Lady put on her public face and brought millions of people into the State rooms of the White House via CBS television. As she and Charles Collingwood toured the rooms, pointing out the changes, discoveries, and additions of the Fine Arts Committee, I stood behind the door, ready to supply any information. But, like the wheelchair when she toured the mansion with Mrs. Eisenhower, I wasn't called for.

Immediately after the taping, we all went downstairs to the movie theater to watch the program.

"CBS is going to give us $10,000 for the Fine Arts Committee," Mrs. Kennedy whispered to me as she came through the door.

President Kennedy sat in the front row to watch the show.

After the runthrough, he asked me, "What do you think?"

"I think it's great," I answered.

"Oh, he *would*," Mrs. Kennedy laughed, meaning I don't know what.

"It's terrific," said the President. "Terrific. Can we show it in 1964?"

Mrs. Kennedy evidently thought it was all right, too. Or else they'd have had it to do over.

6

The millions of Americans who were "invited in" during Mrs. Kennedy's hour-long television special had only a taste of what it was like to be a guest of the White House with Jacqueline Kennedy as hostess. With her official guests, she was as correct, as cool, as formally gracious as she appeared to her television audience. Even so, White House entertaining under Mrs. Kennedy was much less formal than it ever had been, and her style was vastly different from Mamie Eisenhower's.

During the Eisenhower years, we had proudly perfected State dinners down to the second: Always white tie, always one large E-shaped banquet table in the State Dining Room, always a great deal of pomp and circumstance, with the polish of a precision drill team. With the Kennedys, the atmosphere was younger, more glamorous, more informal, because the Kennedys were younger, etc. But it took much more planning to achieve that appearance of spontaneity.

During the Eisenhower administration, I prepared a detailed schedule for every facet of a State function, showing who was to stand where and when, the precise timing of entrances, the orderly procedure from room to room. The President and his wife would study the plan carefully, as would all the military aides, butlers, cooks, doormen, and band.

President Kennedy felt such detail was unnecessary.

On February 14, 1961, for example, at his first State luncheon, President Kennedy entertained the Prime Minister of Denmark, with additional guests. The President received his guests of honor privately, upstairs in the Oval Room. The plan was for them to walk together from the elevator directly to the Blue Room, where the guests were assembled.

At approximately the correct moment, the President and his guests came down on the elevator. Instead of stepping into the Blue Room, however, John F. Kennedy marched his guests directly into the pantry! With his usual aplomb, the President laughed and backed out again. "Oh, this is another room I wanted to show you," he said to the Danes. After that, we had to station an aide outside the elevator door (President Kennedy didn't like walking up or down the curving staircase because of his painful back trouble) to precede the President into the right room.

Mrs. Kennedy made her own rules for protocol and arrangements, mostly thoughtful ones. After the third State function, a dinner for the Prime Minister of Australia, she sent me a memo:

> Mr. West—
>
> Will you tell whoever it is—After this, at *every* occasion where they play Hail to the Chief & just announce Pres—to please also say the V.P. of U.S. and Mrs. Johnson. It is so embarrassing to have them not announced, & just disappear like maids. . . .

The tone of the Kennedy entertaining was lighter, gayer, more fun: Black tie rather than white tie; for the first time, cocktails before dinner; and smoking was allowed. (Despite the denials of such a possibility to the press, our staff even worked out instructions for detecting and removing overindulgent guests. We never had to carry them out, however.)

They had a formal receiving line only at State dinners. At the few large receptions they held, President and Mrs. Kennedy mingled among the guests and "received" as they walked through the room. We set up buffet tables, with roast beef, canapés, salmon and chicken, and served cocktails—a more sumptuous spread than the punch and finger-sandwiches of the past twenty years.

The huge State dinners were fewer in number and were usually restricted to those honoring foreign visitors. René added great variety to the menus with his gourmet cooking.

The Kennedys cut down on the number of courses at meals and changed the tone of after-dinner entertainment (Eisenhowers: 6 courses, with 21 items, followed by Fred Waring and the Pennsylvanians. Kennedys: 4 courses, with 8 items, followed by the Metropolitan Opera Studio). Gone was the formal E-shaped banquet table. Instead, Mrs. Kennedy selected fifteen round tables seating ten each for the State Dining Room. For larger affairs, we set up additional round tables in the Blue Room. Delicate multicolored flower arrangements, yellow organdy tablecloths and candlelight highlighted the formal entertaining.

The powerhouse behind the glittering evenings at the White House was the First Lady's social secretary, Letitia Baldrige. Tish was really a social director, with a background in the diplomatic service, who selected menu, guests, entertainment, decor, and seating arrangements. In one respect she lightened my burden considerably, but in another her creative entertaining set the entire White House spinning.

"If you locked that woman in a closet for twenty-four hours, she'd have enough work to last you a month when she came out," Usher Rex Scouten exclaimed one morning, after Tish had swept through our office.

Messengers trotted upstairs with her "urgent" folders so often that Mrs. Kennedy complained to the President that she could get nothing else done all day. He suggested a solution.

"My husband thinks that I should look for a place for a

285

little office in the east wing near the social office," she told me. "I might spend a couple of hours a day over there, and not be bothered with all the folders all day long. Mr. West, will you take me there now!" she asked.

I walked with her down the glassed-in ground-floor corridor where tourists enter, past the White House police offices, and up the stairs again to the east wing. The First Lady's staff, her correspondence office, files office, press office, and social office cannot be approached from the State floor nor from the family floor.

"I'd have to time my trips over here to avoid the tourists," she noted.

We walked in on Tish's operation, looking for a likely little office for the First Lady. Phones were ringing, papers flying, secretaries zipping from office to office, pacing their moves to Tish's mock hysteria.

"Isn't this a madhouse?" Barbara Keehn asked, apologetically.

No one knew why we were there.

Six-foot Tish propelled herself into the hall, directing a silent orchestra with one arm.

"Oh, I'm so glad I caught you," she said to Mrs. Kennedy. "We're going to have to change the seating for tomorrow's luncheon because the Prime Minister has brought two more in his entourage than we expected. Now if you'll just look at the chart, I think we can squeeze them in. . . ."

"Tish's operation reminds me of an old Rosalind Russell movie," Mrs. Kennedy laughed, as we walked back. And she vetoed the move to a little office in the east wing.

In 1961, Jacqueline Kennedy dispensed entirely with the traditional social season. "The Inauguration was quite enough," she told me.

The next year, she reshaped the "season," combining the dinners for the Vice President and for the Speaker of the House, and adding receptions for Congress, the diplomatic corps, and the military. The same four occasions were repeated in 1963 but the military reception, perhaps to whet patriotism, honored Congressional Medal of Honor winners.

Instead of concentrating on the Washington social season, which had been primarily a series of political evenings, the cosmopolitan First Lady turned to her own strong suit, entertaining foreign visitors. During their three short years, the Kennedys were hosts to sixty-six heads of State.

The Chief of Protocol, Angier Biddle Duke, and the Secretary of State extended invitations for the President. Once the date of a visit was established, they submitted a list of "must" guests—the head of State's entourage, the country's diplomatic corps—all in order of rank, to Tish. She sent out her network of informants to find prominent Americans (especially members of Congress and Democratic contributors) whose ancestors hailed from the honoree's home country.

She then sent the list over in a folder to the President and Mrs. Kennedy. It always came back with the addition of sparkling names from the literary and artistic world, in Mrs. Kennedy's handwriting, and a few more politicians or news-media representatives, in the President's.

The social office sent out the invitations three weeks before the party, and notified me of the date, time, and approximate number of guests. I passed the word along to the housekeeper and head chef, who went to work on the menu, which they soon submitted to Mrs. Kennedy for approval, and then ordered the food from local wholesalers. I also told the head butler, who began lining up the extra help needed for serving at the dinner.

Although René always began cooking two days before a party, we did not start arranging the rooms until the last sightseer had walked through at noon. Then, an army magically appeared, vacuum cleaners roaring, round tables walking upstairs on the heads of moving men, china and crystal, and gleaming, golden vermeil flatware being wheeled up from the depths of the mansion to the Private Dining Room, which was set up as a serving pantry for the dinner.

(My only regret during the restoration was that the Private Dining Room on the State floor wasn't made into a permanent pantry, after the Kennedys had installed the second-floor Presidential Dining Room and kitchen. The hundreds of items necessary for a formal dinner at the

Mansion all are stored in the basement, and the puffing, panting, and grumbling that accompanies this up-and-down hauling of china, flatware, glassware, tables, chairs, *et al.*, can be appreciated by every bride whose kitchen is too small to store the wedding presents.)

The butlers then began setting the tables.

Meanwhile, the carpenters and moving crews had driven out to the warehouse, to fetch our pride and joy, the little red-velvet jewel-box stage, designed by Lincoln Kirsten, inspired by Mrs. Kennedy, and built ingeniously portable by Edgar Shipp and his cheerful crew of White House carpenters.

Finally, as guests began arriving to be checked in by the police at the south entrance, flower arranger "Rusty" Young and his helpers placed their low, colorful bowls of flowers atop each organdy-covered table. The butlers touched the new dimmer switches on the chandeliers and lit the candles and headed for the East Room with their trays of premixed drinks.

I began three hours of wandering around, dressed like any guest, smiling, greeting people, praying for everybody to remember his job, for the guests to stay sober, and for the President to remember that he was supposed to walk into the East Room on "Hail to the Chief," and not to the drum rolls of "Ruffles and Flourishes." (Nobody could understand why he always tried to march off on "Ruffles," leaving the flags, guests, and Mrs. Kennedy standing at the foot of the Grand Staircase.)

There were a few mishaps, such as the time an antique dining chair collapsed under President Kennedy (everybody feared the President had broken his back, and those chairs were banished from the State rooms forever), or when the fuses blew during an after-dinner performance of "Brigadoon" (the President could be heard saying, "It's supposed to be like this," and I ran for the electricians, the Signal Corps, and anybody else in the White House who knew anything about nonpolitical power), or the time a guest knocked over a small table of drinks in the East Room (and I tried to stop a young college student, suave in black tie, from cleaning up the broken glass because I'd forgotten that he had been hired to help the butlers).

My department heads had trained their staff well, and there was usually no need for me to be there at all, dressed in my black tie, white tie, striped trousers, or whatever the occasion called for, to supervise the 150 people called into service for a State Dinner.

And afterwards, the young hostess issued a critic's appraisal of each dinner in a style that could have passed for that of the nation's leading restaurant reviewers. After a dinner party in January, 1963, she complimented housekeeper Anne Lincoln "that the food was fantastic" and that "service was in record time." Having said that, however, she noted: There was a 10 to 15 minute wait for the first course and a consequent lull in the spirit of the party; the wine wasn't served until people had finished their fish; the Brie cheese "was like hard rubber" and should have been left out of the refrigerator all day to get soft. Finally, the name of the dessert was misspelled on the menu. "It is Surprise, not Suprise," she wrote. "If this is your spelling, take note. If it was Sandy Fox (the calligrapher), tell him nicely."

Washington, which had sometimes been described as "culturally latent," woke up to the performing arts during Mrs. Kennedy's evenings at the White House. Bypassing the popular favorites of the era, she invited serious, excellent artists such as Pablo Casals, Isaac Stern, Eugene Istomin, and promoted ballet, chamber music, opera, and Shakespearean drama for the after-dinner enjoyment of guests in the East Room. From the notes I received, I knew that most of the ideas originated in Mrs. Kennedy's head; Tish followed through, made the contacts and built upon the ideas; and I figured out ways to direct the staff to carry them out.

On our most unusual and probably most successful State Dinner, honoring Pakistan's President Ayub Khan, Mrs. Kennedy was involved in almost every detail of the complicated logistics of dining at Mount Vernon.

We made a number of trips down the Potomac on the Presidential yacht *Honey Fitz* *—Mrs. Kennedy standing at the bow like Cleopatra on the Nile—to perfect the

* Née *Barbara Anne.*

timing of transporting our 150 workers, all the food, the National Symphony Orchestra, the Marine Honor Guard, the Army Fife and Drum Corps, the Air Force Strolling Strings, not to mention 132 guests, to the home of the first President, where dinner was served by candlelight on the front lawn overlooking the river.

7

————

Despite Tish's efficiency, Mrs. Kennedy referred to my office rather than to the social office on matters of extreme delicacy. I remember vividly one Sunday morning, October 21, 1962, when Zella and I were at home in Arlington, enjoying our one day of luxurious late sleep. I had followed Mrs. Kennedy's weekend instructions to prepare for the Maharajah and Maharani of Jaipur, who had entertained her so royally during her trip to India:

Mr. West
Could little chest of drawers in Q. dressing room be painted black before Mon. I just want it to look more pulled together by time Maharani of Jaipur comes Oct 23–27. Gold doesn't matter & mirror is OK—just blacken chest.
P.S. Jaipurs will be bringing HIS valet
will you find a place for him—
(over)
Could spread in Lincoln sitting room be ready by Oct

23—for daybed otherwise put my fur rug on it—& some
green & yellow pillows—

The telephone jarred me awake that Sunday. Mrs. Kennedy's voice sounded urgent.

"Could you please come to the White House right away, Mr. West, but come up through the kitchen elevator so nobody will know you're here."

"I'll be there in twenty minutes," I answered—and I was.

I drove down Pennsylvania Avenue, entering the northwest, or "main" gate to the grounds, but noticing, as I passed the President's office, an unusual number of cars parked in the White House driveway—unusual because the Kennedys rarely could be found in Washington on Sunday. As I had been instructed, I drove down to the tradesman's entrance, and rode upstairs on the kitchen elevator.

Mrs. Kennedy, wearing colorful Pucci pants with loafers, and no make-up, as usual, waited in the west hall, alone. Seated on the sofa, she was framed in the large arched window, looking out at the bright Sunday sunshine. Ordinarily, on a day like this, she'd be out in the country, on horseback.

"Thank you for coming, Mr. West," she said softly. "There's something brewing that might turn out to be a big catastrophe—which means that we may have to cancel the dinner and dance for the Jaipurs Tuesday night."

But when she spoke of canceling, her face was impassive, her tone almost casual. I glanced at the Oval Drawing Room door, which was closed, and heard men's voices from the inside.

"Could you please handle the cancellation for me? This is all very secret," she continued, "and I'm afraid Tish would get all upset and rant and rave—*you* know—and I think you could do it more calmly."

"Certainly," I said.

She rose. "I will either call you in the morning, or else you'll hear an announcement of what it's all about. When you realize that it will have to be canceled, call Tish."

As I walked down the hall toward the elevator, Robert Kennedy stepped out of the Yellow Oval Room into the hall. Glancing our way without a smile, he closed the door quickly behind him. Something very grave was happening, but I had no idea what it was.

At seven the next morning I was at my desk in the White House. On the car radio I had heard only the terse announcement: "The President will speak to the nation at seven this evening on this most urgent matter. A special session of the United Nations had been called. . . ." Taking this cue that cancellation of the dinner-dance was in order, I got busy and called the Marines to cancel the orchestra, called the chef to cancel the grocery order, called housekeeper Anne Lincoln and head butler Charles Ficklin, to say, simply,

"There will be no dinner on Tuesday."

Then I called Tish Baldrige in the east wing.

"Because of the urgent nature of the President's message tonight, Mrs. Kennedy wishes to cancel Tuesday night's dinner dance," I announced rather formally.

"I've been listening to the radio," she said worriedly. "We'll begin phoning the guests right away." She did sound rather upset.

Mrs. Kennedy buzzed me at 9:30 a.m.

"I guess you've heard the news?" she asked.

"I've already canceled the party and informed Tish," I said.

"How did she take it?" Mrs. Kennedy wanted to know.

"Calmly," I said.

"Good." She sounded relieved.

That Monday evening, October 22, 1962, President Kennedy spoke to the nation from his office:

Good evening, my fellow citizens.

This government, as promised, has maintained the closest surveillance of the Soviet military buildup on the island of Cuba. Within the past week, unmistakable evidence has established the fact that a series of offensive missile sites is now in preparation on that imprisoned island. The purpose of these bases can be none other than to provide a nuclear strike capability against the Western Hemisphere. . . .

And the Cuban missile crisis began.

For an entire week, top-level, top-secret meetings had been going on all around us, and we didn't know it. The fate of the world was in the balance, and the White House went on as usual.

The Tuesday evening party canceled, the Kennedys dined quietly with their friends, the British Ambassador and his wife, and the Jaipurs, who had been placed in the Blair House.

For the week following, the White House staff, like the rest of the country, was balanced somewhere between war and peace. But, unlike most other citizens, we were not digging bomb shelters and storing up canned goods, because our bomb shelter was there, underneath the subbasement, and our reserve pantries were full.

The President's family stayed close at home, and continued our daily routine as calmly as possible, until Nikita Khrushchev announced publicly that the missiles were being withdrawn.

With the crisis over, Washington and the country heaved a huge sigh of relief. At the White House, we settled back into a heavy schedule of entertaining in the Kennedy style—a style that influenced the nation.

Much of that influence can be attributed to Tish Baldrige and her ability, not only in handling the Kennedy parties, but also in working with Pam Turnure to disseminate the skillful publicity that accompanied them. She had an inner sense of what would catch the public's eye, and knew how to use entertaining to build an image for the First Lady.

Tish was forceful and full of ideas, and she was aggressive by nature. But one didn't push Jackie Kennedy. "You just have to do this," Tish would say, trying to get her to greet some group that she felt warranted an appearance by the First Lady. "Mr. West, I don't *have* to do anything," the First Lady complained. For Mrs. Kennedy also was often forceful and had definite ideas of her own, which at times caused friction between her and Tish.

After two and a half years of spectacular entertaining, and with the restoration project almost completed, the President's wife was expecting a baby. "I just want to sit back and enjoy myself for the next few years," Mrs. Kennedy told me.

And Tish, who Mrs. Kennedy said had been "invaluable to me during those first years," left Washington to work for the Kennedy family's Merchandise Mart in Chicago. Nancy Tuckerman, Jacqueline Bouvier's roommate at Miss Porter's school, and a much calmer personality, stepped in as social secretary.

I arranged a staff farewell party for Tish in the ground-floor China Room (where Presidential dishes from all administrations are displayed in glass cases). Mrs. Kennedy asked to be invited.

"I'd like to bring John and Caroline," she said, "and would you please call in the Marines? I've written a little song I'd like them to sing." She handed me a note with the lyrics.

The Marine Band appeared at 4:00 sharp, their red uniforms matching the brilliant Oriental carpet on the floor, and we all sang, as Tish appeared,

> "Arrivederci, Ti-ish
> Goodbye, goodbye, au revoir
> For you, Tish, our hearts will be yearning
> But we know you'll often be returning
> From afar.
> Arrivederci, Ti-ish
> The time has come to part
> Mr. We-st's heart will keep on churning. . . ."

The authoress of the parody, of course, sang along with the Marine Band.

Although I hadn't realized that I had been "churning," as far as I was concerned things ran much more smoothly under Nancy's calm hand. Mrs. Kennedy had set the style, Tish and I had worked out the procedures, and Nancy stepped into a functioning position. Mrs. Kennedy told her to discuss everything with me, and then to take my judgment.

"Don't bring any questions to me," she told Nancy, "because Mr. West knows what I want, and also what can or can't be accomplished."

Nancy and I worked very closely together during the next few months. She stepped in to handle the President's private forty-sixth birthday party aboard the Secretary of the Navy's yacht *Sequoia*, two stag luncheons, and only two State dinners, while Mrs. Kennedy was in Hyannis, quietly awaiting the birth of her baby.

One advantage that Nancy had was her personal friendship with Mrs. Kennedy. She knew all the First Lady's foibles, and how she wanted to operate. She knew exactly what to send upstairs, when to send it, what to discuss with her, and what subjects to avoid. When Nancy approached her with an idea, she sometimes said, "Oh, Nancy, I don't want to *do* that," and that would be the end of it.

Nancy also made a firm attempt to keep spending down, a task imposed upon her by the President.

Liquor was quite an expense during the Kennedy years —primarily because we had to stop serving bootleg whiskey. During the Eisenhowers, the White House very discreetly accepted bottles of "confiscated distilled spirits" from the General Services Administration, at no cost. However, a new regulation would have forced us to sign purchase orders—which would have put our clandestine bars out in the open. President Kennedy didn't want the publicity, so housekeeper Anne Lincoln shopped around Washington for the lowest-cost liquor.

The President's private liquor supply was stored in a closet on the third floor, to which only the housekeeper and the President's valet held a key. The official liquor supply was stored in the basement of the White House, and Anne kept an account of daily use, purchases, and a running inventory of both the official and the private liquor cabinets.

During the Kennedy administration, we were able to transfer our biggest, costliest failure, the White House grounds, directly to the National Park Service—and just in time, too. It took armies of men, and much more than our budget could bear to get the lawns in shape, and, we found out, so much that the Park Service didn't even have funds set aside to cover it. To do the vast amount of spraying, reseeding, fertilizing, planting, and replanting that President Kennedy insisted upon, the Park Service used funds that had been set aside for various other projects in Washington.

One day, Park Service Director Conrad Wirth was confronted by the President's District of Columbia liaison officer, who was concerned about the shape of D. C. park land. "We just can't do all these other things in the District because we have to spend all our money at the White House," Wirth said.

This remark got back to the President, who bawled him out for making such a statement, and Conrad Wirth was sorry he'd ever opened his mouth, even if it was the truth. The White House grounds project cost nearly $200,000.

Mrs. Paul Mellon, a close personal friend of the Kennedys as well as an authority on horticulture, designed and supervised the President's favorite spot, the Rose Garden outside his office window. But the labor, the biggest expense, came from the Park Service. And most of the plantings that were brought to the Rose Garden were taken from other government property in the area. Mrs. Mellon would drive around the city, and when she saw a cherry tree or a magnolia tree that she liked, she had it dug up and replanted in the White House garden.

At first, President Kennedy spent a good portion of his time with me poring over the mansion's budget, searching for ways to keep spending down. He finally gave up, realizing full well that the $500,000 in our appropriation was too inadequate, too limited to operate the White House, and that we had to siphon quite a bit of our upkeep from other government agencies.

Despite the impossibility of Presidential accounting, I think I can safely say that the Kennedys spent no more of the public's money than did the previous or succeeding administrations. Streamlining the menus helped cut food costs, and, all in all, they held fewer official functions in the White House. The more elaborate functions, such as the dinner for Ayub Khan at Mount Vernon, were partially subsidized by private donors, and, of course, all of the entertainment was free. Nevertheless, President and Mrs. Kennedy certainly spent a lot more of their own money, did more elaborate private entertaining, had more servants, and took more trips.

8

At first, Mrs. Kennedy hated the title "First Lady."

Provy had sent me a note signed "First Lady's Maid," asking if she was to eat in the basement with the White House staff. I took the note up to Mrs. Kennedy, to explain that the maids could stagger their lunch hour, so that someone would be on duty all the time, and the young President's wife spied the words "First Lady."

"*Please*, Mr. West, the one thing I do not want to be called is First Lady. It sounds like a saddle horse. Would you please notify the telephone operators and everyone else that I'm to be known simply as Mrs. Kennedy, and not as First Lady." So I did.

But later on, she realized what her position meant—that there is only one such person in the country. When her husband's mother called, the operators would say, "Mrs. Joseph is on the line . . . ," and Jacqueline Kennedy said to me, "At the beginning I didn't know how it would be. I am *the* Mrs. Kennedy. I am the First Lady."

She had begun to enjoy the title, and the life, more than anyone ever suspected that she would. Proud of her accomplishments, confident of her position, sure of her staff, she was ready to sit back and relax for the next few years.

"Just think, Mr. West," she said as she surveyed the antique-filled White House. "You'll be able to take a good, long rest!"

In the spring of 1963, there seemed to be few hazards for the Kennedys. The President was enjoying greater success in both domestic and international affairs. The dark days of the Bay of Pigs, the Cuban missile crisis, the tough confrontation with Khrushchev, the near-showdown over Berlin were now behind him. The United States and Russia had stopped rattling nuclear missiles at each other, and had signed a nuclear-test-ban treaty.

At home the President seemed to have the economy really humming again, helped by the passage of tax measures to stimulate the economy and by an international tariff agreement. The President was now turning to confront the tough domestic issues of race relations and poverty. Mr. Kennedy already was starting to plan for a reelection campaign more than a year away, and he started venturing out into the country, where he received enthusiastic praise for his peace moves with the Russians.

Also, that spring of 1963, I saw once again how Presidents think ahead about their place in history. They are concerned about how their record on issues of war and peace will be judged in the future, about how the laws that they initiated will be seen in the long, continuing stream of American life. And they also think about monuments to themselves. For example, on April 2, 1963, after only two years in office, President Kennedy already was planning his Presidential library. On that day, Mrs. Kennedy sent me a memorandum:

Would Mr. Arata know of any wonderful wood carver? The absured reason I ask this is that I am thinking very far ahead: In his Library, the President (like President Truman) wishes to have a replica of his office—heaven knows, he picked the worst possible desk to duplicate.

I thought if there was a wood carver around, perhaps, he could do such a thing by stucco, or wax impressions—

would you find this out, perhaps from Smithsonian? You could tell them that some museum wants a duplicate of the desk, the best way this could be done, and let me know when you do.

Unfortunately, the technique turned up by the Park Service for duplicating the elaborately-carved desk was far too costly, and the project was abandoned. (And ironically, the desk itself, presented by Queen Victoria and used upstairs by Franklin Roosevelt and Harry Truman, was shipped all over the world a year later as part of an exhibit of Kennedy memorabilia to raise funds for the construction of the Kennedy Library. The desk itself is now in the Smithsonian.)

Though she stayed away from his official life, Mrs. Kennedy worked lovingly to decorate her husband's office. At one point in 1963, she asked me to push Boudin to finish the office for the President's birthday.

And she was always sensitive to his comfort, whether in his office or the living quarters. After we created the new second-floor drawing room (the Yellow Oval Room, which had been a study for past Presidents), which the Kennedys used for entertainment and for late afternoon or evening business, the President found things that made him uneasy about his new "easy room." He also had similar complaints about his office, and Mrs. Kennedy noted both to me:

> The sofas in the yellow oval room in front of the fireplace are still awfully deep and every one seems to hate to sit on them as they can't get up. . . .
>
> Also, the President says that the softest sofas in his office are a bit low, and everybody doesn't like to be sitting that much lower than he is. . . . Could you see what can be done to raise them. . . . Go sit on one and see if you think they are too "squishy" and deep.

She also was concerned that his surroundings reflect *his* own personality and went to great effort selecting objects and furnishings which would please him. At one point, trying to balance the desires of the President, Boudin, and her own very detailed sense of decor, she noted to me: "I know the President loves a red rug but ask Boudin if he does think it too obvious (or banal? in French) to do the Pres. office in red, white and blue. Let's have no blue. . . ."

When I heard about Mrs. Kennedy's pregnancy, I teased her about planning her life so that she could avoid campaigning in the 1964 election. She laughed and gave me her secret, knowing look. But she set herself a task that spring of 1963, that would give her plenty to do all summer. She was busy planning the gift she wanted to give the President on their wedding anniversary in September.

The gift consisted of three scrapbooks, a project I helped her put together. The elaborate books were entitled: "The White House—Before and After," "The President's Park," and "The Making of a Garden."

Enough work went into those scrapbooks to qualify them as fine art books. We searched historical records for pictures from past White House history. Mrs. Kennedy laid out in great detail the picture scenario from the Kennedy years. The range of photographs she sought covered such simple, loving scenes as "a sweet one of John sniffing tulips and wearing a red jacket." And then there were the events of history, such as President Kennedy ordering the National Guard to restore order at the University of Mississippi, where whites had rioted following the admission of the school's first black student.

In May, before she left for the beach at Hyannis, she wrote me a long, detailed note—planning weekends, matching colors in adjoining rooms, and decorating the President's office. She concluded with plans for the baby she was expecting:

> . . . And that is *ALL*. All I want for the nursery (present childrens dining room) is a pair of curtains like Johns room & (which Lucinda is doing) & white glass curtains you can still see through—like Johns—& a white rug not wall to wall—I don't think the one in the childrens & my room is too practical—I'd just have Anne buy a rather shaggy inexpensive one at Sloanes which we can throw in washing machine—& a rubber pad beneath it.

And for the waiters not to walk through there—& not through my hall either!—or not when I may be around—only for Pres lunch & nap—can they go through—So how will they get out? They may have to use elevator & go upstairs & come down—or you can cut them a trap door in fireplace—but I dont see that they have that much reason to go back & forth there—cleaning boys can learn to come down stairs by elevator or Q room & NEVER go near pantry—unless by servants elevator—as they are only ones who need to go back & forth—& if they would just take a different route—the 2nd suggested —all would be well—

Next yr I wont do one single thing & recuperate for 6 months—so you will have that to look forward to—

Thank you—
JBK

It seems that the baby would live in the "high-chair room," a tiny room between little John's room and the Presidential Dining Room, which had been President Eisenhower's painting room, Mrs. Truman's office, and, before that, Mrs. Roosevelt's office.

The day after Mrs. Kennedy left for Cape Cod, we went to work on the nursery. Even though much touching-up on the house was needed, we scheduled the baby's room as first priority.

By June 15, the stark little room was gone, and a blue-and-white baby's room appeared, with John's white crib and crisp white curtains, and a soft white (washable) rug.

Even though the First Lady was out of town and out of touch, the White House was busy—repairing rugs, repainting walls, and generally keeping tidy for the President, who did a good amount of private entertaining while his wife and children were away.

We received word from the Secret Service of Patrick Bouvier Kennedy's premature birth on August 7 at Otis Air Force Base in Massachusetts, and listened to hourly reports of the baby's progress, from the Base Hospital to Childrens Hospital in Boston, where he died on August 9.

Immediately I called the carpenter shop.

"Get the rug up, the crib back in storage, the curtains off the windows," I ordered. "Bring back the refrigerator and the table and chairs. It should look just like it did before."

Quietly, within two days, we set the children's dining room in order.

When Mrs. Kennedy returned on September 23, nothing was said about the nursery. Tired, worn and sad, she came back to the White House to meet Haile Selassie, the Emperor of Ethiopia, at Union Station. As guests arrived for the stag dinner in his honor, she left on a plane for Greece. She spent six weeks recovering there, and sailed with her sister on Aristotle Onassis' magnificent yacht.

On October 17, Mrs. Kennedy came back from Greece, suntanned but exhausted, and she took her family to the country for the weekend. On Monday morning, she called me into her bedroom. Her dark hair was tousled, her light robe very feminine against the soft blue of her bed. Her eyes were full of mischief.

"Oh, Mr. West," she whispered in her beguiling child's voice. "I've gotten myself into something. Can you help me get out of it?"

"What can I do?" I asked, wondering who was next in line to be fired.

"I've invited someone to stay here," she said, "but now *we've* changed our minds." She cast a glance in the direction of the President's bedroom. "Could you help us cook up something so we can get out of having her as a houseguest?"

Without waiting for a reply, she rushed on, her request becoming a command in mid-breath. "Would you fix up the Queen's Room and the Lincoln Room so that it looks like we're still decorating them, and I'll show her that our guest rooms are not available." Her eyes twinkled, imagining the elaborate deception.

"The guest rooms will be redecorated immediately," I said, and almost clicked my heels.

I called Bonner Arrington in the carpenter's shop. "Bring dropcloths up to the Queen's Room and Lincoln Bedroom. Roll up the rugs and cover the draperies and chandeliers, and all the furniture," I instructed. "Oh yes, and bring a stepladder."

I called the paint shop.

"I need six paint buckets each for the Queen's Room and the Lincoln Room. Two of the buckets in each room should be empty—off-white—and I need four or five dirty brushes."

I met the crews on the second floor. "Now proceed to make these two rooms look as if they're being redecorated," I directed.

"You mean you don't want us to paint?" said the painters.

"No," I said. "Just make it look as if you are."

The crew had a good time, even though they didn't know what it was all about. As I brought in the finishing touches, ashtrays filled with cigarette butts, Bonner shook his head.

"Mr. West, all I can say is that this place has finally got to you," he said.

That evening the President and Mrs. Kennedy entertained a Princess for dinner upstairs in the President's Dining Room. Before dinner, though, President Kennedy strolled down to the East Hall with his wife's guest. He pointed out the bedraped Queen's Room.

". . . And you see, this is where you would have spent the night if Jackie hadn't been redecorating again," he told the unsuspecting lady.

The next morning, Mrs. Kennedy phoned me.

"Mr. West, you outdid yourself," she exclaimed. "The President almost broke up when he saw those ashtrays."

Four days later, Mrs. Kennedy outdid *her*self.

Her caper began when Barbara Keehn called me from the east wing office to ask if we could have a surprise birthday party for Nancy Tuckerman. "Sure," I said and set up the arrangements with the head butler and René.

When Mrs. Kennedy drove in from Wexford later that morning, I told her about the party.

"Great," she said. "I want to come. What time?"

"Four o'clock," I replied. "In the movie theater. All the White House staff and the social office will be there."

At three the telephone rang.

"Would you please come up to my dressing room?" the First Lady asked.

She was seated in a straight-backed chair in front of her dressing table with hairdresser Jean-Paul behind her (Mr. Kenneth only came down from New York for the big occasions), applying huge blue rollers to her dripping hair. Her hands were extended to a manicurist.

As if on cue, Wilma, the second-floor maid, came in.

"Wilma, please bring me one of Miss Shaw's uniforms," Mrs. Kennedy said, smiling at me.

When Wilma appeared with the large, white-starched dress that belonged to Caroline's nurse, the First Lady said, "Now, Wilma, get me one of my wigs."

Wilma opened the closet, and brought out a dark, bouffant head of hair. And Mrs. Kennedy said, "Mr. West, you're going to wear these to the party and be Miss Ward, our housemother from Miss Porter's school. And I want you to put a sign around your neck saying 'Miss Ward,' so people will know who you are."

"I'm not going to do it," I said.

"Oh, yes, you are, Mr. West," she sang.

"No, I'm not."

"Yes, you are. And then you have three of the ushers dress up as our school teams, one as a possum, one as a squirrel, and one as a mink."

"If you want three good ushers to quit on the spot, all I have to do is tell them that," I said.

"Well, anyway, *you're* going to dress up. . . ."

I tried to interrupt.

". . . and I want you to get Betsy Boyd to come down and teach everybody the school song. That's where the animals come in."

About half an hour before the party, I went down and put on Miss Shaw's uniform and Mrs. Kennedy's wig, locking all the doors so nobody, especially not my three ushers, could see me.

Everybody—the east wing staff, the household staff, the curator's office—rehearsed the song in the movie theater. Mrs. Kennedy, now coiffed and manicured, came down at the last minute, and directed the skit.

At 4:15, everybody stood in a circle holding hands,

Mrs. Kennedy in the ring, and I stood in the center of the circle as Miss Ward, when the unsuspecting Nancy walked in.

"Farmington, we sing to thee and to thy dear name . . . ," they sang, and then broke into "Happy Birthday." Nancy couldn't believe her eyes.

"All this without a drop to drink," she exclaimed.

After we had all sampled Ferdinand's birthday cake, I turned to the group. "And now for the entertainment," I announced.

Nancy Hough, from the Curator's office, had perfected an imitation of Mrs. Kennedy's voice, with which she had been known to send people scurrying all over the White House with her whispered instructions on the phone. So she proceeded to mimic the First Lady for Nancy Tuckerman, with Mrs. Kennedy right in the audience. Jim Ketchum, as the irrepressible Boudin, joined in the fun, and the two "restored" the movie theater for five full minutes, with a hilarious take-off on the First Lady.

Mrs. Kennedy howled. Nancy Hough's voice, her intonation, her phrasing so perfectly matched her own.

"Oh, I want you to come up and do it for the President some time," she told Nancy.

Mrs. Kennedy's mischief that month was infectious. All the White Staff followed her teasing style, inventing pranks of their own.

Mrs. Kennedy, glad to be home, played with the children. All we had to prepare for was the Judiciary Reception on November 20. I was not working the party, for a change. My wife and I had been invited as guests of the Kennedys, and it was Zella's first time to meet the President.

"I can't get over how young he looks," Zella remarked.

He did seem youthful, in good spirits, as did Mrs. Kennedy, who was making her first public appearance since her baby died.

They left for Dallas the next morning before I came to work. All day, crews were in the President's office, taking advantage of his absence to carry out Mrs. Kennedy's redecorating plans.

9

I don't know why she decided to go to Dallas. Politicking was certainly not something she enjoyed, and all of us were surprised that she'd step out of character and go. But then I remembered how closely she and the President had stuck together since her return from Greece—even to the point of canceling an invited houseguest to insure privacy on the second floor.

"To think that I very nearly didn't go!" she told me later. "Oh, Mr. West, what if I'd been here—out riding at Wexford or somewhere. . . .

"Thank God I went with him!"

I always seem to hear bad news via the radio. I was at home on November 22, attending to my own redecorating, when the bulletin was broadcast: The President had been shot. Within minutes, I was back in the office. By the time I arrived, he had died.

The White House staff was paralyzed. I summoned everybody, had the butlers prepare to serve coffee, had the maids prepare all the guest rooms, little meaningless gestures, but a signal that our work must go on, until the assassination was confirmed. I tried to remember what had been needed in the house for President Roosevelt's funeral, but I was numb. Then Bill Walton called.

"Mrs. Kennedy has asked me to take charge of the arrangements," he said, "and asked me to get in touch with you." I was so relieved to hear his voice. It told me that Mrs. Kennedy, even in her shock, knew what to do.

"She'd like the house to be just like it was when Lincoln lay in state," he continued.

We ran down to the Curator's office for a reference book, and Jim Ketchum found an old engraving of the East Room draped in black and we worked from there. The President's brother-in-law Sargent Shriver came in, and helped make a list of what we needed. First of all, we had no black cloth at the White House.

I called Mr. Arata, who was doing some upholstery work for us at the time, to ask what kind of material we should use, and where could we get it at that time of night.

"I know just the thing," he said, and suggested webbing—the dark, thin material used underneath chairs to keep the springs from showing.

"But I don't have nearly enough," he said. So we phoned upholsterers until we found one who had enough material. The owner came back downtown, opened the doors, and gave us every bit of webbing in the shop.

Mr. Arata and his wife came back to the White House, and copying the 1865 engraving, they draped the webbing over the East Room chandeliers and windows. They worked all night.

Bill found the Lincoln catafalque at the Capitol, directed the florist to the magnolia tree Andrew Jackson had planted on the South Lawn, and set up the room. Two candelabra, large urns filled with magnolia leaves, and the catafalque waited starkly in the center of the East Room.

The priest also was waiting in the East Room when they arrived with the body, at about 4:30 in the morning. Nancy Tuckerman and I stood in the Blue Room, watching the military guard bring in the flag-draped coffin.

Mrs. Kennedy, with the Attorney General beside her, walked behind it. When Nancy and I saw her, still wearing her pink skirt with its vicious bloodstain, we stepped out of sight. We wanted to spare her the sight of two more grieving friends.

Robert Kennedy took the First Lady upstairs. He slept in the Lincoln Room that night, and Mr. and Mrs. Auchincloss slept in the room adjoining Mrs. Kennedy's, in the President's bed.

There was no sleeping at all for me. I took a shower, changed clothes, and went straight up to my office.

The priest arrived early, and, looking over the State floor, selected the Family Dining Room for the ten o'clock Mass. We removed the table and set up rows of straight-backed chairs for the guests. At ten, however, when Mrs. Kennedy came down, she looked into her most un-favorite of all the White House rooms, and saw her friends and family.

"Oh, no, I want it in the East Room, where Jack is," she whispered, and went back upstairs while we moved all the chairs into the East Room. She returned and the priest began intoning the Mass.

After the service, she came out to the elevator to go upstairs. I was standing in my office door.

She came over, put her arms around me, and said, "*Poor* Mr. West." I couldn't speak. It was all I could do to stand. I just held her for a moment.

"I want you to take me over to look at the President's office," she said.

"I'll come up for you whenever you're ready," I said.

"Oh, no, I'll stop by your office," she whispered.

About twenty minutes later, she came down alone, and we walked over to the west wing. Down the same colonnade she had wanted to enclose so the President wouldn't catch cold. Past the swimming-pool door. Past the Cabinet Room.

But she never got to see the effect of the room she and Boudin had worked so carefully to perfect, for already President Kennedy's office was being dismantled. Movers were carting away books, packing up model ships, carrying out the rocking chair. The President's secretary, Evelyn Lincoln, stood bewildered in the middle of the room.

Without the soft brown wood of his furniture, the new crimson carpet seemed blatant.

"It must have been a grand office," she murmured.

"It was very nice," I managed to say.

As the moving men stood self-consciously by, Evelyn Lincoln said, "Oh, Mrs. Kennedy . . . ," and fled from the office.

"I think we're probably in the way," Mrs. Kennedy whispered, and she looked around uncertainly. Suddenly I remembered that first day she had come to the White House and, like today, how *unprotected* she had seemed.

Her eyes were like saucers, memorizing the oval office —the walls, the desk we had found in the basement, the small pictures of Caroline and John—then she walked out of John F. Kennedy's office for the last time.

We went into the Cabinet Room and sat down at the long mahogany table. She searched my face, as if she might find the truth there.

"My children," she said. "They're good children, aren't they, Mr. West?"

It was a question, not a declaration.

"They certainly are," I said.

We looked out over the sand-pile, the holly-encircled trampoline, the treehouse.

"They're not spoiled?"

"No, indeed."

She stared into my face.

"Mr. West, will you be my friend for life?" she whispered.

I could not make a sound. I only nodded.

Robert Kennedy stayed in the Lincoln Room all that week, the Auchinclosses stayed only one night, and the Radziwills moved in with Mrs. Kennedy. Lee Radziwill slept in a bed in Jacqueline Kennedy's bedroom; her husband slept in the President's bed.

I slept on a couch in the Usher's office.

Sunday morning, the day the body was transferred to the Capitol, Mrs. Kennedy called down, "Mr. West, could you find me a mourning veil?"

"I thought Provy had found one for you," I replied. I knew that "veil" had been checked off my list.

"What she brought was a black lace mantilla, which is all right for today. But for the funeral tomorrow, I want a regular mourning veil like Mrs. Dulles wore."

I called every funeral parlor in town. "Very few people call for them any more," said one director in his apologetic, funereal voice.

Finally we had Lucinda make a black veil. It was, of course, correct.

On the morning of President Kennedy's funeral, Mrs. Kennedy called Jim Ketchum, the Curator, and asked him to perform a very special task. "While we are at the Capitol," she instructed him, "will you please get someone to help you, go up to the Yellow Oval Room, and remove the Cézannes from the wall. In their place, hang the Bennet and Cartwright prints [American aquatints, circa 1810]—and I'll tell you why. . . ."

He was astonished that she wanted the paintings removed—her "glorious" Cézannes, which she'd worked so hard to bring back into the White House, and which hung so prominently in her favorite room.

"This afternoon I'm going to be receiving President De Gaulle in this room," she explained to Jim, "and I want him to be aware of the heritage of the United States, and these are scenes from our own history." So Jim and Bonner Arrington, the carpenter, followed her wishes, and placed a strong stamp of America—prints of Washington, Baltimore and Philadelphia—in the room where the President's widow would receive.

When the procession came back in cars from the Capitol, we had lined up all the guests in the White House: All the visiting Heads of State were in the East Room; the Kennedy relatives in the Green Room; White House staff in the State Dining Room; and Congress in the Blue Room.

Mrs. Kennedy got out of the limousine at the White House, and all those waiting inside joined the procession behind her by order of rank, and walked behind the body to St. Matthew's Cathedral. After the ceremony at Arlington, she returned to the White House. Then she went upstairs to the Yellow Oval Room to receive, one at a time, President De Gaulle, Prince Philip of England, Emperor Haile Selassie of Ethiopia, and Ireland's President Eamon de Valera. Afterward, she stood in the Red Room and received all the other visiting Heads of State.

Following this, exhausted, she turned to me with only one question.

"Mr. West, did you see whether President Johnson walked or not?"

"Yes, ma'am," I said, "I saw both the President and Mrs. Johnson."

"The Secret Service didn't want them to," she smiled wanly.

Robert Kennedy still stayed at the White House, as did I.

Every night until she moved out of the White House, Mrs. Kennedy and the Attorney General went to the President's graveside to pray.

On Wednesday, Mrs. Kennedy and the children flew to Hyannis for Thanksgiving, and I went home, for the first time in six days.

But I couldn't stay. We were fixing up the East Room for the month-long period of mourning, and although I had left instructions on how to do the room, I began worrying about it.

After dinner, I looked at Zella and, though I was about to drop, said, "I have to go back."

"I'm going with you," she said firmly.

As we walked into the East Room, Zella gasped, "Oh my God!"

Lying stretched out on the catafalque in the center of the room was Bonner Arrington, the carpenter. Wearing overalls, arms folded across his chest, eyes closed, he clasped a dead lily in his hand. At first, I was shaken with horror. Then I started laughing, and Zella started laughing, and the week of tension collapsed inside us, as tears of relief flooded my cheeks.

The White House would survive.

Mrs. Kennedy sent me a note from Hyannis, about the manuscript of Jim Bishop's book, *A Day in the Life of President Kennedy*, which he had been writing to coincide with the 1964 election.

Dear Mr. West,

I thought you might be interested to know about the Jim Bishop article, which is so full of 3rd rate cliches I don't care if it appears or not, as no one will ever believe it about our President.

I am referred to as always running up to the President, holding hands and saying, "At last, just us, alone."

"George Thomas (the valet) works harder than anyone in the White House—his light can still be seen flickering at 2 a.m., and he is up at 6 a.m."

But the one time Jim Bishop did pull himself out of the bog and reach great heights was in his description of you—It reads "J. B. West, a man with an elegant smile, the smile of a jaded dandy." Boudin would be pleased!

Affectionately,
Jacqueline Kennedy

We moved Mrs. Kennedy into Averell Harriman's house in Georgetown (the Harrimans moved into a hotel), where she stayed until she bought the house across the street. The next week, she invited Nancy and me for dinner at the Harrimans.

She met us at the door, and I kissed her.

"Oh, Mr. West, you never kissed me when I lived at the White House," she whispered. I started to laugh, and she stepped back, narrowing her eyes wickedly.

"Did you ever kiss Mamie?"

"All the time," I answered.

Mrs. Kennedy came back to Washington for the reburial of her husband, after his permanent gravesite had been finished. She stayed with Mrs. Mellon, who called to invite me to the service.

It was 7:00 a.m., and pouring rain, when I joined Mrs. Kennedy and her family at Arlington.

She greeted me warmly, then looked over her shoulder.

"Oh, Mr. West, you'd better hide. Here comes President Johnson."

But, of course, I didn't have to hide. I was running the White House for the thirty-sixth President of the United States.

The
Johnsons

1

From her very first days as First Lady, Lady Bird Johnson had her own priorities in order.

"Mr. West, I just want you to know that when I move into the White House, I want you to *run* it," she told me, four days after her husband became President. "I've been running a house for thirty years, and I want to devote my time to other things."

It was November 26, the day after President Kennedy's funeral, when Mrs. Johnson telephoned me, the Texas accent strong in her low, alto voice. Mrs. Roosevelt's accent had been Eastern, Mrs. Truman's that of the flat Midwest, Mrs. Eisenhower had no accent at all that I remember, and Mrs. Kennedy's finishing-school training had erased any regional flavor from hers—but Mrs. Johnson spoke pure Southwest.

"Can you come out to The Elms, to discuss our moving in to the White House?" she asked politely.

Armed with blueprints, floor plans, and photos of every room in the mansion, I took a White House car to the exclusive Spring Valley section of Washington.

Mr. Johnson and his wife had bought Perle Mesta's old house, the place where the hostess with the mostest threw some of her most lavish parties. The Vice President of the United States had translated its French name, Les Ormes, to The Elms.

For some reason, I was surprised at the tasteful, French elegance of Mrs. Johnson's home. I hadn't expected to find a ranch in the middle of Washington, of course, but the Johnsons were so publicly and indelibly identified with the state of Texas, I fell into the trap of looking for a stereotype. Instead, I found myself in familiar French territory—Jacqueline Kennedy would have been right at home.

I was met by a uniformed maid, and followed her through a spacious entrance hall, to a small reception room. Mrs Johnson, dressed in black, more petite even than Mrs Eisenhower, came in to greet me. She was accompanied by two ladies.

"This is Bess Abell, who will be my social secretary, and Liz Carpenter, my press secretary," she said.

Little did I realize how important a role these two very dissimilar women, Liz and Bess would play in the White House scheme of things. I barely took notice of the First Lady's two lieutenants that day, I was so intent on introducing Mrs. Johnson to the White House, its floor plans, its patterns.

In every picture I pointed out the new permanent acquisitions from the restoration project, and Mrs. Johnson nodded her approval.

"I especially love the Yellow Oval Room upstairs, where we gathered before State dinners. It's my husband's favorite color."

When I mentioned that it had been a study for Presidents Eisenhower, Truman and Roosevelt, she asserted again, "I love it the way it is."

Mrs Johnson's questions were brief, to the point.

"What furniture shall I bring?"

When she discovered that Mrs. Kennedy was taking only her own bedroom furniture and that of the children, she said quickly, "That's all we'll bring, then. My bedroom and my girls'. I'll ask my secretary, Ashton, to make a list for you."

Then she glanced over at Liz and Bess, who'd been thumbing through the books as well, and they left us alone. As if on cue, I thought.

Mrs. Johnson lowered her voice, confidentially.

"Can I bring my servants with me?" she asked, and when I said yes, "How will they be paid?"

There are two vacancies on the federal payroll, I explained, because Provy and George are leaving with Mrs. Kennedy, and we could stretch to find a third place.

"Let me discuss it with my husband," Mrs. Johnson said, "and I'll get back to you."

As I rose to leave, the new First Lady looked at me intently, and emphasized, "I want *you* to run the White House."

There was nothing tentative about Claudia Alta Taylor Johnson. During those difficult days of transition, she quickly organized her staff, her way of living, her family responsibilities. She was no stranger to the White House. I had seen her at all of the Kennedys' official parties and at quite a few of their private soirées. But as the Vice President's wife she had always seemed to stay quietly in the background, standing beside her towering husband, smiling politely, saying the correct things. In the years to come, I discovered that she was gentle, feminine in manner, earnest, and studious. But always, she seemed to have a cellophane shield around her, through which she appeared, highly visible, dignified, yet somehow *protected*. And I did not run the White House, Lady Bird Johnson did—and in a way no other First Lady had done. She was rather like the chairman of the board of a large corporation.

Her two generals (I'd thought of them as lieutenants, at first) managed the corporation. Liz was in charge of the Public First Lady; Bess the White House First Lady. My role was to operate the Executive Mansion. Indeed, White House management was functioning more efficiently than ever before. With the three able ushers, Nelson Pierce, Ray Hare, and Rex Scouten, and my invaluable assistant, Bette Hogue, the staff performed smoothly, silently, and the mansion seemed almost to run itself, like an automatic elevator.

On Monday, I received a big envelope from Hyannis, where Mrs. Kennedy and the children had spent Thanksgiving. It contained ten pages of notes on the familiar legal-size yellow paper, written in Jacqueline Kennedy's unmistakable scrawl. "These notes are about the operation of the White House," the former First Lady wrote me. "Please send them on to Mrs. Johnson."

I smiled to myself. Even in her grief, Mrs. Kennedy was sure to be thinking of cigarette boxes, flower arrangements, maids—the infinite details of the White House.

Mrs. Johnson phoned that same morning, finding me in the West Sitting Hall, supervising the removal of the Bouvier desk, the De Gaulle commode, and the Kennedy family pictures so we could put in White House furniture from the warehouse.

"Could you come back to The Elms?" the First Lady asked. "I'd like to finish discussing the servants' arrangements."

Again, as I entered the big house, with its off-white expanses, muted greens and yellows, rich rugs and silk draperies, I was struck by the French elegance. This time I was ushered up to Mrs. Johnson's study on the third floor, past a houseful of her friends—Senators' wives, ladies from Texas, Vice Presidential secretaries—who were helping to answer her already voluminous mail.

Lady Bird Johnson was alone in the small, tidy room. She smiled, shaking her head in wordless amazement as I handed her the thick manila envelope. She had already spent two hours alone in the White House with Mrs. Kennedy on the afternoon after our first meeting, touring the second floor, discussing the staff, the rooms, the art.

"How can she be so thoughtful of me at a time like this?" Mrs. Johnson murmured.

The First Lady quickly switched to the business at hand. Once again, Mrs. Johnson asked me if it was "okay" to place her personal servants on the White House payroll.

319

"Every President has done so," I assured her, naming Lizzie McDuffie, Vietta Garr, Rose Woods, the Moaneys, Provy and George.

"There's no way you could be subject to criticism, since the positions are vacant, and quarters for them on the third floor as well," I added.

She smiled, much relieved. "We'd like to bring Zephyr Wright, our cook, and Lee Gregg, our maid, who won't be living in, and Helen Williams, my personal maid, who will need to live at the White House," she said, emphasizing that Helen's and Zephyr's husbands were hired as messengers in the President's office. "They've already been investigated, because they were working for the Vice President."

"You're saving the government money already," I told her, noting that a new Secret Service investigation can cost up to several thousand dollars per person.

"Will we need to adjust their salaries?" she asked, following the same train of thought.

"It's very flexible," I replied—then I suggested that they be paid exactly what they were presently receiving.

Because, I explained, "If their salaries are raised substantially, it might be difficult to get them to go with you when you leave the White House." Mrs. Johnson laughed and agreed, but later I found that I'd have to contend with Zephyr about that suggestion, again and again.

During our meeting that day, Liz and Bess opened the door, then, seeing me in conference with Mrs. Johnson, quickly backed out.

"I like working in a room with one door so I can control my privacy," Mrs. Johnson said.

In the five years that lay ahead, I would learn the significance of that remark—how Lady Bird Johnson could remain a very private person at the same time she involved herself in a swirl of public activity.

It took a week to pack the Kennedys' belongings—furniture, photographs, paintings, toys, animals—everything except Caroline's third-floor classroom, which Mrs. Johnson had graciously agreed to keep in operation until after Christmas. We sent the things to the commercial warehouse where Mrs. Kennedy's own furniture had been stored.

Mrs. Kennedy came back from Hyannis, with two additional requests for me. Dressed in black, a worn, strained look on her face, she handed me a small note.

"Mr. West, can you have a little plaque made, and place it here on my bedroom mantel?" She pointed to a spot near the brass marker stating that Abraham Lincoln had slept in the room.

I looked at the note:

"In this room lived John Fitzgerald Kennedy with his wife, Jacqueline—during the two years ten months and two days he was President of the United States—January 20, 1961—November 22, 1963."

"Of course," I said, but I knew we didn't have time for brass engraving before she moved out. Bonner cut a little three-by-six-inch piece of plexiglass, Rudy Bauss of the Park Service incised the inscription on it, and Joe Karitas painted it off-white to match the mantel and glued it on the next day.

Her next request was simpler. "The Kennedy family has selected this to leave in the White House," she said, indicating a beautiful Monet painting of a waterscape, in lavender, blue and green, "Morning on the Seine." The small bronze plaque would read:

"In the Memory of President John F. Kennedy by his family."

"Can you have it hung in the Green Room? That was his favorite room."

"Yes, Ma'am," I said.

On Friday, December 6, the second floor was empty, the last truckful of Kennedy clothing was delivered to the Averell Harriman home on N Street. Mrs. Kennedy had said her goodbyes.

At about noon, President Johnson conducted an Alliance for Progress awards ceremony in the State Dining Room. Suddenly Mrs. Kennedy appeared on the back elevator.

"May I watch?" she asked. And unseen by anyone, she stood behind a screen in the Private Dining Room, looking on as the new President carried out one of her late husband's wishes.

Just before the ceremony ended, she slipped out quietly through the Rose Garden to the car where her children were waiting.

When the ceremony was over, Lady Bird Johnson walked down the State floor corridor with Mrs. Angier Biddle Duke, wife of President Kennedy's Chief of Protocol. I stood waiting by the elevator door.

"Mrs. Johnson, you may move in at any time," I informed her. "Mrs. Kennedy has moved out."

"Thank you," she said. "I think we'll probably wait until after Pearl Harbor Day." The Johnsons, with a strong sense of history, preferred not to enter the White House on that "date which will live in infamy."

But I had a feeling they might be coming by earlier, so I stayed at the White House that evening. Sure enough, Mrs Johnson, bathing suit in hand, showed up at the President's office at the end of the day, and they went for a dip in the White House swimming pool.

At about eight o'clock three buzzers, indicating the arrival of the President, sounded off. I quickly ordered every light in the house turned on so they could find their way around Then I watched the elevator go up as they went straight from the ground floor to their new second-floor home.

After about half an hour, I thought I might be helpful to answer any questions, so I went upstairs.

As I stepped off the elevator, I heard President Johnson's voice booming, "Where's Mr. West?" Mrs. Johnson was standing in the West Hall, with a few members of the President's staff.

"Here he is now," she called in to the President's bedroom. I hurried down the hall, where I found him sitting on the edge of President Kennedy's king-sized four-poster bed.

He jumped up, and waving his long arms around the room and pointing out to the halls, asked, "Who pays for all these lights?"

"The government does," I answered.

"How much does it come to a month?"

"Approximately $3,000," I said, neglecting to tell him that the bill included air conditioning, kitchen appliances, and all the fancy electronic equipment.

As he walked out of the bedroom, the President reached over and switched off the light. Rather emphatically, I thought.

I walked down the corridor with Mrs. Johnson, talking about moving, with one ear to the President, now in the kitchen opening pantry doors, now in the bathroom trying faucets.

"We'll be moving in tomorrow after all," Mrs. Johnson said.

"Lucy has John-John's room, and Lynda, when she comes home from college, will be in Caroline's. But they will both need much more closet space."

I showed her Miss Shaw's little room, where Rose Woods had pressed Mrs. Eisenhower's dresses in the years before. "We could turn this into closet space," I suggested.

"That would be ideal," Mrs. Johnson smiled.

The commercial moving van arrived from The Elms bright and early the next morning, a Saturday. I stayed on the second floor, directing traffic, setting up the rooms.

Shortly after noon, a white convertible zoomed into the South driveway, and out jumped Miss Lucy Baines Johnson (who became Luci shortly thereafter), with two frisky beagles on a leash.

Immediately following was Mrs. Johnson, with Bess and Liz, in the big, black White House Cadillac. The President's wife was clutching a large, framed photograph of the late Sam Rayburn.

I was waiting at the Diplomatic Room door.

"Welcome to the White House," I said to my fifth First Lady.

"What shall we do with the dogs?" Mrs. Johnson asked me.

"I'll call Mr. Bryant, the electrician," I said. "He took care of Pushinka and Charlie."

"Ours are just Him and Her right now," she said. "I'll think of better names for them later on."

323

Noting all the identical monograms on the luggage upstairs, I thought they'd surely be Lord and Lady Beagle Johnson, but Him and Her they remained.

I accompanied the ladies upstairs, saw Liz and Bess stake out their headquarters in the east wing, and saw Luci to her new bedroom, now outfitted with her own bed, a clutch of stuffed animals, her clothes neatly hanging in the closets. The bouncy sixteen-year-old's eye took in her new room, spying first her bedside telephone.

"Does this extension go just to my room or does it go anywhere else?" she asked.

I explained that each White House phone had a direct line to the switchboard, and to no other phone on the floor.

"Oh, good! In our house all our extensions were connected, and my Daddy was always listening in on me," she lisped, in what her mother called her "little girl voice."

I left the Johnsons alone in the White House that night and all the next day, which was Sunday. It was my first day off since November 22.

On Monday, December 9, Airman Paul Glynn, who'd been assigned to the White House as the President's valet, phoned me just as I walked into my office. "The President wants the Usher to please meet him at the ground-floor elevator landing."

The President stepped off the elevator. "Mr. West, if you can't get that shower of mine fixed, I'm going to have to move back to The Elms." He didn't sound as if he were joking.

There had been no complaints from the Kennedys. And everything in the house had been doublechecked by the engineers after Mrs. Kennedy moved out, as is usual for a change of tenants. I couldn't imagine what had gone wrong.

"It doesn't have enough pressure," he complained. "It's a terrible shower, that's what it is. Now my shower at The Elms . . . ," he went on to describe the special, multinozzled fixture that could direct spray up, down, sideways, wide, narrow, and powerful. Then he repeated, "If you can't get it fixed, I'll just move back to The

Elms." And without a smile, he turned on his heel and walked away.

Immediately we charged upstairs to check the shower. Nothing seemed to be wrong except that it wasn't what he was used to.

A few minutes later, Mrs. Johnson called, asking me to come to the second floor. She was seated in the Queen's sitting room, a small room with one door.

"I guess you've been told about the shower," she said.

"Yes, ma'am," I smiled.

She smiled back. "Anything that's done here, or needs to be done, remember this: my husband comes first, the girls second, and I will be satisfied with what's left."

Out to The Elms we went, with the White House engineer and plumbers, to study the shower. It was an unusual one, but by contacting the manufacturer we felt sure that it could be duplicated. Not so. Word came down from the second floor that the replacement we had installed just didn't work the same. Out it came. Before the second installation, we invited engineers from the factory to look at The Elms bathroom, to provide an *exact* duplication. They, of course, jumped at the opportunity to custom-build a shower for the President of the United States.

But shower number three wouldn't do either. Nor number four, nor number five. The problem was water pressure. We even put a special water tank in the stairwell closet, with a pump of its own, just for Mr. Johnson's shower. The Park Service was called in. Rex Scouten, now the White House liaison officer there, jumped into the shower in his bathing trunks to test the pressure. It was strong enough for Rex, but not for the President. We kept designing, redesigning, tearing out, installing, and fooling with that shower until Lyndon Johnson moved out of the White House. Despite all the talk of savings in electricity, we spent thousands and thousands of dollars, not counting the man-hours, trying to build a shower to please him. It was the strongest, most elaborate shower we'd ever had, with about six different nozzles at different heights, directing spray at every part of the body.

Mrs. Johnson's telling me that "My husband comes first" was a real clue as to how the LBJ White House would operate. More so than in any other administration, it became, as is imprinted in gold on the white souvenir matchbooks, "The President's House." President Johnson was all over the house. With his ever-present Secret Service agents, he roamed up and down the halls, poking his head in doors to find out what people were up to, using all the rooms in the mansion for one purpose or another. He had telephones installed in every room—in the bathrooms, underneath the dining room table— and he kept the lines hot.

It was clear from the beginning that President Johnson was concerned about the lights—and it seemed to us, more than just as a symbol of the budget reductions he'd ordered in all the executive departments during his first month in office.

Since the Eisenhowers, we'd kept the lights on in the State rooms until midnight every night, even when the rooms weren't being used because, as Mrs. Eisenhower had told me, "My friends drive by here at night and they complain because they think nobody's home. Let's keep the lights on!"

But President Johnson wanted them turned off. If there were lights on in a room, he'd call to find out who was in there; if nobody was, we'd hear from him. He'd even prowl around the house at night, turning off lights himself, and we'd hear from him then, too.

One night, though, he heard from one of his employees.

Isaac Avery, a carpenter who'd worked at the White House since the year one, was planing away down in the carpenter shop one night, when suddenly the shop was plunged into pitch-darkness.

"Goddammit, who turned off that light?" Avery stormed at the top of his lungs.

"*I* did," a deep voice boomed back.

The irate carpenter flipped on the light switch,

stomped into the hall—and there, flanked by two agents, stood President Johnson.

"I didn't realize you fellows worked so late," Mr. Johnson said.

"I was finishing the frames for all those pictures you sent over," Isaac Avery stammered.

But Avery never did find out what the President of the United States was doing in the carpenter's shop in the middle of the night.

President Johnson's nocturnal habits concerned his wife, who worried about his erratic dinner hours—sometimes at 10:00 p.m., sometimes at midnight or after—and she worried about the staff waiting around to serve him dinner.

One morning, after a particularly late dinner the night before, when the butlers had gone home at midnight, Mrs. Johnson called me up to her dressing room.

"I am so distressed about the servants having to stay so late," she told me. "I've long since given up on my husband eating dinner at a decent hour. Can't we just have Zephyr fix something that can be kept warm—or I'll go in and warm it up for him—or if I'm asleep he can easily serve himself? Then we can just send the butlers home at eight o'clock every night, the way they're supposed to."

"I'll see what I can arrange," I told her, and passed her suggestions along to the head butler, Charles Ficklin, who went straight through the roof.

"The President of the United States having to serve himself dinner? Never!"

The other butlers were equally indignant.

"We've served the Presidents and First Ladies every meal in formal service as long as I can remember," said John Ficklin. "Even if it's a cheese sandwich or a bowl of chili or a boiled egg. That's a tradition. Let's just work it in shifts."

I went back to Mrs. Johnson. "We're about to have a butler's revolt on our hands," I told her. "They insist upon serving the President, no matter what time."

"I've never seen such a house." Mrs. Johnson laughed in amazement. "First it takes two engineers to light the fireplaces—they won't let me do it. And now the servants don't want to go home at night."

But she realized, as I did, not only that the butlers were proud of their status, but also that traditions, once broken, are difficult to reestablish. The White House staff has maintained a certain continuity of operation through the years, flexible to the demands of the Presidency, yet separate from those demands.

President Johnson's erratic hours (I think he worked *all* the time, and seemed to require less sleep than most people), his impulsive, impromptu entertaining, and the way the Johnsons used the White House kept us all on our toes—as we first found out on December 23, the day that official mourning for President Kennedy came to an end.

Bess Abell called over from the east wing at about two in the afternoon.

"Hold on to your hat," she said. "President Johnson has just invited all of Congress and their wives over to the White House this afternoon. They announced it from the rostrum in Congress. What can we do?"

I looked out my door at the black crepe still draped from the chandeliers. We'd planned to remove it tomorrow.

"How many and what time?" I asked.

She did a quick mental calculation—"Nearly a thousand."

"We'll do the best we can," I offered, and immediately cranked up the kitchen. René pulled in everybody in the house to help make little finger sandwiches. and I think we bought every cookie in Washington. The butlers went to work making tubs of fruit punch and spiked punch, and grabbed outside help from the other government agencies, some of whom grumbled because they'd already accepted bartending jobs elsewhere for the night.

In the meantime, the carpenters and electricians began snatching down the mourning crepe, the florists sticking holly and poinsettias in its place. The Christmas tree had been stashed away out of sight. Now it was quickly set in place in the Blue Room, and the lights and trimmings were whipped out of storage and onto the tree. Amazingly, we really had some decent decorations by the time the people arrived. It was the biggest, most sudden party I'd seen—more than a thousand people showed up—Congressmen, Senators, some with their entire families, the President's top staff and Cabinet.

To me, it was a symbolic celebration, and I think one that reassured the hastily assembled legislators. With the transformation from grief and black mourning to bright, sparkling Christmas decorations, the White House once again proclaimed, "Long Live the King!"

President Johnson, by his speeches to the nation, his determination to carry forward Kennedy administration programs, was also reassuring the country that a confident hand was at the tiller. By his strong emphasis on civil rights, the President from Texas reassured his predecessor's constituency that he was free of any regional Southern bias.

In looking at his background in the Senate—at his legendary record as Majority Leader and his intimate knowledge of Congress—and at his education in the Executive Branch during his three years as Vice President, I personally felt that Mr. Johnson had the strongest professional qualifications of any incoming President I had met. To me, the shower incident, the lights-out directives, all were merely indications that the new President was a no-nonsense man who was accustomed to power. And that snowy December day when we took down the crepe, I felt relieved that the new President was such an experienced politician.

From the moment of that legislative reception, we were in the Johnson White House.

As First Lady, Mrs. Johnson expanded her role into that of a public partner of the President. She was rather like Mrs. Roosevelt in that respect. The exigencies of time—her frequent trips, his nonstop working habits— kept them from spending a great deal of time together. But there was a bond between the two of them, a bond of mutual respect and understanding.

And yet the President was dominant and at times, I felt, almost abusive to her, shouting at his wife as he shouted at everybody else. Mrs. Johnson's daughters also seemed to dominate her, at least in the beginning.

When she told me, "I'll take what's left over," I soon could see that had been her life's pattern.

I'm sure that Mrs. Johnson was not lacking in the normal human qualities of annoyance, irritation or anger. Perhaps the self-control, the clear glass curtain that kept hurt or annoyance out of sight came from a lifetime of public life with a highly volatile politician, who had little inhibition privately in expressing the full, wide range of his very human emotions. Yet Lady Bird's feathers seemed unruffled always—even her husband's impatiently yelling "Bird" in a resounding voice that echoed through the mansion, or the adolescent Luci's exasperated "Mother!"—didn't faze her.

She had an escape valve, some secret little room inside her mind that she could adjourn to when things got tense. When the air got heavy with personalities and pejoratives, a faraway, almost beatific look would spread across Lady Bird Johnson's expressive face. She'd simply tuned it all out.

She hummed a little tune—sometimes a show tune, sometimes a hymn—deep in her own reserve of calm thoughts. Many are the times I'd see Mrs. Johnson, when she obviously had something to worry about, wandering down the halls of the White House, whistling to herself.

At an afternoon meeting upstairs, in the midst of a spirited discussion about which Head Start center in which part of the country the First Lady should visit, Mrs. Johnson suddenly realized that her husband hadn't come home to lunch yet. "Please excuse me," she said, softly, and she walked over to his office in the west wing, to try and persuade him to stop work for a few moments and come back with her. But she returned alone.

She walked down the wide center hall upstairs, and paused before the row of paintings of American Indians. She loved those earliest Americans and the Western lore that had been a part of her earliest childhood. Again she smiled and walked the length of the hall singing quietly. Then, looking across at the dining room where Zephyr was still waiting with the President's meal, she rejoined the meeting.

She had learned, evidently a long time ago, how to compartmentalize her thoughts, how to concentrate solely on one thing at a time. She could be sitting at an informal meeting in the Yellow Oval Room, having tea with fine arts advisors. Her husband would call, to discuss an entirely different matter, and she would "leave" us—to make notes on his call. Or one of her daughters might come in to have some problem solved, and she would "leave" us to plan an event for her. However, Mrs. Johnson stayed at the same table, sipped the same cup of tea. She never allowed interruptions to distract her, but instead directed her full attention to each interruption. Only then would she "return" to the business at hand.

Though she always seemed a bit remote, the First Lady was kind to everyone, with soft compliments for a job well done, and no criticism if it weren't. The person who didn't fit into her scheme of things or didn't measure up to the job might eventually be replaced, but without having to undergo rebukes or feel humiliation from Mrs. Johnson or others on the staff.

On reflection, Lady Bird Johnson, in the course of a long, deeply knit partnership with her husband, may have been making up for what she considered his excesses. For the President handed out lavish praise or hair-curling scorn to his closest staff members or to her with little regard for whoever happened to be in the immediate audience. Perhaps his wife had long since learned to survive in the tough world, first, of Texas, then of national and international politics, and in the always turbulent world of Lyndon Johnson—by appearing to be impenetrable.

Gradually, as Liz and Bess programmed the details of her life for her, Mrs. Johnson took hold and grew in stature as her own person. If they created her role for her, she more than filled it.

The "other things" Mrs. Johnson wanted to do with her time when she asked me to run the White House were not immediately known. But she studied hard as she felt her way into her role of First Lady, working closely with

331

curator Jim Ketchum to acquaint herself with the history of the White House, learning every object, piece of furniture, work of art acquired during Mrs. Kennedy's restoration project.

One of her first tasks was to pick up on the final phases of that project. Mrs. Johnson was anxious that the restoration of the White House not be left in limbo, that the Fine Arts Committee not be dissolved and that the mansion be maintained in perpetuity as a museum.

At the beginning of the restoration, Mrs. Kennedy's first curator was on loan from the Smithsonian; now, four years and two curators later, his salary was paid by the White House Historical Association, which was still doing a land-office business in guidebooks.

"I think the job of curator should be an official position, so that the house will not be at the whim of any First Lady," she said, and talked her husband into making Executive Order #11145, providing for a curator of the White House and establishing a Committee for the Preservation of the White House.*

Before the group's first meeting, on May 7, 1964, Mrs. Johnson worked long and hard to prepare for it—to acquaint herself with the work everybody had done, to memorize the French names for things, to present us with goals and procedures for our work ahead. Our main job would be to report to the President, and to advise the director of the National Park Service on preserving and interpreting the museum character of the White House. We were to make recommendations as to the "articles of furniture, fixtures, and decorative objects used or displayed in those areas, and as to the decor and arrange-

---

* The First Lady was honorary chairman of the committee, which included as permanent members the director of the National Park Service, the director of the National Gallery of Art, the chairman of the Fine Arts Commission, the secretary of the Smithsonian Institution, the Curator of the White House and the Chief Usher. Nash Castro of the Park Service served as executive secretary to the committee, which included, of course, Mrs. Kennedy (although she never attended any meetings), as well as six other "public" members appointed by the President, Mr. du Pont, William Benton, Bruce Catton, Mrs. George R. Brown, Mrs. Marshall Field and James W. Fosburgh, and later Mrs. Charles W. Engelhard, Jr.

ments best suited to enhance the historic and artistic values of the White House. . . ."

It was quite a charge, and a long, long step from the day Mrs. Kennedy had told me to find her a "little curator." Preserving the mansion had become a serious obligation for Mrs. Johnson—and for all of us.

After the meeting, the First Lady held a tea for the various library committees, painting committees, the arts commission and the network of curators Mrs. Kennedy had pulled in for advice. Mrs. Johnson put on an impressive performance that day, conveying intelligence, taste, and sincerity to an audience I'd seen castigate even the "foremost authorities" on matters of style, taste, and authenticity.

"She's great!" my old acquaintances murmured in approval as they were leaving. "Knows what she's doing . . . heading in the right direction. . . ."

I knew she'd been most concerned about how the meeting would turn out. She'd boned up for weeks in advance, working with Jim Ketchum and me, going into the background of every contribution, every contributor. As soon as they all left, I phoned Mrs. Johnson.

"Everything went well," I told her. "The committee thought you were just great."

"I am so relieved," she sighed. "That's the first hurdle."

Over the next five years, she entered enthusiastically into all the committee's choices for the White House. Prior to every committee meeting, Jim and I had at least two or three meetings with her, to work out the agenda. She wanted to be thoroughly briefed on each particular piece, each item. If she made an acceptance speech for the presentation of a painting or anything of that nature, she held discussion after discussion with anyone who knew anything at all about it. She first called in experts to give her advice, then she went into everything very thoroughly herself.

One of her greatest sources was Mrs. John F. Kennedy. The former First Lady never attended any of the Preservation Committee's meetings because she felt, rightfully, that the White House was no longer hers to influence; that her presence among her old friends on the committee might be too dominant. But on major decisions, such as accepting a valuable work of art, Mrs. Johnson conferred privately by telephone with Mrs. Kennedy. Lines of communication between the two were always open, always gracious.

The way Mrs. Johnson tackled the completion of the restoration of the White House showed me a great deal about her conscientiousness and willingness to devote herself to her job, even if it meant that she had to spend a great deal of time learning about new things.

As her knowledge grew, she lent a great deal of her own personality and taste to the selection of gifts to be received, or to the committee's finds, which we could purchase with funds from the sale of White House guidebooks. And she wasted no time in establishing her own White House style.

One of her first visitors was Boudin, who came to report progress on the East Room curtains, which were taking so long to complete because they were being woven in golden-yellow silk in France, by an 88-year-old man. As I ushered the irrepressible Frenchman up to the Queen's sitting room, where Mrs. Johnson was waiting, he kept repeating how "shattered" he was by the news of the assassination.

"Tragedy, a tragedy," he said. "Poor Madame—poor Madame Kennedy!"

Then he whispered to me, "But I will love Madame Johnson."

"I am sure," I said.

"Because she has lived in my *house*."

I looked at him, puzzled.

"My house," he repeated. "I decorated Les Ormes for Madame Perle Mesta." At once, I recalled the very formal French flavor of The Elms—how familiar it had seemed. It was the Boudin touch!

But the meeting did not go well. Boudin's exuberance in describing the draperies, his effusive compliments to Mrs. Johnson spilled over in French, and I, who know little French but knew Boudin, was the only translator.

It was clear that he expected to finish his dreams of the President's Palace. He spoke of his plans for the State

334

Dining Room, and for replacing some fabrics in the Green Room. Mrs. Johnson, however, was clearly uncomfortable. She understood little of what he was saying, and I'm afraid I was no help. I soon realized that even if they had understood one another, they didn't speak the same language.

After he left, Mrs. Johnson walked with me back through the second floor gallery, which was lined with the paintings of American Indians.

"When the curtains are finished, I don't think we'll go any further with Boudin," she told me. Then she smiled, like the knowing politician that she is. "I'd never be able to get away with using a French decorator for the White House!"

The solarium, the West Sitting Hall with new upholstery, rug, and curtains, and one later color change for the girls' rooms—those were the only major changes Lady Bird Johnson made in the newly decorated mansion.

But she made an indelible imprint on the White House in her role as First Lady. She was extremely well-organized, she had each day mapped out in advance, she took her job very seriously.

2

The White House has always had elaborate schedules to take care of dinners, visitors, and every conceivable event. But schedules to Lyndon Johnson were often made to be broken.

He improvised, for example, on the evening meal. Dinner was rarely a two-person or even four-person affair, regardless of what might have been planned. If guests weren't scheduled for the second-floor dining room, Mr. Johnson would round up some. There were usually eight to fourteen people around Zephyr's table, sometimes twenty.

(I've often thought how the Trumans and the Eisenhowers would have loved that second-floor dining room. It probably is the most truly appreciated of all of Jacqueline Kennedy's innovations.)

The President was all over the place, everywhere, from six in the morning until midnight or even two or three a.m. always making his presence felt. Liz Carpenter says that, to her, President Johnson was "The Long Arm."

I remember him as "The Booming Voice."

He spent most of his life on the telephone, although in the mansion he didn't need one, because we could hear him quite clearly from one end of the house to the other.

As the voices of the First Ladies I had known bespoke their varied backgrounds, the origins of their husbands shaped their own style and manners. All were tough, shrewd politicians, and their individuality and backgrounds showed through—no bland organization man at the top of American politics.

I saw Missouri all through Harry Truman—plain as the plains, straightforward and open, and stubborn as a mule; Franklin Roosevelt and John Kennedy had the quick repartee, the urbane, graceful, wealthy eastern manner; Dwight Eisenhower was so military you could imagine brass buttons and polished boots even when he wasn't wearing them, but every now and then, with a "By golly" or two, Kansas flashed through his smile. It was evident that Lyndon Johnson had grown up in the wide open spaces.

Everything about him was oversized—his gestures, his voice, his friendliness, his temper, his work habits, himself, at nearly six foot four. When he swept his arm around the room, you could tell he hadn't spent much time cramped in subways, afraid to touch the next fellow.

When he walked down the hall, you could tell he *had* spent time on a horse, and his long legs covered a lot of territory with each step. He hugged, kissed, patted on the back, arm-around-the-shouldered all he was close to, showering compliments on the same people he thundered at.

Every time he came back from a trip, his luggage was loaded with gifts—sets of china, dresses, or paintings—all presents he'd bought for the people in his office or those who worked closest around him on the second floor of the White House. He made the greatest demands on his staff of any President I worked for, and at the same time he drew the greatest loyalty and devotion from them. As one of his assistants told me, after working until 3:00 a.m. only to be awakened by the President three hours later, "I wouldn't kill myself this way for another man alive!"

337

President Johnson was up at 6:00, into the newspapers and on the phone before breakfast every morning.

At 7:30 or 8:00, the Johnsons had breakfast together in the big four-poster bed which was still outfitted with President Kennedy's special horsehair mattress.

After their breakfast together, Mrs. Johnson went to her bedroom to dress and the President conferred with his top assistants—"the boys"—Jack Valenti, Marvin Watson or Jake Jacobson. They were old Texas friends, to whom he turned for absolute privacy and personal loyalty. In my White House years, I sensed that Presidents seldom develop new friends and confidantes. There is not enough time for that. They turn to people they have known and can count on.

The perpetual-motion President, never losing a minute of valuable time, got briefed while he dressed. Picking up the Secret Service at the elevator he was down to the ground floor and across to the oval office well before 9:00. We didn't see him again until he came home for lunch, usually about 3:00.

Mrs. Johnson also went straight to her "office," which happened to be her own off-white bedroom. She worked there all morning, in the comfortable chair in front of the fire, or propped up in bed with papers and datebooks spread around her, dictating letters to her personal secretary, Ashton Gonella, scanning files of background information for the day's activities, memorizing details about the evening's State visitor, approving speeches written for her by Liz Carpenter and staff, studying the scenario for some program or another. All that preparation was an integral and essential part of how Mrs. Johnson functioned as a corporate First Lady. She was programmed and prepared and then she performed.

Bess Abell and Liz Carpenter, the two women who played such major roles as Mrs. Johnson's advisors and administrators, brought a unique combination of talents with them to the White House. Liz, a veteran Washington correspondent for newspapers in Texas and elsewhere, was a shrewd observer of both politics and the Washington social scene. And from her own background as a newspaperwoman, Liz knew how to use the fine art of public relations in a way that would attract the desired news coverage, rather than repel the reporters.

Bess, the wife of Tyler Abell, who served the Johnson administration as Assistant Postmaster General and later as Chief of Protocol, also knew the political and social life of Washington. She had grown up in it as the daughter of Earle Clements, who served as governor of Kentucky and later in the Senate, where he was one of Lyndon Johnson's closet confidants. Bess had served as a secretary for her friend Lady Bird Johnson when her husband was Vice President.

Mrs. Johnson conferred with Bess and Liz every day and, by prearranged appointment, with curator Jim Ketchum and with me. But we rarely knocked on her door unless we'd been invited first. As before at The Elms, she guarded her privacy in a small room with one door.

Often, if the work was particularly heavy or required a little more concentration, the President's wife worked down at the other end of the hall, in the Queen's sitting room. Actually the room was a dressingroom for the Queen's suite, although guests (including Harry Truman's mother in earlier days) sometimes slept there. The blue-and-white room was attractive, with a day bed in a black lacquer frame, a coffee table—and only one door.

The Johnsons used the Executive Mansion more thoroughly than any other family has ever done. The President held impromptu luncheons and dinners with all the members of his administration; he presided over regularly scheduled "working dinners" for members of Congress and the Senate; he invited labor leaders to stag luncheons; and, in addition to every possible State visitor, every official or diplomatic occasion, he had frequent dinners for the Cabinet, business and manufacturing executives, which always included educators and representatives from the worlds of religion and the arts.

And Lyndon Baines Johnson conducted official business all over the house. There were bill-signing ceremonies and televised press conferences in the East Room; awards presentations in the State Dining Room; White House Conferences and Festivals pouring people in and out.

339

Meanwhile, Mrs. Johnson held small meetings and receptions in the Green Room and Red Room practically every day, sometimes two or three at the same time. For the Johnsons, the White House was like the apartment over the store.

Every day was a logistics triumph, a race against the clock to dismantle the chairs, desks, electronics equipment, and people from a 9:00 a.m. bill-signing ceremony in the East Room so the 10 o'clock tourists (by this time we herded in as many as 26,000 in one four-hour period) could begin trekking through the State Rooms, sweep out their debris after the doors closed at noon and set up the State Dining Room for a 1 o'clock luncheon, and get the Red and Green Rooms ready for afternoon receptions.

The White House was nearly always full of people. There were droves of houseguests—the President's Aunt Olivee and Aunt Josefa, Uncle Huffman Baines, Becky Bobbitt, various Texas friends, friendly governors and their families, famous Americans, schoolgirl friends of Lynda and Luci. The second and third floors were more "open house" than they'd been since the Roosevelts' days.

But there was one relative the President always kept track of.

At one point, the White House served as a long-term way station for Sam Houston Johnson, the President's high-spirited brother whose exploits sometimes gained publicity that bothered President Johnson. At one point, Sam Houston lived on the third floor for months. His principal activity was clipping newspapers, which the President told him would be useful for a future political campaign It seemed, in fact, as if Sam Houston was under some sort of house arrest. At any rate, a Secret Service agent kept a log of his movements and visitors, and his contact with the world was pretty much limited to long conversations with Assistant Usher Nelson Pierce.

I'll never forget the night that Sam Houston brought light into the White House.

The President's sometime tenant had been told, in no uncertain terms, to observe the "electricity-saving" blackouts at the White House. One evening, when President and Mrs. Johnson had been out, they returned late at night to a pitch-dark mansion. Not a light on in the place. They groped their way to the elevator, got off on the second floor and saw, at the end of the hall, only a dim flicker of light.

It was Sam Houston, working at a desk, with only one small candle.

The Johnsons' steady stream of visitors were well attended to. Mrs. Johnson's personal secretary, Ashton Gonella, typed up a daily schedule for the guests' entertainment, suggested sightseeing, White House amenities, and arrangements for meals, all at Mrs. Johnson's direction. Although the First Lady didn't shepherd her visitors around personally, as Mrs. Truman and Mrs. Eisenhower had done, she set aside a definite hour to spend with each of them as part of her busy day's schedule.

Unless there was one of the frequent luncheons on the State floor, Mrs. Johnson had lunch alone in her room, dieting on salads and clear soup before dressing for her afternoon appointments. If she was surrounded by staff at that time, she'd order a tray for them, as well.

The First Lady was always dieting. She kept herself petite and trim and much more attractive than any of her photographs. (She also tried to keep the President on a low-cholesterol diet because he had had a coronary some ten years before.) She concentrated on staying in trim with a will that almost matched that of physical fitness champion Harry Truman, swimming forty or fifty side-stroke laps in the White House pool almost every day. She often bowled in the Executive Office Building with her favorite bowling partner, Lynda Bird, then a nineteen-year-old college sophomore who'd transferred for one semester from the University of Texas to George Washington University per her parents' wishes. (The non-bowling Eisenhowers had moved the bowling alley installed by the Trumans from the White House to the Executive Office Building across the street.)

She occasionally took sunbaths on the White House roof, and although it didn't fit the category of physical exercise, Mrs. Johnson relaxed by playing bridge, sometimes with her old friends from the Senate days, especially Mrs.

Herman Talmadge of Georgia, sometimes with the wife of the Iranian Ambassador, but mostly with Lynda and her young friends.

In the afternoons, she usually made public appearances, and received her advisors on the many projects she had embarked upon. But there was one project that she worked on alone. In the afternoon or morning, when she had an hour (or the evening if her husband was away), Mrs. Johnson went into her little blue-and-white sitting room, after scotch-taping a page from her spiral notebook on the one door: "Mrs. J. At Work!"

She sat on her blue-velvet sofa, in that corner room over the Rose Garden, Jacqueline Kennedy's and Mamie Eisenhower's dressingroom, Bess Truman's and Eleanor Roosevelt's bedroom, and, looking out over the roses, she spoke into her "talking machine"—a small tape recorder always kept on the side table. If she fell behind in her diary, Ashton Gonella kept a daily list of her schedules, her visitors, so she could catch up on several days' worth of recollections and impressions. She stored all the tapes in a closet in that dressing room, and no one, except for Chief Justice Earl Warren, who borrowed the segment for November 22 1963, for use by the Commission investigating the assassination of President Kennedy, heard them until a month before she left the White House, when two secretaries transcribed them for her.*

In the rare evenings she was home alone, Mrs. Johnson usually read for pleasure or dropped in on one of her daughters' movie parties. The Johnsons used the movies to entertain guests, although the President rarely took time out to join the audience. When he did, he usually fell asleep before the first reel was finished.

Like Mrs. Eisenhower, Lady Bird Johnson also was an avid TV fan, but her selections were far more limited. Her one confessed television addiction was *Gunsmoke*, and we took measures to ensure that she never missed a single performance. If she happened to be away during the weekly installments, the Army Signal Corps came to

---

* The daily tapes were edited and published as *A White House Diary*, in 1970.

342

the rescue by videotaping the program, which she could watch later on the television set in her bedroom. *Gunsmoke*'s hero, Marshal Matt Dillon, undoubtedly reminded her of the young Lyndon Johnson. She longed to meet the hero, played by James Arness, until she discovered that he was a Republican. "How *could* he?" she asked, crestfallen. But then she decided *her* hero was Marshal Matt Dillon, not the actor, and Marshal Dillon *had* to be a Democrat! And so she didn't miss a segment.

Like the President, she crowded many appointments into one day, but she had usually moved her meetings away from the second floor—or at least the family end of the second floor—when he came home for lunch at three, usually bringing eight or ten people along to enjoy Zephyr's cooking.

After lunch, almost as regularly as Harry Truman, President Johnson went across to his bedroom for a nap, on the strict orders of Dr. Burkley. Also, Mrs. Kennedy had told Mrs. Johnson how much an hour of rest in the afternoon can mean to the man who must shoulder the burdens of the Presidency, and the First Lady enforced Mr. Johnson's nap.

When he awakened, he went straight back to his office, where he worked until all hours of the night. But sometimes the President swam after his nap. Sometimes he swam with his assistants, with friends such as the minister Billy Graham, or with a visiting Congressman.

The walls of the Johnson White House pool were lined with swimming trunks—huge ones, small ones—swimsuits for every size and shape of visitor who might want to take a dip with the President. Lyndon Johnson used the swimming pool to politick, just as he politicked no matter where else he happened to be, including in his bedroom while changing pants, or in his bathroom, talking on the phone or shouting above the force of running water in his shower.

That shower, and the complicated system of telephones, with scores of direct lines and all the new electronic surveillance equipment, were Mr. Johnson's few "extravagances" in the Executive Mansion. He couldn't resist the new inventions of our technological age. In contrast, however, he thought up endless ways to save pennies, some of which infuriated his employees.

Grappling with our household budget must have given him more satisfaction than trying to control the billions of dollars of national expenditures in the federal budget. These multibillions, to most human minds, become incomprehensible—even to Presidents. The budget of our house, on the other hand, was finite. He could *see* the results of his "economy in government."

The lights-out rule was no joke. And on a winter evening, with dark coming as early as 5 o'clock, someone trying to get from the west wing to the east wing or vice-versa had to stumble along in darkness. "The ground floor of the White House is just like the Black Hole!" fumed Bess Abell. The household staff simply had to accommodate their eyes to the dark.

He told Bess, when she began shopping for gifts for State visitors, "Now I want you to spend all of your imagination, and very little of the taxpayers' money! If you can get it for less, get it for less—if you can get it for free, get it for free—but *no* strings attached."

Savings in the form of "back-to-back" parties also occurred to President Johnson. There'd been a large gathering out on the south lawn, with colorful tents. As soon as the crowds had left, the carpenters began to dismantle the tents, and Mr. Johnson, walking through the ground-floor corridor, asked, "Why are they taking those tents down so soon? As long as they're up, let's invite all the press to come down and bring their children tomorrow."

The press played an almost larger-than-life role in the White House life of Lyndon Johnson.

The President watched television in his bedroom and in his west wing office, three sets going at once. But he limited his viewing to news programs. With a remote-control switch in his hand, he'd turn the sound on one commentator, then another, then another, giving equal time to the networks as they give equal time to politicans. It was the same impulse—he never had enough time to see enough, to hear enough of what the country was thinking and how he and his programs were being portrayed.

From the moment he took the reins of office, he had

very important reasons to be concerned with his image. The country was badly shaken, and much of the liberal Democratic constituency considered him a Southern regional character of suspect political ideology. From November 22 1963, through 1965, it seemed to me that President Johnson exerted an enormous effort to gain acceptance as a liberal, national leader, and to accomplish legislative deeds that far overshadowed any administration's since Roosevelt's first years in the 1930's. And to a remarkable degree, he succeeded. By sheer dint of hard work, helped by a Democratic Congressional victory in 1964, President Johnson succeeded in launching bold new attacks on problems of health, education, poverty, and the environment.

The President's almost superhuman efforts "to reason with" the country to achieve his goals extended into the kitchen, using White House entertaining in a more personal way than any other President I worked for. The principal target was Congress.

Instead of the traditional Congressional reception every winter, the Johnsons held eleven different "working parties"—two for the Senators and their wives and ten separate occasions for the 435 members of the House of Representatives and their spouses. Mrs Johnson and her staff entered in with much preparation and planning to entertain the Congressmen's wives.

We set up the East Room as a meeting room for the men (and Senator Smith of Maine and the women in the House). The President spoke to them then brought on members of his Cabinet to brief them on the world situation, the economic situation and, incidentally, his own programs and problems.

Meanwhile Mrs Johnson took the wives to the theater, where they viewed movies on the history of the White House, or on its art, and then took a tour of the family quarters. The Congresswomen's husbands of course, were invited, and the social office held high-level planning sessions on the subject of entertaining them. "Should we segregate?" Bess asked, fearing that the few gentlemen might be overwhelmed by such a large majority of Congressional wives.

"Let's just let *them* decide whether or not they want to attend," said Mrs. Johnson.

One who did—John Mink, husband of the Representative from Hawaii—had a marvelous time, as did all the ladies, who, even though many had been to occasions on the State floor for years, never had been invited upstairs at the White House.

On other occasions, Mrs. Johnson presented programs for the Congressmen's wives in the Queen's Room upstairs. We would remove the bedroom furniture and install fifty or more of the small gold banquet chairs to make it a meeting room. Mrs. Johnson recruited speakers who were knowledgeable about the White House, as well as previous residents. Children and grandchildren of Presidents, such as Margaret Truman Daniel, Sistie Dall, Anna Roosevelt Halstead, Charlie Taft, Barbara Eisenhower and Lynda Johnson, told personal stories about their lives there.

On one of those evenings, Mrs. Johnson had just begun to take the ladies on their tour of the second floor when Bess ran up to Jim Ketchum and me with Mary Kaltman in tow.

"The Connallys' luggage is in the Lincoln Room and the bed is turned down—the President suddenly invited them to spend the night," Bess said. The then Governor of Texas John Connally and his wife were among the Johnsons' closest friends, and were apt to drop in anytime.

We didn't have time to summon a maid, as the President's wife and the Congressional ladies were in the Treaty Room next door.

"Quick, we've got to make up the bed," Bess whispered, and she and I drew the sheets up over Abraham Lincoln's Victorian bed. While Mary Kaltman put on the white-embroidered spread, we flew around storing suitcases in the closet, and cosmetics in the heavy mahogany dresser and had the room in order within seconds. Just then Mrs. Johnson walked in, to describe the historic room to her guests, and found Bess, Mary, Jim, and me standing innocently beside the bed. She gave us a most puzzled look.

Butlers served cocktails to the wives upstairs as well as to their husbands downstairs. Our only problem arose when the briefings went on too long (President Johnson was confined to no time schedule when he was busy reasoning with Congress), and some of the ladies, who weren't used to such long cocktail hours, began to bob and weave down the halls. Mrs. Johnson soon passed the word to the head butler: "John, the next time, please water the drinks!"

Afterwards, the two groups converged in the State Dining Room for a buffet supper, then swung out to the lobby to dance to the ever-present Marine Corps orchestra.

These evenings were far more costly than the traditional one-shot Congressional reception had been, a fact to which the President was always highly sensitive. When the Chicago *Tribune* reported that they'd spent $5,000 a month for entertaining, the eagle-eyed President saw the article and immediately summoned me upstairs.

"They're saying that we've spent more than anybody else has here." he said. "Is that true?"

"But you don't have to pay it, sir," I replied, thinking of President Kennedy's mortification at his first month's personal food bill. "It's official."

But I had miscalculated President Johnson's concerns.

"That's the whole point," he said. "It's a political thing. They're saying I've spent more of the government's money."

However, the Congressional evenings were worth every cent to the President. Every vote he won with the Johnson "treatment" counted crucially as he sought to move Medicare, a tax cut, aid to education, and civil rights through Congress while he still had a mandate, momentum and a working liberal majority in Congress.

Most of these sessions were off the record, with no reporters in attendance. But Congressmen who gave their own accounts afterwards came away impressed at first with President Johnson's commanding presence and art of persuasion. But as the Vietnam war widened and then widened some more, reports from students at Lyndon Johnson's White House classroom were at best, mixed.

As criticism of his war policies grew some Congressmen took the opportunity to ask sharply critical questions. And when the Johnson treatment and Robert MacNamara's statistics-filled answers no longer satisfied the questioners, the mood of those meetings sometimes became tense. Lyndon Johnson no longer seemed to enjoy entertaining the Congress so much.

Despite all the Johnsons did to be hospitable, though, the President never felt the isolation that surrounds the Presidency so strongly as he did with his old compatriots in the Senate.

"It's so different now," he told an aide after a long, late-night work session when he was feeling a bit philosophical. "There's a wall around me that nobody gets through—people I've known for years, worked with side by side, like (Senators) Jim Eastland or Allen Ellender—they come in here and they don't see me, they see the President. I'm now 'Mr. President' to my oldest friends!"

(I remembered a Secret Service agent telling me about poker games on the yacht *Williamsburg*, hearing Harry Truman's oldest friend call out "Your deal, Mr. President!")

Because of this isolation, Presidents tend to draw closer to their families in the White House. Although by the nature of their responsibilities, the opposite might seem to be the case.

Lyndon Johnson doted on his daughters. He was more indulgent, it seemed to me, than overprotective. For graduation from National Cathedral School, he presented Luci with a Corvette Sting-Ray, in which she buzzed around town with a Secret Service agent in the bucket seat. Lynda had sold her car, preferring to use the White House chauffeurs.

"Why should I spend the money to operate my own car when I don't have to?" she told a Secret Service agent.

The President depended on the Secret Service to protect his young ladies, and Luci teased her guardians unmercifully. She'd bring her record player down from her room, set it up on the ground floor just outside the Secret Service office door, and play, over and over again, the song, "The Secret Service . . . makes me nervous . . . ," from the Broadway show *Mr. President*. Luci was good-natured, playful and friendly to all the staff. Her notes always were signed with a happy-face she sketched from the letters L-U-C-I.

In January, when Lynda Bird transferred from the University of Texas to George Washington University, the second floor of the White House took on the character of a girls' dormitory. Luci's gang of high-school friends had already been in and out, swarming over the house; now Lynda and her Texas roommate Warrie Lynn Smith moved in next door. (Lynda and Warrie Lynn always kept flashlights in their bathrobe pocket—to keep from breaking their necks in the pitch-black corridors at night.) Noise and laughter, dates and dramatics echoed through the historic rooms.

The State Rooms became an essential part of the Johnson daughters' social life. Margaret Truman had held only one ball in the East Room, as had John and Barbara Eisenhower. But Lynda and Luci kept the staid old halls jumping with the frug, the monkey. the watusi.

During the first month, the Johnson girls and their friends explored the second floor, the State rooms, the ground floor—looking for hideouts.

They had their eyes on the third-floor solarium, which at Mrs. Kennedy's request to Mrs Johnson, remained a classroom for Caroline and her little friends until the first semester ended in mid-January. (What a poignant sight to see Caroline ride up to the south entrance every morning, step out and wait with her classmates at the elevator, until Miss Boyd took them up to the third floor. At the end of the school day. off she'd go again. into the waiting car. The six-year-old never stopped off at the second floor to see her old room, never went out to bounce on the trampoline Except for a few sentimental servants, she was generally ignored. Lynda and Luci were the new Princesses.) As soon as the semester ended. and the equipment was packed off to the British Embassy, where the school took residence for the spring term, Mrs. Johnson called me.

"Luci wants to do Caroline's schoolroom over as a hideaway for her and Lynda, so they can study. have dates, and entertain their friends—a teen room, in other words"

So Luci and I got together. We consulted the decorator,

Mrs. Brown from New York, who also decorated the West Sitting Hall for Mrs. Johnson.

"We don't want to spend too much money," Luci kept saying.

We put in a new cork parquet floor, and new gold loose-weave curtains across all the windows. Then we built a bar down in the carpenter shop—a "coke bar" at that time—and Luci sent me out to look for "cheap" barstools. I found some downtown for about $10 each and had them recovered in the shop downstairs. Luci was delighted.

"We're really living it up for ten dollars, aren't we?" she said. She brought up two record players from her room and Lynda's; we installed a huge television set, a couple of sofas, and some chairs; and presto—a teen-age hideway.

Luci had one more request: "Mr. West, can we please have this glass paned door changed to just a plain wooden door? I don't want the servants and everybody looking in here to see what's going on."

I had an idea whom she meant by "everybody."

Somebody had painted a happy-face on the solarium window when it was converted to a dating room, and Luci left it there for years. She delighted in sneaking in and out of the White House in disguises. Once, in a blonde wig, she spent a weekend, unrecognized, with her friend Beth Jenkins at Marquette University, where she met Patrick Nugent, who then began to frequent her inner sanctum on the third floor. That was one place the Secret Service wasn't allowed.

The staff all agreed that Luci was like her mother—friendly, but something of an introvert. Lynda, we thought, resembled her father. She was tall, studious and had a strong emphatic voice. A history major, she drew upon the resources of the White House in preparing her homework, running in and out of the Curator's office in a fast gallop. After graduation, she went to work for *McCall's* magazine.

Lynda went through somewhat of a metamorphosis in the White House. Her "movie star" phase, when she was dating actor George Hamilton, brought her to a

Hollywood makeup artist, and she changed from a tomboy-like college student to a glamorous young woman. But all the time it seemed that Lynda had her eye on the color guard, whose towering young Marine captain was one of the great social assets to a White House evening—a military aide who could present the colors, announce the guests, dance with the ladies, and assist the ushers.

With young romances on the third floor, Congress up and down the stairs, and meetings all over the place, the Johnsonization of the White House didn't involve the decor. it involved people.

The house looked the same, but slowly the Kennedy style was erased, just as the Eisenhower style had been erased previously. Beginning with the departure of Boudin, the gulf between Texas and Paris widened even further at the White House.

3

As the Johnsons slowly injected their own tastes in food and style, I realized that battles would be brewing between new and old help whose styles were as different as Paris, France, is from Austin, Texas.

Zephyr Wright was queen of the kitchen on the second floor, and René Verdon, who'd prepared the Kennedys' personal meals as well as the State dinners, supposedly was limited to official entertaining for the Johnsons.

With the Johnsons, however, the line between official and personal was hard to draw. Most of the time Zephyr cooked upstairs, turning out meals for four to fourteen, the way she'd done for years. She knew their likes and dislikes so well that she rarely even asked Mrs. Johnson what to cook. Every now and then, though, the Johnsons would hold a more formal dinner party in the second-floor dining room, and Bess Abell would get involved, with René preparing the food.

We'd brought Zephyr in at $500 a month, her wages as a cook in the Vice Presidential household. She wasn't in the White House but a few months, however, when she found out that the French chef was making three times that, and immediately thereafter Zephyr came huffing into my office.

"Mr. West, I demand to be put on a pay scale equal to René's. Why, I do four times as much cooking as he does!"

"René is the official White House chef," I explained. "He runs a big staff, and is in charge of the very important State entertaining. He has very specialized skills and training, and is paid commensurate with his background." (Although, in truth, René also felt that he was being paid mostly in prestige. No White House salaries, none of them, are on a competitive level with private business.)

"But I cook for official entertaining, too," Zephyr argued. "Practically every night! And I have to turn out a big dinner for twenty people on a few minutes' notice, and I have to stay here until midnight. . . ."

Zephyr Wright did have a point. On the other hand, those impromptu dinners, late though they were, of necessity involved much use of the can-opener and quick-thaw method of cooking (at which Zephyr was indeed skilled), not the seasoned hands of a gourmet chef.

Nevertheless, I took up the matter with Mrs. Johnson.

"It *is* necessary for her to be on duty to prepare late night dinners," the President's wife agreed, and we raised Zephyr's salary to $625 a month. But Zephyr stuck to her guns, and kept us in a constant battle to have her salary raised to equal the French chef's.*

The Johnsonization of the White House was discreet, subtle, but firm. As with each of the First Ladies, Mrs. Johnson was aware of the sensitivities and loyalties of those employees closest to her life. And, also like every other First Lady, she required total loyalty to *her* family.

Presidents are peculiar people. They can take public criticism and even abuse, and shrug it off as a political by-product. But close up, they develop ways of examin-

* When she finally left the White House, her salary had been raised to $9,000 a year.

ing, scrutinizing, testing every employee. "Are you with me?" is an unspoken question—and somehow the President and his wife can always tell if the answer is "No," or even "I'm not sure." The White House employee whose loyalties remain with the previous administration rarely survives long, as in the case of Henrietta Nesbitt—and Anne Lincoln.

Anne, I believe, truly wanted to remain as housekeeper of the White House. There was always an undercurrent, a feeling that her ties with the Kennedys were too deep. Perhaps she felt a bit frustrated at taking directions from the social secretary, when she'd worked directly with the previous First Lady.

Mrs. Kennedy had hired the French chef René, whose huge stainless-steel kitchen was like a kingdom unto itself. Anne worked closely with René, because the two of them understood the type of menu the Kennedys wanted to serve. When the Johnsons came in, Anne and René would work up a menu, then they'd have to submit it to Bess, who then would discuss it with Mrs. Johnson. So Anne had very little contact with Mrs. Johnson.

At any rate, Anne was replaced by Mary Kaltman, a Texan who reflected Mrs. Johnson's tastes. Mary was primarily a food person, having been in charge of food operation at the Driscoll Hotel in Austin. But she tried at first to take the housekeeping in hand. Mary came in full of vim and vigor, and tried to put into effect a system that would work, in supervising the maids and housemen. She even held little staff meetings with them in the mornings.

One day she had a call from Mrs. Johnson—"Could you take it a little easier, please," the First Lady told her, laughing. "You're ruining the morale of the staff." One of Mrs. Johnson's own maids had filtered the word to the First Lady that Mary Kaltman was really going to run a tight ship—and the staff didn't like it.

Mrs. Johnson's rebuke—or advice—took some of the fire out of Mary. She decided she would have to go along with the way the operation was. As Mr. Crim would have said, this was another case of White House tradition prevailing—where the tail sometimes wags the dog. Mary's

354

heart was in the kitchen anyway, so she looked to that arena as the next place to establish her authority. But the kitchen was run by someone else. I could see that another battle was inevitable.

It was a personality clash, pure and simple, matching Texan versus French egos. Mary was accustomed to supervising a kitchen in an Austin, Texas, hotel, but nobody supervises a kitchen when there's a French chef around. Nobody, that is, except the French chef.

Not only did René feel that his sacred territory was being invaded, but he also was less than enthusiastic about some of the Texas innovations in the official menus. One of the Johnson favorites, chili con queso, which is really a hot, gooey cheese dip, he christened "chili concrete." And after the President sent his tapioca pudding back to the kitchen, suggesting that he go upstairs and take lessons from Zephyr, René allowed as how Zephyr must put glue in hers.

"The President eats so much tapioca pudding that Zephyr doesn't even cook it herself," René fumed. "She has the pot washer do it."

The friction between chef and housekeeper and between rival cooks was beginning to send sparks up and down the White House halls. So one day I stopped by the kitchen when I knew René would be alone.

Tall and regal in his immaculate white chef's hat, René leaned over the immense wooden chopping block in the middle of the room, studying not a cookbook but a French newspaper.

"René, how are you getting along?" I asked, quietly.

He knew what I meant but rejoined with equal subtlety, "I don't know." He paused a long moment, "What do *you* think?"

"I don't know either, I'm not able to assess it too well myself."

It was my turn to pause. "Are you happy here?"

"No," he said.

"What would you think of making a change," I said. It was not a question.

He agreed and it was all handled on a very calm basis. He left.

Actually another French chef was waiting in the wings, swiss-born Henri (which the Johnsons soon converted to "Henry") Haller. Like René, a Cordon Bleu food artist, Henri had been discovered by Mary Kaltman in the Essex House Hotel in New York. He arrived in 1966, and Zephyr once again was up in arms about her salary.

"He's just beginning here," she complained. "Why should he get more than I do when I have seniority?" I took it up with Mrs. Johnson and once again Zephyr won her raise. The First Lady took that opportunity to bring up another point.

"Zephyr has been used to shopping for our groceries for all these years and feels a little tied down when the housekeeper orders everything wholesale. She thinks she might be able to keep our food bills down by doing her own shopping for our personal meals."

Then Mrs. Johnson sighed, running her hand over her forehead, smoothing down her dark hair. Confronting the food bills once a month gives every First Lady a shock. Somehow, it seems much less when a housewife buys and pays for a weekly load of groceries than it does when the same amount of food is billed in a cold, itemized ledger at the end of the month.

So once a week Zephyr hopped in the food truck with a security man and made the rounds of her favorite grocery stores. I don't know whether the Johnsons saved anything on their food bills that way. Zephyr, however, got to save a big batch of trading stamps by going to the supermarkets—a bonus that may have eased her grudge against the higher-paid French chefs.

Following the Johnson's economy directives, Mary Kaltman balanced the budget with the zeal of a home economist, keeping her four separate sets of accounts—official expenditures, personal spending, State Department accounts, and food for the help—juggled neatly and confidentially within the limits of the appropriation. Mary was the first housekeeper we'd ever had with a background in actual institutional management, and Mrs. Johnson was delighted with her efficiency.

Because Congress had permitted us to feed the servants since the beginning of the Trumans, Mary had $1,000 a month to spend for two meals a day (the servants worked on two shifts) for the thirty-two-person staff. They selected their own menus—not chili or pâté, but plain American Southern-style cooking: fried chicken, pork chops, pigs' feet, cornbread, blackeyed peas. They ate family style, in the help's dining room in the lower basement.

One day, Mary Kaltman called me, all alarmed.

"We're missing a ham down in the servants' kitchen," she stated. "I bought a whole ham to feed the extra help we hired for tonight's party, and now it's gone. Somebody stole it!"

"Do you have any suspects?" I asked.

"No, but I think you ought to have everybody searched as they leave tonight."

I didn't, of course, ask the police to search our employees. I did ask Piedro Udo, who cooked for the domestics, to keep a closer watch on things from then on.

About a month later Udo called, asking for help.

"There's an awful stink in the help's dining room. It's like something dead. I think it's in the walls."

Shades of Edgar Allan Poe, I thought, calling in the engineers and plumbers.

"Here it is," cried "Red" Arrington, as he pried away a section of wall underneath the sink.

The offending item—even more pungent as it was brought into the air—was a well-chewed ham bone!

"Your mystery is solved," I explained to Mary. "The rats dragged the ham off the counter and carried it away."

"Rats!" the housekeeper screamed in horror. "Rats in the White House?"

"Well, we're in the middle of downtown Washington," I told her. "And don't be alarmed. It's not the first time we've had rats."

Actually, rats were an old story for us. Once, during the Trumans, Reathel Odun called me out to the South Portico, where she and Mrs. Wallace were eating dinner. We watched, fascinated, while a large, brown rat walked up the steps, across the portico and down the steps on the

357

other side, before I called the gardener to chase it away.

Later the unwelcome animals became more of a problem. We found that they came from underneath Lafayette Park across the street, where they'd built acres and acres of catacombs. At night, the police told us, Pennsylvania Avenue looked as if Napoleon's army was crossing the street to the White House grounds.

We called in an exterminator, who came in every couple of weeks and worked on the grounds and in Lafayette Park until the worst of them were eliminated. But every now and then they came back, at least once during each administration. Fortunately, after the hambone incident, we sneaked the exterminators in and out very quickly.

"We'll have to keep the dogs away from the rat poison," Mary worried. The exterminator assured us that their poison only affected rats, so we were able to get rid of the vermin without having to inform the First Lady.

At one of our discussions about kitchen expenses and rivalries, Mrs. Johnson apologized for violating her own rule to stay out of day-to-day management of the mansion. "I realize," she said, "that there are some things we have to discuss now and then."

There were quite a few such discussions over the years, in which Mrs. Johnson had to arbitrate disputes or settle matters both large and small. Throughout all those discussions I never heard Lady Bird Johnson with a sharp word for anybody, with complaint or anger in her voice, with anything but a pleasant expression on her face.

Once, her press secretary and her curator became embroiled in an argument over the nature of the "White House history" exhibits in the ground-floor corridor. Liz had been offered an exhibit of campaign memorabilia; Jim felt strongly that the mansion belonged to all the people and should display only White House artifacts such as Mrs. Grover Cleveland's sewing box.

Mrs. Johnson listened patiently to their presentations, which grew more and more heated. Then she interrupted.

"You're acting like children," she said firmly in her most schoolteacherly voice. "That will be quite enough argument. *I* will make the decision." And she did. The exhibits were limited to First Ladies' sewing boxes and the like.

She often showed the practical side to her nature, as when we were revamping the West Sitting Hall on the second floor. We reupholstered in the same fabrics, but added new curtains and a rug. Mrs. Brown from the McMillen Company in New York, who was helping out, suggested new lampshades as well. Mrs. Johnson called me up to inspect the decorator's photographs.

"These lampshades cost a hundred dollars each," she said. "Don't you think that's awfully expensive?"

"I do, but most of them around here cost a lot more than that," I pointed out.

"Well, if this old house is used to that sort of thing, go ahead and order them," she said, half-disapprovingly.

4

Though she had become an avid student of art appreciation and art history, Mrs. Johnson, as First Lady, wanted her own project. Making the State rooms a museum was, after all, Jacqueline Kennedy's idea, and no matter how many paintings or pieces of furniture she acquired, she knew the end product would be referred to as "adding to Mrs. Kennedy's restoration."

The White House politicians—including those stationed in the east wing—had discovered what a natural asset the President had in Lady Bird Johnson. She was a poised public speaker, an intrepid, articulate question-answerer, and she did her homework.

Mrs. Johnson became an ambassador of sorts to various projects and programs of her husband's "Great Society," taking well-publicized trips to Head Start classrooms, job training centers, homes of poor mountaineers. Her visits, always accompanied by Liz's thoroughly briefed press corps, drew national attention wherever she went. At the White House, she initiated a monthly series of

"Women Do-ers" luncheons for prominent women leaders, professionals and volunteers.

Shortly before Mrs. Johnson went out to campaign for her husband's election in 1964, Liz Carpenter and staff began looking for a project for Mrs. Johnson, one that would be uniquely hers. Liz called me for ideas.

"You ought to be able to figure out something," she said.

Unfortunately, I wasn't.

Off they went on the Lady Bird Special, whistling through Dixie on a red-white-and-blue train, and when they came back, winning the election to the tune of 61 percent of the vote, they had discovered Beautification. It fit Mrs. Johnson to a T.

The beautification project helped Mrs. Johnson become a national figure in her own right. It took her out of her husband's shadow, but not away from his side. If at first the project appeared to be "manufactured" for her as a quasi-political vehicle, she more than grew into the job, giving it unmatched energy and zeal, and gained respect from conservationists throughout the country.

Behind her, providing inspiration, speeches, information, and locale, was the entire Department of the Interior and its National Park Service. Liz Carpenter, though, was the brains of the operation, thinking up occasions, grinding out press releases, setting up conferences, all to obtain the maximum amount of publicity for the First Lady and her goals of preserving and reclaiming the scenic beauty of America. It caught on.

Her numerous speeches, raft trips down rivers, and ceremonial tree plantings became a forerunner of the ecology movement that began to sweep through the country in the late 1960's.

The White House seemed always to be full of beautification people. From the meetings there, they'd board special buses and go on an inspection tour of Washington, D. C. with Mrs. Johnson as tour guide. She pointed out little triangles of earth that could be transformed into beautiful flower gardens, and the Potomac River, which sadly was becoming almost a running sewer.

Her friend Mary Lasker largely underwrote the beautification program for the nation's capital, donating millions and millions of bulbs for the Park Service gardeners to plant in nooks and corners and mini-parks in the city. As Mrs. Johnson and Mrs. Lasker scouted the city for unplanted areas, I began to remember all the trees and bushes that Mrs. Mellon had absconded with when she scoured those same parks for President Kennedy's lawn.

In the White House grounds, tourists were startled to hear the recorded Texas drawl of Lady Bird Johnson, speaking to them from loudspeakers in the bushes and trees. "This is a Grandiflora Magnolia, planted by President Warren G. Harding, two linden trees set out by President Franklin D. Roosevelt; you are now looking at a dogwood, one of my favorite. . . ."

We had our own little nature walks at the White House.

I remember the night President Johnson wanted to bring Mrs. Johnson a present from the House of Representatives floor, the night of his "Salute to Congress" party at the White House. The gift would be House passage of the Highway Beautification Act, which would severely restrict billboards, and which was related to Mrs. Johnson's pet project.

The only trouble was that the House Republicans generally didn't have much to salute in 1964–65, and the bill's opponents were in no hurry to let the measure come to a final vote. They were taking their time, employing the usual parliamentary delaying tactics, calling for innumerable quorums and attempting to pierce the bill with weakening amendments.

The Democrats felt they had earned a good party, and most of their wives were dressed and impatiently waiting to go to the White House, as the hours slipped away into evening and on past the starting time for the White House reception. The Democratic leadership was ready to call it quits for the night, but the White House Congressional liaison staff—acting on Presidential orders —said the President wanted them to *stay there* and finish the bill. The President stressed he wanted that bill for his Lady Bird. The party would just start later.

A further complication was that President Johnson was scheduled to go into Bethesda Naval Hospital after the party to have his gallbladder removed in an operation scheduled for seven o'clock the next morning.

It turned out to be some evening. The House finally passed the bill not too long before midnight. By the time a few dozen Congressmen straggled through the White House gates, the President was persuaded that he'd better leave for the hospital and get some rest before major surgery.

The movie stars, singers, and jazz musicians who'd lined up to salute Congress in the State Department Auditorium went on, despite the fact that most of the audience wasn't there. But enough Democrats finally got to the White House to make quite a party. By 3:00 a.m., the scene in the East Room had a little of the spirit of the rollicking days of Andrew Jackson. Most of the Marine musicians, who had by then been playing for many, many hours, loosened or unbuttoned their tight tunics. Vice President Hubert Humphrey was the center of attraction, dancing with everyone in sight. By the time the party broke up, the President had long since gone to sleep at the hospital. And the law became known as the "Lady Bird Act."

5

Like everything else in the Johnson White House and life, it soon became apparent that the entertainment would be served up on a grand scale. From Shakespeare to musical comedy to ballet to American Indian dancers, Bess Abell began to put on a really big show after dinner. She needed more facilities to accommodate all the performers, however. There would be no more "jewel-box theater" in the East Room. The little red velvet stage Mrs. Kennedy had designed was too small for extravaganzas.

"Can't we expand the stage?" Bess asked, and when I shook my head, explaining the technical unfeasibility, she countered:

"Can't we build a bigger stage?" After I explained our budgetary situation, Bess announced "What we need is an angel!"

One flew in, in the form of Rebekah Harkness, who had created her own ballet company. She commissioned Jo Mielziner, the premier Broadway designer, to create "something that fits in with the East Room decor."

"It has to be portable," I cautioned. "Something that

two or three men can put up and take down in a few hours' time."

Knowing the Johnson's penchant for using the East Room and our time and manpower limitations, one could really get into a bind if there were three events scheduled for the room in one day and our crews were scheduled to put up a stage. Which is exactly what happened.

When the stage was completed, instead of taking three men eight hours, it took eight men three days to put the thing together for a performance, and about the same time to take it down again. It took up a full third of the East Room and was fashioned with columns to match the room's classical Greek detail. It was painted to match the room's white paneling.

At first, the designer wanted a gold silk stage curtain to match those now hanging over the windows. I pointed out that the curtains cost $26,149, that the fabric design —taken from an old document—was extremely complex, and that the curtains had been woven by an old Frenchman who could only turn out six inches a day. The designer settled for an American-made silk curtain of a matching color.

When the new stage was finally in place, Mrs. Johnson stood back to take a look.

"Well, at last this room has a stage that fits in with it," she said.

It was so large the East Room looks like part of the stage, I thought to myself.

But our work in the theatrical business was not yet done. When *Hello, Dolly* came to the White House, we had to build a runway in front of the stage for Carol Channing to do her famous "number," which incidentally had been used as a 1964 Democratic campaign song, retitled "Hello, Lyndon."

Bess was always looking for something different for a party, and her imagination was considerable. We'd have dances on the east terrace, barbecues on the west terrace, formal dinners with Japanese lanterns in the Rose Garden, carnivals with circus tents on the south grounds. But once was enough. It's just a lot simpler to put on a do in the State Dining Room.

During State dinners, Bess and I would sit in the Private Dining Room, which was set up as a pantry, eating the same food, having the same service as the other guests, and joking with each other about being the "official tasters," wondering who would get the poison first.

At one State luncheon, a very irritated President Johnson decided that *he* had gotten the poison first. The butler who served him (the President always is served first) came running in to Bess and me.

"The President says not to serve any more meat. He says it's rotten!"

Bess and I jumped and ran to the door to hear Mr. Johnson say to his table: "Don't anybody eat it. It's spoiled!" And he called for Marvin Watson, his trusted first assistant.

Meanwhile, the President's plate had been carried back to the kitchen. Bess, Mary Kaltman, Henry Haller and I all steeled ourselves and took a bite, hoping it wouldn't be our last. It tasted exactly the way filet of beef with pâté de foie gras in the center is supposed to taste.

"It's perfect," said the dismayed chef Haller, who'd been so proud of his Tournedos Rossini.

Marvin relayed the word to the President. "It's supposed to taste like that."

At the end of the dinner the President had only one comment: "Don't ever serve that stuff again in this house."

Sometimes others joined Bess and me in the pantry and we'd have quite a party. Our dinner partners would be members of the President's staff who'd been edged out of their seats by last-minute guests, or staff members who came to listen to the dinner toasts or entertainment.

One lovely evening we were joined by James Symington, the Chief of Protocol, and by Joe Califano, the President's chief assistant on domestic issues. Joe and Jim were in the midst of a spirited conversation, which we all thoroughly enjoyed. That is, until Joe gave a sweeping gesture to make a point and knocked a full glass of red wine down the front of Jim Symington's snowy white evening shirt.

Everyone jumped up, mopping and blotting, and Bess, who always knew what came next, said:

"Oh my God, Jimmy, you've got to escort President Saragat [of Italy]. What are we going to do?"

"You can have my shirt," I said, and flew down the hall to my office to pick up a discarded one for me to wear.

Back in the Private Dining Room, the Chief of Protocol and I solemnly disrobed and exchanged shirts. It was all done in a flash, and just as we heard chairs scraping the floor in the State Dining Room, Mr. Symington popped in, starched and snowy breasted, to do his official duty.

He returned my shirt freshly laundered the next day, writing, "to J. B. West, who literally gave me the shirt off his back."

Music was an integral part of Bess's parties, from beginning to end! "If you didn't see so many people sitting around with fiddles, you'd think they had Muzak around here all the time," said one butler, hearing the strains of "Hello Dolly/Lyndon" for the umpteenth time.

The Marines sat in the lobby playing show tunes while the guests entered the White House; the Air Force Strolling Strings moved in and out among the round tables during dessert, somebody or other was always singing or playing on the East Room stage—Dave Brubeck or the New Christy Minstrels or Robert Merrill. And at the end, the Marine Orchestra and their rock combo turned up for dancing.

The Johnsons were the dancingest First Family I'd known. Perhaps it was urged on by their daughters, perhaps it fit in with their informal "get-to-know-everybody" entertaining. Or maybe Lyndon Johnson just liked to dance. Watching him dance at midnight after a Lyndon Johnson-style workday gave me one further glimpse into the superhuman energy of this President.

After every official dinner and reception, even in the

afternoon, the white marble lobby and main hall were transformed into a dance floor.

"How funny that we should do more dancing after fifty than at any other time in our lives," wrote Mrs. Johnson.

The President did his foxtrot smoothly, instructing the military aides to cut in on him after a few twirls around the floor with every lady. Everybody danced. Even I did a few turns now and then. The President sat out the wilder dances, however, when his daughters and a few from his own generation cut into the gyrations of the 1960's. And the Johnsons, contrary to White House tradition (in which nobody goes home until the President goes upstairs), were the last to leave.

The liveliest party we ever had was a dinner dance in honor of England's Princess Margaret and her husband, Lord Snowdon. The east wing staff worked long and hard on the guest lists—it was known that this "madcap Princess" liked a good time—to bring together a group of important people who in those days could be called "swingers." The swingers were drawn from the town's Anglophiles, Lynda Bird's friends in the movie community, the younger politicians, and, as always, the wealth of America.

Representing the latter category were auto manufacturer Henry Ford and his Italian-born wife, Cristina, who almost outshone the diminutive princess.

Mrs. Ford was endowed with all the personal magnetism of a Sophia Loren—even the President paid a great deal of attention to the lady—and considerable physical charm as well. There was a lot of open-mouthed gaping at her enthusiastic version of the frug, especially when some of her charm popped out of the top of her white gown.

Another time a guest came close to losing her jewels. Jane Engelhard, an old friend since the Kennedy days, a benefactress of the White House restoration and wife of the platinum magnate, wore a pair of dangly earrings that Bess Abell declared must have dropped off the White House chandeliers.

At dinner Jane sat at the same table with philanthropist

Mary Lasker, who had meant so much to Mrs. Johnson's beautification-of-America campaign. As happens to everybody at some time or another, Mrs. Lasker spilled a drop of wine down the front of her gown. Jane Engelhard quickly took off one of her big diamond earrings and pinned it over the wine spot on Mary's dress.

But after dinner they became separated. When everybody moved into the East Room for the entertainment, Mary Lasker took a seat in the center of the third row and the Engelhards stayed at the back of the room.

"We have to get our jet out of National Airport before 11:00 p.m.," Jane told me, "because they've got a noise pollution ban on jet traffic after that time." At about ten, the Engelhards left their seats and slipped into the Green Room where I was standing.

"We want to leave now," Jane whispered, "but Mary Lasker has one of my earrings on the front of her dress. Do you think you could retrieve it without all the press ladies noticing?"

Seeing Bess Abell standing against the East Room wall, I passed the word along to her, thinking it would be less conspicuous for *her* to unpin the jewels. Agreeing, Bess sidled into the third row, whispered to Mary, palmed the earring and dropped it into my closed fist. I took it to the Green Room and handed it to Jane.

"Do you know the value of what you just held in your hand?" Mrs. Engelhard asked.

"No," I said.

"$100,000," she announced.

"More like two hundred thousand dollars," her husband corrected, hurrying her toward the door.

"I should have walked right out the front door," I told him.

During the Johnson years, we geared up for more entertaining than at any other period. And each party was uniquely Johnsonian.

The President absolutely refused to wear white tie and tails; his most formal social occasions called for black tie. Bess Abell, a long-time friend of the Johnsons, knew how to shape White House entertaining to fit their informal, expansive Texas style.

369

Invitations, except for State occasions, might come in every color, every style of printing. For the after-dinner entertainment, the printed programs were mighty fancy, as in a regular theater. Some were covered in red velour, some in green silk, and some contained cartoons or drawings.

Many times, Bess set themes for her parties with decorations. Sometimes there were big paper flowers for a "Mexican" party; other times the trees wore live flowers.

Once Lynda had a dinner dance in the East Room and we moved in trees, "planting" them in wooden tubs around the room, trying to achieve a garden effect. There were potted geraniums, cherry blossoms stuck on the trees, and greenery hanging from the chandeliers.

In planning for these affairs, I was on the phone with Bess Abell sixteen times a day, for Bess was indeed the White House social director. In addition to directing the thirty-person social office, handling the traditional duties of guest lists, calendar, and correspondence, Bess was the impresario of the Johnson White House. We called her Sol Hurok.

Utilizing a crew of knowledgeable outside advisors, she garnered performing artists from concert stage to Indian tribes, directed rehearsals, perfected timing, and set up dressing rooms for the after-dinner entertainment. She designed theater programs, named the dishes on the menu, selected gifts for State visitors, decorated the State rooms, coached the military social aides, and acted as assistant hostess at all the parties, introducing guests, starting conversations, choreographing the crowds from one room to another.

Her instruction sheets were called scenarios, and the staff performed according to instructions like actors on a Hollywood set. Because the gregarious Johnsons used all the house all the time, combining official business with entertaining, Bess was on duty all the time. She coordinated menus with the chef, gave instructions to the housekeeper, directed the activities in the flower shop.

The evolution of the White House social secretary has paralleled the growth of the mansion as an institution. When I first went to work at the White House, Edith

Helm served, simply, as a secretary for social occasions. She worked only in the mornings, went home for lunch and returned only if she'd been asked to help pour afternoon tea. Her main responsibility was to have her staff find the correct addresses of the people who were to be invited, instruct calligraphers to write the invitations, keep records of the acceptances and rejections, and provide the social calendar to the newspapers. She appeared at the White House parties only if she'd been invited.

"She invites the people," Mr. Crim told me. "After they come in the door they're our responsibility."

Mrs. Helm knew social Washington from one end to the other, having served as social secretary to Mrs. Woodrow Wilson as well as Mrs. Roosevelt and Mrs. Truman. She had memorized Emily Post and the New York Social Register and the Washington Green Book, and the guest lists stayed rather closely within those confines.

Mrs. Truman depended on Mrs. Helm and her knowledge of Washingtonians for most of her guest lists, as well, and because Mrs. Truman didn't follow Mrs. Roosevelt's precedent of weekly press conferences, Mrs. Helm met with the newspaper ladies to announce social occasions, describe Mrs. Truman's clothing, and fend off questions about Margaret's beaux.

Mary Jane McCaffree followed the same format and served as Mrs. Eisenhower's personal secretary, as well. Mrs. Eisenhower, of course, was her own social director, decorator, guest-list selector, seating arranger. She worked directly with the Usher's office.

But Mary Jane came to every party, "mixing" with the guests, keeping an eye out for reporters taking notes (a military social aide would quickly appear and ask the lady to stow her notepad), making introductions and organizing conversations. Before every State dinner, Mary Jane would usher in the press ladies—asking them please not to step on the rugs—to show off the table settings and guest lists.

(The working press was not invited to the Eisenhowers' affairs. "I think it ruins the party to have some questioner running around," Mrs. Eisenhower told me.)

Tish Baldrige didn't enter into the decorations, but she

ran around like a stage director while a party was going on. She'd even have the girls in her office get dressed up and come over to State dinners, to see if guests were being taken care of, talked to, danced with. Tish was the first social secretary in charge of programming for the East Room, but her great flair for directing activity sometimes came in conflict with Mrs. Kennedy's.

Bess Abell directed everything. She was in on everything for the Johnsons' private parties as well as for official entertaining. She dreamed up the decorations, she told the chef how to cook, told the housekeeper what needed to be cleaned and where the ashtrays should be placed. She did for Mrs. Johnson what Mamie Eisenhower and Jacqueline Kennedy had done for themselves.

After our first open house for Congress, miraculously put together in just a few hours, Bess was amazed at the instantaneous response of government agencies, and private companies as well, to White House requests.

"Mr. West, I never realized what power went along with the title 'Social Secretary of the White House.' You ask for something and it's delivered immediately, if not sooner!"

From then on, Bess never hesitated to use that power.

The entertaining bills were higher under the Johnsons because there simply was more entertaining. Some months the bill might run $10,000 or even $12,000. More than 200,000 guests received invitations to the Johnson White House during the five years they lived there. The Democratic National Committee picked up the tabs for some political evenings, and we tried to keep as many parties as possible "official," under the auspices of the State Department and its budget.

"Official" entertaining came out of the President's travel account, because with the Air Force now paying for his transportation—on Air Force One or the smaller Jet Star— we had no more need for White House Pullman tickets.

Mrs. Johnson, however, almost always traveled by commercial airliner, paying her own way, grabbing the shuttle to New York like everybody else. Jerry Kivets, her Secret Service agent, made the arrangements.

Over in the west wing, there was a public austerity

campaign going on, with Marvin Watson in charge. Marvin was the President's right-hand man for a wide range of duties, ranging from issues of state to carrying out the President's slightest passing whim. In matters of White House expenses, he was known as the President's tight fist.

While the President carried on about the electricity bills, Marvin cut down on salaries, travel, telephones, even newspaper subscriptions. The east wing was always up in arms about some new directive from the west wing. Bess soon learned, like Jacqueline Kennedy, that the only way to operate under the west-wing limitations was by devious methods. One crafty move was the time she sneaked a promotion for Jeff.

The most popular man in the social office, Fred Jefferson worked as a messenger and driver. He carried memos from the east wing to the west wing and all over the house, he drove around town delivering invitations and printing orders and anything else. Full of dignity and kindness, the tall, lanky messenger also worked extra in the mansion as a butler, filling in at parties in any capacity he was needed. He'd been there since the Eisenhowers; Tish had adored him, and Bess thought he was great. Jeff was indispensable, Bess told me, and she thought he deserved a raise. She went to Marvin Watson (the social office came under west-wing jurisdiction; it was not my bailiwick, although I could vouch that Jeff was a very good butler) to request a promotion. Marvin denied the request. He said, in effect, that there just wasn't any place to which he could promote Jeff.

Not to be outdone, Bess pulled as neat a bureaucratic coup as I'd ever seen. She wrote a very stiff and formal memo about how badly she needed an "assistant to the social secretary," and how the member of her staff she'd like for the position had been performing above and beyond the call of duty. She sent the request through regular channels and it came back "approved."

After the State of the Union message in early 1967, the Johnsons were having a little party on the second floor, just for family, friends, and close staff. Marvin Watson was there.

"How do you like your new assistant?" he asked Bess.

"Just fine! In fact, here he is now," she said sweetly, as Jeff served Marvin his ginger ale.

As one staff member said, "It's more important to keep the President and Bess Abell happy around here than it is the First Lady." It wasn't just that Bess *assumed* more authority than the previous social secretaries, she'd been *granted* that authority by Mrs. Johnson. The "Chairman of the Board" approved or disapproved all Bess's written plans and scenarios with a "yes—CTJ" (Claudia Taylor Johnson, as she signed her checks), or "no—CTJ."

And although she didn't get involved in the details, the final word of the First Lady always counted.

When Marvin Watson was appointed Postmaster General, Bess set up a noon reception in the east garden as a farewell party. Mrs. Johnson, housekeeper Mary Kaltman and I were in conference in the Lincoln sitting room, discussing the month's finances. The First Lady, looking out the window, noticed butlers carrying tables out to the garden.

"Oh, that's right. I have to be downstairs to say farewell to Marvin at twelve o'clock," she said. "What are you serving?"

"Canapés, sandwiches and liquor," I answered.

"Oh my gosh, no!" she exclaimed. "Marvin Watson is probably the *only* teetotaler among our friends." I quickly had the bar removed.

When we set about to select the new White House china, which would be known to future administrations as the Johnson china, "CTJ" became very much involved. The new china, a set of 220 rather than 120 (because, since the Kennedys, we'd been using the Blue Room as well as the State Dining Room for dinner parties), was made by Castleton through Tiffany and Company. It was to be a gift to the White House from a generous, anonymous donor.

Mrs. Johnson decided first on a cream background for the dinner service, then they came up with suggestions for designs for the plates. They'd leave mock-ups of the patterns for the First Lady to look over. And look them over she did. She would even come down at night and try the "dummies" in the dining room, just to see what it was going to look like under candlelight.

She finally decided that she wanted a border of wild flowers for the base plate, and right away, they came up with a design that she approved. The design was duly affixed, and we ordered 220 each of the service plates, dinner plates, salad plates, soup bowls, coffee cups and saucers, and demitasses. For the dessert plates, she suggested that they use the state flowers from each of the fifty states.

But when those arrived, somebody had goofed. There was a big blob of color, hardly recognizable as a flower, in the center of each dessert plate.

"I'm just sick about it," said Mrs. Johnson.

"They look like the dime-store special," said Bess Abell.

"Rotten!" said Jim Ketchum.

"Just terrible," said Jane Engelhard, who was advising.

"Back to the drawing board," said the Chief Usher.

There was no question that the plates had to be redesigned. "They're certainly not representative of our work," agreed Walter Hoving, the president of Tiffany's, seeing them for the first time.

But the Johnsons had learned, with a certain portrait of the President, what a delicate matter it is to turn down something you've commissioned. We couldn't just say "no thank you" and ship them back. We didn't want Tiffany's to have them; we didn't want *anybody* to have them. But Bess solved the problem.

"Come down to the lower basement," she stopped by my office to say. I followed along, trying to decipher her mischievous look. We stopped at the ground floor Curator's office, now tucked into Harry Truman's old broadcast room. Bess beckoned to Jim.

"We're going to a party," she told him, and picked up Carol Carlyle, Connie Carter, and Bonner Arrington along the way.

In the basement, Bess led us to a storeroom with reinforced concrete walls. In the center of the floor, neatly stacked, were the dessert plates. And on the wall was a poster, with freshly painted caricatures of Bess's favorite Presidential assistants.

"Heave away!" she shouted—and we had the time of our lives.

It took us less than an hour to smash all 220 pieces of china against the concrete walls. We aimed at our targets with unadulterated glee. And I must say, it was totally satisfying. The china had to be destroyed by law. But perhaps we also were letting off steam at the end of an era.

The broken pieces were sent to the incinerator, and Jim asked Connie Carter, a researcher from the Library of Congress, to help him select good source pictures of the state flowers for Tiffany's artist. In due time, Mrs. Johnson approved all fifty flowers.

6

As I learned with my own Kathy and Sally, the transformation from girl to woman can occur almost overnight. It happened to both Lynda and Luci during the Johnson White House. Within the same five years, they grew up quickly, married, and had children of their own.

By 1966, Luci, the tiny brunette with her own ideas about everything, had embraced Catholicism (her mother was Episcopalian, her father a member of the Disciples of Christ), was a student nurse at Georgetown University, worked part-time in an optometrist's office, and, since Christmas, was engaged to be married to Patrick Nugent.

Luci's was my first White House wedding, and even though she was married in the Shrine of the Immaculate Conception, near Catholic University, the White House was decorated to the hilt for her reception. Bess Abell decorated, choreographed, stage-directed, rehearsed. Liz Carpenter dangled tidbits of information to the press about every possible detail involving the wedding with the exception of the wedding gown.

Luci's gown was such a closely guarded secret—she thought it would be bad luck for the groom to see it before the wedding day—the Secret Service met designer Priscilla of Boston at the plane. The designer hand-carried the big box into the White House and locked it in the Lincoln bedroom. No one was permitted to go in there, not even to dust.

A few days before the wedding, which was scheduled for August 6, Bess called me.

"Can everybody stay put for a while? Luci wants to be photographed in her wedding dress in the East Room, and she doesn't want *anybody* to see her."

"Right," I answered. And at one o'clock, we shut off the entire house. There was tighter security than there'd been during the Roosevelts' air-raid drills or the Cuban missile crisis. For an hour and a half, everyone stayed in his own position, in her own spot. No one was permitted to move on the elevator or walk through the corridors while Luci Johnson posed for her wedding portrait.

It had been a whirlwind week. In the midst of all the bridesmaids and buffet suppers, we'd had a full-scale State dinner for Israeli President Shazar in the State Dining Room.

The last two days before the wedding, I held the White House together, staying late at night, seeing to the setup of the white canopy tent in the garden, the installation of hundreds of flowerpots in the hallways, and banks and banks of flowers in all the State rooms.

The morning of August 5, I asked Bess to walk around the house with me, inspecting every room, going over the reception scenario, being sure there were to be no changes. I was planning to make an escape that afternoon, and I didn't want any last-minute phone calls about details.

I'd had a call from Mrs. Paul Mellon, inviting me to attend a surprise birthday party for Jacqueline Kennedy, at the Mellon estate in Osterville, Massachusetts.

"You've *got* to come," she urged. "I'll make all the arrangements for you."

So off I went, on the eve of the biggest event in the Johnson White House to date, on the *Caroline* with Bobby,

Teddy, the Robert McNamaras, and Kay Graham, publisher of the Washington *Post*.

When she saw me, Mrs. Kennedy came as close to a shriek as I'd ever heard her.

"Mr. West! What's *Luci* doing?"

I just smiled.

Grinning wickedly, she chided, "If this were the French revolution you'd be the first one on the guillotine!"

The party—and I with it—lasted until three. I slept for two hours at the Oyster Bay Harbor Club, jumped into the limousine Mrs. Mellon had sent, rode to the Hyannis Airport, took a plane, chartered for me, to the Boston airport. At eight a.m., I just barely boarded a jet for Washington, where I hurried home in time to change clothes for the wedding.

I must say, as Zella and I left the White House after the reception, that I did feel a bit heady. It was a fabulous twenty-four hours.

Zella and I were perplexed about one thing: What do you give a President's daughter?

Luci received gifts from all over the world. We had cleared two large storage rooms in the basement, lining the walls with shelves to display the gifts, and installed two desks, one for a secretary to work at cataloguing the gifts, and one for Luci to write thank-you notes.

Our gift, an antique Chinese export porcelain plate, to my surprise rated a telephone call at home from Mrs. Johnson, a few days after the wedding. "How did you ever think of such a lovely gift?" she asked.

We have two daughters the same age as Luci and Lynda who are just beginning to appreciate such things, I explained, and we thought Luci might, too.

But however much Mrs. Johnson appreciated our gift, I appreciated her thoughtful call much more.

In December, 1967, December 9, to be exact, Bess had another wedding on her hands. Lynda, marrying her color guard captain, Charles Robb, was the first President's daughter to be married in the White House in fifty-three years. In the days before the wedding, the house was full of Robbs, bridesmaids, hairdressers, and TV cameramen, all trying to stay out of the way of Bess and her crew of assistants, florists and electricians, all of whom were trying to decorate the East Room for a Protestant ceremony and the entire State floor for a wedding reception.

Mrs. Johnson didn't want television, really, but with the press demanding coverage it was difficult to shut them out completely. We had to figure out a way to hide the lighting equipment. Finally, the poles were all wrapped in white to match the walls of the room. The networks were permitted to shoot twenty minutes of film during the procession and the beginning of the reception, and then they had to clear their equipment from the rooms so they wouldn't look cluttered, all in five minutes' time.

Half the employees in the house stood in for Lynda and Chuck at one time or another, to help Bess Abell choreograph crowd movements from one room to another.

From the East Room military ceremony, where Lynda and Chuck marched out through a tunnel of crossed swords, the crowd of 640 or so moved into the State Dining Room for a buffet and champagne, and spilled out onto the terrace into a big, pink, electrically heated tent, while we furiously dismantled the East Room wedding altar and installed Peter Duchin and his orchestra, who played for dancing.

It was at that wedding that we observed how Mrs. Johnson could "handle" her husband. As the bride and groom and all their relatives lined up in the Yellow Oval Room to be photographed, out wandered Luci's little white dog, Yuki, dressed in his best red velvet sweater.

President Johnson reached for the dog, a friendly mongrel who accompanied him everywhere. He'd taught it to "sing"—and, in fact, often knelt down to sing along with the dog.

"We've got to get Yuki in the picture," said the President. "We can't have a family portrait without him."

Lady Bird Johnson drew herself up to her full five feet three and backed off until she could look her husband in the eye.

"That dog is *not* going to be in the wedding picture," she said.

The President started to argue. But Mrs. Johnson whipped out a most Lyndon-like command.

"Mr. Bryant, get that dog out of here right now! *He will not be photographed!*"

Nobody, not even the President, stood up to that tone in her voice. And Lynda, the bewildered bride, breathed a great sigh of relief and everybody smiled for the wedding camera.

The next day, wedding debris had disappeared, the huge blue spruce Christmas tree was up in the Blue Room and the White House once again absorbed another Grand Event.

For a short while, the Johnson White House was without daughters. Then, they both came back, Luci with her funny white dog, Yuki, and her baby son, Patrick Lyndon, and Lynda, who was pregnant. Their soldier husbands had gone to Vietnam.

The most dramatic and publicly startling event of the Johnson Presidency really did not surprise those of us in the White House who had learned to sense or guess at the President's moods and thoughts. The President went on television, March 31, 1968, and announced he would not seek reelection. The public's growing disenchantment with the seemingly endless war in Vietnam had cut into the President's popularity at the polls. It looked as if his own political party would be torn apart by bitter disagreement over the war. If he sought reelection, the New Hampshire primary indicated, he would have to fight for the nomination.

I think President Johnson sensed that his efforts to lead, personally and publicly, had started turning sour. The war in Vietnam was a large part of the problem. But the President's overwhelming effort at wooing the media and projecting himself on television may have backfired. Because the press, and through it the public, began to see this President's outsized flaws as well as his virtues.

Lyndon Johnson had shown the news media his scar from gallbladder surgery and his image never seemed to heal after that. He kept switching back and forth on those three television sets but he less often found a satisfying picture.

I had thought almost from the beginning that the President's and Mrs. Johnson's advisors had overscheduled them, had stretched publicity efforts to the point where they overexposed their bosses. And, of course, Lyndon Johnson seldom cooperated even when his staff finally decided to cut back on his public exposure. I can remember those afternoons when I was called to a south window to see the President, pursued by a horde of reporters and television cameramen, walking rapidly round and round on the broad circular driveway surrounding the vast "backyard."

When he found the personal publicity and war news increasingly unfavorable, the President for lengthy periods stopped seeing the press.

Lyndon Johnson didn't like to lose.

But I would also say that he had worked at a hectic pace for five long years in the most pressure-filled, demanding job in the world. The President was determined to spend his last nine months in the White House trying to gain a negotiated peace with honor in Vietnam.

But after his momentous announcement, a whole series of events spread shame, violence, confusion, and even further discord through the country, making it extremely hard for the President to glimpse peace at the end of his journey. The spring and summer were filled with events that cast a pall over life in the White House—the assassinations of Martin Luther King and Robert Kennedy, the constant concern about the lives of 500,000 American sons in Vietnam, including the Johnsons' two sons-in-law, the Senate rejection of the Johnsons' close friend Abe Fortas to be Chief Justice of the Supreme Court, the souring of the economy as the President fought desperately to stop inflation with a tax hike without utterly demolishing the domestic programs he had hailed as the goals of a "Great Society," the violence and discord at the Democratic National Convention. The splendid misery of the Presidency seemed to have turned to just plain misery.

The difficulties of Lyndon Johnson and the times we lived in were brought home to me when Charles Lindbergh and three astronauts visited the White House. Their respective feats of lonely bravery spanned a good portion of my lifetime. There was a difference, of course. The Lone Eagle had braved the Atlantic literally alone, while the astronauts were backed up with all the sophisticated technology of the computer age.

But the computer age, I thought, could not master the mysterious essence of man's relation with man. The computers did not keep Lyndon Johnson from becoming sucked into the most tragic, divisive conflict since the Civil War. And during the last nine months in office, this oversized man, with all his arts of persuasion, could not get us out of that war in Vietnam.

I have seldom seen the fortunes of the Presidency change so rapidly in a brief five years—from the courage with which he took office and rallied the country, to his landslide election and historic domestic legislation, to the quagmire war and a bitterly divided America.

But the Johnsons left office as they entered, with their heads held high. After Richard Nixon won the 1968 election, the President and Mrs. Johnson immediately made clear that they planned to leave with dignity and with utmost courtesy to their successors.

On November 11, just six days after the election, Mrs. Johnson invited her successor to the White House, beginning the most orderly transfer from one occupant to another I had witnessed. Mrs. Johnson briefed Mrs. Nixon on everything and instructed Curator Jim Ketchum and me to provide as many details as possible. She was determined that the new First Lady should get a thorough advance orientation to help smooth her transition to her new life. And Mr. Nixon, with the help of a new law and appropriation, had a staff especially to handle the transition of the Presidency.

During the last two Johnson months in the White House, there were few State dinners and little pomp and circumstance. Rather, the Johnsons appeared to be reaching back for their roots in the hill country of central Texas. They invited droves of Texas friends up to spend the night with them, giving those Texans a thrill of White House glory but giving the Johnsons perhaps much more. The owner of the chili parlor in Johnson City came, as did Mrs. Johnson's hairdresser from the small town nearest the LBJ ranch.

Mrs. Johnson expressed a great desire to get back to the ranch, but I could tell she hated to leave. They all do.

It is difficult to imagine the deference that is paid to the First Lady every day that her husband is in office. All the Presidents' wives I have known appreciated the services and status that went with their role, no matter how much they yearned to be out of the spotlight of the glass White House.

Mrs. Johnson left the White House a somewhat different person than when she had arrived.

She had developed self-pride in her own accomplishments and won greater respect from her husband. She had come to the White House admitting frankly that she had been cast in a role for which she had not rehearsed.

She mastered the role, and yet she retained the same sense of inner privacy, which kept all but her family at a respectful distance. She had been far more accessible to the press and to the public than anyone since Eleanor Roosevelt. She survived the tempests of her husband's life and of the times. And, yet, when she finally walked out the White House door for the last time, Lady Bird Johnson still wore an invisible screen.

The
Nixons

1

And once again, the changing of the guard.

Inauguration Day, that greatest American festival, always turns Washington upside down. Hundreds of thousands of citizens pour into the city for the swearing-in and celebrations, hoping somehow to get a glimpse of the man they helped elect President of the United States.

On January 20, 1969, I worked in the White House as usual, directing the astonished staff to arrange the most unusual transfer of power any of us had witnessed.

From election day onward, the transition of administrations had been carried out without a hitch. The mood of the switchover was evident from that first greeting between Claudia (Lady Bird) Johnson and Thelma (Pat) Nixon on November 10, at the White House door. They embraced and kissed each other.

The Nixons were back several times before the Inauguration, visiting, measuring, planning their lives there. You could hardly believe that they were of different political parties, much less that Richard Nixon and Lyndon Johnson had once been bitter campaign opponents.

This changing of the guard felt different to me in another way. It was to be my last as Chief Usher of the White House.

In my twenty-eight years in the White House I never saw the President take the oath of office at noon on the Capitol steps, never watched the marching bands strut smartly down Pennsylvania Avenue, never saw the elaborate floats roll by the parade stands while the new President and his family stood shivering but radiant in their glass-enclosed booth, never dressed in my tuxedo to take Zella to the mad crush of bejeweled ladies and thirsty gentlemen to search for an inch of dance floor at one of six hotels or two exhibition halls during the Inaugural balls.

I reflected a little that morning, in the midst of checking the supply of orange juice for the morning's reception. In all my years in the mansion this was the fifth time I'd seen the government change hands. Two Presidents had died in office; their two successors had already been living in the White House when they were elected; one had been elected to two terms. This was only the third time we'd changed tenants on Inauguration Day.

The atmosphere had been considerably chillier during the other two transfers—when General Eisenhower rode down to the Capitol with President Truman and, later, with President Kennedy.

Now, as the thirty-seventh President was about to take office, the thirty-sixth had invited him and his family for breakfast.

The night before, the Nixons had slept at the Statler-Hilton Hotel but their dogs spent the night at the White House.

The family, the President, Mrs. Nixon, Tricia, 22, Julie, 20, and the same David Eisenhower who'd asked "Mimi" why she lived in such a big house, stepped out of their limousines at the North Portico at 10:30 on Inauguration morning. But before Bruce, the elegant senior doorman, could bring them in with his usual flourish, out ran Pasha the yorkshire, and Vicky the poodle, to greet their masters.

"A dog's welcome to the White House—that's what they'll write," muttered one staff member.

But nobody did.

The Nixons, the Johnsons, the Agnews, the Humphreys —all gathered in the Red Room to drink orange juice and coffee, and nibble on sweet rolls and toast. At 11:30, laughing and cordial, the group set out for the Capitol. President Johnson, who had delivered his own Inaugural address in a business suit, even wore a cutaway coat and striped trousers to please Mr. Nixon.

As he repeated the Oath of Office, Mr. Nixon laid his hand on a verse from Isaiah in his family Bible: "And He shall judge among the nations and shall rebuke many people; and they shall beat their swords into plowshares and their spears into pruning hooks; nation shall not lift up sword against nation, neither shall they study war any more."

The new President had pledged to end the war in Vietnam.

While Richard M. Nixon delivered his speech in that dreary, freezing weather, the truck from New York pulled up to the south entrance, and maids began unpacking trunks and boxes of the Nixons' clothes. Not until one minute after 12:00 could we ever do this.

When they came back into the house after the parade, their rooms were ready—Tricia in Lynda's bedroom, Julie and David in the Queen's Room.

But the real queen—some of the staff now called her the Dowager Empress—didn't spend the night in the White House. Mamie Eisenhower, beaming in delight, joined the Nixons for coffee in the State Dining Room but she went back to Walter Reed Hospital to the side of her General.

The former First Lady, regal as always, had definite ideas for the new administration. As she came in from the parade, accompanied by her son, John, and his wife, she gave me a big kiss, then said, right off, "I think it's terrible the way they've been using the East Room in this House—using it like an office. Can't you do something about it?"

"Why don't *you?*" I said, smiling.

"Well, don't think I won't!" she said, with her old "I'm in charge here" look, and a twinkle in her eye.

About a hundred Nixon relatives milled around in the

State Dining Room, then left for their own hotels to dress for the Inaugural Ball.

And Pat Nixon's first White House request threw the kitchen into a tizzy.

Chef Haller and Mary Kaltman stood by, tense as we all are on the first day of a new administration, to order the President's first dinner in the White House. It was well after dark when Mrs. Nixon called to the chef.

"Tricia, Julie, David, and the President would like steak for dinner in the upstairs dining room," she said. "I'd just like a bowl of cottage cheese in my bedroom."

Steaks we had—juicy, fresh, prime filets carefully selected by the meat wholesaler, waiting in the White House kitchen for a family who, we'd heard, loved steak.

But cottage cheese?

Chef Haller called to request a White House limousine. "For two weeks we've laid in supplies in the kitchen," he wailed. "I think we could open a grocery store in the pantry. We've tried to find out everything they like. . . . But we don't have a spoonful of cottage cheese in the house. And what in the world would be open at this time of night—and Inauguration night to boot?"

So the head butler, in a White House limousine, sped around the city of Washington until he found a delicatessen open with a good supply of cottage cheese. The kitchen never ran out, after that.

I'd worried that Mrs. Nixon was so thin. Now, I realized, she intended to stay that way.

Later that evening, we saw them off to the inaugural balls, Mrs. Nixon wearing a long-sleeved yellow satin gown with a jeweled jacket, the President in white tie and tails.

At the last of the six crowded affairs, at all of which he declined to dance, the President announced, "They gave me the key to the White House—I have to see if it fits."

It did, of course. The White House always adjusts to its new occupants.

The only initial change was the President's bedroom.

"Take out the big canopied bed and put in a simple double bed," Mrs. Nixon requested. We went to the storehouse, and there we found President Truman's old bed, the one that also had been in the room during the Eisenhower Administration, but seldom was used by the President then.

The First Lady liked Mrs. Johnson's bedroom.

"I'll have to have a room of my own," she confided to me in her mellow, throaty voice. "*Nobody* could sleep with Dick. He wakes up during the night, switches on the light, speaks into his tape recorder or takes notes—it's impossible," she laughed.

But although the new President kept two dictaphones by his bedside, he quickly got rid of most of the electronic equipment, wiring, and recordings in Mr. Johnson's bedroom.

On a first tour around the living quarters, President Nixon peeked underneath the oversized four-poster bed President Kennedy and Johnson had used.

"What on earth is all this?" he asked, amazed at the cat's cradle of electric wires, all tangled on the floor.

I explained that they were telephone connections, from the elaborate, console phone system of dozens of direct lines that Mr. Johnson had used, remote control wires to the television sets, tape-recording devices, and heaven knows what else.

"I don't want any of that under here," Mr. Nixon told me. "Take it all out, whatever it is. All I need is one line to the operator. She can find anyone else for me."

We took out all the phone extensions from the bathrooms, the West Hall, and the dining room. The three television sets went, too, right away. And the Rube Goldberg shower. Mr. Johnson had proudly pointed out that shower to his successor, describing its pleasures in great detail.

"Please have the shower heads all changed back to normal pressure," the new President requested after the first blast of Johnson-strength spray had almost knocked him right out of the bathroom.

And Mrs. Nixon eliminated the big television set in the West Sitting Hall.

"What did Mrs. Kennedy have here?" she asked me.

"Nothing," I replied. "She used a portable set in her bedroom."

"Then let's get rid of this," she said.

389

Like Lady Bird Johnson, Mrs. Nixon loved Jacqueline Kennedy's favorite Yellow Oval Room.

"It was the Trophy Room when Dick was Vice President, wasn't it?" she asked.

It was indeed, I assented and smiled to remember the Trumans with their night work in that room, and Franklin Roosevelt with his ships' prints, when it was the President's study.

Now three First Ladies had agreed it was the loveliest room in the house.

"I'm crazy about the French furniture," Pat Nixon said, indicating the sofas, commodes, tables and chairs chosen so carefully by Boudin, Mrs. Parrish, and Mrs. Kennedy.

"Do you have some French bedroom furniture in storage that we could use in Tricia's room?"

"No," I replied. "The Altman reproductions are strictly Grand Rapids."

The First Lady leaned against a yellow silk sofa, arms across her chest.

"Then we'll have to order some from New York."

But the Catlin Indians, the oil paintings Mrs. Kennedy had borrowed from the Smithsonian and hung in the center hall, had to go. After Mrs. Nixon requested that they be removed, Jim Ketchum and I went up to hang replacements for the fierce-looking chieftains.

Blond, petite Tricia Nixon stepped out of her bedroom. As usual, she was dressed to the nines.

She saw us removing the paintings.

"Oh, I'm so glad to see those things go," she said. "I felt like I was about to be scalped every time I walked down the hall!" And tossing her long hair over her shoulders, she rang for the elevator.

I seldom saw Tricia during her first few weeks in the White House. When she was "in residence," she remained behind closed doors. When she went out, she requested that no one enter her room, except for the maid.

Her sister, Julie, a junior at Smith College, was living in Massachusetts with her bridegroom, David Eisenhower. (President Nixon once introduced himself jokingly as "General Eisenhower's grandson's father-in-law.")

Her mother, looking at the floor plans I'd given her,

thought we'd be able to make a little sitting room for Tricia in the tiny room adjoining her daughter's bedroom, the room that President Eisenhower had used for painting portraits, that Bess Truman and Eleanor Roosevelt had used as an office.

But when the Kennedys put in the kitchen, part of the room was sacrificed to divert traffic from the elevator to the kitchen. Now the small room was little more than a passageway.

"I'm disappointed," the First Lady told me. "It looked like a cozy little room and very private."

The President found his spot of privacy at the other end of the hall, in the Lincoln sitting room. Directly across from Mrs. Johnson's retreat, the Queen's sitting room, it, too, "has only one door."

At night, or on weekends when he took work home, Mr. Nixon worked there alone, sometimes listening to music from the stereo set Mrs. Nixon had rigged up for the little room. I believe he listened to classical music most of the time.

At first, there were only a few changes. Mrs. Nixon promptly had installed in her bedroom an historic marble mantelpiece, which had been designed by Benjamin Latrobe. Out, and into storage with the old mantel went the little plaque that Mrs. Kennedy had requested on her last day there, "In this room John Fitzgerald Kennedy lived with his wife Jacqueline . . . ," and the Kennedy family gift, the Monet landscape which she'd hung in the Green Room "because that was his favorite room," was banished to an obscure place in the ground-floor vermeil room. The Jacqueline Kennedy Garden, which Mrs. Johnson had dedicated and which Mrs. Kennedy—by now Mrs. Aristotle Onassis—never came to see, became the "First Lady's Garden."

It seemed to many that there was concerted effort to de-Kennedyize the White House. As time went by, Mrs. Nixon hired a new Curator, Clement Conger of the State Department, who became, it appeared, decorator as well, and one by one, the Boudin touches disappeared. The color scheme went back to Truman renovation, the restoration became Mrs. Nixon's. But Jacqueline Kennedy

Onassis would be the first to agree that each First Lady should, certainly, decorate the White House any way that suits her.

"I never intended for Boudin's work to remain in the White House forever," she told me. "Every family *should* put its own imprint there."

After all, it had been six years, and the walls were getting streaked, the upholstery threadbare. The White House gets a lot of use and did so, especially, during the Johnsons.

It was the antique furnishings, the paintings, the sculpture that Jacqueline Kennedy wanted so much to remain a part of the national treasure. And they have. As for Mrs. Nixon's decor, the former First Lady liked it. She and her children came to dinner privately with the Nixons, her first visit to the White House since leaving in 1963.

"I think it looks lovely," Mrs. Onassis told me afterwards.

Of all the changes that have been made in the old mansion from one administration to another, the only one that affected me was removal of the swimming pool.

I've always contended that the First Family could ask me to have their quarters painted purple with pink polka dots, and I'd do so without question, for the house, so far as I'm concerned, belongs to the President in residence.

I think all the First Families would agree with me. When the daughter of Theodore Roosevelt, Mrs. Nicholas Longworth, ate dinner with the Nixons in the upstairs family dining room, someone remarked that she was eating in her old bedroom.

"I wouldn't say it was *my* bedroom," Mrs. Longworth replied. "Helen Taft had it. And I suppose the Wilson girls did." Lorena Hickok slept there, too, I could have added. And Margaret Truman and Mrs. Doud.

The house "belongs" to whoever lives there.

But I hate to see history disappear. When a tree dies on the White House lawn, a tree planted by some earlier President, it is removed very quietly and replaced to keep the continuity. Most people don't even notice that the old tree is gone.

For that reason, I was sorry to see the swimming pool

go. It was not in the mansion proper, nor was it in the west wing, but rather between the two. It was a gift to President Roosevelt from the schoolchildren of America who collected millions of dimes to pay for constructing the heated indoor pool, which that President used every day in his first years of office for post-polio therapy. I remember President Truman swimming there, his glasses all fogged up, as part of his fitness regimen; the Eisenhowers' grandchildren, coming over on weekends, splashing around with the greatest glee; the mural, a colorful sailing scene, commissioned by Ambassador Joseph Kennedy and painted by artist Bernard Lamotte, that brightened up the walls for the swimming races between President Kennedy and his Cabinet; the scores of bathing trunks hanging from the hooks for President Johnson's guests—in all sizes from King Farouk to Mahatma Gandhi.

I miss that swimming pool, which President Nixon tore out to make way for the Fourth Estate. Congress should have let President Truman make that addition onto the west wing—so there'd be room for the press over there.

2

———

President Nixon put the press in the swimming pool; he put the preachers in the East Room.

On their second evening in the White House, the President and his family asked for a "historical" tour by Jim Ketchum and me.

As we went from room to room, Mr. Nixon asked a hundred questions—about each piece of furniture, about how each room had been used. His wife was strangely silent, saying little about the State rooms, reserving her comments for the living quarters. But President Nixon seemed to be making plans for his White House.

When we got to the State Dining Room, I mentioned the official events that had taken place there. And he nodded in recognition, remembering State occasions when he was Vice President.

"Have any of the Presidents used this dining room just for family?" he asked, indicating the long, classical table with its James Monroe mirrored plateau centerpiece and gold compotes and candelabra.

"Herbert Hoover dined at this table every night, even when he was alone," I answered.

The President laughed. "That figures," he said.

The tables were set with the small gold banquet chairs Mrs. Kennedy had ordered for her round-table entertaining.

"I don't really like these," he said, lifting one easily. "They don't really look very comfortable."

"Sometimes they aren't too stable, either," I said, telling him about a few instances where they'd come crashing to the floor during Johnson dinners.

"Do we have any other kind of chairs?" he asked, as we walked down the marble hall. "You know, we are going to have church services in the East Room."

Appropriately, after that announcement, the President and his family went down to the movie theater to watch *Shoes of the Fisherman.*

The next day, I ordered samples of all our chairs brought out to the East Room—Mrs. Kennedy's French banquet chairs and Mrs. Truman's bentwood chairs that Mrs. Eisenhower had called "fit for a children's party."

I also brought up the altar we'd rigged up for Lynda Bird Johnson's wedding, but President Nixon decided against an altar.

"No, the services are going to be interdenominational," he pointed out. "I don't want an altar, just a podium."

But by the time we set up the room with Mrs. Truman's bentwood chairs for a congregation of 200, we discovered we'd have to put in risers for the choir and bring in an electric organ.

The Reverend Billy Graham, evangelist friend of my last three Presidents, as George Allen had been the humorist friend of my first three, preached the first East Room sermon, his longtime soloist George Beverly Shea singing "How Great Thou Art."

Except for Mass before President Kennedy's funeral, and services for Franklin Roosevelt, the only time I'd seen church services in our Grand Ballroom, the East Room, was at President Roosevelt's last Inaugural.

All my Presidents were churchgoers, some more than others. There were special ramps in St. John's Episcopal

Church for President Roosevelt's wheelchair, although his bodyguards "walked" him to his pew. President Truman often walked to the First Baptist Church on 16th Street, while Mrs. Truman and Margaret attended St. John's Episcopal Church, across Lafayette Square from the White House. More often they took turns, one Sunday after another, and all went together, first Baptist, then Episcopalian.

Dwight D. Eisenhower never joined a church until after he was elected President. Thereafter, to the great delight of his wife, he attended the National Presbyterian Church regularly, and confessed that he made some White House decisions "on his knees." John F. Kennedy went to Mass every Sunday without fail, usually in the little churches in the Virginia countryside or Massachusetts seaside where they spent their weekends.

Lyndon Johnson, like Harry Truman, was a fundamentalist married to an Episcopalian. He belonged to the Disciples of Christ (Christian) Church but kept popping up in any church, any denomination in town. In the late evenings, sometimes, he'd go with Luci to a small monastery in southwest Washington to pray.

President Nixon, a Quaker, who was not a member of a meeting in Washington, added a new chapter in the social history of the East Room.

In most other uses of the State rooms, it appeared that the influence of Mamie Eisenhower was to be felt. Her particular style of formal entertaining was brought back by the Nixons.

On her first full day in the White House, January 21, Pat Nixon stood on a black-carpeted stage in the East Room and told a thousand Republican campaign workers, who'd come in for the inaugural: "You'll all be invited back. We're going to have our friends here, instead of all the bigshots!" she told them.

Gerry Van der Heuvel, the First Lady's new press secretary, winced.

"I wish she wouldn't use that phrase," she whispered to me.

"Of course, *all* our friends are bigshots," President Nixon quickly broke in.

Mrs. Van der Heuvel and Lucy Winchester, the First Lady's social secretary, took a little time to get in step with Mrs. Nixon's wishes. For that first official reception, at ten in the morning, they'd ordered champagne.

Remembering Mrs. Johnson and Marvin Watson, I checked with Mrs. Nixon before sending word to the wine cellar.

"Oh, definitely *not!* I don't think we want to serve alcoholic beverages in the morning," she told me.

Instead, the butlers served coffee to the Inauguration-weary campaigners.

For the first, back-to-formality white tie affair, the diplomatic reception on January 31, Lucy and Gerry walked off the State floors with me, arranging to place the Nixons in the Green Room, the Agnews in the Blue Room, the William Rogerses, the new Secretary of State, in the Red Room to receive the 115 ambassadors and chiefs of mission and their wives.

"Mrs. Nixon would like the Marine band in the State Dining Room," Lucy told me.

"But how could the guests hear each other talk?" Mrs. Nixon said, when I asked her. We'd placed the long, narrow table against the west wall to serve hot and cold buffet to the guests.

As it turned out, we stationed the Marines in their usual spot in the foyer and sent a combo to the East Room.

"She'd like white linen tablecloths on the buffet table, just like Mrs. Eisenhower's," the social secretary reported.

Mrs. Eisenhower had called this white linen "bed sheets" and directed that the tablecloths be draped with smilax.

When Mrs. Nixon came down to look at the table, I questioned her about the smilax, too.

"Oh, heavens, no," the First Lady said. "That would keep people from getting up close to the table."

The reception, like those during the Eisenhowers, began at 9:00 and Mrs. Nixon, like Mrs. Eisenhower, received with a gloved hand.

All that week, the Nixons entertained at small, seated dinners in the family dining room.

One night there was FBI Director J. Edgar Hoover,

Secretary of State and Mrs. Rogers, National Security Advisor Henry Kissinger, Assistant to the President and Mrs. John Ehrlichman, Mrs. Longworth, and longtime Republican hostess Mrs. Robert Low Bacon.

The next night they invited Secretary of Defense and Mrs. Melvin Laird, Consultant "Bud" Wilkinson, and the Apollo Eight astronauts and their wives.

Mrs. Nixon had asked Chef Haller to "surprise us" with a menu.

After the first dinner, Henry Haller came running into my office. "The President came into the kitchen tonight and told me it was delicious! Can you imagine?" The chef was so happy I thought he would burst into tears.

"The President himself," he repeated, almost unable to believe it. "That never happened before."

Mrs. Nixon's first seated luncheon in the State Dining Room on February 18 was for ladies of the press. Everybody drew numbers for a seat at the table, and Pat Nixon drew a number, too.

The First Lady had just announced that she'd have no White House "projects"; instead, she would like to instigate a national recruitment program, to enlist hundreds of thousands of volunteers to "help others."

Some of those volunteer projects, she told the press women that day, might include teachers' aides, home care for the mentally retarded, services for the ill in hospitals and institutions, and volunteer bookmobiles to serve the aged.

But I never got to watch Mrs. Nixon carry out those plans—for my thirty years in government service were coming to an end (I'd spent two years in the Veterans Administration before joining the White House Staff in 1941).

Mrs. Johnson had told Mrs. Nixon of my impending retirement during that first visit, when we all pored over the White House blueprints in the West Sitting Hall.

Mrs. Nixon's reaction did please me.

"Oh, but Mrs. Eisenhower has recommended you so highly," she said. "And so has everybody else."

Rex Scouten was the perfect man for the job of Chief Usher, I thought. He'd been through all the paces. He

398

knew the house—he'd been an usher during the Kennedy administration; he knew the grounds—he'd gone from the White House to the National Park Service; he knew the Fine Arts collection—he'd come back as executive secretary for the Committee for the Preservation of the White House; and he knew the Nixons—he'd been their Secret Service agent when Mr. Nixon was Vice President.

On March 1, 1941, I'd walked up the steps of the White House, awed by the liveried doorman, by the immense white columns, by the majesty of the mansion.

On March 1, 1969, my last day, I had lunch in the White House kitchen. Just Zella and me. They'd asked to give me a retirement party, but this was the way I wanted it. (Later, to my surprise, a crowd of about 300 of my friends took over the Carter Barron Amphitheatre in Washington to celebrate the fact that I was no longer in the White House.)

After lunch, Rex, who'd been there all week, Zella and I went upstairs to see Mrs. Nixon. It was our own little changing-of-the-guard ceremony. I said goodbye to the First Lady, and we went home.

I feel that I caught only a fleeting glimpse of Pat Nixon during her first six weeks in the White House. I saw only her First Lady face, the public poise, the correct mannerisms, the erect posture of a woman who, through no fault of her own, had been photographed almost constantly for twenty-three years.

She always seemed to be too thin; she wore high-necked, long-sleeved dresses, tasteful but subdued. Her facial expression, always pleasant, rarely changed, and at times was almost rigid.

Yet she often showed warmth and spontaneity—it seemed perfectly natural for her to scoop up a crying child in her arms; to say "I just *love* you," to an old Senate friend; to embrace a former First Lady in as close to a bearhug as somebody her size could give.

Gestures such as these always seemed somewhat of a surprise coming from Mrs. Nixon—because she was always so *composed*.

There was a serenity about Pat Nixon, that, I think, may have covered a lot of tough scar tissue. She'd had to work hard, very hard as a child on a farm in Nevada; she was orphaned and had to educate herself; she had to survive in the national spotlight; and live through two heartbreaking political campaigns.

All the First Ladies I've known have been exceptionally strong in spirit. They came in that way, because they'd been able to share their husbands' grueling political road to the White House. They'd all learned to be on display, and at the same time to find some way to guard their private moments. They'd learned organization, discipline, self-control, composure—all their tools before they got to the White House. They'd learned how to be of use to their husbands, and what their husbands needed from them.

And each of them has performed a great public service to the people of America, filling a role that is non-appointive, nonelective, certainly nonpaid, the most demanding volunteer job in America.

Far from being a "glamorous prison" or as Harry Truman called it, "This jailhouse I'm in," the White House is a pretty wonderful place to live, I think. Because of the constant protection from the outside world, families get to spend a lot more time together than they ever did before. Despite all the pressures and burdens, the White House is great for family life. They're all insulated *together*. The distance between the west wing and the second floor is not a long commute.

There are drawbacks to living in the White House, certainly. Even inside, it's a goldfish bowl, unless you're sequestered behind closed bedroom doors. The second floor is like a long one-story house—house guests are right in your lap. (How would *you* like it if the Queen of England were sleeping right down the hall?) And there are always *eyes*. Not the Secret Service so much —they're looking at everybody else. It's the eyes of the public, the visitors, the help, always staring, perhaps involuntarily, trying to catch the President and First Lady being human. Their only escape is with each other.

I think all the First Ladies would agree that life there, even for four short years—or "one shining moment"— was worth all the effort.

I came back as a guest at a ceremony celebrating Mrs. Nixon's acquisition of a fine portrait of James Madison, one that Mrs. Johnson had wanted for the White House.

As I went through the receiving line, President Nixon said to me, "Mr. West, after all you've done for this house, you're welcome here any time."

"Thank you, sir," I replied.

I do think rather highly of the place.

The material in this book was compiled from tape recordings, from the rich store of memory of J. B. West, and from his extensive personal files.

To prepare for interviewing Mr. West, I read the following books, as a background on White House History. I am also grateful to James R. Ketchum, a true White House historian, for his assistance in research and preparation of the manuscript.

M.L.K.

ALBERTSON, DEAN, *Eisenhower as President*. New York, Hill and Wang, 1963.

ALLEN, GEORGE, *Presidents Who Have Known Me*. New York, Simon & Schuster, Inc., 1950.

BALDRIGE, LETITIA, *Of Diamonds and Diplomats*. Boston, Houghton Mifflin Co., 1968.

BISHOP, JIM, *A Day in the Life of President Kennedy*. New York, Random House, 1964.

———, *A Day in the Life of President Johnson*. New York, Random House, 1967.

BLACK, RUBY, *Eleanor Roosevelt: A Biography*. New York, Duell, Sloan & Pearce, 1940.

Blair House, Past and Present. An Account of Its Life and Times in the City of Washington. United States Department of State, MCMXLV.

CARPENTER, LIZ, *Ruffles and Flourishes*. Garden City, New York, Doubleday & Co., Inc., 1970.

DONOVAN, ROBERT J., *Eisenhower, The Inside Story*. New York, Harper & Brothers, 1956.

EISENHOWER, DWIGHT D., *The White House Years*, Vol. 1. *Mandate for Change, 1953–1956*. New York, Doubleday & Co., Inc., 1963.

————, *The White House Years,* Vol. II. *Waging Peace, 1956–1961.* New York, Doubleday & Co., Inc., 1965.

————, *At Ease; Stories I Tell to Friends.* Garden City, New York, Doubleday & Co., 1967.

FIELDS, ALONZO, *My 24 Years in the White House.* New York, Coward-McCann, Inc., 1961.

FURMAN, BESS, *Washington By-Line.* New York, A. A. Knopf, 1949.

————, *White House Profile.* Indianapolis, New York, The Bobbs-Merrill Co., Inc., 1951.

GALLAGHER, MARY BARELLI, *My Life With Jacqueline Kennedy.* New York, David McKay, 1969.

GERLINGER, IRENE HAZARD, *Mistresses of the White House: A Narrator's Tale of a Pageant of First Ladies.* New York, Hollywood, Samuel French, 1948.

HATCH, ALDEN, *Red Carpet for Mamie.* New York, Henry Holt & Co., 1954.

HELM, EDITH BENHAM, *The Captains and the Kings.* New York, G. P. Putnam's Sons, 1954.

HOOVER, IRWIN HOOD, *Forty-Two Years in the White House.* Boston, Houghton Mifflin Co., 1934.

JEFFRIES, ONA GRIFFIN, *In and Out of the White House . . . from Washington to the Eisenhowers.* New York, Wilfred Funk, Inc., 1960.

JENSEN, AMY LA FOLLETTE, *The White House and Its Thirty-Two Families.* New York, Toronto, London, McGraw-Hill Book Co., Inc., 1958.

LADY BIRD JOHNSON, *A White House Diary.* New York, Chicago, San Francisco, Holt, Rinehart, and Winston, 1970.

JOHNSON, GEORGE, *Eisenhower.* Derby, Connecticut, Monarch Books, Inc., 1962.

JOHNSON, LYNDON B., *The Vantage Point.* New York, Chicago, San Francisco, Holt, Rinehart, and Winston, 1971.

KALTMAN, MARY, *Keeping Up with Keeping House.* Garden City, New York, Doubleday, 1971.

LARSON, ARTHUR, *Eisenhower, the President Nobody Knew.* New York, Charles Scribner's Sons, 1968.

LASH, JOSEPH P., *Eleanor and Franklin.* New York, W. W. Norton & Co., Inc., 1971.

MANCHESTER, WILLIAM, *The Death of a President*. New York, Harper & Row, 1967.

McCALLUM, JOHN, *Six Roads from Abilene*. Seattle, Washington, Wood & Reber, Inc., 1960.

McLENDON, WINZOLA, and SMITH, SCOTTIE, *Don't Quote Me!* New York, Dutton, 1970.

McNAUGHTON, FRANK, and HEHMEYET, WALTER, *Harry Truman, President*. New York, Toronto, London, Whittlesey House (Division of McGraw-Hill Book Co., Inc.,) 1948.

MEANS, MARIANNE, *The Women in the White House, the Lives, Times and Influence of Twelve Notable First Ladies*. New York, Random House, 1963.

MONTGOMERY, RUTH, *Hail to the Chiefs*. New York, Coward-McCann, Inc., 1970.

MORROW, E. FREDERICK, *Black Man in the White House*. New York, Coward-McCann, Inc., 1963.

NESBITT, HENRIETTA, *White House Diary, F.D.R.'s Housekeeper*. Garden City, New York, Doubleday & Co., 1948.

NIXON, RICHARD M., *Six Crises*. Garden City, New York, Doubleday & Co., Inc., 1962.

PARKS, LILLIAN ROGERS, in collaboration with Frances Spatz Leighton, *My Thirty Years Backstairs at the White House*. New York, Fleet Publishing Corp., 1961.

Report of the Committee for the Preservation of the White House, 1964–1969, George B. Hartzog, Jr., Chairman, 1969.

ROOSEVELT, ELEANOR, *The Autobiography of Eleanor Roosevelt*. New York, Harper & Brothers, 1961.

SHELTON, ISABELLE, *The White House*, A Fawcett Special Edition, 1962.

SMITH, MARIE, *Entertaining in the White House*. Washington, D.C., Acropolis Books, 1967.

SMITH, MERRIMAN, *Merriman Smith's Book of Presidents*. New York, W. W. Norton & Co., 1972.

SNYDER, MARTY, *My Friend Ike*. New York, Frederick Fell, Inc., 1956.

STEINBERG, ALFRED, *The Man from Missouri: The Life and Times of Harry S. Truman*. New York, G. P. Putnam's Sons, 1962.

TAYLOR, TIM, *The Book of Presidents, 1972*. New York, Arno Press, A New York Times Company, 1972.

THAYER, MARY VAN RENSSELAER, *Jacqueline Kennedy: The White House Years*. Boston, Toronto, Little Brown and Company, 1971.

TRUMAN, HARRY, *Memoirs by Harry Truman*, Vol. I, *Year of Decisions*. Garden City, New York, Doubleday & Co., Inc., 1955.

————, *Memoirs by Harry Truman*, Vol. II, *Years of Trial and Hope*. Garden City, New York, Doubleday & Co., Inc., 1956.

TRUMAN, MARGARET, *Harry S. Truman*. New York, William Morrow & Co., Inc., 1973.

————, with Margaret Cousins, *Souvenir: Margaret Truman's Own Story*. New York, Toronto, London, McGraw-Hill Book Co., Inc., 1956.

————, *White House Pets*. New York, David McKay Co., 1969.

WHITE, THEODORE H., *The Making of the President, 1960*. New York, Atheneum, 1961.

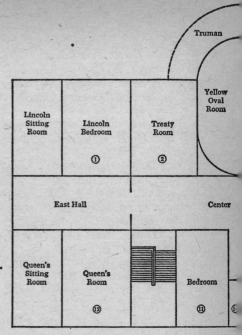

UPSTAIRS AT THE WHIT.

1. Harry Hopkins' Bedroom under Roosevelt

2. Monroe Room under Roosevelt, Truman and Eisenhower

3. President's Study under Roosevelt and Truman
   Trophy Room under Eisenhower

4. The First Lady's Sitting Room under Roosevelt and Truman

5. The First Lady's Bedroom under Roosevelt and Truman

6. Lorena Hickok's Bedroom under Roosevelt
   Margaret's Bedroom under Truman
   Mrs. Doud's Bedroom under Eisenhower

7. Lincoln Bedroom under Roosevelt
   Margaret's Sitting Room under Truman
   Family Sitting Room under Eisenhower

8. First Lady's Office under Roosevelt and Truman
   President's Painting Room under Eisenhower
   Children's Formula and High Chair Room under Kennedy
   Luci's Study under Johnson

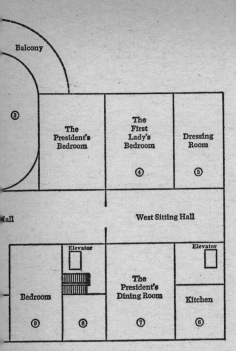

HOUSE FROM 1961 ON

9. Guest Room under Roosevelt (reserved for Joe Lash)
   Guest Room under Truman (Reathel Odum's Room for first year)
   Guest Room under Eisenhower
   John's Room under Kennedy
   Luci's Room under Johnson

10. Book Storage under Roosevelt and Truman
    Rose Woods' Pressing Room under Eisenhower
    Nurse Maude Shaw's Room under Kennedy
    Dress Storage Room under Johnson

11. Guest Room under Roosevelt
    Mrs. Wallace's Room under Truman
    Guest Room under Eisenhower
    Caroline's Room under Kennedy
    Lynda Bird's Room under Johnson

12. Called the Rose Room under Roosevelt—
    later referred to as the Queen's Room
    after five Queens had slept there

Index

Abell, Bess, 317-18, 320, 323, 324, 328, 331, 339, 344, 345, 355, 364, 366, 367, 368-70, 371-74, 375, 377, 378, 380

Abell, Tyler, 339

Acheson, Dean, 90-91

Acheson, Mrs. Dean, 85

Adams, Charles Francis, 269 n.

Adams, Sherman, 171 n., 184

Agnew, Spiro, 387, 397

Agnew, Mrs. Spiro, 387, 397

Allen, Eugene, 241

Allen, George, 161, 185, 395

Allen, Mrs. George E., 156 n.

Alsop, Mrs. Joseph, 273 n.

Arata, Mr., 300, 309

Arden, Elizabeth, 175

Arness, James, 343

Arrington, Bonner, 305, 312-13, 321, 375

Arthur, Chester A., 268

Astor, Mrs. Vincent, 231

Attlee, Clement, 118

Auchincloss, Hugh D., 310, 311

Auchincloss, Mrs. Hugh D., 260, 310, 311

Avery, Isaac, 326-27

Ayub Khan, 289, 297

Bacon, Mrs. Robert Low, 398

Baines, Huffman, 340

Baldrige, Letitia "Tish," 228, 238, 244, 257-58, 279, 285-87, 289, 291, 293, 294-95, 371-72, 373

Barkley, Alben, 108, 257

Bartlett, Charles, 258

Bartlett, Martha, 258

Baruch, Bernard, 47

Bauss, Rudy, 321

Benton, "Tojo," 179

Benton, William, 332 n.

Bernhard, Prince, of Holland, 34, 122

Bethune, Mary McLeod, 32

Biddle, Francis, 78

Billings, Lemoyne, 261

Birdzell, Officer, 115-16

Bishop, Jim, 314

Black, Mrs. James C., 156 n.

Blair, Elizabeth, 103

Blair, Francis Preston, 102-3

Bobbitt, Becky, 340

Boettiger, Anna Roosevelt, 20, 24, 39, 48, 54, 57

Boettiger, John, 39, 54

Boettiger, Johnny, 48, 54

Boring, Secret Service Agent, 116

Boudin, M. Stephane, 270, 301, 307, 310, 314, 334-35, 351, 390, 392

Bouvier, John Vernou, 235

Bowen, Janet, 244

Boyd, Betsy, 258, 306, 349

Bradlee, Benjamin, 258

Bradlee, Toni, 258

Brooks (chauffeur), 145

Brown, Mrs., 350, 359

Brown, Mrs. George R., 332 n.

409

Brownell, Herbert, 171 n.
Brubeck, Dave, 336
Bruce (senior doorman), 386
Bryant, Mr., 323, 381
Buchanan, James, 268
Bulganin, Nikolai, 165 n.
Burkley, Dr., 343
Butcher, Mrs. Ruth, 156 n.
Byrnes, Mrs. James F., 84

Caesar (valet), 46-47
Calhoun, John C., 103
Califano, Joe, 366
Campbell, Mary, 28
Cannon, Clark, 105
Carleson, Joel, 174
Carlyle, Carol, 375
Carmichael, Leonard, 277 n.
Carpenter, Liz, 317-18, 320, 323, 324, 331, 338, 339, 358, 360-61, 377
Carter, Connie, 375, 376
Carter, M. O., 88
Carter, Tom, 246
Casals, Pablo, 289
Castagnetta, Grace, 14
Castro, Nash, 332 n.
Catlin, George, 230
Catton, Bruce, 332 n.
Chaney, Mayris, 34
Channing, Carol, 365
Charnley, Harry, 88
Chiang Kai-shek, Madame, 45-46
Churchill, Sarah, 85
Churchill, Winston, 40-43, 51, 62, 85, 105, 120
Churchill, Mrs. Winston, 85
Clark, Gilmore, 95
Claunch, Charles, 13, 15, 16, 36, 55, 57, 58
Clay, Henry, 103
Clements, Earle, 339
Cleveland, Mrs. Grover, 358
Clifford, Clark M., 277 n.
Clifton, Gen., 233
Coffelt, Officer, 116

Collingwood, Charles, 281
Conger, Clement, 391
Connally, John, 346
Coolidge, Calvin, 63, 94, 101
Collidge, Mrs. Calvin, 101
Cowdin, Mrs. J. Cheever, 273 n.
Cox, Tricia Nixon, 386, 387, 388
Crim, Howell G., 7, 11, 12, 13, 14, 15, 19, 20, 22, 26, 27, 28, 30, 31, 32, 33, 37, 40, 44, 46, 48, 49, 50, 52, 53, 54, 55, 56, 57, 58, 67, 74, 77, 78, 80, 83, 86, 87, 89, 94, 95, 96, 100, 102, 106, 107, 108, 112, 113, 115, 116, 119, 123, 126, 128, 129, 132, 150, 155, 165, 173, 174, 354

Dall, "Sistie," 23, 346
Dall, "Buzzie," 23
Daniel, Margaret Truman, 54, 59, 60, 61, 64, 67, 68, 70, 74, 77, 82, 83, 99, 100, 101, 109, 110, 114, 118, 120, 121, 122, 125, 126, 127, 140, 141, 142, 241, 346, 348, 392, 396
Daniels, Jonathan, 55
Davis, Leroy, 269 n.
Davison, Officer, 116
De Gaulle, Charles, 312, 313
Delano, Laura, 51
Dewey, Thomas E., 99, 124
Dillon, Mrs. C. Douglas, 269 n.
Doud, John Sheldon, 131
Doud, Mrs. John S., 142, 153, 159, 165, 392
Dougherty, Richard E., 104 n.
Downs, Officer, 116
Draper, Colonel William, 173
Dry, Sergeant, 162, 163, 187
Duchin, Peter, 380
Duke, Angier Biddle, 287
Duke, Mrs. Angier Biddle, 322
Dulles, John Foster, 138, 139, 164, 171 n., 184
Du Pont, Henry Francis, 259, 269 ff., 332 n.

410

Early, Steve, 24, 25, 54, 55
Eastland, Jim, 348
Eden, Anthony, 165 n.
Edgerton, Glen E., 104 n.
Edinburgh, Duke of. See Philip, Prince
Ehrlichman, John, 398
Ehrlichman, Mrs. John, 398
Eisenhower, Barbara, 158, 185, 346, 349
Eisenhower, Barbara Anne, 158
Eisenhower, David, 154, 158, 386, 387, 388, 390
Eisenhower, Dwight David, 62, 86, 120, 121, 124, 126, 128-32, 135-39, 140-46, 147-60, 161-66, 167-70, 171-76, 177-89, 255, 273, 303, 317, 336, 341, 386, 387, 395
Eisenhower, Dwight Doud, 158
Eisenhower, John, 158, 181, 349
Eisenhower, Julie Nixon, 386, 387, 388, 390
Eisenhower, Mamie, 10, 85, 126, 128-33, 134-39, 140-46, 147-60, 161-66, 167-70, 171-76, 177-89, 190-91, 192-226, 227, 234, 242, 267, 268, 283, 314, 316, 323, 326, 341, 342, 372, 387, 395, 396, 397, 398
Eisenhower, Mary Jean, 158
Eisenhower, Milton, 171 n.
Eisenhower, Susan, 158
Elder, Bill, 280
Elizabeth, Queen of England, 43
Elizabeth II, Queen of England, 120, 177-80
Ellender, Allen, 348
Engelhard, Charles, 369
Engelhard, Jane, 269 n., 332 n., 368-69, 375

Farouk, King, 393
Faubus, Orval, 180
Faure, Edgar, 165 n.
Felton, Janet, 258, 259

Ficklin, Charles, 70, 133, 148, 156, 225, 240-41, 245, 327
Ficklin, John, 241
Field, Mrs. Marshall, 332 n.
Fields, Alonzo, 14, 69, 97, 112, 116, 130, 148
Fields, George, 24
Finley, David, 269 n., 272, 277 n.
Fleischman, Mr. Lawrence, 273 n.
Fleming, Gen., 54
Ford, Henry, II, 124, 368
Ford, Mrs. Henry, II, 269 n., 368
Fortas, Abe, 382
Fosburgh, James, 273 n., 332 n.
Fox, Sandy, 289
Frankfurter, Felix, 36
Franklin, Benjamin, 280
Frederika, Queen of Greece, 43

Gallagher, Mary, 238
Gandhi, Mahatma, 393
Garr, Vietta, 77, 81, 142, 320
Gaspar, Master Sergeant, 67
Geaney, Victoria, 111-12
George, King of Greece, 43
Glynn, Paul, 324
Goldberg, Rube, 389
Gonella, Ashton, 306, 318, 338, 341, 342
Graham, Billy, 343, 395
Graham, Kay, 379
Gregg, Lee, 320
Grosvenor, Melville Bill, 277 n.
Gruenther, General Alfred, 185

Hagerty, James, 171 n., 182-83
Hall, Leonard, 171 n.
Halle, Mrs. Walter, 273 n.
Haller, Henri, 356, 366, 388, 397
Halstead, Anna Roosevelt, 346. See also Boettiger, Anna Roosevelt
Hamilton, Alexander, 281
Hamilton, George, 350

Hannegan, Robert, 64
Harding, Warren G., 361
Hardy, Tom, 73
Hare, Ray, 172, 246, 318
Harkness, Rebekah, 364
Harriman, Averell, 314, 321
Harriston (doorman), 191
Helm, Edith, 29, 44, 86, 89, 341
Hickok, Lorena, 20, 392
Hitler, Adolf, 34, 62
Hoban, James, 107
Hogue, Bette, 319
Holness, Wilma, 239, 307
Hoover, Herbert, 62, 64, 254, 281, 395
Hoover, Irwin H. "Ike," 7
Hoover, J. Edgar, 397-98
Hopkins, Diana, 23-24, 43-45, 46
Hopkins, Harry, 12, 17, 23, 25, 30, 43, 44-45, 48-49
Hough, Nancy, 307
Hoving, Walter, 375
Hughes, Mrs. Everett, 156 n.
Humphrey, George, 139, 169, 171 n.
Humphrey, Hubert, 363, 387
Humphrey, Mrs. Hubert, 387
Huth, Hans, 267

Istomin, Eugene, 289

Jackson, Andrew, 48, 103, 105, 254, 309
Jacobson, Jake, 338
Jean-Paul (hairdresser), 306
Jefferson, Thomas, 95, 107, 281, 373
Jenkins, Beth, 350
Jett, T. Sutton, 277 n.
Johnson, John, 241
Johnson, Lady Bird (Claudia Taylor), 10, 257-313, 316-35, 336-51, 352-59, 360-63, 364-76, 377-84, 385, 397, 398, 401
Johnson, Luci. See Nugent, Luci Johnson

Johnson, Lynda. See Robb, Lynda Johnson
Johnson, Lyndon Baines, 257, 313, 315, 316-35, 336-51, 352-59, 360-63, 364-76, 377-84, 385, 387, 392, 395
Johnson, Sam Houston, 340
Jones, Bobby, 138
Jones, W. Alton, 139
Juliana, Queen of Holland, 34, 43, 122

Kaltman, Mary, 346, 354, 356, 357, 366, 374, 388
Karitas, Joe, 321
Keefe, Frank B., 104 n.
Keehn, Barbara, 286, 305
Kennedy, Caroline, 229, 234, 237, 249, 250, 251-52, 256, 295, 311, 349
Kennedy, Edward "Teddy," 379
Kennedy, Jacqueline, 10, 190-235, 236-48, 249-61, 262-82, 293-98, 299-307, 308-15, 316 ff., 332 n., 333, 336, 342, 343, 349, 354, 360, 372, 378, 390, 395
Kennedy, John F., 190 ff., 236 ff., 249 ff., 262 ff., 283 ff., 299 ff., 308 ff., 316, 337, 393, 396
Kennedy, John F., Jr., 191, 229, 234, 237, 249, 250, 251, 256, 295, 302, 303, 311
Kennedy, Joseph, 245, 266, 393
Kennedy, Patrick Bouvier, 303
Kennedy, Robert, 310, 311, 313, 378, 382
Kennedy, Rose, 260
Kenneth, Mr., 306
Kensett, J. F., 280
Kent, Duke of, 34
Ketchum, James, 279, 307, 309, 312, 332, 333, 339, 346, 358, 375, 383, 390, 394
Keyes, Frances Parkinson, 14
Khrushchev, Nikita, 183-84, 256, 294
412

King, Admiral Ernest, 62
King, Martin Luther, 382
Kirsten, Lincoln, 288
Kissinger, Henry, 398
Kivets, Jerry, 372
Kung, Miss, 46

LaGuardia, Fiorello, 34, 37
Laird, Melvin, 398
Laird, Mrs. Melvin, 398
Lamotte, Bernard, 393
Lanin, Lester, 257
Lash, Joseph, 20-21, 27, 39
Lasker, Mrs. Albert, 269 n., 272, 362, 369
Latrobe, Benjamin, 391
Leahy, Admiral William, 54
Lee, Richard Henry, 103
Lee, Robert E., 103
LeHand, Marguerite, 22
Lincoln Abraham, 103
Lincoln, Anne, 244, 258, 289, 296, 353
Lincoln, Evelyn, 311
Lindbergh, Charles, 382
Lingo, Jane. 74
Lodge, Henry Cabot, 171 n.
Loeb, John L., 269 n.
Longworth, Mrs. Nicholas, 392, 398
Louvat, Ferdinand, 246, 307
Lovell, Dr. James, 102

MacArthur, General Douglas, 114, 118, 119
Macy, Louise, 43-45
Madison, Dolley, 97
Madison, James, 401
Malraux, André, 256
Marcus, Stanley, 273 n.
Margaret, Princess, of England, 368
Marshall, General George, 57, 62
Martha, Princess, of Norway, 21
Martin, Edward, 104 n.
Martin, Joseph, 54

Marx, Louis, 152
Mays, John, 50, 51, 75
McCaffree, Mary Jane, 170, 341
McCarthy, Joe, 114, 153, 164
McCormack, John, 54
McDuffie, Lizzie, 320
McInerney, James, 247
McKellar, Kenneth, 104 n.
McNamara, Robert, 347, 379
McNamara, Mrs. Robert, 379
McShain, John, 106
Mellon, Mrs. Paul, 269 n., 297, 314, 362, 378-79
Merrill, Robert, 367
Mesta, Perle, 108, 317, 334
Mielziner, Jo, 364
Miller, Earl, 31
Miller, Mrs. Pell, 156 n.
Mink, John, 345
Moaney, Delores, 163, 187, 320
Moaney, Sergeant, 137, 142, 155, 157, 163, 320
Molotov, Vyacheslav M., 45, 62
Monroe, James, 30, 268, 394
Montgomery, Robert, 153
Moore, Elizabeth, 28
Moore, Ellen, 159, 186
Moore, Frances "Mike," 156 n., 159, 186
Moore, Mamie, 159, 186
Morgenthau, Elinor, 30, 33
Morgenthau, Henry Jr., 12, 78
Morman, Lucinda, 243, 302, 312
Murphy, Chief, 88

Nelson, Pearl, 238, 245-46
Nesbitt, Henrietta, 15, 27, 28, 38, 45, 77, 78, 79, 354
Nixon, Julie. See Eisenhower, Julie Nixon
Nixon, Pat, 10, 185, 385-93, 394-401
Nixon, Richard M., 139, 182, 185, 383, 385-93, 394-401
Nixon, Tricia. See Cox, Tricia Nixon
Nugent, Patrick, 350, 377

413

Nugent, Lucy Johnson, 323, 330, 340, 348, 349-50, 377-78, 379-81

Nugent, Patrick Lyndon, 381

Odum, Reathel, 63, 68, 86, 109, 329, 357

Ormsby-Gore, David, 258

Orr, Douglas William, 104 n.

Paley, Mrs. William S., 273 n.

Parades, Providencia "Provy," 238, 239, 242, 243, 299, 318, 320

Patterson, Mrs. Robert, 84

Parish, Mrs. Henry, II, 229, 230, 232, 263, 269, 274, 390

Pearce, Lorraine, 278-80

Persons, General Wilton, 171 n.

Peter, King of Yugoslavia, 43

Philip, Prince, of England, 120, 177-80, 313

Pierce, Nelson, 318

Powell, Adam Clayton, 91

Powers, Dave, 261

Prettyman, Arthur, 24

Price, Vincent, 273 n.

Priscilla of Boston, 378

Pulitzer, Joseph, 273 n.

Pyle, Howard, 171 n.

Rabaut, Louis C., 104 n.

Radziwill, Lee, 259, 311

Radziwill, Stanislas, 311

Ramos, Ramon, 84

Rayburn, Sam, 54, 323

Redmond, Robert, 56-57, 113, 186

Rigdon, Lieutenant Commander William, 88

Robb, Charles, 379-80

Robb, Lynda Johnson, 323, 340, 341-42, 346, 348, 349-50, 370, 377, 379, 380, 381, 395

Roberts, Clifford, 139

Robinson, Bill, 139, 185

Rogers, William, 397

Rogers, Mrs. William, 397, 398

Roosevelt, Anna. See Boettiger, Anna Roosevelt

Roosevelt, Eleanor, 10, 11-17, 18-35, 36-51, 52 ff., 71-72, 73, 77, 83, 85, 86, 122, 123, 141, 143, 163, 263, 268, 316, 329, 342, 371, 384, 391

Roosevelt, Elliott, 20, 39, 57

Roosevelt, Franklin D., 11-17, 18-35, 36-51, 52 ff., 71, 77, 84, 85, 99, 236, 254, 281, 301, 309, 317, 337, 362, 390, 392, 395

Roosevelt, Franklin D., Jr., 20, 39

Roosevelt, Hall, 34

Roosevelt, James, 20, 50

Roosevelt, John, 13, 20, 39

Roosevelt, Mrs. John, 13

Roosevelt, Sara Delano, 31

Roosevelt, Theodore, 82, 107, 132, 249, 281, 392

Ross, Charlie, 118

Rutherfurd, Lucy Mercer, 25

Salinger, Pierre, 247

Saltonstall, Mrs. Leverett, 85

Saltonstall, Nathaniel, 273 n.

Saragat, Guiseppe, 367

Schulz, Robert 137, 157

Scott, Hazel, 91

Scouten, Rex, 246, 318, 325, 366

Searles, Wilson, 13, 27, 58

Selassie, Haile, 304, 313

Sharpe, Mary, 79-80, 81, 112

Shaw, Maude, 230, 306

Shazar, Zalman, 378

Shea, George Beverly, 395

Shea, Gerald, 269 n.

Shipp, Edgar, 288

Shriver, Sargent, 309

Slater, Ellis, 185

Smaltz, Mrs. 53

Smith, Helen, 185

Smith, Margaret Chase, 345

Smith, Warrie Lynn, 349

414

Snowden, Lord, 368
Snyder, Drucie, 74
Snyder, General Howard, 163, 168, 172, 181, 189
Snyder, Mrs. Howard, 156 n.
Spessot, Julius, 244-47
Stalin, Joseph, 51, 62
Stephens, Thomas, 171 n.
Stern, Isaac, 289
Stettinius, Edward R., Jr., 55, 78
Stevenson, Adlai, 124, 125
Stimson, Henry L., 12, 78
Stone, Harlan F., 48, 55
Stout, Stewart, 152
Stover, Major, 256
Suber, Fate, 241
Suckley, Margaret, 51, 57
Summerfield, Arthur, 171 n.
Symington, James, 366

Taft, Charlie, 346
Taft, Helen, 392
Taft, William H., 103
Talmadge, Mrs. Herman, 342
Tartiere, Mrs. Raymond, 263
Thomas, Albert, 119
Thomas, George, 238, 239, 265, 314, 318, 319
Thompson, George, 132, 143
Thompson, Malvina "Tommy," 22, 26-27, 29, 44
Tkach, Dr. Walter, 163, 172, 189
Truman, Bess, 10, 51, 52-75, 76-92, 93-114, 115-27, 130, 136, 144, 147, 155, 187-88, 242, 268, 303, 316, 341, 356, 371, 391, 395, 396
Truman, Harry, 48, 50, 52-75, 76-92, 93-114, 115-27, 136, 137, 139, 177, 229, 281, 301, 317, 336, 341, 343, 348, 357, 375, 386, 388, 391, 393, 396, 400
Truman, Margaret. See Daniel, Margaret Truman
Truman, Vivian, 108

Tuckerman, Nancy, 258, 259, 295-96, 305, 307, 309, 314
Turnure, Pam, 238, 256, 294
Tully, Grace, 22, 24, 25

Udo Pedro, 357

Valenti, Jack, 338
Van Buren, Martin, 103
Van der Heuvel, Gerry, 396
Van Loon, Henrik, 14
Verdon, René, 230, 244, 258, 283, 287, 305, 328, 353-55
Victoria, Queen of England, 301

Wade (doorman), 116
Wallace, Henry, 46-47
Walker, John, 269 n., 277 n., 278, 280
Walker, Mabel, 112, 116, 143, 149, 152, 225, 229, 242-44
Walker, Mrs. Walton, 156 n.
Wallace, Fred, 73, 108
Wallace, Henry, 78
Wallace, Margaret Gates, 63, 68, 69, 76, 77, 115, 125, 357
Wallace, Mary, 71
Walton, William, 257, 309
Waring, Fred, 178, 184, 285
Warren, Earl, 139, 175, 342
Warren, Mrs. George Henry, 269 n.
Warren, Whitney, 273 n.
Washington, George, 97
Washington, Martha, 281
Watson, Edwin "Pa," 24, 25, 47, 56
Watson, Marvin, 338, 366, 373, 374, 397
Webster, Daniel, 103, 280
Webster, Mabel, 28, 123
West, Kathy, 151, 192, 377
West, Sally, 151, 377
West, Zella, 45, 52, 151, 163, 173, 174, 307, 313, 379, 386, 399
Whitman, Ann, 130, 171

415

Whitney, "Jock," 139
Wickard, Claude, 78
Wilhemina, Queen of Holland, 43
Wilkinson, "Bud," 398
Williams, Helen, 320
Wilson, Charles E., 139
Wilson, Mrs. Woodrow, 371
Winchester, Lucy, 397
Wirth, Conrad, 277 n., 297
Woods, Rose, 128, 129, 142, 163, 179, 320, 323

Woodward, Stanley, 90
Woollcott, Alexander, 14
Wright, Annette, 74
Wright, Zephyr, 320, 330, 336, 343, 352-56
Wrightsman, Mrs. Charles, 269 n.

Young, "Rusty," 288

Zurcher, Susette Morton, 273 n.